"Youth and politics – in conventional thinking, they don't mix. In this lively and well-informed book, Judith Bessant shows that they do mix, and have been mixing for a very long time. With examples ranging from mediaeval France to 1950s Australia to global climate activism today, Bessant shows that youth engagement and activism, in many different forms, really matter."

— *Raewyn Connell, Professor Emerita, University of Sydney, Australia, www.raewynconnell.net*

"More than ever, the young generation is presented as a source of fear, given its presumed cynicism and disillusion, but also of hope, given inclusive values, progressive visions and broad participation in protests for social and environmental justice. In this brilliant book, Judith Bessant addresses the historical evolution of the mainstream social representation of the young people connecting it with the capitalist development, that has expelled young people from the stable labour market. Building upon a relational approach, the analysis convincingly points at the youth resistance to their recursive stereotypization and at their fundamental political role."

— *Donatella della Porta, Director of Centre of Social Movements Studies, Scuola Normale Superiore, Italy*

"*Making-Up People: Youth, Truth and Politics* is a cornerstone book for the sociology of youth. With searing insight, Bessant takes the reader to the central issues for contemporary youth sociology and youth studies, challenging many taken for granted assumptions. Drawing on insights about the nature of youth political action in the 18th and 19th centuries, Bessant shows that youth is always represented in ways that are embedded in a specific place and time and that in order gain some traction on the analysis of young people's lives, a 'relational perspective' is required. She takes the reader through a compelling and highly accessible analysis of the profound transformations occurring in our contemporary world, that 'change the very nature of reality and human nature' and place us at a political crossroad. At this juncture, Bessant's book is signpost to a future in which young people take a key role in decision-making forums and shape new political spaces to address pressing issues of environmental preservation, social transformation and social justice."

— *Johanna Wyn, Redmond Barry Distinguished Emeritus Professor, Youth Research Centre, The University of Melbourne, Australia*

"Having written extensively on how young people have galvanised and led recent global social movements and been at the vanguard of new forms of political participation, the prolific Judith Bessant now turns her attention to their involvement over the longue duree. From Joan of Arc to Greta Thunberg, and many more in-between, Bessant is at her best in carefully tracing how young people and children have been represented and how they have in fact shaped our current sensibilities. Written with engaging detail, theoretical acumen and kaleidoscopic insights, *Making-Up People: Youth, Truth and Politics* is a fabulous contribution to global youth studies."

— *Sharlene Swartz, President of Sociology of Youth Research Committee, University of Fort Hare, South Africa*

"Judith Bessant is a leading international authority in the field of youth studies. Full stop. She is also a prodigious writer on the subject. *Making-Up People: Youth, Truth and Politics* offers another incisive contribution that considers how young people's lives – and especially their politics – has historically been (mis)represented by professional commentators and casual observers alike. At a time when young people are stepping-up to take the vanguard in global campaigns for environmental and social justice, this book will be of critical importance to serious scholars interested in making sense of their interventions and contributions to social and political life."

— *Matt Henn, PhD, Chair of Social Research, School of Social Sciences, Nottingham Trent University, UK*

"In this wonderful new volume, Judith Bessant does a brilliant job of documenting the ways in which we 'make up' young people. She details the gaps between reality and representations of youth and politics and the paradox linked to critiques of youth apathy. Youth have spearheaded political movements throughout history, from the French Revolution to 1968, to current protests and sit ins. This thoughtful and deeply original new book is sure to engage anyone interested in these important issues."

— *Maria Grasso, Professor of Political Science and Political Sociology, Queen Mary University of London, UK*

MAKING-UP PEOPLE: YOUTH, TRUTH AND POLITICS

This book is about modern politics and young people. Judith Bessant revises some long-standing myths about children and young people's politics. She highlights the huge gap between the many ways young people and politics are talked about and how they have long been politically active.

Bessant draws on a relational historical sociology to show how since the nineteenth century certain historical dynamics, political interests and social imaginaries have enabled social scientists, writers, political leaders and policymakers to imagine and 'make up' different kinds of young people. Given these representations of childhood, adolescence and youth, everyone knows that young people are cognitively immature, inexperienced, morally under-developed and lack good judgement. For these reasons, they cannot possibly be allowed to engage in the serious, grown-up business of politics. Yet in just one of the many contradictions, young people are criticised by many of their elders for being politically apathetic and disengaged from politics.

Many think recent global warming movements largely led by quite young people are a novel phenomenon. Yet young people have been at the forefront of political movements of all kinds since the French revolution. Since the 1960s, children and young people increasingly played a major, if sometimes obscured, role in civil rights, anti-war, anti-globalisation, anti-austerity and global-warming movements. This accessible book is rich in theoretical and historical insight that is sure to appeal to sociologists, historians, youth studies scholars and political scientists, as well as to the general reader.

Judith Bessant is a Member of the Order of Australia (AM) and a Professor at RMIT University, Australia and writes about politics, youth studies, policy, sociology, media-technology studies and history. She also advises governments and non-government organizations.

MAKING-UP PEOPLE: YOUTH, TRUTH AND POLITICS

Judith Bessant

LONDON AND NEW YORK

First published 2021
by Routledge
2 Park Square, Milton Park, Abingdon, Oxon OX14 4RN

and by Routledge
52 Vanderbilt Avenue, New York, NY 10017

Routledge is an imprint of the Taylor & Francis Group, an informa business

© 2021 Judith Bessant

The right of Judith Bessant to be identified as author of this work has been asserted by her in accordance with sections 77 and 78 of the Copyright, Designs and Patents Act 1988.

All rights reserved. No part of this book may be reprinted or reproduced or utilised in any form or by any electronic, mechanical, or other means, now known or hereafter invented, including photocopying and recording, or in any information storage or retrieval system, without permission in writing from the publishers.

Trademark notice: Product or corporate names may be trademarks or registered trademarks, and are used only for identification and explanation without intent to infringe.

British Library Cataloguing-in-Publication Data
A catalogue record for this book is available from the British Library

Library of Congress Cataloging-in-Publication Data
A catalog record has been requested for this book

ISBN: 978-0-367-27629-4 (hbk)
ISBN: 978-0-429-29697-0 (ebk)

Typeset in Bembo
by codeMantra

This book is dedicated to
  Dr. Ahmed Nazir Ahmed Elsousi (ICU Physician)
  Dr. Cecille Bernadette Dabu-Fortun (Anaesthetist)
  Dr. Maher Abdalla Omer El-Hamarna (ED Physician)
  Dr. Mirza Saima Mahmud (Cardiology Physician)
  Ms. Jismy Antony Padathuparambil Varthu Antony (RN)
  Ms. Jane Flores Bamero (RN)
  Mr. Mark Aries Esquivel Fresco (RN)
  Ms. Aideleen Gonzalez David (RN)
  Ms. Sheena Mae Gilamon Beliganio (RN)
  Ms. Yasser Kintanar Fuentes (RN)
  Ms. Shiela Aira Esteron Villareal (RN)
  Mr. Abdul Mateen Shabu Sab Shaikh (Anaesthetic Technician)

CONTENTS

List of figures xi
Acknowledgements xiii

Introduction 1

1 Thinking about social representations 20

2 A minor omission: children, young people and politics 43

3 'The past is a foreign country...': young people in the eighteenth century 66

4 Civilising little savages: children and the dangerous classes 89

5 Girls politics and delinquency in the 1950s 122

6 Representing student politics in the 1960s 153

7 The great transformation: the young precariat and young entrepreneur 183

8 Making the waves: contemporary youth action 210

x Contents

9   Answering back and the politics of recognition   237

     Conclusion   256

Bibliography   *261*
Index   *303*

FIGURE

7.1 The number of job seekers and job vacancies (marginally attached not included) 1958–2018   194

ACKNOWLEDGEMENTS

Like most book projects, this one began some time ago and would not have seen the light of day without the support I was fortunate enough to receive.

I dedicate this book to staff from Emergency Department of Dubai Hospital without whom this book, quite literally, would not have happened. I 'met' them around this time last year while making one of my regular work trips from Australia to Europe. The plan was to present a research paper on refugees at a conference organised by colleagues at the Scuola Normale Superiore in Florence. It is a very long flight from Australia to Italy, and as usual, we stopped for a short transit in Dubai after 13 hours in the air. I slept all the way, woke up refreshed and feeling very pleased with myself for managing such a big sleep. As it turned out however being still and curled up asleep on a plane seat for such a long time is not a good thing to do.

During that trip unbeknown to me, I grew a rather large blood clot that became a 'massive pulmonary embolism'. As I walked off the plane, it went straight to the pulmonary artery and I collapsed.

As we entered the emergency room (ER), I went into cardiac arrest and my heart stopped for ten minutes. Rob, my partner, was told: 'she's gone'. Luckily however that wasn't to be thanks to the skill, expertise and professionalism of the 12 staff mentioned in Dubai Hospital's ER. They resuscitated, intubated me before putting me in a coma for a few days. To the doctors and nursing staff who brought me back into 'the land of the living' I am most grateful.

I woke a few days later to find my children and their partners beside my bed staring at me. Fearing the worst, they flew over to help and to be there. I realised then just how lucky I was not just to be alive but also for having such a wonderful family.

Besides being an eventful stop-over in Dubai, it gave me pause to think. I was on my way to Italy to give a conference paper on Australia's appalling treatment of young refugees. And there I was, a stranger in Dubai, so far from my homeland, in a land full of sounds, colour and sights that were so very foreign to me.

Perhaps it was because I had been researching the experiences of asylum-seekers and refugees who arrive on Australia's shores, that I could not help but think how different my Dubai experience was to the way so many of those who come to my country as strangers in desperate need of help are treated. I not only experienced the professionalism of the Dubai public hospital, which was first rate, but also got to encounter the generosity of Arabic hospitality.

It was a hospitality and generosity that came from everyone, and not so much a one-off kindness to a stranger as an ethical practice embedded in the Arabic culture.

One year later in a world marked by global pandemic, continuous refugee crises, closed international borders and increased hostility between nations, I keep thinking of that hospitality as a deep and rich oasis in the middle of a desert, which we might all visit to refresh our soul, and from which we may learn how to better treat each other and live better lives.

I also acknowledge and thank my family, Rob, my children, Rebekah and Macgregor and their wonderful partners Emma and Flynn. Of course, my grandchildren Harry and Matilda, Anouk and Sebastian who give me joy every single day that I could not live without. My mother Laura has also been a big part of my life while this book was written, and I thank her for being there.

A big thanks also to my university RMIT and to all my good colleagues and students.

Rob Watts my partner in crime and all things is someone you always want in your corner. As I have said before, he has a generous soul, and as all who know him would agree, he is also the brightest star in the universe. Without his daily support, this project would not have happened. Of course, I am always indebted to the National Tertiary Education Union (NTEU) and especially to my good colleague Linda Gale.

Finally, a big thanks to the Routledge staff. In particular, to the former commissioning editor Gerhard Boomgaarden who encouraged and supported me in the development of the proposal for this book; to Rebecca Brennan, now senior publisher at Routledge, and Mihaela Diana Ciobotea, editorial assistant. For their patience and support I am most grateful. Of course also thank Rajamalar and colleagues at Codemantra who provided patient and expert copy editing assistance.

INTRODUCTION

In 1428, a 16-year-old French girl called Jehanne left her village of Domremy in the north of France.[1] She travelled to Vaucouleurs, a town held by supporters of the Crown Prince of France, Charles of Valois. Charles had recently been disinherited by his father, enabling Henry V of England to claim France as his own. Jehanne, who could neither read nor write, claimed she had been told by the Archangel Michael to save France by expelling its enemies and installing Charles as its rightful king. Initially rebuffed by the magistrate of Vaucouleurs (Robert de Baudricourt), she persevered, gathering a small group of devotees who believed she was the virgin who, according to a popular prophecy, would save France.

When magistrate Baudricourt finally relented, Jehanne cropped her hair and dressed in men's clothes set off on an 11-day journey across enemy territory to Chinon, site of the Crown prince's palace. She is said to have exhibited supreme horse riding skills on this journey. Jehanne promised Charles that she would see him crowned king at Reims, the traditional French royal capital. Jehanne then asked Charles to give her an army to lead to Orléans, which was then under siege from the English. Against the advice of most of his counsellors and generals, Charles granted her request, and Jehanne set off to end the siege of Orléans. She succeeded in doing this in March 1429, dressed in white armour and riding a white horse, displaying remarkable strategic skills (Richey 2003). Charles was enthroned as Charles VII of France in July 1429. Soon after, Jehanne fell victim to political intrigue among warring French factions and was burned to death as a witch in 1429. She is now known as Joan d'Arc and is France's patron saint.

Nearly 600 years later, on 23 September 2019, Greta Thunberg, a diminutive 16-year-old Swedish girl, crossed the Atlantic by boat to speak to world leaders at the United Nation's (UN) Climate Action Summit in New York. A year earlier,

2 Introduction

she began a solo protest outside the Swedish parliament in Stockholm. She used her *Skolstrejk för klimatet* (School Strike for Climate) to draw attention to government inaction in the face of a climate catastrophe. At the UN, she said:

> This is all wrong. I shouldn't be up here. I should be back in school on the other side of the ocean. Yet you all come to us young people for hope … People are dying; entire ecosystems are collapsing … We are in the beginning of a mass extinction and all you can talk about is money and fairy tales of eternal economic growth. How dare you!
>
> *(Cited in Scott 2019)*

By 2019, Greta Thunberg had galvanised a global social movement, which, like her lone protest outside the Stockholm parliament, is called #Strike4Climate. It is a movement that has energised and mobilised large numbers of children, young people and older people. On 15 March 2019, around 1.4 million protesters worldwide joined the youth strike for climate change (Barclay and Amaria, 2019). In early December 2019, *Time* magazine acknowledged her global political impact by declaring her their *Person of the Year 2019*.

It seems that medieval French people had little trouble accepting that an illiterate 16-year-old girl could be assigned a role as military leader, able as one contemporary English writer observed to demand that she

> …have and… carry the very noble and excellent arms of France [and] to lead men-at-arms and command great companies to commit and exercise inhuman cruelties in shedding human blood in causing popular sedition and disturbances, inciting them to perjuries and pernicious rebellions.
>
> *(Devries 2011: 1)*

Yet if you had been listening to parents, social scientists, teachers, politicians, the media and various 'thought leaders' in the second decade of the twenty-first century, what young women like Greta Thunberg were doing should not have been happening.

There is a long-standing animus about the very idea that young people are, or could ever be, taken seriously as political agents. Acknowledging that children and young people can be political is offensive to common sense. After all, everyone knows that young people are cognitively immature, ethically defective, inexperienced and under-developed and for these reasons are not able to engage effectively in political activity. And if for some reason, they are silly enough to try, they should be kept well away from politics for their own sake and for that of the community. Recent versions of this idea relied on claims about 'the adolescent brain', which it is claimed, is not fully mature or developed like the 'adult brain'. Proponents of this argument point to 'scientific research' based on the use of functional magnetic resonance imaging (fMRI) brain-imaging technology to assess adolescent development. 'Science informs us that young people are neurologically not full adults even at 18 years of age' (Toumbourou et al. 2014:568–570). According to Chan and Clayton, e.g., owners of 'the teen brain' are not ready to vote at 16 (Reyna and Farley 2006:1–44, Steinberg 2007:55–59, Chan 2006, cf. Bessant 2008:347–360).

Notwithstanding the common sense idea that politics is no place for young people and that they need to be protected from entering the public sphere, another more recent argument paradoxically complains that young people are politically apathetic and disengaged (Martin 2012, Sloam 2016). Since the 1990s we have seen a lot of public discussion and research on young people and their political disengagement characterised by alarm about young people's lack of interest in politics (Norris 1999, 2002, Benedicto 2012:719). Numerous surveys of young people's political attitudes and voting behaviour have been carried out to confirm this (Kimberlee 2002, Print et al. 2004).[2] It seems that participation in traditional or conventional forms of politics is now rare among young people (Galston 2004, Martin 2012:485).

Yet something seems wrong here. It is clear now that children and young people are engaging in politics and doing so in considerable numbers. Recent academic research has tracked standout examples of such action. This research reveals that children and young people are using what scholars like Pickard call 'Do it Ourselves' politics. This is a politics that is often impromptu, issue-oriented and collective in form, using new social media like Facebook, Twitter and smart phones to inform and mobilise other young people (Bessant 2014, Bäck et al. 2019, Dennis 2019, Pickard 2019). As I document later in this book, this is not a recent phenomenon: there is a long and rich history of political action by children and young people.

If this is the case, then why is there a disconnect between dominant ideas about what children and young people should not be doing and what they actually do?

How to make sense of this incongruity or gap is what animates this book. Why, e.g., have young people like Greta Thunberg elicited such enormous support and admiration from supporters and vitriolic abuse from others? Consider, e.g., how 'opinion-makers' like Michael Knowles, an American conservative commentator, called Greta Thunberg a 'mentally ill-child'. Knowles continued: 'What is shameful is exploiting a child – particularly a child with mental disorders - to advance your political agenda' (Scott 2019). US President Donald Trump followed suit drawing on the long-standing idea that children and young people are incapable of rational political thought or action, describing Thunberg as an angry child who needed to 'chill out' (Trump 2019, @realDonaldTrump).

One possible reason for such responses is that it is one way of ignoring what they say. Attacking the messenger rather than the message is an old device. This kind of attack was not uniquely directed at Thunberg. Many other young leaders like Cameron Kasky, Sarah Gonzales and David Hogg who mobilised the 'March for Our Lives' in 2018 attracting around 1.4 million young people across America were given the same kind of treatment.

This does not however address the problem raised as children and young people are continually inserted into dire political situations and crises whether they want to be or not. Typically, this is because children are victims of horrendous circumstances over which they have had no say or influence. Consider, e.g., of the iconic image of the unknown Jewish 'ghetto boy' photographed bare-legged in his 'little boy shorts', standing fearful with hands in the air as Nazi paramilitary troopers point a machine gun at him during the eviction of Jewish people from their Warsaw homes in 1943.[3] Or think of nine-year-old Kim Phuc, photographed in 1972 as she runs, with other children, naked and screaming toward the photographer as they flee a napalm air strike by South Vietnamese forces incinerating their village of Trang Bang'.[4]

A few years later in 1976 Soweto outside Johannesburg, 15-year-old Antoinette Sithole is photographed running alongside her 18-year-old friend Mbuyisa Makhubu as he carried the limp body of Sithole's dying 12-year-old brother, Hector, in his arms, a casualty of a police bullet.[5] This is testimony to the brutality of the apartheid regime and the ways young people are so often central political actors in such political crises. Significantly, it was action that also helped bring about the demise of the apartheid regime.[6] Or consider the Argentinian 'dirty war' of 1976–1982 when around 30,000 people mostly aged between 16 and 35 years 'disappeared' as part of the junta's bid to eradicate a generation of young people represented as political subversive.

Think too of the famous 'David and Goliath' photograph of 15-year-old Palestinian Faris Odeh at the Gaza Strip in 2000. It's a powerful image of a boy standing alone facing-off a huge Israeli military tank. Faris Odeh has a stone in his hand prepared to throw it at the tank (Hockstader 2000).[7] Ten days later, (8 November), Odeh was once again throwing stones when he was shot in the neck by Israeli troops and killed (*Hockstader* 2000).[8] For many Palestinians, he epitomised heroic Palestinian defiance and resistance to Israeli military occupation. This image of Faris Odeh became a central icon in graffiti and street art, in calendars, political posters and in social media. Closer to our own time, in 2015, is the confronting image that ricocheted around global media outlets. Who can erase the 2015 image of the body of three-year-old Syrian refugee Aylan Kurdi, whose small body lay on the beach of Bodrum in Turkey, bearing mute witness to the greatest refugee crisis in modern history?[9]

Consider finally, the powerful video footage of the child as witness, Gianna the six-year-old daughter of George Floyd, the unarmed African American man killed in May 2020 by police officers in Minneapolis, USA. They were images swept across traditional media and social media amidst world-wide protests staged during the COVID-19 pandemic and lockdowns. Footage of Gianna shows her standing beside her mother Roxie Washington bearing witness to her grief and personal tragedy, the murder of her father. The caption reads 'this is what life will be like for George Floyd's young daughter', 'without her dad'. Gianna's mother says she wants everyone to know 'this is what those officers took … Gianna does not have a father. He will never see her grow up…' (Silva 2020). In another video, the figure of the child Gianna is again pictured as she sits on the shoulders of Stephen Jackson, a famous former basketball player with her arms extended and smiling out to the world, as she says 'daddy changed the world'. Her words are echoed by those around her. The video went viral with 83.9k 'retweets' and 83.9k 'likes' (ABC News 2020).

Whether valorised as sad, injured or dead victims of state terror, freedom fighters, as climate warriors or excoriated as school truants, delinquents, petty criminals, young people are present in the political domain. They are constituted in representations that position them in ways that help serve the interests of those with the power to win out in struggles over recognition, over what counts as political and what 'kind of person' they are.

What we see as writers from Jenks (1996) and Prout (2000) to Hartung (2017) have argued, are some of the contradictions that have endlessly circled around the figure of the child and youth over the last century or so. It seems that children and young people have always been caught in all various politics and political controversies whether as unwitting victims, purposeful political actors or as objects of anxieties and fantasies. We get some insight into the complex array of contradictory and competing representations epitomised in the way Greta Thunberg herself played with these contradictions. She did this when referring to herself as a schoolchild conspicuously not in the place she should have been. As she stood before some of the most powerful adults in the world 'gathered together at the United Nations in New York' Thunberg argued: 'I shouldn't be up here. I should be back in school on the other side of the ocean. Yet you all come to us young people for hope. How dare you!' (Thunberg 2019).

It seems whatever you are or want to be, if you are a child or a young person you are caught in this cross-fire of contradictory representations. As Bray and Nakata argue, these contradictions in the representation of children and politics reflect how, in spite of what has been said about keeping children out of politics, this has never actually been possible (2020:1). Whatever the debates about whether children should, or should not be, part of political processes, the fact is that children and young people are already political, whether as political 'objects' or as political 'subjects'. This indicates there are more substantive normative and theoretical questions to explore in the ways children and young are represented, and in the ways young people react to, or push back at some of these representations.

This book is about modern politics and young people. More specifically, it is about the politics that informs how children and young people are represented. I attempt to address the following questions.

- What value is there in inquiring about how young people and children are represented?
- What do we mean by representations?

- What is meant when we refer to political representations of young people?
- What is politics and what is political?
- Who makes these representations and why?
- Do the representations change over time?
- Do these representations provide an accurate account of what children and young people are doing?
- Do these representations influence how young people variously represent themselves and experience their lives?
- How should we understand these often paradoxical ways young people have been represented and how can their often conflicting nature be understood?
- Do young people push back against these representations and if so how?
- How have young people represented themselves and how have they interacted and responded to representations of them?
- Could those interactions change representations?

This book observes that there is, and has long been, a gap between how children and young people are represented politically, *and* the realities of those young people's lives. I also see that gap between reality and representation as a political artefact, as something that is itself part of a political process. Talking about representations is to talk about how experts, intellectuals, writers, journalists, policy-makers 'make up' certain kind of people. This is why I refer to the idea of 'making people up'. With this in mind, I briefly discuss in an introductory way some of the relevant theoretical issues.

Theoretical observations

Two insights inform this book. One is the historical nature of representations, which means recognising how being human is always something experienced in a specific place and time.

While this may seem to be a truism, as Anderson argues, even historians are by default 'presentists' who use present day frameworks and concepts, usually in unacknowledged ways, to explore the past (2018). And even though we may never be able to escape the present entirely, an effort needs to be made to at least acknowledge the 'taken for granted thought about givens of existence and beliefs, ideas, and perspectives, orthodox or heterodox, that comprise the particular worldviews of particular subjects' in times past (Anderson 2018:124).

The other insight informing this book involves a 'relational perspective', an approach that is gaining some traction in the social sciences. It's an approach that involves recognising the typically unspoken, but powerful influence of substantialist thinking in contemporary western natural and social sciences. It involves recognising how for much of their history, those working in these fields have seen the social world as if it has been made up of actual things, of structures or forces that interact in causal and predictable ways resulting in controversial binaries or oppositions, like 'individual–society or structure–agency'. A relational perspective focuses on relations rather than 'social things', in ways described by theorists like Norbert Elias (2012) and Pierre Bourdieu (1998). I discuss this in detail later in the book. What follows is an introductory discussion about the idea of representations and 'making up people'.

Making up people

Debates about whether the ideas we have about what is real correspond with the world have a long history in western philosophy and the social sciences. In early discussions about how we know the world, Plato used a cave allegory to say that our ideas about the world are at best understood as shadows. The shadows are produced by a fire at the entrance to a cave implying they are ideas or illusions that prevent us from seeing and knowing things in the world as they actually are. (One political implication of this was Plato's claim that we need philosophers to tell us what the truth is.) His pupil Aristotle was less pessimistic, seeing representations whether they were mathematical, artistic, political or theoretical as necessary, because they provided a medium based in language or in different kinds of mimetic art. These representations gave us access to the world. In short, Aristotle thought we can access the real world through the practice of *mimesis* or imitation in literature, painting or dance (Zoran 2015:470–472). In this way, Aristotle was a naive realist who thought we can know things as they are. This could be done, Aristotle believed, by using symbolic forms such as language, inductive reasoning (empirical or sensory data from our eyesight, smell or touch) and deductive logic (e.g., geometry or syllogistic deduction).

Two thousand years later, the eighteenth-century philosopher Kant developed an account of scientific concepts, laws and theories as representations. He believed we experience mental events that allow us to produce representations of the world and thus become aware of 'something else'. Boniolo draws on Kant arguing that a representation is simultaneously what we know *and* the means by which we know it is through an act of cognitive constitution (Boniolio 2007: xiv).

Twentieth-century social theorists like Stuart Hall (1977), social psychologists like Serge Moscovici (2000) and anthropologists like Pierre Bourdieu (1991b) also developed theories of representations. Their work acknowledges that in large modern complex societies like ours, we rely less on direct experience and increasingly on a range of descriptions, images or representations. They are representations produced by experts in the social sciences or the biological and medical sciences or journalists, novelists, film-makers and policy-makers (Sercombe 1996:2). This means that any categories we use to talk about 'indigenous people', 'gays', 'teenagers', 'Muslims', 'feminists', 'teachers', 'politicians', etc., are usually not based on any wide, long-term personal experiences with 'those people', but on mediated representations of these 'types' of people. In this way, we rely on networks of experts, writers and creative people to 'make-up people'. I say more about this in Chapter 1.

Historians like Mary Poovey also developed these ideas in histories of social statistics and the invention of the modern census in the nineteenth century that were then used to help 'make-up people' (1995). The use of a census, e.g., which became increasingly common in the nineteenth century required classifying people in terms of attributes like their gender, age, occupation or religion so they could be classified and counted. It was a practice that involved imposing certain categories, attributes or characteristics on people that may or may not have been true and that may also have been resented.

At this point, I need to say why readers will not find here, or anywhere in this book, a definition of who what a child or a young person is. This might seem strange because as Sonia Livingstone and Mariya Stoilova say, if we are writing about children and young people what do 'we call them, children or young people? 'Youth or adolescents? Teens or teenagers? Or perhaps just kids?' (Livingstone and Stoilova 2020:1). Does this mean we need some kind of definition based on age?

Typically, such definitions refer to one's calendar age, which has become standard practice with its origins in the emergence of the census and of social science researchers. Today, it is expected that governments, international bodies like the United Nations and most researchers define 'children' as anyone, e.g., aged 0–18 or 0–14 years, depending on the jurisdiction and time, while 'youth' is defined as a person aged 15–25. If I do not do this, then perhaps the reader will expect me to say that the child or youth is 'socially constructed'. I do not however say this either because it is not true.

Yet clearly a six-month-old 'infant' is very different in appearance and body shape and in many other ways to a 13-year-old or a 30-year-old. They are differences that are real in the same way that differences can be observed when we enter puberty. Dismissing those differences by saying they are social constructions will not make them disappear. Nor will it help clarify how we come to have such categories.

This is not to deny as many people like Margaret Bucholtz (2002) and Margarete Gullette (2004) observe, that when different societies at different times call someone a child, a young person or an adult, they are engaging in a cultural practice. As anthropologists have observed, in many cultures, a pre-pubescent person may be called a 'youth', while in others, people in their thirties or forties may be referred to as a youth (Bucholtz 2002). In the USA, pre-adolescent children accused of violent crimes may be classified as adults in the justice system (Bucholtz 2002:525–526).

For Durham, use of the linguistic term 'shifter' is a helpful way of understanding how societies use age as a marker to identity categories such as child or youth (Durham 2004: 592). As she says, 'shifter' is a representation or word that cannot be understood fully without also having additional contextual information. It is to attribute relationships between people and they carry with them ideas about what counts as a child, youth, adult or the elderly. Seeing youth or adolescence as a shifter means situating those categories within a particular context, appreciating how the meanings of those categories shift – even within the same space and time according to the message being communicated. As Durham argues, to refer to someone as a youth is to position them in terms of various social attributes, including not just their age but also independence–dependence, authority, rights, abilities, knowledge, responsibilities, etc. (Durham 2004:593).

As I explain in later chapters, the idea of the shifter is what Pierre Bourdieu (1992) develops in his relational approach to categories or representations like youth to show how they are involved in reproducing *and* contesting certain social relations.

As I also argue in this book, social representations or categories like youth, child and adolescent are *symbolic* and thus exist as a result of *collective a*ction by members of a given community. They become embedded in our social and political lives, they express and shape identities, and the social conditions of all the people who play a role in bringing them in to existence, in replicating them, changing and in becoming them (Moscovici 2000). In short, to say what a child or youth or adolescent is, it is necessary to study the culture and individual mind. Defining or representing the youth or child involves defining how those 'kinds of people' are 'made up' or are constitutively imagined in the setting of human relations marked by power differences and by the material, social and symbolic worlds in which we live. As symbolic phenomena, the content, structure and processes of social representation making needs to be studied if we are to understand the interest and politics that informs them.

These representations are also recursive. That is they are not just descriptions of 'children', 'youth', 'the unemployed', 'Muslims' or 'the poor'. They also help constitute or make up those *types* of people and inform how those people being talked about, how they come to understand themselves, how they respond to those representations and how they act in the world. This is what Ian Hacking calls a feedback or 'looping effect' (1983, 1986). That is, any representation, in this case of children and young people, affects those people it is said to 'describe'. This is also what Giddens referred to as the 'double hermeneutic effect' (1984).

The words used to *describe* people are never literal descriptions of the qualities or attributes said to define them: they also carry overlays of interpretation and evaluation that can shape the way those people see or understand themselves. As writers like Bernard Cohn showed, when British imperial officials imposed alien census categories on Indian people based on caste or religion, this was initially resented, but came later to be adopted by certain groups as true (1998). In short, this active relationship between how we describe or classify other people and the ways those descriptions can affect those who are being described is a distinctive feature of the human and the social sciences. It differentiates the social sciences from the natural sciences because objects of social science are humans affected by how they are known or represented.

This focus on representations challenges the common sense notion that the 'kinds of people' in our world are 'real' or 'natural' objects that are just 'there' and are relatively amenable to description. A focus on representations also highlights why it's problematic to assume that all 'children' or all 'young people' share basic defining or *essential* qualities. This is essentialist thinking that involves inventing or exaggerating certain qualities and then applying them to all those deemed to belong to the group in question (e.g., all 'young people', all 'women' or 'all Chinese'). There are good reasons to be sceptical about such essentialist thinking given the diversity or heterogeneity, e.g., of children and young people.

In what follows, I provide an account of social representations by critically adapting insights provided by scholars like Stanley Cohen (1972) and Christine Griffin (1993) and by drawing on Moscovici (1981) and Bourdieu (1993). Like Bourdieu, I argue that categories like 'childhood', 'youth' and 'adolescence' are part of a symbolic order constructed in *fields* of cultural power that owe much to expert knowledge and practices carried out in institutions like universities, the state and its legal systems, churches and schools, the media and the law (Bourdieu 1991b). The dominant modern scientific and common sense (western) representations of children and young people are a product of certain practices and institutions.

Paying attention to these representations over the past few centuries helps highlight the various ways young people have been represented. Some of those representations changed over time, whereas some continue and recur over time. What we have are changing realities *and* semantic-conceptual variation (Kosselleck 2002, Palti 2011:5).

Historian Reinhart Kosselleck (2002, 2004) offers an account of historical thinking and narratives by tracing how changing conceptions of time and of history itself influence the ways we tell stories about political ideas. His history of historical and political concepts helps to think about relations between changing ways of enacting politics and the categories or concepts that are used to understand political practices. Kosselleck also highlights the value of paying attention to the social context in which concepts emerge. In this way, we can recognise how they are manifestations of particular political conflicts rather than eternal categories (2002). One insight Kosselleck provides is that, we should not expect or attribute any coherence or rationality to the processes that generate representations or indeed to the social representations themselves. Indeed, the representations of young people identified in this book are rarely characterised by logical thought reliant on static evidence (Moscovici 2000). Rather they involve 'everyday thinking' that is typically characterised by different, irrational and contradictory forms of knowing or 'cognitive polyphasia' where different knowledge with different rationalities co-exist side by side (Moscovici 2000).

Moreover, while social representations tend to affirm the knowledge we have already created, they also help create ways of ignoring and denying what is actually happening sometimes in front of our noses. These representations can be seen, e.g., in journalist reports, in cultural images produced for mass audience and markets and in popular collective memories. That is, they not only help 'mediate' our knowledge about 'the young' (youth unemployment, politics and poverty) but they may also obstruct, fragment and negate our knowledge of people and issues. This indicates that what we come to know about certain kinds of people may be a political process. Developing this approach to representations also involves identifying and moving beyond the substantialist thinking that dominates western thought and sciences (Bessant et al. 2019:1–17).

A relational approach

According to Bourdieu, the social representations are the product of relations *and* processes in which our ideas about types of people such as children and young people, function 'as the relay mechanism in exchanges of power, value and publicity' (1993).

Bourdieu's approach to representations positions him in a relational philosophical tradition.[10] This tradition is not generally acknowledged by English-speaking scholars and researchers partly because most scholarly traditions are embedded, often unknowingly, in the western substantialist tradition (Cassirer 1923). Substantialism, in its various forms, provides the dominant epistemological framework for modern English-speaking sociology and mainstream social sciences.[11] It is a tradition that goes back to Aristotle who claimed reality is made up of a 'multiplicity of existing things', and that we can create concepts that allow us to know what is in the world. This was to be done by identifying and isolating all the elements common to the various things that exist and then putting them into classes (Vandenberghe 2001:482). Aristotle thought the world is naturally made up of animate and inanimate entities or things that are clustered together into species. For Aristotle, constructing a concept involves uncovering the *substantial form* of the things that exist in reality. A species is defined by its essential attributes. All 'dog', e.g., have fur, four-legged, a long tail and bark. All 'tables' have four legs and a flat surface on top. These attributes are essential to that 'thing', and they are also invariant and timeless.

This substantialist approach permeated western thinking over nearly two millennia in the natural sciences and philosophy and it continues to do so in the social sciences. According to proponents of the substantialist tradition, *substances* are the 'things' that make up components of the world, they constitute the objects we know. These substances, depending on whether you subscribe to a materialist view or an idealist view, are 'hard' natural and material entities or 'soft' ideational, 'spiritual' or cultural.[12] This is why regardless of whether the social scientist is doing quantitative and qualitative research, the shared and underlying belief is that there are natural-biological things or social-cultural-symbolic substances that define categories like the 'child' or 'youth'.

Bourdieu drew on the philosopher Ernst Cassirer and his critique of Aristotle's theories of substance to develop his relational perspective. Cassirer (1923) rejected Aristotle's ideas about substance as 'objects and things' and developed a relational theory that privileged 'functions and relations' (Vandenberghe 2001:483). Thus, according to Cassirer, what is 'real is dissolved into different relational structures that are mutually inter-linked by a whole system of laws which mutually condition each other' (Cassirer 1923:288).

Though this point is to be elaborated in Chapter 2, Bourdieu developed the idea that scientific concepts and representations do not and cannot stand alone and function separately either from the reality that they represent or form each other *as if* they are unrelated to each other. In short, Bourdieu's emphasis was on the mutual relations between 'words' and 'things' that are produced by intellectual practices being in various practice-based 'fields'.[13]

This involves showing how networks of ideas, metaphors and images as different collective cognitions and common-sense systems of thought come together (Moscovici 2000:153, Hoijer 2011:3–16). These representations come into being within fields and they are formed politically through constant struggles or competitions over various capitals (Bourdieu 1993, Isin 2002). This is why it is useful to give attention to the political struggles involved in the making of social representations if we are to see how some people get to exercise more power than others in constructing and challenging certain representations. As I demonstrate in later chapters, we can see how representations of young people are produced in different fields such as scientific, educational, political and cultural fields.

The argument

This book is about modern politics and in particular it is about modern representations of young people from the late nineteenth century to our own time with a focus on the west and in particular on countries such as America, Britain and Australia. The practical constraints of writing one book meant that I could not address the global south, something that I hope to do in a second book.

While the primary focus is on the twentieth and twenty-first centuries, I go back to the eighteenth and nineteenth centuries. It is a timeframe I use for three reasons. One is practical and has to do with what is possible in one book. The second reason is because while there is much debate about the 'starting point' for the emergence of the modern categories of youth and child (Aries 1962, Gillis 1974, Mitterauer 1992, Heywood 2001, Foyster and Marten 2010), it is generally agreed that between the 1880s and early 1900s, the modern idea of the child and youth was becoming well entrenched in many parts of the world.[14]

This does matter because I argue that the incongruity or disjunctures that exist between what we see and what we know about children and young people today *can largely be explained by reference to modern scientific ideas* about young people that emerged and flourished during this period.

Third, I focus on this period because it marks the rise of the modern western capitalist economy and as I and others argue, we are now witnessing the beginnings of its demise (Streeck 2016, Mason 2017, Bessant 2018, Zubov 2019). It was an industrial order and period of change described by its proponents positively in terms of progress, enlightenment and an inevitable linear development toward 'civilization' (e.g., Comte, Hegel, Weber, Durkheim) (Wallerstein 1974:387–415).

In this book, I document the ways we have come to know children and young people in the past few centuries. I argue that this owes much to 'modern' ways of constituting or making up certain representations of them as 'child', 'adolescent', 'juvenile', 'minor', 'teenager' and so forth. The modern privileging of 'scientific method' based on careful definition and measurement of the 'essential attributes' of children or young people interlaced with meta-narratives about human evolution and economic and social development generated a powerful and influential account of children and young people as 'incomplete adults' (Hall 1905, Burt 1925, 1965, Piaget 1940, 1967, Erikson 1950, 1963, Kohlberg 1981).

The dominant tendency operating here has been to continually represent children and young people as inherently apolitical because they are morally and cognitively immature.

Yet as I demonstrate, there are also many inconsistencies that characterise official and popular thinking about young people and politics. This in part is because young people and children do actually play a major role in politics and have done so historically. Yet their presence and status as political actors is rarely acknowledged or valued. Indeed, the political nature of their action and their presence tends to be ignored, rejected or recognised as something else. We have seen, e.g., how young people are held responsible for the crisis of democracy because they are 'politically apathetic' and 'disengaged'. Yet at the same time, there is talk and images of young people as victims of various socio-economic or geo-political processes from unemployment, the global refugee crisis or family violence, constantly filling our public airways, government reports and policy documents, our news programs, films and music.

How the book is set out

In what follows, I outline the key arguments in this book.

In the first chapter, I ask what are representations and why paying attention to them is important.

I begin with Christine Griffin's book *Representations of Youth* (1993), arguing that while her book is admired for its insight into how experts created discourses about young people in the twentieth century, it does not provide an account of representations. This is a curious omission given Griffin is a social psychologist working in the same field as Serge Moscovici, an international figure in social psychology whose work specifically focused on developing a theory of social representations. I consider Moscovici's theory of representations and why he says it is important to pay close attention to this topic. I identify and critically assess key features of Moscovici's social representations theory, which he sees as the products of experts and scientific researchers.

Attention is then given to Bourdieu's ideas about symbolic capital and symbolic orders, which provide helpful insight into the practices of representing 'Others' within social orders marked by continuous, ubiquitous and diverse inequalities. I note how Bourdieu pays close attention to the unequal nature of social relations that shape representations, how e.g., people with greater access to various kinds of capital tend to win out in the constant struggles over who gets to represent whom. Bourdieu's relational perspective provides a helpful way of thinking about representations, and it is one that breaks with the dominant substantialist epistemological paradigm that continues to permeate social sciences. This also has implications for how we understand politics.

In Chapter 2, I ask what is meant by politics and the political. Given that politics is central to this book, I devote a chapter to getting some clarity about what it means. This is needed if we are to consider the various ways young people's politics is represented or misrepresented.

It argues that politics informs how young people represent themselves and their action, and it informs arguments that deny or exclude young people from the field of politics. And yet there is no consensus about what is meant by politics. Moreover, politics as it is understood in the social sciences is narrowly defined in terms of electoral politics and the business or mechanics of the state of government.

How politics is conceived also matters because it determines whether we recognise its influence in shaping scientific and popular ideas (e.g., developmental theory) about the capacity of young people to be political. All this has implications for how young people are variously represented. I argue in this chapter that politics is best understood as inclusive of various actions that involve contesting power relations, the *status quo* and conventional categories and imaginaries. Understanding politics in this way allows for a recognition of the many ways young people are political.

In Chapter 3, I ask how children and young people were represented in the eighteenth century. The chapter establishes how often quite young people were able to assume leadership roles in government or in military services and politics in ways that in the twenty-first century are unthinkable. A survey is provided of some contemporary historian's understandings of the eighteenth century as a period in which significant changes occurred in the ways children and young people were represented and how they lived in their communities. I document how some young people responded to and engaged in the crossfire of political ideas and movements coming out of the French revolution (1789–1796). This helps reveal the politics that informed the identification of 'youth' with democratic motifs like human rights, democracy and equality, which then as now were and are dangerous and disruptive ideas.

Attention is also given to how ideas of novelty and change were seen as a threat to the old order whose defenders were committed to defending what was seen as a natural divinely inspired hierarchy and social order. I argue that reactions to the French revolution provided a new interpretative framework in which children and young people came to be seen as sources of disorder and trouble, representations that were developed and amplified in the nineteenth century, which is the focus of the following chapter.

In Chapter 4, an account of the ongoing ripple effect generated by the French Revolution is offered. It was an event that terrified European elites and established young people as sources of democratic disruption and as key members of 'dangerous classes'. By the 1840s, the idea that the children and young people found in the 'lower orders' were delinquents and criminals became a fixed idea that continues into our own time.

By the 1880s, when European imperial rivalries and contests over colonial acquisitions peaked, political and scientific elites everywhere showed a strong interest in 'racial fitness' based on the fear that the 'white race' needed to address social problems like poverty, unemployment, slum dwelling, illegitimate births, crime and mental health by racial scientific means. An international eugenics movement committed to promoting a 'science of breeding' and to promoting 'racial fitness' produced a science quantifying the number of delinquents, deviants and physically and mentally degenerate members of society. It also encouraged a great interest in children and young people.

Enter the science of child development that evolved into the science of 'adolescence', usually attributed to G. Stanley Hall (1904). The advent of this science generated the figure of the adolescent represented as undeveloped, moody, immature, inexperienced, irresponsible, irrational, lacking in impulse control, incapable of good judgement and ill-suited for self-determination – and thus required close management. It followed that 'they' were to be excluded from politics and the public sphere generally: their presence in the political space was a danger to them and a direct threat to the community and to the state.

Chapter 5 documents the rise to public prominence of young women called 'Widgies' in Australia and New Zealand in the 1950s. The emergence of this sub-culture paralleled the evolution of similar youth cultures in the UK, Europe and the USA all of which generated a much public concern and scholarly attention. The rise of such a youth culture occurred in the context of decades of eugenic discourse and developmental framings of 'adolescence' that evolved through the twentieth century, providing a point of reference for the evolving industry of youth experts.

Not surprisingly, conventional accounts of human cognitive and moral development developed by academics and professional experts were conceived in overwhelmingly masculine ways. In one sense, girls and women were marginalised, if not rendered invisible. Widgies however were determined to be noticed. Following on the rise of rock n roll and a culture of consumption of clothing, music and cars, widgies challenged long-standing gendered assumptions about how women should behave and what they should aspire to. Widgies subverted conventional ideas about how girls should use their bodies when they spread their legs to ride a motorbike 'as men did', or when they wore tight-fitting clothes, cropped their hair short, smoked cigarettes 'like a man', occupied public spaces by attending rock n roll dances or the movies, or just hung out like boys in public spaces.

They challenged prevailing ideas about the place of young women and an imagined future social order in which they were good wives and mothers (Carrington 1993). Widgies were denigrated, pitied and characterised as 'maladjusted' or psychologically troubled. While the outrage directed at them focussed on their subversion of gendered ideas about how women should be adjusted, it also ignored and misrepresented the political character of their interventions. Under the disapproving gaze of experts, widgies openly violated the clearly stipulated expectations of women and what it meant to be a 'good girl'. In some ways, widgies were a social movement *avant la lettre* though this was not acknowledged then because their conduct did not fit the conventional category of the political.

There can be no such mistake made in the 1960s, a decade which saw a global explosion of dissent by children and young people on issues such as war, civil rights and the quality of education.

Chapter 6 documents what some scholars refer to as the 'Long 68' as students in schools and universities engaged in serious and continuous protest in many countries. Politicians, the media and public opinion were generally not well disposed to this action, with governments and commentators representing student protestors either as impulsive, infantile and deranged or as the dupes of extremists and communists. It was a reaction designed to deny the distinctively political nature of student dissent. This chapter documents how once more we see a pattern of continuing efforts by experts, commentators and policy-makers to represent young people in ways that suppress any acknowledgement of the political character of the critical responses coming from young people to the emerging crisis of liberal-democracy and the old Left.

Chapter 7 documents key representations of young people generated in the 1970s and 1980s by politicians, policy-makers and experts in governments, universities, global consultancies and think-tanks. This chapter shows how governments, economic actors and various professionals tried to explain early signs of the far-reaching changes occurring in the economy. Those changes included shifts in the labour market that began in the late 1970s, which accompanied 'new' representations of young people. One way of trying to understand the transformation involves asking whether human labour or work has a future. It was a question raised in a context marked by a real and unprecedented transformative process driven by a confluence of political and policy shifts, continuing technological disruption and major structural changes in capitalist economies. Given how these changes have led to high youth unemployment, young people came to assume a central role in various political and cultural discussions encapsulated in categories like 'unemployed youth', 'early school leaver' and 'youth underclass'.

The expulsion of young people from the full-time labour market became especially apparent in the 1990s. Between the 1970s and 1990s, government and business commentary converted the problem of mounting unemployment to one 'best explained' by deficits of skill, experience and motivation in the unemployed.

Apart from being used to justify harsher welfare systems in many advanced economies, these representations and policy discourses of which they were part, masked other changes occurring in capitalist economies. A raft of neoliberal polices were launched in a bid to restore the 'natural' dominance of capital over labour, that had been unsettled after 1945 by the co-evolution of full employment policies and welfare state interventions.

By the late twentieth and twenty-first centuries, concern about the 'young precariat' was countered by an enthusiasm for the redemptive qualities said to characterise the 'young entrepreneur'. And while representations of young people were centre stage, the political significance signalled by their apparent absence as political actors in this period should not be read as inferring the decades of change described here saw no evidence of political pushback by young people. Far from it. As argued in the following Chapter 8, the political response of young people was yet to come.

Chapter 8 addresses repeated instances of significant political action by children and young people around the globe over the past few decades. This is clearly a response to and product of deepening fault-lines evident in the confluence of technological disruption, failed neoliberal policies, mounting inequality and the global warming catastrophe. Both these waves of protest and the matters in contention suggest that the west is facing a total systems crisis, similar in some ways to the crisis confronting the French state in decades before 1789, a period in which as we have seen, young people also played a key role. This chapter highlights the way children and young people continue to be being represented as half-adults lacking the experience, cognitive skills, self-control and judgement apparently needed to take on the role of citizen. This contrasts strikingly with how many children and young people now represent themselves as political actors and assume highly visible leadership roles in social movements. One distinctive feature of this action, e.g., compared to the 1960s, is the increasing reliance on new media used to inform, recruit and mobilise campaigns. Several vignettes of online action are offered to illustrate this.

Chapter 9 highlights the increasingly contradictory ways children and young people continue being represented in the scholarly literature. Arguably this reflects the uncertainties generated by the many ways young people are now rejecting the conventional ways in which they have long been represented. As I show here, this also includes the often hostile responses to the very idea that children should ever be engaged politically. This includes repeated claims that student protestors are variously 'spoiled', 'ungrateful' or 'disobedient', who are either 'dupes' being manipulated by unscrupulous adults or are 'shallow' and just looking for any excuse to play 'truant'. These representations have been vigorously contested and rebutted by young activists, concerned as they might well be, to keep paying attention to the issues that have mobilised them to take action.

These young activists are living evidence of the Arendt's point that natality is indeed a key feature of the political: These young activists are interested in moving beyond established arrangements towards something better, because although it may sound a little clichéd, they want to 'create a different and better world'.

Conclusion

This book is about the politics that shape how young people are represented by others and how they represent themselves. I will attempt to identify and explain some incongruities between the key role many young people play in politics, modern conceptions of children and young people and claims they are incapable of political thought and action and therefore should not enter the public domain.

How young people are represented in our time is diverse and contradictory. The tendency to see young people as puppets of exploitative adults depends on the long-standing normative ideas of the child or young person as inherently innocent, vulnerable and immature who should not be exposed to 'the adult' world of politics or public things. Others however represent those same young people as heroic and praiseworthy political activists and harbingers of a future. They are representations that draw on quite different understandings of young people and their capacities.

The fact that many children and young people are now actively participating in a range of political actions and assuming leadership roles in various social movements can be understood as a reminder that historically that is exactly what children and young people once did. The slow and steady expulsion of young people from political activity and public deliberation that began in the nineteenth century is not so much testimony to an inherent deficiency, but a reflection of the interests of power elites in maintaining their own social status and a particular social order. These representations also reveal much about how politics between the generations now operate.

Normative ideas based on modern concepts of youth, the child and adolescent imply that they should not be victims of crisis, war or civil strife and should be protected from those situations. Those same concepts inform the view that young people should not be taken seriously as political actors engaged in various kinds of protests or civil disobedience. The fact remains that many are. The same thinking says they cannot possibly be political leaders able to grasp what is happening, to demonstrate strength of character, to create new possibilities and energise millions of people across the globe. Yet they do.

Notes

1 Most people at this time in France did not have surnames. Jeanne referred to herself when she was on trial for witchcraft as Jehanne la Pucelle.
2 See Kimberlee (2002), Henn and Weinstein (2006:517–534), Edwards (2007) and Furlong and Catmell (2012). A lot of research refers to low rates of electoral turnout among young people. In 2009, e.g., European Parliament elections, 50% of those over 55 years of age voted, whereas only 29% of 18- to 24-year olds voted.

3 https://en.wikipedia.org/wiki/Warsaw_Ghetto_Uprising#/media/File:Stroop_Report_-_Warsaw_Ghetto_Uprising_BW.jpg
4 https://edition.cnn.com/videos/tv/2015/06/18/the-seventies-vietnam-war-iconic-photograph-orig.cnn/video/playlists/atv-in-case-you-missed-it/
5 The photograph was taken by Sam Nzima in 1984.
6 A series of photos taken by Sam Nzima working for *The World* of the boy being taken to the car and hospital where he was pronounced dead on arrival. https://www.flickr.com/photos/panr/2590874830
7 The picture was taken by photographer Laurent Rebours.
8 Reporting on the event Hockstader describes the boy as standing:

> …about 5 feet 4 inches in his socks. He might have weighed 100 pounds if he had eaten recently and well, which he rarely did. He was good at soccer, naughty at school, and before he died- shot in the neck by Israeli troops and left to bleed to death on the battlefield- he told his friends he was intent on becoming a martyr for the Palestinian cause.
>
> (Hockstader 2000)

9 http://100photos.time.com/photos/nilufer-demir-alan-kurdi
10 See also Spinoza, Hegel, Marx, Whitehead and Cassirer.
11 The following discussion draws on Bessant et al. (2019:1–17).
12 Dewey and Bentley identified two substantialist approaches. Proponents of the first, referred to as the *self-action* approach see 'things … as acting under their own powers' (1949:108). It's an idea of substance that began with Aristotle, it characterized classical and medieval philosophy and continues now to inform many projects like rational actor theory, the sociology of deviance (based on Parson's and Merton's structural-functionalism), micro-sociology involving everyday social interaction – and the sociology of youth (1949:131, see also Emirbayer 1997:281–317).
13 Bourdieu did not see structure as a real phenomenon. Rather 'it' is 'a method of scientific representation'. The idea of 'structure' helps sociologists group various facts. It is what social scientists use to create 'the whole system of relationships … by forcing one to relate each opposition to all of the others'. For Bourdieu, using 'structures' as a concept can only be done when they are understood 'for what they are … models giving an account of the observed facts in the most coherent and most economical way' (Bourdieu 1990a:4). These 'models … become false as soon as they are regarded as the real principles of practices' (Bourdieu 1990a:11).
14 While there is evidence of these ideas as far back as the seventeenth and eighteenth centuries in the work, e.g., of Locke and Rousseau, it can be safely said that by the late nineteenth early twentieth centuries, the modern scientific categories were well in place.

1
THINKING ABOUT SOCIAL REPRESENTATIONS

A common lament amongst many academics and researchers is about the difficulty they experience in defining concepts that are central to their work. In the social sciences, sociology and youth studies in particular, many writers observe how concepts vital to their field of study, like 'youth' or 'adolescence', have been contested, and the difficulty they experience in defining 'its' precise nature. As Steven Threadgold notes, one reason for this is that we have many different 'figures of youth', that include 'stereotypes, clichés, memes, targets, scapegoats, folk devils, stigma, discourses and signifiers' (Threadgold 2019:3).

Given this, it may seem reasonable to ask: why can't common sense prevail? Surely, it cannot be that hard. Why don't we just look and see what is in front of us, and identify certain people 'as they are' as 'children' or 'young people'? While this may sound sensible, it is not so easy for reasons explored in this chapter. Clearly, there are children and young people 'out there', but how and what we know of them is not so straightforward. If, e.g., we assume that everyone including scientists and statisticians all see the world in the same way, we might expect everyone to use the same words to describe the same things and thus we could have unanimous agreement. That however is something we cannot assume as most words have multiple meanings and there is considerable disagreement about what is happening in the world.

Why then are there so many different ways of seeing, knowing and representing concepts that are central to our lives and work. It was this question that led Christine Griffin in 1993 to publish a widely cited and well-received book called *Representations of Youth: The Study of Youth and Adolescence in Britain and America*.

This book begins with the observation that while children and young people do sometimes get to talk for and about themselves, most of the dominant, powerful and enduring representations about them are produced by experts, academics and media workers.[1] Griffin describes how young people have been talked about or 'represented' by academics and various experts in British and North American research through the twentieth century. As she says, her interest was in 'the ideological role played by youth research in the construction and reproduction of academic common sense about young people' (Griffin 1993:2). She said her aim was to 'throw a conceptual spanner into the workings of ... youth research by examining the discursive processes through which "youth" and "adolescence" were represented in the 1980s' (Griffin 1993:214). Griffin also observed the tendency to represent young people as 'problems'. Her focus was on young people represented as potentially 'troubled' and subject to 'disorders of consumption and transition'.

This representation, she argued, relied heavily on G. Stanley Hall's account of adolescence as an inherently troubled and turbulent period in the 'life-cycle' (Hall 1904). According to Hall that turbulence was due to a conflict between biological urges and the need for social restraint. With puberty he argued came the release of sexual hormones. This produced hyper-sexualised adolescents seeking sexual release, but who needed to control their impulses until they could legitimate sex with people of the opposite sex – and form their own family. This became the dominant model or *representation* of adolescence as a physiologically driven period of 'storm and stress'. Griffin demonstrated how experts addressed a series of 'crises' about young people in relation to unemployment, crime and delinquency, their sexuality, including 'teenage pregnancy' and leisure.

Without detracting from Griffin's achievement and the many qualities of the book, there are one or two conceptual problems in her work. In what follows, I highlight those as they relate specifically to the question of representations. The main problem is that Griffin did not say how she understood representations. This is a curious omission given that Serge Moscovici, a major figure in Griffin's own discipline of social psychology, produced a body of work on social representations. Rather than representations, Griffin considered other categories, namely discourses and ideologies, which *it seems* she saw as synonymous with representations. Griffin, e.g., described a 'representation' as a kind of 'discourse' or 'discursive configuration', which in 'treatment regimes' is used to 'construct' and manage 'troubled teens'. This might lead one to think a discourse analysis was going to be offered (Fairclough 1989, 1992). However, what Griffin provided was a discussion of 'ideologies'. In what follows, I discuss the concepts 'ideology', 'discourses' and 'representations', beginning with discourse and ideology.

Discourse and ideology

Griffin's work is reflective of the time in which she wrote. In the 1980s and 1990s, many academics developed and applied 'discourse theories' and 'discourse analysis' – typically under the *aegis* of Foucault and Derrida. In Griffin's book however Foucault makes a fleeting appearance – and Derrida not at all. Griffin seems more interested in the traditional idea of 'ideology' than discourse. It was

22 Thinking about social representations

a preference that created certain difficulties for her. Griffin's decision to talk about discourse and ideology also seems to have distracted her from focusing on representations.

For Griffin, discourses are 'constructions' of the 'age stage of youth' or 'adolescence' that involve making 'distinctions between "normal" and "deviant" forms of adolescent behaviour itself...' (Griffin 1993). Moreover, these 'constructions' are the product of:

> ...complex interactions between research funding agencies, academic career moves, research designs and techniques, publication of research results –*and the practices of young people* and other adult groups with whom they are involved.
>
> *(Griffin 1993:6) (My stress)*

The idea that these 'constructions' or 'discourses' are produced through interactions with 'the practices of young people' creates a problem because Griffin also says 'constructions' or 'discourses' are produced by experts with – or *without* – any relation with or connection to young people.

The mixed messages are amplified when Griffin says drawing on the work of Ian Parker that:

> I have viewed *discourse* as 'a system of statements which constructs an object. This *fictive object* can then be reproduced in the various texts written or spoken within the domain of discourses (that is within the *expressive order of society*).
>
> *(Parker 1989:61–62)*

This interpretation of discourse includes a number of different ideas. One is that 'discourses' about young people reflect 'the practices of young people'. Yet Griffin also says there are naturally occurring 'objects' like the 'practices of young people'. Moreover, 'discourses' are said to 'construct fictive objects'. The claim that discourse 'invents an object' (even if a 'fictive object') implies that some kind of world-making exercise is happening.

Thus, it seems Griffin thinks discourses about young people are simultaneously 'fictive objects' *and* 'real objects' (i.e., 'reflections of real practices'). She does not however say how such a distinction might be made. Here Griffin falls into a formulation that begs a number of questions. On the one hand, the idea that discourse 'invents an object' implies there is an ontological world-making exercise taking place. Contrarily, it also implies there is a distinction between 'fictive objects' and 'real objects' but without identifying what that distinction is.

There is also a question about Griffin's reference to 'the expressive order of society' and what that means. It seems Griffin saw (like Durkheim or Parsons) society as an 'objective' entity that can be understood as a single, unitary symbolic order that is independent, unitary and separate from any individual. However, no modern society exists that exhibits such unity. All such societies are characterised by major economic, political, religious, moral and sexual differences. These are evident in important moral disagreements, in political conflicts, major inequalities in people's access to cultural and economic resources – all this framed by differences apparent in categories such as class, gender, religion, ability, status, ethnicity and age. Given these differences, it is not possible to say we have a single or unitary expressive order.

Besides overlooking those differences, such an understanding of society also creates a difficulty for someone (like Griffin) who claims a Marxist provenance when thinking about ideology. Talking about a society as a unitary entity while also using a Marxist framing of ideology that presumes major class differences is bound to cause some problems.

In short, while Griffin declares a commitment to using the category of 'discourse', at the same time, she also uses the Marxist idea of 'ideology':

> I have retained what may seem (to some) an unfashionable use of concepts such as ideology and hegemony alongside an examination of discourses ... I have tried to show how specific discourses operate in the ideological domain.
>
> *(Griffin 1993:7)*

The problem with doing this is that talking about 'ideology' means acknowledging that societies are not unitary. It means recognising how they are characterised by major inequalities, conflicts, differences of experience and diverse cultures and do not constitute a singular 'expressive order' (Parker 1989:62).[2]

Those working in the classical Marxist tradition see ideologies as false ideas or forms of false consciousness.[3] The Marxist idea of 'ideology' refers to belief-systems designed to persuade particular groups such as 'working-class people' or 'women' that they should not complain about their place in what is actually an unequal social order. This may involve claims that this is a natural and timeless order that benefits everyone, or that it is a society which is committed to equal opportunity, etc. Indeed, 'workers' or 'women', etc. believing these ideas to be true assist in their continuation and in the reproduction of the social status quo (Eco 1995:17). As Žižek argues, ideologies are used to secure the voluntary consent of people about contestable political policies or social arrangements. Typically, this is done by representing those arrangements as natural and so unchangeable (Žižek 1989).

Using this Marxist framing, Griffin says she demonstrates why various representations of 'youth' are ideological and perform the social function of binding young people to a hegemonic capitalist culture of consumption. As she explained earlier:

> How are we to understand these contemporary constructions of young people, and especially young women, in texts from all parts of the political

spectrum? ... For many young women (and young men), dominant representations of 'normal' family life appear as pervasive if increasingly distant images, strongly associated with a particular set of consumer goods – including a VCR and a CD player ... What if the bait (steady job, nice things, lovely home/car/baby/husband) fails to materialize at all?

(Griffin 1977:18)

Griffin also did not say how she understood the 'representations of youth' as a political practice.

Having said that, a failure to explicitly discuss the concept of 'politics' is both common and hardly unique to Griffin. Many researchers in sociology and political science don't define politics perhaps because we all assume we agree on what we are talking about. When pressed, the default position usually is that the political is synonymous with the exercise of power. This may be why, when Griffin does touch on the subject of the political, she refers to power but does not go on to develop that idea.

She does however, at the start of her book, briefly refer to power differences between young people and the academics researching them, noting that most research participants have minimal 'material, cultural or ideological power', while their voices are frequently pathologised, criminalised, muted or silenced altogether (Griffin 1993:2). Moreover, academic researchers also possess and deploy their privileged 'intellectual expert status about other people's lives' (Griffin 1993:2). This is why Griffin says she pays attention to 'power relations' because power is an element of social structures and cultural and ideological practices. She notes too that ideologies are constructed through 'relations of power and dominance which are also disputed and contradictory' (Griffin 1993:8).[4] Here, we hear echoes of Max Weber's axiom that 'power' is (apparently) best thought of as being about as successful domination. Besides these brief allusions, Griffin does not develop her understanding of power with any more clarity than she addressed the idea of representations.

Rather than an exploration of what she meant by representations and how young people were represented, Griffin provides a granular detailed account about how youth researchers talked and wrote about young people across the twentieth century.

How then can Griffin's work be built on? How can representations be understood?

The approach I offer here draws on insights provided by the social psychologist Serge Moscovici's and his work on social representations (Moscovici 1973, 1981:181–209, 1982:115–150, 1984a, 1984b, 1988:211–250, 1990, 1993:160–170, 2000). It also draws on Pierre Bourdieu's work on power and symbolic order that canvass the idea of representations. I draw on both Moscovici and Bourdieu to clarify how we might understand representations, and specifically of children and young people.

Moscovici helps in the task of articulating representations of youth. Like Griffin, Moscovici was interested in the role of experts in developing representations:

> Social representations, thus, appear to us almost as material objects, in so far as they are the products of our actions and communications. *They are in fact the product of a professional activity: I am referring to those pedagogues, ideologues, popularizers of science, cultures and priests, that is the representatives of science, culture and religions* whose task it is, is to create and transmit them, often, alas, without either knowing or wishing it.
> *(Moscovici 2000:27) (My stress)*

In what follows, I position his work in the context of a long-standing interest in the sociology of knowledge and outline the key features of Moscovici's account of social representations. I then draw on Pierre Bourdieu's account of representations, situating it in the context of his 'theory-method' that centres on his concepts, *practice, habitus, capitals* and *field*. Like Moscovici, Bourdieu offers a way of understanding social representations, but in ways that extend Moscovici's work. This provides the theoretical framework used in this book.

Why have a theory of social representations: Moscovici?

Serge Moscovici was a social psychologist who developed an academic career in France, eventually becoming the Director d'Etudes at the *Ecole des Hautes Etudes en Social Sciences* in Paris. His career was dedicated to developing a 'social psychology of knowledge'. To do this, he built on the work of Marx, Durkheim, Weber, Freud, Mead, Lévy-Bruhl, Bartlett, Piaget and Vygotsky. As he explained:

> ...the study of how and why people share knowledge and thereby constitute their common reality of how they transform ideas into practice -in a word, the power of ideas – is the specific problem of social psychology.
> *(1990:164)*

Moscovici offered an historical cross-disciplinary theory of social representations that stood at the 'cross roads between a series of sociological concepts and a series of psychological concepts' (Moscovici 2000:3). His disciplines were psychology, sociology, anthropology and history. Unlike most mainstream social psychologists, he steered clear of the dominant positivist epistemology that characterises the natural sciences.

Moscovici provided a rationale for why a theory of social representations was needed. He explained this by making a distinction between what he called 'primitive thought' that was 'based on a belief in the mind's unlimited power to shape reality and to determine the course of events' and modern scientific thought (Moscovici 2000:18). He added that in the first case thought acts on reality, whereas in the second, thought is seen as a reaction to reality. 'In the one, the object emerges as a replica of thought, and in the other, thought is replica of the object'. The modern scientific perspective which sees 'thought as a replica of the object' is exemplified in the empiricist and positivist traditions.

Moscovici says modern scientific thought (and social psychology as a sub-set of scientific thought) relies on two hypotheses:

> (i) 'normal individuals react to phenomena, people or events in the same way as scientists and statisticians do',
> and
> (ii) We 'perceive the world, such as it is, and all our perceptions, ideas and attributions are responses to stimuli from the physical or quasi-physical environment in which we live'.
>
> *(Moscovici 2000:19)*

This is what Latour calls a 'double-click' model of knowledge. Latour uses this computer–mouse metaphor to ridicule the idea that a simple, unmediated process of looking or thinking can give us direct access to reality (Latour 2013:173).

As Moscovici argues, there are three reasons why these two hypotheses are wrong.

First, on many occasions, we fail to see (or acknowledge) what is before our very eyes. He cites as one example, the way a class of people, e.g., women, young people, the elderly, or people of colour, become 'invisible' in the eyes of others.

Second, the facts we take for granted and that appear to be verifiable because they are based on solid perceptions, turn out to be untrue: the classic case is a belief such as the idea that the sun goes around the earth.

Finally, we rely on a particular representation to make sense of something we see: the example he uses is the case when we see an overturned car and nearby emergency services. We immediately call this an 'accident' (i.e., an unpredictable event arising from chance or randomness), even though it is likely there nothing accidental about that occurrence.

The tradition of 'sociology of knowledge' acknowledges the problem that while we have one (objective) world, we also have many symbolic belief systems and knowledge claims. Those working in that tradition also acknowledged that what we believe can work to bring into being social institutions and practices that are real. As Berger and Luckmann explained:

> A 'sociology of knowledge' will have to deal not only with the empirical variety of 'knowledge' in human societies, but also with the processes by which any body of 'knowledge' comes to be established as 'reality' [...] And in so far as all human 'knowledge' is developed, transmitted and maintained in social situations, the sociology of knowledge must seek to

understand the processes by which this is done in such a way that a taken-for-granted 'reality' congeals for the man in the street. In other words, we contend that *the sociology of knowledge is concerned with the analysis of the social construction of reality.*

(Berger and Luckmann 1967:15 stress in original)

Moreover, the everyday life-world:

...is not only taken for granted as reality by the ordinary members of society in the subjectively meaningful conduct of their lives. It is a world that *originates* in their thoughts and actions, and is maintained as real by these.

(Berger and Luckmann 1967:30) (Their stress)

Thus, as Berger and Luckmann say: 'knowledge about society is a *realization* in the double sense of the word, in the sense of apprehending the objectivated reality, and in the sense of ongoingly producing this reality' (1967:8) (Their stress). Given this, the task of those working in sociology of knowledge is to understand how the objectifications of subjective processes create an *intersubjective* and *common*-sense world, a world shared with others and that appears to be self-evident and taken-for-granted.

Like Berger and Luckmann, Moscovici drew heavily on Durkheim and Weber. Berger and Luckmann's debt to Durkheim is evident when they argue that 'society does indeed possess objective facticity'. They also said society is 'built up by activity that expresses subjective meanings' (Berger and Luckmann 1967:30). It seems that Moscovici accepts these ideas suggested when he says the theory of social representations 'focuses as much on the way in which men think or create their shared reality as on the content of their thinking' (Moscovici 1981:181). Moscovici is also interested in the processes by which 'each representation realizes, literally, a different degree of objectification which corresponds to a different level of reality' (Moscovici 1981:198).

Moscovici tries to understand the dialectical relationship through which a social representation 'is converted into a property of the phenomenon and thereby becomes the reference point' (Moscovici 1981:200). He says that an 'overlapping disjunction' exists between the object and the subject (Moscovici 1981, see also, e.g., Moscovici 1981, 1984a, Jodelet 1989). In this way, social representations mediate between the world they constitute *and* the subjects who create them.

Representations 'variously direct us towards that which is visible and to which we have to respond, or which relate appearance and reality or again, which define this reality' (Moscovici 2000:20). Moscovici also says he doesn't want to 'imply that such representations don't correspond to something we call the outside world' (Moscovici 2000:20). What he says matters is one's capacity to judge when it can be said that a representation corresponds to the

28 Thinking about social representations

external or natural world as distinct from the social or symbolic world, and when they do not.

This raises two questions, one is about knowledge and the other is about reality. These are questions that have been addressed by philosophers going back to Plato. They are also questions that have been asked by people working in the social sciences and humanities. Philosophers have long inquired into how we can know anything with certainty – as distinct from having an opinion or belief. This relates to questions like: What is truth? How do we know? And what justifies a belief? Philosophers have also asked about the nature of reality.

Those working in the social sciences and humanities in fields like the sociology of knowledge, the sociology of science and technology and social psychology have addressed parallel questions. Their work has focused on how social relations, institutions and practices shaped our representations of the natural and social world.

Drawing a distinction between epistemological questions about the nature of reality and ontological questions about knowledge (about being) in the social sciences is not always easy or indeed possible. It involves questions like whether reality an epistemological effect? In other words, is what we know of reality, e.g., that 'a young person is a victim', the effect of the knowledge we have about a reality? And does what we know about that young man reflect the particular ways we see, hear, smell things in the world? Does what we know of that young person reflect how we calculate, count, construct definitions to explain or understand?

Or is reality an ontological effect. In other words, does 'reality' refer to the nature of things or entities that actually exist? Does 'X' refer to things we encounter in the world and make distinctions between?

While these questions may be fascinating, elaborating on them takes me too far away from the focus of this book. To cut to the chase, how can we determine the truth of claims that social reality is just a social construction, a claim posed by Berger and Luckmann in their sociology of knowledge?[5] At the same time, philosophers like Richard Rorty showed why claims that what we know of the world is a mirror the 'real world' are not justified (Rorty 1980). More recent work by Ian Hacking points to the problems with arguing reality is 'just' a social construction (Hacking 1999).

The social psychologist Kenneth Gergen offers a 'weak' version of social constructionism. Social constructionism, he says, is an inquiry 'concerned with explicating the processes by which people come to describe, explain, or otherwise account for the world (including themselves) in which they live' (Gergen 1985:266). Moscovici, on the other hand, advocates for the 'strong' version of social constructivism claiming that social representations are *constitutive* of reality:

> [Social] representations are capable of *creating* and stipulating a reality by naming and objectifying notions and images, by directing material and symbolic practices towards this reality which corresponds to them. In

short, giving a kind of public reality 'out there' and *ontological status* to our representations and to the verbal and iconic symbols that represent them and act on our relationships and practices. Thereby, we situate ourselves in a world of shared reality.

(Moscovici 1994:7 – italics added*)*

Given that Moscovici sees social representations as having constitutive power (i.e., the power to give existence to parts of the world), he does not provide a causal explanation of relations between people, what they do, or what they think. Rather, he supports a dialectical understanding of social representations. That is, Moscovici's theory encourages a *relational* approach for understanding why and how a social group converts their representations into social relations and practices, material objects, and social institutions that shape reality.

Moscovici (2000:30) draws on Durkheim's argument that the categories we use to understand the world have their origins in human cognition citing Durkheim's work on religious thought and its role in making science and philosophy:

It is because religion is a social thing that it could play this role … a new kind of thought had to be created: collective thought. If collective thought alone had the power to achieve this. [It required] … the hyperexcitation of intellectual forces that is possible only in and through a society.

(Durkheim 1912–1995:239)

According to Durkheim, we do not experience reality as a *direct* response to empirical stimuli or direct observation. Rather, we know reality through social categories of understanding – and through particular communal beliefs and theories. Durkheim used the term 'collective representations' in talking about categories that express and construct reality. Like Durkheim, Moscovici assumed we can talk about a 'collective representations', 'collective thought', 'common representations', etc. Moscovici also points to the ways social representations have a 'collective origin' and are 'shared by all and strengthened by tradition' (Moscovici 2000:27).

For Durkheim, collective representations are historically constituted and continue across generations because they are produced, reproduced and disseminated across an entire society which he says generates society-wide consensus. Moscovici revises this holistic Durkheimian account of society-wide collective representations. He did this by adding the idea that lower-level entities or institutions (e.g., governments, communities, non-government organisations, professional bodies or social movements) also produce social representations (Rubtsova and Dowd 2004).

Moscovici emphasises how social representations, i.e., 'concepts, statements and explanations originating in daily life through inter-individual communications' are produced in various social sites, creating a diversity realities and different common senses (Moscovici 1981:181). However, the down-side of Durkheim's influence on Moscovici can be seen in his talk about a:

> ...vision of the whole of society. And in this vision stamped by the symbolic and the ritualistic, social representations are constitutive of bonds and common actions. [...] Then the theory is a particular theory of the collective forms of thought and belief and of the communications produced under the constraints of society. [...].
> *(Moscovici 1993:161)*

The problem with this view of an organic order that imagines a socially cohesive, integrated and undifferentiated society is that it overlooks the divisions, fractures, diversity and inequalities that actually characterise all modern societies. Apart from this organicistic perspective, reflected in his work, Moscovici assumes a general equality in the relations existing between members of groups or communities as they build consensual, 'common-sense' knowledge around important themes. The assumption 'the social is a construction' seems to encourage the idea that 'the social' is an integrated whole. This can be seen in Moscovici's claim that social representations constitute a 'common sense', as they are a:

> ...set of concepts and explanations originating in daily life in the course of inter-individual communications. They are the equivalent, in our society, of the myths and belief systems in traditional societies; they might even be said to be the contemporary version of common sense.
> *(Moscovici 1981:181)*

For Moscovici, social representations are *symbolic*. For this reason, social representations cannot exist without being realised *collectively*. They are embedded in social life, expressing and structuring the identities and social conditions of those who create, reproduce, change and become them. Thus, to appreciate social representations, it is critical to study the given culture and individual mind. For Moscovici, social representations are *constitutively informed by the* material, social and symbolic worlds in which we live. As symbolic phenomena, the content, structure and processes of social representation making need to be studied if we are to understand the interest and politics that informs them.

Thus, communication processes and social interaction are central to his account. As Moscovici explained:

> A social representation corresponds to a certain recurrent and comprehensive model of images, beliefs and symbolic behaviours. Envisaged in this way *statically,* representation appear similar to *theories* which order around

a theme (mental illnesses are contagious, people are what they eat, etc.) (2000:152). To this we can add 'teenagers are trouble'.

These propositions:

> ...enable things or persons to be classified, their characters described, their feelings and actions to be explained, and so on. Further the 'theory' contains a series of examples which illustrate concretely the values which introduce a hierarchy and their corresponding models of action.
> *(Moscovici 2000:152)*

Surprisingly however Moscovici seems disinterested in the social context.

Yet if we are to name the significant socio-economic dynamics operating along with the many intersecting gendered, ethnic, age-based, religious and other reasons for inequality, then we would name the context as a capitalist order comprising a variety of logics of inequality and difference. Moscovici pays little attention to the existing conditions of capitalism. This is a significant omission, especially given the extent of the commodification of so many 'things' like scientific knowledge and representations (e.g., in advertising, intellectual property). Moscovici also overlooks how access to and competition over economic capital (Marx) and many other kinds of capitals (Bourdieu) create inequality. Given the asymmetric nature of age- or generation-based relations, competition over capitals and the commodification of certain capitals, this is a significant omission.

For a theory, of representations to be sound, the relations of inequality cannot be ignored. In other words, being sensitive to the influence of social context and especially to the politics that shape it is critical for understanding how certain representations came to be.

This is why there is value in establishing what Bourdieu has to say and whether he overcomes some of the problems with Moscovici's work.

Bourdieu and representations

Compared with concepts like 'field', 'practice', 'habitus' or 'capital', Bourdieu does not use the category of representations very much. Having said that he does address the idea clearly and in ways that are aligned to his larger theory-method. Bourdieu's concept of 'symbolic capital' or the symbolic dimensions of social life is what comes closest to Moscovici's concept of social representations. For Bourdieu, 'symbolic capital' refers to prestige, honour and celebrity. It rests on a recognition that a person has the ability or knowledge to do a task successfully signifying 'the acquisition of a reputation for competence and an image of respectability and honourability...' (Bourdieu 1984:291). Bourdieu's notion of 'symbolic capital' relies on the idea that as with all forms of capital, the acquisition and use of 'symbolic capital' involved in the making of representations requires the labour of representations.

Like Moscovici, Bourdieu said social representations provide a 'systematic view of the world and human existence' (Bourdieu 1987:126). Bourdieu also saw in the making of representations and classifications older forms of authority that can be religious in nature. Like Durkheim, Bourdieu observes the religious-like practices operating in the making of representations that involve tracing the lines that limit and delimit, 'the realm of the sacred and the realm of the profane'. As Bourdieu argued, the drawing or tracing out of 'national territory and foreign territory',

> ...is a *religious* act performed by the person invested with the highest authority, the *rex,* whose responsibility it is ... to fix the rules which bring into existence what they decree, to speak with authority, to predict in the sense of calling into being, by an enforceable saying, what one says, of making the future that one utters come into being.
> (Bourdieu 1991:222, 1992:220–226)

However, there is one critical difference with Bourdieu. Unlike Durkheim and Moscovici, Bourdieu does not assume that experts, scholars or scientists generate a single set of social representations. Quite the opposite, modern scientists are involved in a:

> ...game whose stake is the power of governing the sacred frontiers, that is, the quasi-divine power over the vision of the world, and in which one has no choice, if one seeks to exercise it (rather than submit to it), other than to mystify or demystify.
> (Bourdieu 1992:228)

Bourdieu says he is interested in '*representations* through which people imagine the divisions of reality and which contribute to the reality of the divisions' (Bourdieu 1991:228).[6] And unlike Durkheim and Moscovici, Bourdieu does not presume that a single, unitary or homogenous symbolic order exists, but rather that any society is characterised by inequality, struggle and competition.

Bourdieu carried out an extensive inquiry into the different forms of symbolic capital,[7] and like Marx, he defined capital as accumulated labour. Bourdieu revised Marx's economistic theory of capital by pointing to the many different kinds of capitals that are distributed unequally. It's an account that highlights how different resources are struggled over, distributed and how that competition shapes a larger political-economy of power.

For Bourdieu, 'capital' includes money and property as well as many other social, technical and intellectual resources. (Notably, he recognised how education, social networks, arts and cultural knowledge are obtained through labour.)

Symbolic capital (cultural capital, social capital, political capital, etc.) is also subject to the same laws of accumulation, in exchanges that govern material productive practices. Like economic capital, these other capitals involve labour because they have to be worked for, while competition and conflict characterise and help determine who gets what share of the resources. These *capitals are also always involved in producing representations*. Bourdieu's emphasis on the fractured and unequal distribution of capitals involved in producing representations makes his approach different to Moscovici's.

Another difference between them is that while Moscovici and Bourdieu both consider how expert or scientific knowledge works, Bourdieu makes a distinction between categories and representations that are produced by scientific practice and lay or 'common-sense' categories that are developed in the everyday life-world (Bourdieu 1991). Bourdieu has a more sophisticated relational grasp of what is happening. This is because he focuses on the connections *and* differences between scientific research and practical everyday judgement. These connections and differences '...transcend the opposition that science, in order to break away from the preconceptions of spontaneous sociology must first establish between representation and reality' (Bourdieu 1991:222). In short, Bourdieu is saying that sociologists *as scientists* need to avoid accepting the categories or hypotheses that lay people use and or construct- to describe and explain social phenomena. And, sociologists as scientists also need to acknowledge how their own sociological categories and theories go back into or re-enter the world and circulate as representations. This can only happen:

> ...*if one includes in reality the representation of reality*, or, more precisely, the struggle over representations, in the sense of mental images, but also of social demonstrations whose aim it is to manipulate mental images...
> *(Bourdieu 1991:116) (My stress)*

For Bourdieu, this raises political questions about the relationship between scientific categories used in research and the everyday, common-sense ideas and practices used by people in families, schools and workplaces. Bourdieu highlights the distinctions between categories like 'unemployment', 'working class' or 'poverty' that academics use and analyse in their research, which often have little or no connection with the experience of being jobless or living on inadequate incomes. Bourdieu's interest is in the different consequences that practices of academics and experts and ordinary people have.

What Bourdieu is saying is that the interests that inform the development of representations and the efforts to create them are very different when academics and experts do it and when 'ordinary' people do it. For example, age-based categories and distinctions used by experts to classify people as a 'child', 'adolescent', 'young adult' or 'adult' as part of their scientific research, typically involve assessments using scientific criteria that draw on models of 'normal' adolescent development. In a context where the state is promoting and has a direct interest in that research, the goal may be to create a specific social-political effect by imposing regulatory regimes on young people (e.g., night curfews or bans on certain activities). In the life-world however, we can see different age-based categories or distinctions of various kinds made, e.g., inside families and communities.

In both cases – scientific and lay – these representations are political struggles. As Bourdieu explains, if a representation involves assigning people to classes (categories of people), this always includes classificatory struggles or *struggles over representations*. There is always a 'struggle over classifications' constituted by the struggle over the definitional criteria used to say who belongs to such and such a class (Bourdieu 1992:116). This is because:

> Struggles over classifications involve struggles over the monopoly of the power to make people see and believe, to get them to know and recognize, to impose the legitimate definition of the divisions of the social world and, thereby, to *make and unmake groups*.
>
> *(Bourdieu 1992:116)*

The work of some academics, e.g., and their efforts to increase and use their symbolic or intellectual capital, is often informed by an interest in advancing their career and employment security. Similar but different struggles happen in families or workplaces. Between both fields, there are certain kinds of contests operating. People on low incomes may, e.g., reject the use of categories such as 'poverty' or 'underclass' that some academics, policy-makers and politicians impose on them. For Bourdieu, common-sense categories result from 'everyday judgement'. Scientists say they use logically controlled and empirical criteria to produce objective descriptions, explanations and predictions. Yet as Bourdieu argued:

> Nothing is less innocent than the question, which divides the scientific world, of knowing whether one has to include in the system of pertinent criteria not only the so-called 'objective' categories (such as ancestry, territory, language, religion, economic activity, etc.), but also the so-called 'subjective' properties (such as the feeling of belonging), i.e. the *representations* through which social agents imagine the divisions of reality and which contribute to the reality of the divisions.
>
> *(Bourdieu 1991:119)*

Intrinsic to scientific processes are political struggles:

> When, as their education and their specific interests incline them, researchers try to set themselves up as judges of all judgements and as critics of all criteria, they prevent themselves from grasping the specific logic of a struggle in which the social force of representations is not necessarily proportional to

their truth-value (measured by the degree to which they express the state of the relation of material forces at the moment under consideration).

(Bourdieu 1991:119)

As I argue later in this book, we see recurring attempts 'to impose the legitimate definition of the divisions of the social world'. In this case, my interest is in *how age-based criteria informed by developmental theory and similar models which have the effect of denying those represented as such many of the capacities they do have.* While Bourdieu rarely makes explicit reference to youth and age, his interview on 'representations of youth' highlights the classificatory 'struggle between the young and the old' (Bourdieu 1993:95).

Bourdieu and representations of youth

In his only explicit discussion about the category of 'youth', Bourdieu said 'Youth is just a word' ('La 'jeunesse' n'est qu'un mot') (Bourdieu 1978–1993).[8] However, having said that, he went on to show how that is not actually the case, and that youth is more than a word. He did that in ways that pertinent to this book (Jones 2009:1).

In 1978, Bourdieu gave an interview in which he discussed 'youth' acknowledging that age is natural because some people are young and others are older, but this fact is understood or classified in ways that are 'variable and subject to manipulation':

> One is always somebody's senior or junior. That is why the divisions, whether into age-groups/brackets or into generations, vary and are subject to (deliberate) manipulation... What I want to remind you, quite simply is that youth and age are not self-evident facts, but are constructed socially, *in the struggle between the young and the old.*
>
> *(Bourdieu 1993:95) (My stress)*

Bourdieu states the obvious here: to have a concept like 'youth', someone has to *represent* it. And, like other classes (based on ethnicity, gender, control of economic resources, religion, etc.), the classificatory process that informs those representations is part of a relationship marked by struggle. Bourdieu's argument is that social scientists need to refrain from thinking about 'youth' ('working class', 'middle class', etc.) *as if* these are natural or objective facts and *as if* they refer to naturally existing 'objects'. In short, for Bourdieu, 'youth' and 'age' are constructed 'through struggles between the people'.

Bourdieu also gives attention to the representations of 'youth' and other concepts (e.g., gender, class) by highlighting how power relations function to mark particular spaces of cultural action (Purhonen 2016:100). This is critical for showing how those who own or control various capitals (e.g., symbolic capital, economic capital, political capital or cultural capital) use their capitals in ongoing struggles to gain and keep more of that capital. He emphasises the exercise of power in these continuous political competitions or classification struggles that shape – in this case – how young people are variously represented:

> ...the logical division between young and old is about power, about the division (in the sense of sharing) or the distribution of power with classifications according to age (but also gender or social class).
>
> *(Bourdieu 1993:95)*

Understood as elements in 'classification struggles', age-based classes like 'youth', or 'the elderly', are constituted *in and through* those struggles (Bourdieu 1998:10–11, Purhonen 2016:101). In addition to *not* seeing 'age', 'gender', 'class', etc. as natural entities, Bourdieu says there is value in thinking about these concepts within the context of the relations between the people who bring them into being. What, for example, is represented as gender, age, ethnicity, region or nation are 'relations of union and separation, of association and disassociation already at work in the social world' (Bourdieu 1990:14). The significance of this can be seen when we consider how Bourdieu deploys his concept of 'field'.

For Bourdieu, the classificatory struggles over 'youth' happen within fields (Bourdieu 1998:1–13, 31–33). Such 'fields' are 'spaces' regulated by 'laws':

> Each field, ... in relation to fashion, as well as artistic and literary production, has its specific laws about aging. In order to know how to divide up society into generations, we have to know the specific laws at work in that particular field, and what is at stake which that struggle makes possible ('new vague', 'new novel', 'new philosophers' etc.).
>
> *(Bourdieu 1993:96)*

How Bourdieu understands and uses 'field' connects to his observations about competition, conflict and struggle. Bourdieu's appropriation of the metaphor 'field' (from Cassirer and Lewin) highlights how he belongs to a relational philosophical tradition of intellectuals[9] who say 'the reality of the objects of the human or social sciences is relational rather than substantial' (Caws 1990:1, see also Vandenberghe 2001:479).

Bourdieu's relational theory-method

Bourdieu's representation of 'youth' highlights his place in a philosophical relational tradition that rejects the dominant substantialist tradition in western philosophical and scientific thought (Cassirer 1923). This is why Bourdieu called on social scientists to abandon their substantialist ways (1991:129).

Mindful that Bourdieu is not a substantialist, many of those working in the social sciences who develop representations of young people and who claim to represent 'youth', do.

There are a number of ways the social sciences such as sociology are substantialist. This can be seen by considering the debates between the antagonists in the long-running 'structure' versus 'agency' debate, or the clash between protagonists of the 'objective-quantitative' and 'subjective-qualitative' methods divide in the social sciences.

The very framing of this binary itself assumes a substantialist perspective. The distinction made between 'objective-quantitative' and 'subjective-qualitative' methods in the social sciences relies on different kinds of substance to construct binaries like 'society'-'structure'-'objective' versus 'individual'-'agency'-'subjective'. Each part in this binary assumes that a 'structure' (class, gender or religion) is a substance that can be identified and used to explain why something happens. For example, one might say: 'Being middle-class determines an age-appropriate form of conduct'. If one sees 'ideology', 'belief systems' or 'discourses' as a substance, then it might be argued that 'Linda's feminist "ideology" disposed her to reject the idea of marriage'. In both cases, the substance is used to make causal connections. This is done while reducing 'the social' to a binary, i.e., 'society', 'class structure' or 'the individual', or 'discourses', 'ideology' or religious belief.

As Emirbayer notes, the idea of 'structure as a self-acting substance' links various kinds of:

> ...theories and structuralisms that posit not individuals but self-subsistent 'societies', 'structures,' or 'social systems' as the exclusive sources of action. Proponents of these approaches, from neo-functionalists and systems theorists to many historical-comparative analysts, all too often fall back upon the assumption that it is [these kinds of] durable, coherent entities that constitute the legitimate starting points of all sociological inquiry.
>
> *(Emirbayer 1997:285)*

Escaping the influence of substantialism is difficult. As Norbert Elias argued, our language makes it hard for us to see the ways in which substantialism has become the naturalised, almost common-sense way of thinking about the world – and how to do research (Elias 1978). Elias observes that thinking about the social world in substantialist ways is embedded in grammatical patterns involving nouns (the names of things) and verbs (names of the actions that things do), so much so that it has become common sense to English-speakers to focus on 'things' and ignore the relations and processes:

> Our languages are constructed in such a way that we can often only express constant movement or constant change in ways which imply that it has the

character of an isolated object at rest, and then, almost as an afterthought, adding a verb which expresses the fact that the thing with this character is now changing.

(Elias 1978:111)[10]

For Bourdieu, the substantialist tradition is part of the 'commonsensical perception of social reality of which sociology must rid itself' (Bourdieu and Wacquant 1992:15). Like Elias, Bourdieu called on social scientists to reflect on their substantialist habits of mind and give away such thinking:

> ...the 'entities' sociologists or criminologist are interested in are presumed to be independent of a social world made up of relations and processes – a perspective reinforced by a language better suited to express *things* [rather] than *relations, states* than *processes*'.
>
> *(Bourdieu and Wacquant 1992:15) (My stress)*

Relying on this substantialist approach is why we create paired concepts that 'are unthinkingly used to construct social reality' (Bourdieu 1987:1). To this Bourdieu adds: 'This is in fact a false opposition. In reality, agents are both classified and classifiers, but they classify according to (or depending upon) their position within classification' (Bourdieu 1987:2).

As a relational theorist, Bourdieu's theory of practice replaces things with relations. He was clear about the implications of such a focus when he said: 'What exists in the social world are relations – not interactions between agents or intersubjective ties between individuals, but objective relations' (Bourdieu and Wacquant 1992:97). It's a perspective that highlights how practices constitute individuals, as much as individuals create practices: indeed, all social action is relational (Burnett 2017, Dépelteau 2018).

This has implications for understanding how young people are represented.

Bourdieu's relational perspective also meant he rejected the idea we can provide causal explanations because whatever we do, it always occurs within mutually constitutive relations (Emirbayer 1997). In short, for Bourdieu's categories like '*habitus*', 'capital', 'practice', 'field' and 'power' are not amenable to conventional kinds of empirical description or research because they are not standalone 'entities' or things *but relations and events*. For this reason, they cannot be subject to study assuming that they can be measured or counted as if they are dependent or independent variables. Bourdieu warned about seeing 'products' such as three-dimensional diagrams generated by factor analysis and produced as a result of an empiricist research practices as if they were standalone entities or objects (1992a, 1992b:4). This has implications for scholars who rely on conventional empirical research methods who say they can subject Bourdieu's categories like 'habitus' or 'symbolic violence' to empirical testing.

Bourdieu also rejected the idea that we can split people into 'bodies' and 'minds', 'behaviours' and 'beliefs'. His notion of *habitus* embodies this. In this way, his debt to Piaget is evident for Piaget's did not emphasise cognitive structures as static symbolic representations, but on *bodily schemas*. As Piaget argued: we think with the body' (Piaget 1932). This is also why Bourdieu argued that practice and our belief in take-for-granted, self-evident social orders (*doxa*) is cognitively embodied:

> Practical belief is not a 'state of mind', still less a kind of arbitrary adherence to a set of instituted dogmas and doctrines ('beliefs'), but rather a state of the body...
>
> *(Bourdieu 1990a:68)*

Bourdieu's focus on practice and his emphasis on studying the embodied nature of knowing and creating highlights the value he attributed to close, ethnographic studies of how, e.g., children and young people learn to 'think with their body' as they play, make art or music, do jobs, dance, playing sport or use digital technology.

Finally, Bourdieu's relational focus is why he was interested in reflexivity and the value of scholars or researchers thinking about their own practices, which includes reflecting on their relations with the people they research. Bourdieu scholarly perspective or 'academic vision' creates problems because it encourages an 'odd point of view':

> The scholastic view is a very peculiar point of view on the social world, on language, on any possible object that is made possible by the situation of *skhole*, [the scholastic or academic space] of leisure, of which the school ... an institutionalized situation of studious leisure.
>
> *(Bourdieu 1990b:381)*

For Bourdieu, being a scholar means being free from the stressors of practical necessity. *Homo academicus*, he said, get paid to play 'outside the urgency of a practical situation and oblivious to the ends which are immanent in it, he or she earnestly busies herself with problems that serious people ignore – actively or purposely' (1990:381). This, he says, means a loss of reflexivity as scholars can easily overlook the social conditions that make their own scholarly practice possible. This retreat from the world influences how they-we think.

Conclusion

A theory of representations is needed to help understand how most people (including experts and scientists) claim to know certain groups, when that 'knowledge' too often does not align with how those being researched and talked about experience their own lives and understand themselves.

This misrecognition or misalignment is particularly important when there are major differences in the resources, abilities or power between those being representation and others who play an influential role in saying how they are represented. Consider, e.g., groups historically and in the twentieth and twenty-first centuries like people with disabilities, people of colour, indigenous people, the unemployed, women, the elderly, single mothers, and children and young people.

These 'kinds of people' have been – are – subject to a range of practices. They can be controlled, punished and have their rights violated with relative immunity from criticism or prosecution. Today, in many places, children and young people can still be hit in ways that would incur charges of criminal assault if done to an adult. Each of these groups lack many civil and political rights (e.g., they don't have an effective say about matter that directly affect them, for many under the age of 18 years, this includes not being able to vote, or to make decisions about their own bodies or lives, etc.). These are practices that define what it is to be young, 'a minor' or 'under-age'.

It is also common practice that those deemed to fit these categories have others (e.g., experts, authorities or professionals) speak on their behalf even when they are themselves present, well able to speak and have something they want to say. Typically, this is done without permission or invitation, thereby usurping the young person's ability to identify and speak themselves using their own words. This has the effect of rendering 'them' mute and dumb, reinforcing the idea that young people cannot and should not speak about certain, and especially substantive, matters.

Finally, as Griffin, Moscovici and Bourdieu argue, children and young people are the 'object' of 'representations' of various scientific studies, which re-produce a diversity of fears, fantasies, hopes and misunderstandings. These representations take many forms, including the long-standing and popular tradition of scientific studies claiming to show the alleged innate or natural deficiencies of people with an adolescent or teen brain. This 'teen brain' is analogous to the 'negro brain', or the 'female brain', each characterised by deficits used to underpin claims that those with these 'brains' cannot and should not be political and should not exercise basic rights such as voting.

Like Moscovici, Bourdieu offered a theory of representations, one that was informed and animated by his thinking on symbolic order and symbolic capital. Bourdieu offers a relational perspective that can be used to integrate the politics of representation (e.g., as relations between groups representing young people, how young people engage with those representations and engage generally in politics).

While we can all be represented in different ways, some representations are more significant and have a greater effect than others because they reproduce representations that have relational authority. As Bourdieu argued, representations are always part of classification struggles. In particular fields, some people who possess considerable capitals (e.g., economic, social, symbolic and cultural capitals) are the ones who get the most say in shaping and authorising certain representations that produce important and real effects.

As Bourdieu explained, one problem with representations made by those who talk on behalf of or in the name of others is that it encourages the belief we can see 'those kinds of people' clearly and what is happening when in fact we cannot. As he explained:

> A whole series of symbolic effects that are exercised every day in politics rests on this sort of usurpatory ventriloquism, which consist of giving voice to those in whose name one is [allegedly] authorised to speak.
> *(Bourdieu 1992:211)*

This 'usurpatory ventriloquism' has become the norm when it comes to young people.

Notes

1 There are a number of major studies of representations of youth, including Cohen (1972) and Pearson (1983): see also Sercombe (1996), Bessant and Hil (1997), Dunkels et al. (2010) and Gordon (2018).
2 Griffin conflates two different concepts, i.e., 'ideology' and 'discourse', which as Teun van Dijk argues, are significantly different categories and need to be recognised as such (van Dijk 2013:177). van Dijk emphasises how the study of 'ideology' involves an inquiry into 'false consciousness' or of 'false belief systems'. In the theory of ideology what was (true) *knowledge* and what was (false) *ideology* were seen as being different even antagonistic (van Dijk 2013:177). According to Van Dijk, discourses are social practices through which ideologies are learned or acquired, used and spread (van Dijk 2013).
3 Writers drawing on the Marxists tradition see ideologies as cognitive representations (i.e., ideas and beliefs shared by particular groups with shared interests typically within systems of domination). In this way, ideologies are taken-for-granted ideas and beliefs shared within a group and not across the whole society (van Dijk 2013:177). Within this tradition, 'ideology' refers to belief-systems designed to persuade certain groups ('the working-class', 'people of colour' or 'women') that the existing and unequal social order is natural and timeless arrangement, and even the best of all possible worlds.
4 What Weber actually said was: 'Power … is the probability the one actor within a social relationship will be in a position to carry out his own will despite resistance…' (Weber 1947:152). Weber did not see 'power' as a thing, but part of our relations. As Uphof explained:

> For Weber, any attribution of power is a statement about *the probability that someone can achieve his or her own goals,* relative to the goals of others… What exists is not 'power' but rather these means and the relationships they establish. While one can speak abstractly about power just as physicists talk about 'energy', an analysis is best done in terms of specific kinds [of relationships].
> (Uphof 1989:299)

5 Berger and Luckmann say how a social representation can be transformed into a property of the phenomenon:

> …the symmetry between objective and subjective reality cannot be complete. *The two realities correspond to each other, but they are not coextensive.* There is always more reality 'available' than what is actually internalized in any individual consciousness, simply because the contents of socialization are determined by the

social distribution of knowledge. No individual internalizes the totality of what is objectivated as reality in his society ... On the other hand, there are always elements of subjective reality that have not originated in socialization [...] Subjective biography is not fully social. The individual apprehends himself as being both inside and outside society. This implies that the symmetry between objective and subjective reality is never a static, once-for-all state of affairs. It must always be produced and reproduced *in actu*.

(Berger and Luckmann 1967:153–154) (My stress)

6 Here, we see also a difference between the social constructionism offered by Gergen, Berger and Moscovici and Bourdieu's approach.
7 For Bourdieu, representations take various forms. He noted differences between:

...*mental representations which are* acts of perception and appreciation, of cognition and recognition, in which agents invest their interests and their presuppositions, and ... *objectified representations,* [embedded in]... things (emblems, flags, badges, etc.) or acts, self-interested strategies of symbolic manipulation which aim at determining the (mental) representation that other people may form of these properties and their bearers.

(Bourdieu 1991:221)

8 This part of the discussion draws on Bessant et al. (2019).
9 That tradition implicates significant philosophers including Leibniz, Spinoza, Hegel, Marx, Whitehead Cassirer Heidegger and Latour, and social scientists like Durkheim, Mauss, Lévi-Strauss, Bachelard, Simmel, Mannheim, Elias, Emirbayer, Isin and Depelteau.
10 Elias offers an example of how this works:

[W]e say, 'The wind is blowing,' as if the wind were actually a thing at rest which, at a given point in time, begins to move and blow. We speak as if a wind could exist which did not blow. This reduction of processes to static conditions, which we shall call 'process-reduction' for short, appears self-explanatory to people who have grown up with such languages.

(1978:112)

2
A MINOR OMISSION
Children, young people and politics[1]

In September 1957, Little Rock, the capital of the southern American state of Arkansas, USA, became a site of national controversy. At issue was whether nine African-American children who enrolled following a Supreme Court ruling would be allowed to actually attend the hitherto whites-only Central High school. In the ensuing campaign for desegregation paid by the National Association for the Advancement of Coloured Peoples (NAACP), the children began attending the school protected by police and surrounded by jeering, abusive white racists. A photograph of one of the children, 15-year-old student Elizabeth Eckford as she was verbally attacked by angry white protestors, flashed across America's media.

The respected modern political philosopher, Hannah Arendt was outraged. Adding to the controversy, Arendt wrote an essay in which she argued the parents of the children involved in the incident were abusing their children. She said they had failed to guide and protect them: 'The girl, obviously was asked to be a hero, something neither her absent father nor the equally absent representatives of the NAACP felt called upon' (Arendt 1959:45). The children who Arendt saw as vulnerable and innocent should not have been expected, let alone allowed to participate in such a political process. The implication was that they were being manipulated by their elders who should have known better.

Arendt's essay provoked further debate. One critic was Ralph Ellison, an award-winning African-American writer, who said Arendt failed to see what was actually happening. He argued that an important clue to the meaning of the African-American experience was 'the idea, the ideal of sacrifice' something that Hannah Arendt failed to appreciate (Ellison 1995:343). Arendt he said had:

> ...absolutely no conception of what goes on in the minds of Negro parents when they send their kids through those lines of hostile people. Yet they

are aware of the overtones of a rite of initiation which such events actually constitute for the child, a confrontation of the terrors of social life with all the mysteries stripped away. And in the outlook of many of these parents (who wish that the problem didn't exist), the child is expected to face the terror and contain his fear and anger precisely because he is a Negro American.

(Ellison 1995:344)

Here, we see not only different conceptions of the status of children, but also of politics. For Arendt, children belonged to the social world and not the public or political world. In terms that later attracted the ire of feminists, Arendt drew a distinction between the private, social world and the public, political world (Arendt 1958, Pitkin 1998). For Arendt, citizens had a right to control their private life and household, which included their choice about who marry and how to rear their children. However, when people come together in public, they constituted a 'common world' or 'political realm' with their fellow citizens. Given Arendt believed only two political rights counted, namely the right to vote and the right to be eligible for public office, the idea of politics could only refer to practices like electoral campaigning and voting.

Ellison in contrast did not draw a line between the social and the public worlds. As Allen explains, Ellison believed African-American parents were obligated to teach their children that the political and legal world is part of a social context, which for African-Americans is often terrifying. Indeed, the circumstances experienced by African-Americans, especially in the southern states, were so dreadful that the rule of law provided them with little or no protection. Given that representative democracies were also responsible for making the laws that liberals thought provided the foundation for the rule of law, it was feasible, as this American case suggests that democratic majorities could enact laws that denied minorities their fundamental rights. As Allen explains, this could be done in ways:

...that constrains the possibilities for action supposedly protected by law. Ellison argued that African-American parents and their children were acting politically while articulating positive visions about new political forms ... For Ellison a citizen's participation in public life introduces her to pains and disappointments that, though generated in the public sphere, will be experienced in the social and personal realms.

(Allen 2001:862)

Ellison argued that learning this and how to negotiate the losses African-Americans regularly experienced was central to becoming a political actor, not only for minorities suffering political abuses, but for all citizens.

I return to this debate between Arendt and Ellison later in the chapter. It is a debate that reiterates the point that children and young people have always been central to various politics and political crises and controversies. If we reflect on political debates in the twentieth and twenty-first centuries, this is demonstrated in debates about stolen generations, child poverty, gay and lesbian marriages, youth unemployment and educational policies, through child sexual abuse to the politics of asylum-seekers and refugees. Even quite young children regularly figure in high-stake political crises when, e.g., asylum-seeking children drown on beaches, or are separated from their families and put in detention after being trapped on borders after governments have attempted to block the entry of refugees (Davis and Shear 2018). As Bray and Nakata observe in such cases, we are compelled to consider 'a representation of children made for political purposes, with important constitutive effects on the terrain of political contestation' (Bray and Nakata 2020:2).

While many older people may say that children should have nothing to do with politics until they vote, the fact is that in many ways, children and young people are engaged in politics, whether as *political objects* such as child refugees or as *political subjects* protesting about climate action or university fees. In spite of the endlessly claims about the need to keep children and young people out of politics, this has never been possible. As writers like Brocklehurst observe, the 'political world is not separate from children, but is constitutive of children's roles and presence [because] they have a political capacity as agents and actors' (Brocklehurst 2003:79).

It is an argument I develop and defend in this book. Yet it is a truth that is denied and resisted by many contemporary social scientists and other experts and by major political theorists like Hannah Arendt. We see in the work of these experts the continuing argument that because children and young people are psychologically, biologically, socially and morally different to adults, they should be treated differently in a number of ways. This ignores the point Brocklehurst makes that the 'political world is not separate from children, but is constitutive of children's roles and presence'. That is, decisions about who is, and who is not political, are made by people within the political field. In what follows, I explore some of substantive normative and theoretical issues involved in determining who is, and who is not a full citizen.

How do those working in the social sciences and political science in particular represent children and young people as political beings? I ask this because those conceptualisations inform common-sense understandings of politics and the place of young people in that field? If these representations depend on a particular characterisation of politics, as I argue they do, what are those understandings? If there are problems with how social scientists conceptualise the political, how should we think about politics and the political in ways that acknowledge that children and young people can and do engage politically?

I begin with an historical account of some of the ways children and young people have been constructed as objects owned by their parents, or as minors needing to be protected until they can become adults and can exercise the affordances of adulthood like political participation. I then suggest reasons for the representation of children and young people as unsuited to political life. This involves showing how they are represented as inadequate, deficient or defective adults. Showing how and why children are ill-suited for political life also depends on a quite narrow and state-centric way, conception of politics, something highlighted in the way citizenship has been represented in the west. While the focus is on political science, the arguments and claims made here apply more generally to the social sciences as well as popular common sense.

Representing children and young people as unfit for political life: paternalism

One popular contemporary way of describing the political status of children and young people is to describe them as semi or partial citizens. This can be seen in Elizabeth Cohen's suggestion that modern children occupy a political status somewhere between aliens and full citizens. Minimally, they can have passports and may be assigned a nationality but are 'judged to be incapable of citizenship in that they cannot make the rational and informed decisions that characterize self-governance' (Cohen 2005:221). Like Arendt, Cohen observes how children like women were for a long time 'consigned to the private world of the family, removed from public life – ostensibly for the good of themselves and the polity in general' (Cohen 2005:222).

While Cohen is sympathetic to the effects of the 'stifling of children's interests' and argues that children should be assigned a semi-citizen status, she also says 'children cannot hold a citizenship that is identical to full adult citizenship'. Cohen argues this because 'children are not equal to the demands of citizenship' and the reasons for this are clear and unchangeable: 'We don't give children full citizenship in part because they aren't ready for it, and would not fare well as independent political actors' (Cohen 2005:236). Significantly, Cohen uses the language of citizenship to frame the discussion. This is evident, e.g., when she observes that: 'As things stand, children form the largest group of unrepresented people in every liberal-democracy in the world' (2005:181).

Cohen's work highlights how children and young people have long been the object of adult political, legal, cultural and philosophical representations. This can take the form of paternalism involving representations of children and young people as minors.

Children and young people have long been subject to paternalism in which the child or adolescent, or youth, *belongs to* or is *owned* by parents or guardians. The idea of ownership provided a justification for segregating 'the young' to the confines of the private realm of the family and for excluding them from political and public life. Paternalism involves restricting 'the freedom of persons so that their interests may be better served' and is based on the idea the person in question needs protection because they cannot defend or look after themselves (Miller 1995:367–368). Traditionally, those who practice paternalism have not acknowledged that children and young people (or other groups like women and indigenous people) have any rights or autonomy to say what they believe is in their interest (Howard-Warner et al. 2018). It's an approach that relied heavily on a politics of mis-recognition whereby the child or youth is represented as the 'Other' (i.e., to the adult) (Taylor 1994).

This produces a contradictory mix of assigned attributes: children and young people are natural or natives, dependent, emotional, playful, naïve, irrational and under-developed. At the same time, they are fierce, wild, aggressive and dangerous. Yet they can also be innocent, pure, incomplete unable to assume adult responsibilities (Kioupkiolis and Pechtelides 2018:229)

Paternalism has historical roots, at least in the west, in Roman law. Pocock demonstrated how Roman law provided the precursor for modern, legalistic and rights-based conceptions of citizenship (Pocock 1995). Under Roman law, parental rights were extended from labour and property to their children.[2] The fact that children were so completely dominated under Roman law children might help explain why they were excluded from more recent conceptions of citizenship that followed the Roman model. John Locke's seventeenth-century liberal model, e.g., amended this ownership idea by limiting parental entitlement to authority over children. Locke argued that god is the maker of children, not parents. Given there are no rights without labour, Locke argued that parents do not have an absolute right to control and punish their children (Shapiro 1999:73).

The effect of this liberal revision was not dramatic. If parents do not own their children, they cannot physically punish them without limitations, but they do retain emotional and affective ownership of their children. Parents can and do compel certain kinds of behaviours like church attendance, schooling, the choice of friends or leisure by reference to the idea of their 'best interests', which typically reflects only what parents believe are in the child's best interest. As women, children and many young people discovered the liberal conception of the private–public distinction meant the home and the lives lived within it are ostensibly protected spaces in a liberal-democracy.

A more recent form of paternalism relied on the idea that children are immature and incapable of the rational deliberation and decision-making that contemporary democratic political life ostensibly requires. That kind of paternalism lingers on in our time in numerous sociological and psychological studies that confirm this deficit account of children and young people. These studies have in turn been used by liberal-democratic states to justify their unwillingness to assign substantive civil and political rights to children and young people (Pocock 1995:37–39).

Representing children and young people as unfit for political life: children as minors

Representation of children and some young people as 'minors' refers to their status as inferior, secondary, and of lesser significance. Being a minor means having lesser status and a potential adult. In this respect, it is a representation that has a principle of futurity built into it. This future-oriented representation emphasises what the child or adolescent will become as a citizen and provides a vision of the society they will fit into as it welcomes children as they slowly become full adult members.

The status of children and young people as minors is generally described as temporary and preparatory. As such, the policies and laws that affect them are designed not so much with a mind to acknowledging the individual people that comprise the population of children and young people, but to the kind of people various adults wish them to become. One result of this has been that any idea that children either can and or should participate in political life or activities has generally been opposed or resisted. This rests on the idea that adults are obliged to protect children from what sensible adults know is a dangerous world:

> …[children] either need to be better protected (better policed from the evils of the adult world) or better controlled (because of the failure of certain families to police properly their children).
>
> *(Roche 1999:477)*

Like paternalism, representations of childhood and youth as 'minors' see 'stages' on the road to adulthood. Children and young people are incomplete, non-adults in a state of becoming rather than being (Jenks 1982, Chesters et al. 2018). This stadial framing generated a vast scholarship in fields like psychology, child development, legal studies, education, youth studies and social history (Griffin 1993, Zaff et al. 2003, Melkman 2017, Haggman-Laitila et al. 2019). As Zhao explained, they are representations that signify how children and young people have been 'used for different social, cultural, economic, and political purposes' (Zhao 2011:242). In the modern era, this 'adult power' was increasingly been applied in ways that talk about pursuing the 'best interests of the child'. However, as Prout notes, while claiming to prioritize the future of the child and society over the child's present well-being, adults still practise control, which many scholars say is distinguishing feature of modernity (2000, see also Freeman 2000).

As I argue later in this book, there are a number of overlapping representations that cohere around the idea that children and young people should not be allowed to participate in political activity. These rely on the idea they are in various ways vulnerable, frail, naïve, or emotionally troubled, dysfunctional, deviant trouble-makers and need protection. It can rest on the claim that because they are not adults they lack the requisite cognitive, ethical, emotional skills or experience to participate in political life that requires them to know certain things and to exercise judgement, which they are naturally incapable of doing.

This framing also generated a vast amount of academic and practical scholarship in fields of sociology, psychology, social history child development, legal studies, education, youth studies and social work (Griffin 1993, Zaff et al. 2003, Melkman 2017, Haggman-Laitila et al. 2019).

This also points towards better understanding the purpose of these representations?

The purpose of representations of children and young people

For those who automatically accept as obvious the idea without proof that children and many young people cannot be citizens, or do things citizens do like vote or stand for public office, there is no need to query or attempt to explain these representations. Bruno Latour calls this the 'double click' conception of knowledge (Latour cited in Tresch 2013:302–313). That is, we can have 'the illusion' of having immediate, direct reference to reality and truth by going back and forth between objective, knowledge and the world as easily 'as we move from an icon on our computer's screen to the page it links to, by clicking on it' (Latour cited in Tresch 2013:309–310).

Some writers however reject this common-sense representation of children and young people saying they do not capture the richness and complexity of children's lives and experience. They highlight how these representations fail to acknowledge what is actually happening. One way of explaining how it is possible to accept representations of this kind without question, is to point to the reliance on certain assumptions that inform these scientific or common-sense narratives about children and young people.

Writers from different traditions including Michel Foucault (1972), Quentin Skinner (2002), Ian Hacking (2002) and Richard Tuck (2016) emphasised the value of tracing out how these representations came about through time. This entails reconstructing the history of 'constitutive schemes' that operate in those traditions (e.g., sociology, political science, psychology, youth studies and so forth) (Danziger 1990). Doing history in this way involves paying close attention to the language categories that are used and especially the role played by key metaphors. It's an approach that allows us to see how the practices, vocabulary and interests of experts create and shape the problems to be addressed, the questions asked, as well as the methods of inquiry and the descriptions and explanations offered. This vocabulary and associated practices also help shape the boundaries that distinguish one discipline from another.

Reinhard Kosselleck developed an historical method of inquiry drawing on the Heideggerian and Gadamerian hermeneutic tradition (2004). Rather than talking about 'constitutive schemes', Heidegger and Gadamer, e.g., spoke of 'horizons'. As a metaphor, horizons speak of how far we can and cannot see. It is through our encounters with others that we construct horizons that determine the entirety of what we can realise or think about within a specific context. The limits of our horizons are influenced by the attitudes, feelings and understandings of the world we have before we even start to think about 'it' directly. The fore-judgements or prejudices we have constrain our capacity to see or encounter the world 'as it actually is'. Thus, we always approach the world through existing horizons. This involves projecting on the world our horizons that are shaped by our particular experience, prejudices or traditions of inquiry, which mediate our views of what we are able to grasp (Gadamer 1977). For hermeneutic philosophers like Gadamer, if we extend or look beyond those horizons, then it is necessary to reflect on our own life and 'look beyond what is close at hand – not in order to look away from it but to see it better' (Gadamer 2004).

This helps highlight the effect of interpretative frames that inhibit our capacity to see what children and young people are actually doing and experiencing. For example, according to Mary Nolan, children's political engagement has been underestimated because social scientists 'narrowly defined concepts of civil society and socio-political participation at the macro level' (Nolan 2001:308).

One effect of these scholarly 'horizons' can be seen in the vast literature that snowballed since the 1990s as governments and various researchers discovered the 'crisis of democracy'. This was described in part as caused by young people who had 'disengaged' politically, evident, e.g., in a disinclination to vote or join political parties. Many social scientists have been measuring evidence of political disengagement since the 1990s, showing e.g., how only between a third to a half of young voters are voting in Britain, the US or Australia (Eckersley 1988, Bhavnani 1991, Jowell and Park 1998, Mellor 1998, Mellor et al. 2002, Johnson and Marshall 2004, Edwards et al. 2006, Saha et al. 2007). Much of the time and effort has been spent examining this and proposing solutions that typically involve more or better civics education (Crick 1998, Henn et al. 2002, Bang 2004, Furlong and Cartmel 2007, Bennett 2008, Eckstein et al. 2012, Hart and Youniss 2017, Giersch and Dong 2018).

Yet a number of critics noticed how this concern about young people's political disengagement relied on a very narrow idea of politics. Cockburn argues that if political activity is constrained conceptually by thinking about young people's politics in terms of their engagement with formal organisations or practices like voting, then it will be underestimated. This will enable 'media and government continue to portray children and young people ... as "politically apathetic" and disinterested in politics and the life around them' (Cockburn 2007:446). Similarly, Manning argued that if the activities of political parties and institutions like voting are seen as constitutive of politics, then drawing on a 'particular model of politics to measure young people's political knowledge and participation ... privileges the conventional wisdom and dominant paradigm for understanding young people and their relationship with politics' (Manning 2010:12).

A key feature of this literature is its dependence on a quite narrow conceptualisation of politics. Manning calls for some reflexivity in how the term politics is used and for the need to be more attuned:

> ...to the ways in which the dominant liberal model of politics works to close down what counts as political. Researchers need also be aware of political repertoires operating outside mainstream politics.
> *(Manning 2010:21, see also Vromen 2003:79–99, Bessant 2014)*

This indicates that another way of understanding the nature of dominant representations of children *and* politics is to focus on the restricted ways politics has been understood. Following Bourdieu's relational approach implicates the connections between the field of politics (the state) and relevant academic fields.

Conventional understandings of politics

Today, when academics and researchers discuss political matters, many assume that everyone knows what 'we' are talking about. Accordingly, there is no need for any extended discussion. It seems, there is no need to say much about what everyone knows. While I focus on the political science in what follows, I also refer to general tendencies in the social sciences.

Bourdieu spoke of the serious risks we face when thinking about politics or socio-economic problems. The danger he spoke of was of 'being taken over by a thought of the state, that is, of applying to the state, categories of thought produced ... by the state' (Bourdieu 1998:35). Bourdieu saw this as a problem because science is 'on the side' of subordinated people and groups. That is, the social sciences as an interdisciplinary ensemble have a key role to play in creating emancipatory thought and practice. It was this thinking that prompted Bourdieu's critique of social or political science as a 'false science'. As Bon and Schemeil argue, Bourdieu's:

> ...condemnation of political science is final as an 'official science' or 'practitioner's art', it cannot claim the status of an established scientific discipline ... Pierre Bourdieu asks them one question that they cannot evade: is political science an enterprise aimed at legitimizing the political world and the social hierarchy on which it is founded?
> *(Bon and Schemeil 1980:1203)*

As practical knowledge, social sciences are designed to assist professional politicians and policy-makers to advance their interest in the political field, i.e., the state. In effect, social science and political science in particular, have become handmaidens to the state.

To paraphrase Bourdieu, researchers and scholars generally risk applying to our understanding of politics and the state, 'state thinking' whereby 'our thinking, the very structure of consciousness by which we construct the social world and the particular object that is the state are very likely the product of the state itself' (Bourdieu 2014:3). There is a danger that the state is an 'unthinkable object' because:

> ...one of the major powers of the state is to produce and impose (especially through the school system) categories of thought that we spontaneously apply to all things of the social world – including the state itself.
> *(Bourdieu 1998:35)*

More than most of the social sciences, political science tends to avoid critical reflection about the nature of the political. This led the Australian political scientist Hugh Emy to observe some time ago that: 'To study Australian politics is to be aware of a vacuum. ...there is no thematic core to research, unless it stems from a personal belief in the suitability of some particular '"answer"' (Emy 1972:12). Writing decades later, Gregory Melleuish said little had changed:

> Emy's comments made in 1972 still have a ring of truth in 2015. Reading the pages of the [Australian Journal of Political Science] one can discern that there is a lot of particular research going on with Australian politics as its focus … it is difficult to see what that research means for creating an overall and intelligible, larger picture of Australian politics
> *(Melleuish 2015:732)*

Much of the problem seems to relate to the narrow, constrained and largely implicit understanding of what counts as politics. Melleuish himself seems happy to accept Archer and Maddox (1975) view that political science centres on four themes or problems in which we can easily be trapped. This matters because it sets horizons, limits or constrains our thinking about what is politics, what counts as political action and who are political agents. Each theme relates to the character and regulatory functions of government. They include:

1 Politics as administration, 'the managing of the state as corporation'. Such an approach concentrates on policy formation;
2 Politics as 'a high level of competition between rival interests';
3 Politics as 'a framework of legally defined institutions';
4 Politics as 'constitutionalism', the conduct of rulers being limited by a tradition of behaviour, by 'ethical considerations' (Archer and Maddox 1976:7).

As standard histories of British and American political and social science indicate, things are not much better in those countries (Collini et al. 1983, Ross 1991, Farr and Seidelman 1993, Hayward et al. 1999, Adcock 2014).

When academics and researchers discuss politics, many assume that everyone knows what we are talking about, so there is no need to spend time describing what is already clear, namely, the nature of the political. There is no need to say much about what everyone already knows. Many working in mainstream social science overlook the core concepts being studied and continue with accounts of politics that are uncritical and unreflexive. Jose and Motta argue that political science is unwilling to reflect on the nature of the political (2017). Like all other disciplinary knowledge, political science claims it has a distinctive field of knowledge. As they argue, there is '… no discipline-wide consensus concerning the discipline's boundaries let alone its content and the acceptable or preferred means of arriving at it' (Jose and Motta 2017:651).

How we understand politics and the political matters because the interpretative 'horizons' that defines a concept and a discipline like political science and the social sciences generally significantly influences what we see and look for, what we identify as important problems and how we research politics (Leftwich 2004:2). A lack of clarity and reflexivity about what we mean by words like 'politics' and 'political' has serious effects.

One effect is to render young people and their politics invisible.

As Leftwich observed, the absence of clarity about what political scientists mean when they use words like 'politics' or 'the political' has not discouraged many from developing many styles or traditions of inquiry that rely on tacit or implied understandings of 'politics' as they research political things (2004). Indeed, as Jose and Motta acknowledge:

> …paradoxically, there is agreement, or perhaps it is more accurately described as mutual recognition, as to what makes political science 'political science' and not something else.
>
> *(Jose and Motta 2017:651)*

Presumably this is why, Leftwich points to various types of political science.

An older political science tradition e.g., focused on the rules, procedures and formal organization of government. This 'institutionalism' used research methods akin to those used in law and history and privileges research on a narrow range of formal institutions and practices (Heywood 2013:17) Then there was a tradition of political 'behavioural science' that co-opted the methods of the natural science to create quantitative accounts of voting behaviour, the behaviour of legislators, links between parties and special interests, etc. Another tradition such as 'New institutionalism' was concerned primarily with 'formal' political reasoning (Downs 1957, Becker 1976). It included ideas like rational-choice theory and public-choice theory (Dunleavy 1991, Heywood 2013). Each of these political science approaches have been underpinned by implicit understandings of what is political. It is an understanding that prioritises the use of legitimate institutions like political parties, elections, constitutions, codes of law or parliaments. Added to this are local issues specific to a given polity like the United Kingdom, Australia or America such as federalism, immigration policy, corruption, gender equity in parties, pro-republican movements or the regulation of political donations (Melleuish 2015). Each of these approaches shares a strong interest in the mechanics of government, policy-making, sampling public opinion and electoral processes. Again typically, this is framed by a privileging of the liberal-democratic paradigm and notions like citizenship, constitutionality and rule-of-law principles.

This liberal account is set out by Philipe Schmitter who says that if we want to understand this preoccupation with the state, or ideas like citizenship and the mechanisms of rulership, then there is value in acknowledging the extent to which the European tradition of thinking about the political that can be traced to Aristotle (2016). This is a tradition that produced many variations on Aristotle's writings on the role of government in our collective lives.

According to Schmitter, most political and social scientists have, since Aristotle, been committed to a substantialist perspective. Schmitter cites Aristotle to the effect that: '…the mark of an educated man is to look for precision in each class of things just so far as the nature of the subject admits.' This is why Schmitter stresses the importance of defining concepts (like politics), which involves what he says is the most important and contested of all concepts, namely power (Schmitter 2016:14). Schmitter also positions himself in the European tradition arguing that politics is 'a (if not the) quintessential human activity' and humans have agency, i.e., freedom to act. Moreover, humans are intrinsically 'restless':

> Some are dissatisfied with their existing situation and, hence, willing to try to change it. In so doing, they are very likely to provoke a response from those who are not so dissatisfied. The latter will react to defend the status quo and, therefore, also become agents.
>
> *(Schmitter 2016:4)*

Schmitter's Weberian provenance can be seen when he says 'politics rests on the exercise (or the threat of the exercise) of power and of resistance to it' (Schmitter 2016:4). The influence of the liberal social contract is evident in Schmitter's highlights the role played by rules:

> What is unique to human beings is their capacity to 'domesticate' this activity by inserting rules and practices that serve to channel the actions and reactions of agents according to mutually agreed upon rules and/or reliably applied practices. These regulated exchanges, negotiations, deliberations and decision-making allow conflicts to be resolved pacifically and, thereby, preclude the resort to violence that would otherwise be needed to resolve the differences in resources and preferences that give rise to political activity in

Finally, political science or theory tends to retreat to Max Weber and his discussion of power. This is an idea of power grounded in the claim that we need to understand the state as an institution that possesses a monopoly control over legitimate use of force. This encouraged generations of political scientists like Ian Shapiro to argue that 'politics is concerned in the last instance, as well as in the first, with managing power relations' (2016). He adds that 'the power to coerce is…a natural monopoly[much] as Max Weber did when he defined the state by reference to its capacity to monopolize legitimate coercive force in a given territory' (Shapiro 2016:33).

Likewise, Jose declares 'the idea of "the political" is specifically concerned with that domain that has as its focus, how relations of power between rulers and ruled are constituted, justified, and exercised' (Jose 2017:719–720).

It is worth noting that a failure to read Weber carefully has generated many books and journal articles discussing Weber's approach to power as a relation of dominance. What Weber actually says is this:

> Power [*Macht*] is *the probability* that one actor *within a social relationship* will be in a position to carry out his own will despite resistance, regardless of the basis on which this probability rests
>
> *(Weber 1947:152) (My stress)*

Far from seeing 'power' as a substance, Weber suggests it is best understood relationally. Weber understood the indeterminacy of 'power' when he emphasises that it is only a probability and not a certainty that in any relationship, someone will be able to achieve her objective at the expense of someone else. As Uphof explained:

> For Weber, any attribution of power is a statement about *the probability that someone can achieve his or her own goals,* relative to the goals of others, using one or more of a number of means. What exists is not 'power' but rather these means and the relationships they establish. While one can speak abstractly about power just as physicists talk about 'energy,' an analysis is best done in terms of specific kinds [of relationships].
>
> *Uphof (1989:299)*[3]

A number of things can be said about framing the political as the study of government that sees power-as-dominance and leads to an emphasis on the rules, procedures and formal organisation of government, voting behaviour, the behaviour of legislators or political leaders, or notions like citizenship. This disposition to privilege an implicitly state-centric framing is not always obvious in conventional political science and social science approaches to the political. This suggests why those who use the conceptual vocabulary and problematics of social sciences find it difficult to explain how the political is constituted. One reason given for this is that 'these disciplines have not, by and large, addressed the question of how the political is imagined' (Brown and Diehl 2019). In general, the preoccupation with political institutions, governments, policy-makers and politicians, and the traditional practices of political parties and electoral campaigns (Almond and Verba 1963), has preferred to document and describe those practices rather than inquire into how the political is imagined. Another way of getting at this 'horizon' is recall how the Greek experience of the *polis* has encouraged a deep and continuing state-centric story. This is a story that repeatedly tells us we are political *because* we are 'members' of a 'polity' or 'citizens' of a state. This preoccupation with citizenship, has the effect of discounting the possibility of children or young people ever 'being' political actors.

Citizenship

There is a long tradition in the west of seeing politics as coterminous with being a citizen (a member of a political space or community). As Aristotle suggested, if we are 'political animals' this is because we are born into political communities or a *polis*. Indeed, the city-state's where many Greeks lived 2,500 years ago is where much of the conceptual vocabulary used today came from. From those 'city-states' a *polis* came key words like 'political', 'politics', 'police' and 'policy'.[4] Many *poleis* also had designated spaces for public assembly, for political purposes or for entertainment.

Aristotle writing in the fourth century BC assumed as did most other men of his time that living in a Greek *polis* was the original source of politics: all male citizens ostensibly had equal political rights conferred on them by their ownership of property. (This idea of property included their slaves, women, children, land, technologies, livestock, dwellings and furnishings.) Aristotle's *Politics* offers an exploration of a political system with choices ranging from tyranny, aristocracy, oligarchy through to democracy. It is also likely that Aristotle understood that political power in the *polis* was dominated by a few aristocratic families who controlled the important positions like membership of elite councils, magistracies and higher military ranks.

As mentioned, there is a tradition in the west of seeing politics as coterminous with being a citizen. From the Greeks 'city-states' or *polis* and the Romans *civitas* came a continuing state-centric story in which citizenship referred to the 'rights, duties and membership in a political community of some kind' (Brown 1994:874)[5]. It was the city space the *civitas* that constituted and fostered citizenship as a 'special status of being *of* the city' (Isin 2008:268). Citizenship also referred to the 'rights, duties, and membership in a political community of some kind' (Brown 1994:874). As Isin argues, the Greco-Roman tradition assumed being a citizen entailed a right and a responsibility to be political involving 'a right to constitute oneself as an agent, to govern and be governed, deliberate with others and enjoin determining the fate of the polity to which one belongs' (Isin 2002:1). (This is why being sent into exile and forced to leave a city was a dire punishment for Greek and Roman citizens alike.)

Yet Isin is critical of the historical and political narratives found in modern textbooks that tell a timeless story of citizenship. It is a narrative that says how successive communities simply looked back to previous examples in a more or less smooth narrative arc that started with the Greeks, went through the Roman and Medieval period ending in the modern period. According to Isin, if there is a 'harmonious unity and unbroken continuity in the images we are given of citizenship', that is *not because of a natural growth* but rather a 'strategic emulation and appropriation – invention – of tradition that has made it possible' (Isin 2002:3).

Here Isin also makes an important observation that the idea of citizenship involves not just inclusion but also exclusion. Recalling, e.g., that the number of citizens in Athens 500 BC was small, Isin notes that this small size was because many people – namely, slaves, foreign residents, women, and artisans – were excluded from ancient forms of citizenship as they would be in medieval and into modern times. Identifying who is a citizen is a political process that involves saying who is not. As Isin explained:

> …In almost every discussion of citizenship [there is the idea that] while ancient citizenship was "revolutionary" it did exclude these groups. But did it? The logic of exclusion assumes that the categories of strangers and outsiders such as women, slaves, peasants, [foreign residents], immigrants, refugees and clients pre-existed citizenship, and that once defined it excluded them.
>
> *(Isin 2002:3)*

This inclusion–exclusion logic assumes that those excluded are to be represented in negative ways. This is why as Isin says the qualities defining those who are excluded such as 'strange, hidden, frightful or menacing' were all qualities understood as negations of the citizen-as-norm. Isin maintains that all those 'others' (other than a citizen) did not exist before the idea of the citizen came into being. Rather, they were constituted by it because citizenship requires the constitution of others who are not (Isin 2002:4). This helps make clearer what Brocklehurst was saying when she argued that the 'political world is not separate from children, but is constitutive of children's roles and presence' (Brocklehurst 2003:79).

This a reminder that since their inception, social sciences like political science have emulated this political practice by obscuring and excluding subjects, objects and processes. A politics is operating when a discipline claiming to be a science, blanks out certain kinds of people and their ideas, experiences and need for recognition. Jose and Motta, e.g., observe how it took many decades for political scientists to acknowledge issues like sex, class, gender, race and political and social movements as worthy subject of study (2017).

Given young people's exclusion from formal politics and their engagement in 'other', i.e., 'non-political' modes of action (as understood by many the

58 Children, young people and politics

social sciences), it is not surprising that because they were and are excluded from formal political processes, they are defined as 'apolitical', 'disengaged' and 'inactive'.

Yet it is paradoxical and characteristic that major political theorists like Arendt and progressive writers like Jose and Motta and Isin – along with other critical theorists – have not acknowledged young people in their account of who has been excluded or rendered invisible. Even these progressive critics of mainstream political science obscured and excluded children and young people. This is a problematic because of an inconvenient truth, namely children and young people have long been engaged politically. The fact that is not acknowledged suggests there are some problems with the ways children and young people are represented, and also with how politics is represented.

The political: what Mouffe and Arendt say

The popular and dominant view in the social sciences suggests that when talking about politics we are referring to formal institutions, rules, conventions and the practices of governance originating in and regulated by the state (Srnicek and Williams 2015). This includes recruiting and mobilising party members, staging political debates, regulating political advertising, donations and electoral campaigns, running elections, passing legislation, using the courts to interpret legislation debates and regulating and managing the negotiations between civil society interest groups such as trade unions, business peak bodies and the media.

A revisionist reimaging of the political that enables review of how children and young people engage politically is beyond the scope of this book, let alone this chapter. Having said that, several insights have been offered critics of contemporary liberal-democratic politics that point to some useful ideas about the possible directions such a project might take. Mouffe offers an agonistic or conflict-ridden conception of politics (e.g., Mouffe 2005, also Unger 2014). Another is Arendt's idea of the political as a source of rebirth, novelty and change – or what she calls natality.

Informing the liberal-democratic political imaginary is the idea that rational consensus is possible and desirable. This is because as political subjects, citizens are rational responsible subjects. From this perspective, conflict is a surplus and indeed gets in the way of politics. Modern exponents of the deliberative democratic idea include Jurgen Habermas. For Habermas, the public sphere connects rational deliberation to the democratic political process providing a rational basis for consensus (1989). Many deliberative democratic theorists influenced by Habermas also argued that a strong public sphere in combination with electoral politics are essential institutional devices for consensus making, albeit if only temporarily, in a democratic polity (Macedo 199, Dryzek 2006). The elimination of conflict can be eliminated is preferable to a politics based on conflict, dissent and protest.

Chantal Mouffe

The past few decades have seen a growing body of critical political theory arguing that a genuine democratic politics is one characterised by conflict and disagreement rather than consensus. This is what 'agonistic' theorists like William Connolly (1995, 2005), Bonnie Honig (1993a, 1993b, 2009, 2017), James Tully (1995, 2008) and Chantal Mouffe (2005) say. The classical Greek idea of 'agon' means contest or competition. Having plural of value systems and diverse conceptions of social goods that are constitutive of democratic politics involves conflict between 'us' and 'them', based on relations of identity-difference, which cannot always be resolved. This is because any democratic society is always incomplete, uncertain and open. A democratic society is not characterised by consensus and a harmonious existence.

To protect this pluralism and openness that exemplifies democratic life, differences and disagreements need not be acknowledged, affirmed and expressed. As Honig says, this is because the agonistic expression of differences like gender, class and, in this case, age:

> ...challenge existing distributions of power, disrupt the hegemonic social, and proliferate political spaces when they interrupt the routine, predictability, and repetition on which [...] dominant patterns of private realm identity depend.
>
> *(Honig 1993:359)*

Mouffe has been a major critic of conceptualising politics in terms of rational consensus and reconciliation. Mouffe argues for the subversion of a key premise or underpinning assumption of the liberal political tradition that politics is what rational, well-integrated individuals – who are also adult – do. According to Mouffe, this account of the rational self and political consensus presupposed by liberal-democratic theorists is implausible. As Mihai et al. note (2017:501–531), Mouffe along with other theorists like Slavoj Žižek (1989) draws on a Lacanian account of the self.

Lacan's idea of the self refers to how we are split beings, devoid of essence and not reducible to a conscious, rational well-integrated ego or self. Mouffe agrees, saying the self is far from having a clear, stable identity and one that is always open or amenable to reason (Mouffe 1993:75–76). For those not so convinced of such a Lacanian account of a non-rational subject, reference can be made to those working in the field of modern behavioural economic science. It is work that documents the often irrational psychological, cultural and emotional factors that often inform economic and political decision-making in ways that subvert the model of rational economic individual found in neo-classical economic theory (Frank 1988, Kahneman 2011).

Mouffe's approach however is one that sees the 'self' as perpetually seeking an elusive identity in which to invest libidinally. She uses Derrida's idea of the 'constitutive outside' to argue that collective identifications presuppose a 'they' against whom the libidinal force of aggression is directed. In effect, passionate attachment to socially constructed collective identifications keeps individuals politically engaged and enables political action (Stavrakakis 1999:26). This is why Mouffe says the valuing of political consensus presupposed by liberal-democratic theory is not possible and is inadequate: it rests on a deeply flawed account of the human subject. Mouffe was also critical of the conventional accounts of citizenship that require an often unspecified level of cognitive, emotional competence and judgemental experience said to be associated only with adults. This is why Mouffe argues that many working in the social sciences or politics are 'blind to … the political in its dimension of conflict decision' and cannot see the value of opposition in political life (2005:3). Mouffe rejects this emphasis on consensus. She argues that conflict is an inevitable quality, because we are libidinally charged creatures and so cannot be got rid of. Thus, we need to reflect on the conditions under which the field of politics and the public sphere can flourish as spaces, given the public sphere is where various collective identifications grounded in class, sexuality, ethnicity, religion, etc. are contested.

Mouffe also distinguishes between agonism and antagonism. Drawing on Schmitt's definition of the political as the relation between 'friends and enemies', she says antagonism is a 'we-they' relationship between 'friends' and 'enemies' who do not share common ground. Agonism is a 'we' relationship in which conflicting parties declare commitments to shared principles (e.g., to liberal-democracy). While agonists acknowledge there may be no immediate, or even long-term, solution to their differences, they nonetheless recognize the legitimacy of their opponents' opposition and its value for democratic processes. Significantly that shared commitment makes them 'adversaries' not 'enemies'.

For Mouffe, while differences are 'natural' and 'normal', making pluralism axiomatic, it is also, at a different level, of agonistic struggle itself. While plural values and interests – conflicting and often irreconcilable – reveal the need for agonism (for a different way of negotiating ever-present and inevitable conflict), agonism also nourishes and protects democratic pluralism. Mouffe argues there is value in looking more closely at what the modern democratic discourse offers, which involves securing the possibility of radical democratic conflict. This entails the rediscovery of contingency plurality and agon conflict as its foundation.

This points to an important moral–political role for the kinds of political contest that involve protest and various forms of dissent that many children and young people have been generating, but which have often been rendered invisible by conventional ways of conceptualising as or reducing politics to state-sponsored regulation and the use of techniques designed to promote consensus.

Hannah Arendt

Mouffe shares Arendt's emphasis on treating the political as action oriented to freedom. As Menga notes, Arendt's concept of plurality reveals the same focus on contingency and conflict that Mouffe advocates (Menga 2017:533). Arendt was committed to the idea of freedom and to new beginnings in politics.

No human activity, she argued, is more revelatory of being human than the free activity of politics. Indeed, contingency and freedom are constitutive conditions of human interaction (Arendt 1958:175–177). Human existence she says is characterised by freedom, it is the power to begin something new. Freedom is also self-grounding within a political space of appearances as opposed to being grounded, e.g., in a sphere of divine or metaphysical laws. Her idea of freedom is not based (as it is within the classical liberal tradition) on an idea of a will that masters itself or directs its actions from predetermined principles, whether metaphysical or religious or laws of reason or nature.

For Arendt, politics is uncertain and unregulatable. Uncertainty in fact is central to her understanding of political action: the success of any political action is never certain and the effects of our actions are unpredictable in an agonistic political world of plurality of actors and spectators with conflicting wills and cross-purposes (Tchir 2017:25). It is not grounded in a conception of political sovereignty, where a ruler crafts laws that subjects then obey. The political field is intrinsically interactive and reflects the intricate interplay of what Arendt calls the 'twofold character of equality and distinction among individuals.' Plurality, being structurally informed by a contingent dynamic of interaction between equal and distinct beings, cannot give a final unitary formation of common space or collective order (Menga 2017:549). Rather, politics constitutes a realm of commonality, which inevitably displays conjunction *and* disjunction (consensus and conflict).

The distinctive idea Arendt adds to this emphasis on contingency, plurality and contest is natality. Arguably natality is central to Arendt's conception of politics. As Canovan observes, Arendt's 'most heartening message' in *The Human Condition* (1958) 'is its reminder of natality and the miracle of beginning' (1998:xvii). For Arendt, natality is 'the central category of political [thought]' because politics has to do with 'the task to provide and preserve the world for, to foresee and reckon with, the constant influx of newcomers who are born into the world as strangers' (1958:9).

She traces the source of political action to there being two births that bring forth something new. The '…new beginning inherent in birth can make itself felt in the world only because the newcomer possesses the capacity of beginning something anew, that is, of acting' (Arendt 1958:9).

Critical to her concept of natality is the idea that when each human being is born that new being comes into the world as a stranger. Human action (political action) is a second birth and is when we enter the political field. It is through words and deeds that we insert ourselves into the human world, and this insertion is like a second birth (1958:176). That second birth occurs when we address political questions like: *who* are you? (Arendt 1958:178–179).

Arendt also argues that transformative conflicts take place, not 'inside' or 'outside' of democratic orders but *on their borders*.

As Menga argues natality, which is characterised by a uniqueness and divergence within plurality, can make unprecedented claims such as making demands to alter a given way of life and introduce 'new beginnings' into an established political order (Menga 2017:551). Natality as such does not figure in or already have a place inside the political order: if it did, it would be unlikely to represent or offer a real challenge or disturbance. Equally, natality is not the same as 'Other', typically understood to exist beyond or outside the order. If it were outside the polis, it would be invisible enabling it to be immediately rejected. Rather, natality and its promise are situated on the boundaries of the public realm between the inside and the outside. On the border, natality is engaged in pushing across the threshold through repeated and renewed demands for shared recognition (Menga 2017:551).

In this way paradoxically given Arendt's critique of children and young people acting politically, her notion of natality is nonetheless an invitation to consider the role children and young people can play in politics on the border of the political order.

This seems the point at which Arendt might have considered the role, indeed the responsibility, children and young people have to play as sources of renewal, novelty and in Mouffe's words, agonism. Yet she did not.

Even political theorists like Arendt are sometimes prone to contradiction, to considering the implications of their own thinking or to denying the obvious. As I indicated at the start of this chapter, in 1959, Arendt wrote about the politics of the emergent civil rights movement and the role children played in that disruptive movement. In her response to the political actions of children such as Elizabeth Eckford, she exhibited an antipathy to the idea they should be involved in the civil rights campaigns. This is surprising because as I have just noted, Arendt was committed to the idea of freedom and the idea of new beginnings in politics. And yet as Hannah Arendt wrote, no-one:

> ...will find it easy to forget the photograph reproduced ... throughout the country, showing a Negro girl [Elizabeth Eckford], accompanied by a white friend of her father, walking away from school, persecuted and followed into bodily proximity by a jeering and grimacing mob of youngsters.
>
> *(Arendt 1959:50)*

Arendt was critical of 15-year-old Elizabeth Eckford's participation in politics. As Arendt argued, the girl was required to be a 'hero' by her irresponsible elders and that she was being used for a political cause that was really theirs. For Arendt:

> ...neither her absent father nor the equally absent representatives of the National Association for the Advanced of Coloured People (NAACP) felt called upon to be.
>
> *(Arendt 1959:50)*

Arendt then asked: 'Have we now come to the point', 'where it is the children who are being asked to change or improve the world? And do we intend to have our political battles fought out in the schoolyards?' (1959:50).

Why did Arendt deny young people's capacity to be political when her idea of natality seems to envisage exactly that possibility? Perhaps it can be seen as a consequence of her own understanding of political thought. Do we see here what Arendt herself describes, the kind of uncertainty and unpredictability that she saw as inherent in politics? It is an uncertainty that comes about as each of us interpret and respond to words and actions in ways that cannot be anticipated by those who do the speaking and acting. In short, it is unlikely that Arendt would have anticipated others interpreting her account of natality in support of young people's capacity to be political.

Another possible way of understanding her refusal to encourage young people to engage politically is to consider how Arendt thought about what happens between our first birth (when we physically come into the world) and our 'second birth' when we act politically? She addressed this in her essay on 'The crisis in education' when she asked: 'What concerns us all' and answers that it 'is the relation between grown-ups and children in general or, putting it in even more general and exact terms, our attitude toward the fact of natality' (Arendt 2006:193).

In this way, natality is seen as a balancing act, because 'the child requires special protection and care so that nothing destructive may happen to her from the world'. The world also 'needs protection to keep it from being overrun and destroyed by the onslaught of the new that bursts upon it with each new generation' (Arendt 2006:182). Here, Arendt does seem, to some extent, to recognise the capacity of young people as the manifestation of natality, as a 'new generation' with the capacity to bring forth 'new bursts', to be transformative, of the social order.

Here too, Arendt fills the gap between our first birth and our 'second birth'. Children 'are not finished but in a state of becoming', and it is the responsibility of those with (temporary) authority over them to ensure that education is orientated to 'the task of renewing a common world', which is home to adults and children alike. However, she continues by saying that this must be done 'without striking from their hands their chance of undertaking some- thing new, something unforeseen by us' (Arendt 2006:174, 182–183, 193).

Arendt's argument reflects a common idea, one that pervaded the twentieth century and that continues today: namely, participation in the politics is adult business and no place for young people. It was a view that relied on distinctions Arendt drew between 'the private' and 'the public' and between 'the social' and 'the political.' Schools she argued are social institutions designed to support the child's movement from home and family to the public life of the world (the political). For this reason, the school is a social, i.e., a non-political site. Moreover, children are 'becoming' adult and for that reason they require protection, which includes being prevented from exercising positive freedom.

All this matters she said because a young person's entry to the political sphere can harm them as individuals and their acting politically (second birth) can seriously disrupt or indeed destroy of the prevailing order. This Arendt argued is because each 'new generation' has the capacity to create unexpected possibilities, make 'something new happen' and thereby disrupt the politics of the day (Arendt 1959, Nakata 2008:19–25, Bessant 2014:138–153, Bessant 2018). For these reasons, young people like 15-year-old Elizabeth Eckford can and should only have limited positive freedom.

Conclusion

Seventy years after Arendt's essay and the same ideas about children, young people and politics continue being promoted in the public sphere and in academia and elsewhere. Even contemporary 'capability' theorists like Amartya Sen and Martha Nussbaum, who are strongly committed to ideas of justice and freedom, support the idea that young people cannot and should not be political.

Yet this seems to be an aberration on the part of Arendt. It seems that on this occasion Arendt failed to see what was actually happening. Her critic Ralph Ellison at the time saw more clearly that African-Americans, one of the major among many other subordinated groups, faced frightening existential challenges imposed by centuries of racialised terror violence and oppression. As responsible parents, the African-American parents trying to enable their children to attend a previously segregated school were obligated to teach their children that America was for many, if not all African-Americans, a dangerous society where the liberal-democratic order provided little effective protection. In that context, children and young people had a legitimate role in being political.

Here, we see what I return at the end of the book, namely a paradigm case of a politics of recognition. Elizabeth Eckford was part of a political movement of children and young people. They did not have a place inside the order, nor were they absolutely 'Other' and outside the order. Rather, that movement demanding basic civil rights (like the 'Black Lives Matters' movement today) was located at the boundary poised on the liminal point between inside–outside, engaged in the radical and contested process of pushing to cross the threshold through repeated and renewed demands for recognition. It is an irony that Arendt could not on that occasion see what was actually happening.

Notes

1 This title is taken from Hecht (2002).
2 Cohen notes that Roman men had similar 'ownership rights' over their wives, who had no legal claim in the fate of their children. Husbands could not appoint their wives as guardians in the event of their death and wives were considered unfit to be guardians if fathers died intestate (Cohen 2003:225).

3 Parenthetically though this needs to be said, Weber is clearly signalling a departure from a substantialist approach to power – and presumably to other political things. Recall that a substantialist approach to power involves treating 'power' as some kind of 'force' or 'thing', which, e.g., has a certain quantity, that can be measured and that can even be divided up amongst a group of people. Weber is clearly pointing to a relational conception of power.
4 A *polis* was an urban space typically fortified from the seventh century BCE on by walls centred on a sacred space and built on a natural *acropolis* or near a harbour. Those cities also had a marketplace *(agora)*.
5 As Isin notes, the Romans distinguished between the city as *civitas* (virtual) and the city as *urbs* (actual) (Isin 2008:263). In the Roman tradition, *civitas* was the place for the religious and political association of familial and tribal units while *urbs* was the actual place of assembly, dwelling or sanctuary (Isin 2008:263).

3
'THE PAST IS A FOREIGN COUNTRY...'
Young people in the eighteenth century[1]

By December 1783, relations between Britain's King George III and his government headed by his Prime Minister Lord North had broken down. The North government had been in office since 1770, but was being crippled by bitter recrimination as it struggled to deal with Britain's disastrous defeat by its American colonies in the American War of Independence (1775–1783). Prime Minister North's government was widely considered responsible for starting the war – and for losing it. During 1783, a series of Prime Ministers came and went, each in the space of months. By December 1783, King George was fed up and cajoled the House of Lords into rejecting an important bill. That action gave him the excuse to invite William Pitt the Younger, son of a previous Prime Minister, to form government. Pitt was already a prominent Tory MP, When he became Prime Minister Pitt was 24 years old.[2]

Pitt's rise had been rapid. Pitt was elected to parliament at the age of 21 when he took his seat in the House of Commons in January 1781. Within 20 months, he was Chancellor of the Exchequer, and within three years was Prime Minister (Evans 1999:8–9). Pitt remains Britain's youngest and its longest serving Prime Minister. Today it would be inconceivable that someone as young as Pitt could assume the role of head of government.[3]

In the eighteenth and early nineteenth centuries, the experience of William Pitt was not unusual. The King who invited him to form government himself assumed the throne in 1760 at the age of 22. When Britain became involved in the French revolutionary wars after 1803, Pitt's military and political opponent was Napoleon Bonaparte, the First Consul of the French Republic and soon to be Emperor of France. Bonaparte enlisted as a lieutenant in the French army at 16 years of age and by 24 he was a general in the French Army.[4] Admiral Horatio Nelson, Prime Minister Pitt's 'greatest' naval commander, became a naval officer at the age of 12 and received his first command of a British naval vessel at age 20. (Nelson later repeatedly defeated Napoleons' navies in the late 1790s and early 1800s before dying heroically at the Battle of Trafalgar in 1806.) Major-General Arthur Wellesley (and later the Duke of Wellington), who would defeat Napoleon at the Battle of Waterloo in 1814, was a lieutenant in the British army at 18. He became an MP at age 20 and was a Lieutenant-Colonel by age 24 in command of a brigade which saw action in Europe in 1794.

Now it is unimaginable that people as young as Pitt, Bonaparte, Nelson and Wellesley would assume significant positions as political leaders or take on military command roles while in their teens or early twenties. Back then however this was not that unusual. Understanding how and why this change happened is my task here.

I address the following questions. How have contemporary historians understood the ways children and young people were represented up to, and into the eighteenth and early nineteenth centuries? How were children and young people represented during the eighteenth century by others and to what effect? How did they represent themselves? To what extent, if any, were children and young people engaged in political activity?

I draw on various historical resources to consider how children and young people were represented in the eighteenth and early nineteenth centuries. Children and young people were represented across the eighteenth century in diverse and fluid ways. There was no attempt to prevent children and young people from engaging in activities defined today as adult-only activities. This included involvement in various political and public activities as well as active military and naval service. Acceptance of the idea that young people could engage in public affairs was amplified when popular discontent in Paris launched the French revolution in July 1789, an event with wide repercussions in Europe. Young people would play an important role in the politics of the French Revolution – and in its aftermath. In what follows I start by considering what modern historians have had to say about how children and young people were represented in the centuries up to and into the eighteenth century.

What the historians say

Modern historians demonstrate how representations of the child, the adolescent, youth and associated categories are neither timeless, biological nor natural phenomena. Rather, they are the product of historically located social and representational practices. While the work of French historian Philippe Ariès was controversial, he provided a detailed explanation of 'the birth of childhood' in Europe that occurred in the shift from medieval societies to early modern societies. It was a change that reflected the evolution of bourgeois families, producing a transformation in how many came to understand human time and how childhood and children should be understood and experienced.

Ariès' primary argument was that childhood was not recognised as a distinct stage in human life until the fifteenth century and that 'childhood' is a modern idea. He documented how children played games with 'adults' and wore smaller versions of adult clothes. Once the modern conception of childhood gained traction children increasingly were placed in child-specific spaces. They were considered to be sexually innocent, socially dependent and emotionally and psychologically vulnerable. Ariès argued the idea of childhood also brought forth new practices intended to protect vulnerability and dependency children who soon after started wearing age-specific clothes, engage in childish leisure, play and games, who enjoy prolonged periods of education and protection from adult activities like labour, sex, alcohol and gambling.

One controversial claim made by Ariès was that medieval parents were colder, more detached from their children compared to the sensibilities of modern parents. This he argued was evident in the common medieval practice of fostering out children as apprentices-servants to other families at an 'early' age, and in the high child mortality rate. The fostering out and high infant death rates referred to what Areis saw as weak emotional bonds between parents and their children (Ariès 1962:411).

Ariès also argued that some medieval communities recognised *phases* in human life as infant, youth, senescence (half-way between youth and old age) and old age. These categories he said were not age-based, but referred rather to habits and appearance so, e.g., a 50-year-old could be considered a 'youth' (Ariès 1962). Later historians have also noted that since antiquity human life was often discussed in terms of stages. Some stages were elaborate, like the medieval 'stages of man' that divided life into 3, 4, 7 or 12 stages (Burrow 1986, Sears 1986). In the pre-modern period, reference to the 'ages of man' typically involved stages like youth or adolescence,[5] while semantic distinctions between children and youth were said to be non-existent in the seventeenth century and remained rare in the eighteenth. It was however a distinction that became increasingly common in the eighteenth century (Kett 1971).

Ariès also highlighted the emergence of new professional and institutional practices in western Europe that accompanied the 'discovery of childhood'. In medieval communities, schools were the preserve of a small numbers of boys wanting to become religious leaders or professionals like lawyers and doctors. With these modern educational institutions, we saw new modern representations of young people. Along with the expansion of education institutions, boarding schools and early modern schools, came age-based segregation and the practice of defining young people according to their 'stage' in the 'life cycle'.

Since the publication of Ariès' work, other historians explored the evolution of childhood and related categories like adolescence, youth, etc. (e.g., Demos and Demos 1969:632–638, Kett 1974, Stone 1977, Elder 1980, Gillis 1975). In 1971, Rothman asked whether age groups have histories (1971:367). According to Kett, the origins of modern conception of adolescence can be tracked to the early twentieth century and owed much to the work of G. Stanley

Hall – something I return to later in this chapter (Kett 1974:1). A decade later, Lawrence Stone agreed with Kett about when the concept adolescence emerged as a 'clearly defined period of life after puberty during which a young person remains in a position of dependence', noting that:

> Hall saw it emerge only in the late nineteenth century. Demos and Gillis place it in the early nineteenth century. Kett puts it later, and others – including myself – much earlier.
>
> *(Stone 1981:69)*

To this Stone added that: 'the dispute seems to be more about boundaries and definitions than about concrete social realities, and the difference between "youth" and "adolescence" to be mainly one of terminology' (Stone 1981:69).

In 1982 Lowe disagreed, arguing that the 'phenomenon of adolescence' did not occur before the late nineteenth and early twentieth centuries:

> …youth had been not so much an age, but a semi-dependent status in society, when one had already left the family to become an apprentice, a servant, a page, or a student elsewhere, but had not yet gotten married or set up an independent household. It had been, in effect, an intermediate space between family and society at large.
>
> *(Lowe 1982:67)*

This he argued was happening in the eighteenth century:

> …in bourgeois society, youth became yet another age separating childhood from adulthood. Industrialization and urbanization both strengthened and prolonged the bourgeois family. Bourgeois youth now reverted from that intermediate space into the family. One stayed at home much longer after childhood, and had to go to school to acquire the necessary virtues of rationality and discipline, in preparation for the mature, adult.
>
> *(Lowe 1982:67)*

Gleadle argues that by the 1960s historians were saying the modern idea of 'childhood' began to crystallize in the eighteenth century (2016). And for Plumb the eighteenth century was 'the new age of the child' pointing to different sources to support this idea (1975:64–95).

Ages of child and youth

In the eighteenth century Europe, representations of who was and what defined a child or youth – and the associated practices – were very different to the ways young people are generally understood today (Aries 1962). The eighteenth century saw changing conceptions of childhood and youth as ideas about human nature began changing. The eighteenth century also ushered in a proliferation of new ideas about human physiology and psycho-perceptual schemes. They included the Cartesian idea of 'hydraulic mechanism' and John Locke's ideas about the self as a *tabula rasa* or blank-sheet 'written on' by experience (Yallop 2014). John Locke's *Some Thoughts Concerning Education* (1693), e.g., had a major influence on the English middle-classes (Ezell 1983), promoting the idea that children's intellects should be cultivated and that they should be recognised as rational beings (Manly 2007). Locke's thinking also led to pedagogical schemes in which children were encouraged to be creative learners (Stewart and McCann 1967:ch. 2).

Indeed over the eighteenth century, ideas about a post-pubescent stage during which young people became restless, as suggested by writers like Rousseau, began providing content for the literature of the time (Lowe 1982). Typically this accompanied a general agreement about the importance of young people's submission to their elders. By the 1790s the category 'youth', which had long been associated with passion, was often linked to political exuberance and energy, especially within progressive circles. At the same time, new ways of thinking about education and childhood came into being.

Educational opportunities also began to grow and the 'cultural and intellectual horizons of the child' widened from the 1740s (Plumb 1975:64–95). Accompanying this were early signs of a growing interest in the science of childhood (Benzaquen 2004). A century after Locke and his persuasive metaphors used to represent children as passive 'soft wax' or 'fertile gardens', Jean-Jacques Rousseau's *Emile* (1762) highlighted the role of giving children (boys) freedom. According to Rousseau distinct stages of human development existed that inherent made them unable to be rational.

> Childhood … has its own way of seeing, thinking, and feeling; nothing is more foolish than to try and substitute our ways. And I should no more expect judgment in a ten-year-old child than I should expect him to be five feet high. Indeed, what use would reason be to him at that age? It is the curb of strength, and the child does not need the curb.
>
> *(Rousseau 1979:60)*

For Rousseau childhood was a 'presocial developmental stage of life'. That is, 'the child was best understood as *becoming* but not yet *being* a political subject' (Beier 2015:5). It was a position that encouraged discussion as some well-informed parents and educators considered the question of freedom and the degree of freedom that children should be allowed to exercise (Ezell 1983:14).

Following on the heels on these new ideas were innovations like the development of children's literature.[6] What emerged was a new mainly middle-class market for juvenile literature and educational games (O'Malley 2003, Woodley 2009). As Margaret Kinnell argued, eighteenth century children's literature assumed young readers could exercise moral judgement and had intellectual autonomy: the growing number of stories, books, magazines and poems produced for children played a role in the further development of their political consciousness (1988).

In turn this encouraged an interest in children's rights to social goods like shelter, protection, education, recreation, etc. This did not mean however that a new single or dominant representation of children and young people emerged by the end of the eighteenth century. As in previous centuries and has been so since, we saw diverse ways of representing the child or young person.

As today, full legal capacity and responsibility with being adult was set at 21 for men and women in England and British America (Gillis 1974:2). In England and British North America, the age of minority was restricted below 21 for men and 25 years of age for women. In these countries being a minor was equivalent to the absence of a legal or civic identity. As a minor, a boy e.g. was not permitted to negotiate contracts or make other financial decisions independent of a guardian, parent or master. Unsurprisingly girls were deemed to be almost legally incompetent. In France and Spain childhood as a legal category was also expressed in terms of the age of minority. Through the French and Spanish empires, a minor was a young man under the age of 25. For children this was a temporary category shared by non-slaves, non-'natives' white males. Slaves and 'native' peoples were barely seen to exist as autonomous legal identities with rights. For Europeans the categories of 'slaves' and 'natives' denoted their status as commodities (slaves) and in some cases as vermin to be cleared from the land (Premo 2005, Coolidge 2016).

In criminal law, the age of criminal responsibility (the age at which a child is held responsible for their criminal actions) had been 7 years since the thirteenth century.[7] In England, according to Blackstone's *Commentaries on the Laws of England* (1765), anyone under 21 convicted of a 'common misdemeanour' would 'escape fine, imprisonment and the like'. However those under 21 convicted of a felony were liable to punishment, (although with 'certain mitigating considerations' would be taken into account). Those mitigations or discretion would depend on *doli capacitas*, that is, when it was determined that a child could understand what they had done wrong. According to Blackstone a determination of *doli capacitas* was linked to age (Cited Magarey 1978:11–27).[8]

Yet, as Blackstone argued, age categories were fluid. Sometimes people spoke about 'childhood' as opposed to an earlier stage of 'infancy', suggesting there were various conceptions of childhood. Others talked about the age at which 'youth' began (Muller 2006). Legally a girl could marry at age seven. The marriage however could not be consummated until she reached 12 years – the age of discretion and sexual consent for girls when she was legally considered to have the knowledge and competence needed to make decisions and be responsible for her actions (Toulalan 2013:17). The age of discretion for boys was not reached until the age of 14. According to Samuel Johnson, the famous author and poet (1709–1984), this was the point at which 'youth' commenced which lasted until one's late twenties. However, as Alysa Levene discovered English Poor Law registers sometimes recorded 18-year-olds as 'children' (2012:17).

It seems however that these legal definitions had little effect on popular consciousness or everyday practice through the early modern period. This is reflected, e.g., in the way that by age seven, children were usually able to act with some independence and self-direction in their local community (Ronald 2015:14). It was common for children to do productive labour from quite a young age in and outside the household. Similarly, leaving home to be a domestic or farm servant or apprentice marked a break in a young man's legal, socio-economic and social position in early modern England. For girls it was a different transition as they moved from one form of dependence on an older male to another (De Moor and Van Zanden 2009). Thereafter, boys and girls were normally no longer dependent on their family for food and lodging, because they were subject to the authority of their employer, were on the path to acquiring income, experience and skills that would allow themselves to establish an independent household of their own when the time came (Laslett 1965).

The early modern apprenticeship system provided a 'transition' from childhood to youth in the eighteenth century (Wallis et al. 2009). The move from one's family to employment was a key point of change for many young people in early modern England. Usually it involved geographical and economic change: whether entering agricultural work or a craft or trade, young men and women usually left home and lodged in their employers' households or near their employment. The age at which apprenticeship began varied widely across Europe, suggesting the nature of the work also varied.

Some examples illustrate the wide range of age when that 'transition' took place (Epstein 1991:104–105, Rahikainen 2004:5–6). In French cities, apprenticeships began at age 12 in the sixteenth century and increased over the seventeenth century, with young people becoming journeymen in their mid- to late teens. By the eighteenth century, Parisian apprentices were bound at an average age of 15 years (Davis 1971:41–75, Kaplan 1993:452). In seventeenth and eighteenth century Antwerp, apprentices were 15 years old when they began work (de Mucnk 2007: 85–110). However by 1800, Hamburg carpenters' apprentices were 18 or 19 years old when they entered apprenticeships (Rahikainen 2004:5–6). By contrast, in eighteenth century Vienna, three quarters of silk weavers' apprentices were between 13 and 15 years of age when they started, while in Florence the *Ospedale degli Innocenti* put children into apprenticeship and service at the age of 6 or 7 years (Steidl 2007).

There were other ways a young man could move from minority status. For instance, a 16-year-old boy who inherited a large estate could be deemed adult when his father died even if he had not reached the age of majority. Similarly, a successful young merchant under 25 years of age could negotiate contracts on his own, essentially transitioning to majority, because he ran a prosperous business. In these ways, it was the ability of a young man to achieve economic solvency that was more important to attaining majority than reaching a certain age (Brewer 2007).

According to Gleadle, the combination of practices and philosophies of the enlightenment like 'the rational education of children; the sociable and political opportunities of the [England's] public sphere; and the emergence of juvenile literature and reading practices had empowering possibilities for young subjects' (Gleadle 2016:144). This had implications for the politicisation of children and young people that would be amplified by the French revolution. The French revolution promoted 'a phenomenon that was tangible to many in the 1790s – the radical politicization of the young. This included males and females; and it involved small children as well as teenagers and young adults' (Gleadle 2016:144).

Young people and the French Revolution, 1789–1796

The French Revolution (1789–1796) dominated the last decade of the eighteenth century in Europe. It was a defining political event that shaped the lives of young leaders like George III, Pitt, Nelson, Wellington and Napoleon as well as millions of Europeans at the end of the eighteenth century and into the nineteenth century. It was an event that also introduced a framework of Enlightenment values, the idiom of modern science, and a powerful colonial ethos and politics which touched the lives of most people across the world. The French Revolution is also directly relevant to this book because it was initiated and led by young men and women as well as being supported by many young people across Europe.

If we understand the agonistic nature of politics then the Revolution was a deeply political event, characterised by contest, struggle, competition and conflict. The French Revolution not only issued in a new conception of revolution as a novel process of change, but it also challenged some of the most persistent and deeply cherished ideas about tradition, and a naturally hierarchical order.

Those opposed to the French revolution and supportive of the old order (*ancien régime*) believed fervently in a divinely inspired naturalized social order expressed in terms of the right of monarchs, aristocrats and priests to rule the Rest.[9] For those people the revolution was not merely dangerous, it was catastrophic, spreading disorder, moral decay and terror.

The French Revolution was initiated and led by young men and women and supported by young people all across Europe (Déplanche 2011:225–237, 2018). Déplanche has observed how the key figures in the French Revolution of 1789 were relatively young. They included Antoine de Saint-Just who was 22 in 1789 while Robespierre, Danton, Brissot and Hébert, were then in their early thirties. Sociologists like Goldstone highlighted certain patterns in the period leading up to rebellions and revolutions like the English Revolution of 1640 and the French Revolution of 1789 occurred. They related to the expansion of university enrolments that in a context where there was not a proportionate increase in positions in the state and church bureaucracies which were the typical destinations for university graduates (Goldstone 1991). In the early seventeenth century, enrolments at Oxford and Cambridge rose by 400%, an increase that was twice as fast as the rate of population growth. In France, between 1730 and 1790 law graduates increased by 77%. The result was a rapid growth in unemployed and underemployed professionals (doctors, lawyers, journalists and itinerant preachers) many of whom became staunch opponents of the monarchy and conservative elites.

The symbolic coming together of the role of young people and the idea of the revolution as a source of novelty, renewal and regeneration is epitomised in Schama's history of the revolution when he tells the story of Jean Jacob, then 120 years old, who spoke to the National Assembly in 1789. Jacob said that he 'lived to be a free man' and that 'like France he had been given a second life'. He experienced 'the blessing of regeneration' (Schama 1989:472). As young people became 'an inherent part of the symbolic order of the first French republic' (Déplanche 2011:226) it also underwrote the popularity of the metaphor of regeneration which got traction in France after 1789. The motif of a new beginning served to define the 'message' of the French Revolution later providing Arendt with an example of the politics of natality.

In his study of the revolutionary movements of Anjou and Brittany in western France during 1789–1790, Déplanche noted how they consisted mainly of young people aged 18–25 years. He documents how those young people created political associations, assemblies and dispatched addresses and delegations to Paris after the fall of the Bastille. In short, young people became increasingly politicised. The novel character of this movement and claims to belong to a specific political class did not rest on factors like social origins, professions, ethnicity or gender, but on its generational position. Noticeably most of those politicised 'youth' in Brittany and Anjou were law students. According to Déplanche, this meant they had the intellectual, rhetorical and organisational skills and confidence, to constitute a cohesive, well-articulated and assertive political movement (Déplanche 2011).

It was a collective who also defined themselves in generational terms. They 'found their legitimacy in the spirit of regeneration that occurred with the calling of the Estates General in 1789'. Déplanche continued, by 1790 this youth movement established a dialogue with the National Constituent Assembly to achieve citizenship status through the institution of the National Guard. As Déplanche argues it was an accomplishment resulting from 'intergenerational dialogue and negotiation'.

This demographic feature may indicate why the French revolutionaries identified themselves as 'brothers'. That was a key difference between them and the American revolutionaries. The lead protagonists in the American revolution were men such as George Washington, John Adams, Patrick Henry, Thomas

Paine and Thomas Jefferson, all in their forties and fifties – or like Franklin then in his late sixties: they preferred to describe themselves as the 'founding *fathers*'. More significantly as Hunt argues, countries like America, France, Britain and Holland all experienced the 'Atlantic democratic revolution' of the eighteenth century, but did so differently:

> What most separated the French Revolution from the others... was the French insistence on breaking absolutely with the national past and installing a completely new and self-consciously innovating regime.
> *(Hunt 1989:612)*

Hunt argues that while much of the political discussion in eighteenth century French political writing focussed as it had done in England, America, and the Dutch Republic, on restoring an ancient constitution, that was not the case in France, when the Bastille fell to the citizens of Paris in July 1789. In 1788, French writers were more interested in the virtues of the English and American constitutions as models for a new French constitution, than they were with the imagined virtues of an ancient French one.

Novelty was very much the order of the day in the first major revolutionary document: the French *Declaration of the Rights of Man and Citizens* proclaimed on 26 August 1789. It was a document signalling novelty and a major departure from the Anglo-American constitutional tradition. As Berman argues the French 'rights of man and citizen' was the product of people influenced by the rationalist and individualist belief system of the *philosophes* of the two previous generations (Berman 1992:311–334). The distinctive features of the revolution were made clear in the French *Declaration of the Rights of Man and Citizens*. It was not 'the lords spiritual and temporal and commons' that enacted the French *Declaration* but the 'representatives of the French people'.

There were no statements about 'the ancient rights and liberties of Englishmen': rather the focus was on 'the natural, inalienable, and sacred rights of man'. It also makes no reference to the past. Instead the Declaration identified 17 'natural and imprescriptible rights of man'. Those rights began with the idea that all 'men are born and remain free and equal in rights' and for this reason 'social distinctions can be based only upon public utility'. The Declaration also stated that 'liberty, property, security, and resistance to oppression' were 'natural and imprescriptible rights'. The third set of rights declared that 'the source of all sovereignty is in the nation'. Likewise we hear echoes of Voltaire in statements that the right to speak, write and print freely is 'one of the most precious rights of man' (Berman 1992:311–334).

The determination to make a new beginning encouraged the historian Hunt to argue that it was 'predominantly young' French revolutionaries who opted for a perpetual 'mythic now', for the restoring of an earthly paradise that relied on continuous attempts to re-enact and mythologize the social contract (Hunt 1989:161–176).

We see here an affinity between this interest in novelty and the re-generative capacities of young men and women who played key leadership roles in the revolutionary process. Supporters of the new order of rights and citizenship constantly referred to the 'new moment', to the 'new national character', and to newness in general. This reflected the dispositions of the *sans culottes* even as it also highlights the contested character of ideas about citizenship that came about after 1789.

The contested politics of citizenship

The French Revolution was a historic moment when modern democracy and citizenship first appeared on the European stage. As the French historian Francois Furet observed, it was 'the first experiment with democracy' (Furet 1981). Universal male suffrage was introduced in elections to the Convention in 1792 and then enshrined in the Revolutionary Constitution of 1793. They were years marked by lively discussions about the rights (and duties) of citizens, the extension of political participation to poor people, the rights of black slaves in the colonies and whether women should vote. Indeed, the word 'citizen' (*citoyen*) was more prevalent by the 1790s than it had been a century earlier.[10] Yet from day one of the French revolution, the conception of citizenship was and remained highly contested (Hammersley 2015:468–485). This, as I argued in Chapter 2, reflects the relational nature of citizenship: citizens were defined, e.g., in relation to those who were not citizens.

For some citizenship was understood as referring to the 'bourgeois man' indicating that citizenship was seen as a right determined by one's status as a man of property. By 1832 that idea of citizenship was articulated as 'workers are outside political life, outside the city. They are the barbarians of modern society. They should enter this society but can only be admitted to it after passing through the novitiate of owning property' (cited Merriman 1991:59).

For others however, citizenship was about rights, based on whether or not one was born in France – and born a man. Prominent Enlightenment figures like Diderot had argued for a conception of citizenship based on rights, but restricted this to civil rights and not political rights. As Diderot explained:

> A citizen is someone who is a member of a free society with many families, who shares in the rights of this society, and who benefits from these freedoms… Someone who has been divested of these rights and freedoms has stopped being a citizen. One accords the title to women, young children, and servants, only as family members of a citizen, … but they are not truly citizens.
>
> *(Diderot 1753)*

This idea that citizenship meant possessing civil, but not political, rights continued through the Revolution. Emmanuel-Joseph Sieyes, a leading political writer and constitutional theorist of the French revolution, defined citizenship in his 1789 pamphlet (*Vues sur les moyens d'execution dont les representants de la France pourront disposer en*) in a way that echoed Rousseau:

> In general, any citizen deprived of the right to consult his own interests, to deliberate, and to impose laws upon himself is rightly taken to be a serf. It follows that the right to consult its own interests, to deliberate, and to impose laws upon itself must necessarily belong to the nation.
>
> *(Sieyes 2003:9)*

Sieyes seems to have influenced a law passed by the National Assembly in late 1789, that allowed men who were either under 25 years of age or who paid less than 3 livres a year in tax to be 'passive citizens'. Even though they gained civil rights articulated in the *Declaration des droits de l'homme et du citoyen,* they were not entitled to political rights that allowed them to vote in elections, nor were they eligible to stand for political office.

The leading Jacobin and radical democrat Maximilien Robespierre opposed making a distinction between 'active' and 'passive' citizens. In his speech to the National Assembly on 22 October 1789, Robespierre argued against any new 'conditions of eligibility' being proposed. Citing statements from the *Declaration des droits* declaring an end to privileges, distinctions and exceptions, Robespierre argued: 'All citizens, whoever they are, have the right to aspire to all levels of office-holding':

> The Constitution establishes that sovereignty resides in the people, in all the individuals of the people. Each individual therefore has the right to participate in making the law which governs him and in the administration of the public good which is his own. If not, it is not true that all men are equal in rights, that every man is a citizen.
>
> *(Cited Hammersley 2015:477)*

Here the fracture lines can be seen between the middle-class (bourgeois) interest in preserving citizenship for themselves and the radical Jacobin (and the 'common peoples' or *sans culotte*) commitment to ensuring that citizenship was available to all men as a right.

The *sansculottes* were mostly working-class urban poor, young apprentices, workers, artisans, shopkeepers and teachers. In Paris they led the attack on the Bastille and consistently supported the radicalisation of the revolution (Soboul 1980:25–40). One *sans culottes* group in Lyon described their commitment to novelty and revolutionary change in 1793:

> …to be truly Republican, each citizen must experience and bring about in himself a revolution equal to the one which has changed France. There is nothing, absolutely nothing in common between the slave of a tyrant and

the inhabitant of a free state; the customs of the latter, his principles, his sentiments, his action, all must be new.

(Commission Temporaire of Lyon 1957:224)

In this way everything written at the time and shortly after became a story of regeneration, a motif of perpetual youthful regeneration.

However not every young person was enamoured of democracy and the new republic. Quite different groups of young people espousing a different politics would play a major part in suppressing the revolutionary impulse represented by the *sans culottes,* the Jacobins and splinter groups like the Hebertists.

The revolutionary democratic project ended violently in July 1796 when the ring leaders of the coup of 9 Thermidor toppled Maximilien Robespierre, bringing the radical democratization process to a halt. In that process and in the counter revolution that followed, young people again played a key role. The coup began when the 24-year-old Jean-Lambert Tallien, a former President of the National Convention, stood up in the Convention attacking Saint-Just before denouncing the tyranny of Robespierre. Other members of the convention like Billaud-Varenne then joined in, yelling 'Down with the tyrant! Arrest him!' Robespierre tried to appeal to the deputies of the Right, but failed.

The National Convention ordered the arrest of Robespierre and his followers. On 29 July, Robespierre and his key supporters were guillotined. Following the execution of these key Jacobins, the Convention established a Directorate that issued a new Constitution in August 1795 installing a bourgeois conception of citizenship. While it preserved the 1789 Declaration of 'the Rights of Man and Citizen' (the rights of 'liberty, equality, security, and property'), the new constitution made eligibility to vote in the elections for the Councils dependent on whether a person met certain minimum property criteria.[11]

The other key element in this counter-revolution involved closing down the revolutionary committees established in 1789 to oversee the *sections* of the City of Paris. Those committees were key supporters of the Jacobins and did much of the recruiting and mobilisation for demonstrations and invasions of the Convention by the *sans culottes*. On 24 August 1794, the National Convention abolished these revolutionary committees. On 31 August 1794, the municipality of Paris itself, previously the domain of Robespierre and Danton (and other leading revolutionary figures, was also abolished. The city was then placed under the direct control of the national government. In this counter-revolution young men *(les jeunes gens)* and better known as the 'Gilded Youth' *(les jeunesse doree)* played a decisive role

By 1794–1795, as the historian Francois Gendron has documented, a group of young men known as the 'Gilded Youth' emerged as a street-based right-wing vigilante militia to play a significant role in this counter-revolution. Under the direction of the bourgeoisie the 'Gilded Youth' helped take down the radical-democratic institutions that had driven the Jacobin reign of terror, that came to a violent end in 1796 with the arrests and executions of Robespierre and St. Just (Gendron 1993).

In ways that anticipate the urban 'youth cultures' of the second half of the twentieth century, these 'gilded youth' had their own distinctive dress styles, behaviours and interests. They were easy to recognise given their distinctive bright and colourful 'extravagant' dress. They wore tightly-cut coats with large lapels, typically in different colours, with elaborate cravats and sashes round the waist. The colours were vivid and contrasting and stripes were generally popular. They also wore musk perfume, powdered wigs and whitened their hands with almond paste. The Guilded Youth also had their own anthem or 'hymn of fraternity', 'The People's Awakening' ('*Le Reveil du Peuple*'), as well as war slogans, secret passwords, and regular meeting places. They revelled and fought pitched street battles against the *sans culottes* of Paris and other major French cities in brutal fights to clean up whatever remained of Jacobinism (Gendron 1993).

Yet the direct involvement of young people in French politics after 1789 does not tell the whole story about the dramatic effects of the Revolution on other young people at the time. As I show now, their political engagement highlights further the conspicuous differences between young people then, and now.

Children, the 'Juvenile Enlightenment' and the French revolution[12]

In the 1790s, children and young men and women across the English Channel were inspired by and involved in the fervour of revolutionary change taking place in the streets, cafes and halls of Paris. In 1798, 11-year-old Thomas Love Peacock wrote a letter to his local newspaper about Prime Minister Pitt's war policies, declaring himself 'impassioned with those sentiments which fire my breast when the dearest rights of humanity are at stake' (Peacock 2001:8–9, Gleadle 2016:149). Similarly 12-year-old William Hazlitt declared to his mother that 'In a state of liberty men improve'. The next year he wrote a letter to the *Shrewsbury Chronicle*, protesting against the religious persecution of the radical Joseph Priestley in Birmingham. Quoting Addison, he declared that Priestley's name 'shall flourish in immortal youth' (Hazlitt 1978, 48, 57–59, Gleadle 2016:149). Between the ages of 12 and 16 years young Leigh Hunt wrote political essays on topics like the navy, Nelson, Robespierre and war with Switzerland (Gleadle 2016:149).

Gleadle also takes readers into the world of 11-year-old Louisa Gurney (1784–1836), one of a family of 11 children. Louisa kept a diary in the 1890s that offers valuable insights into the many political issues she was thinking about including the 'uneven notions of selfhood' and her own political awakening. Her father John Gurney (1749–1809) was a prosperous Quaker wool-stapler lived in the city of Norwich, and his wife Catherine (nee Bell) (1754–1792). In her diary in July 1796 Louisa expressed her enthusiasm for the democratic principles of the French revolution:

> I do from the bottom of my heart hate the preference shown in all things to my elders merely because they have been in the world a little longer. I do love equality and true democracy.
>
> *(Cited in Gleadle 2016:143)*

A year later Louisa recorded her 'great satisfaction' with Helen Maria Williams's *Letters from France*, that she read, and that was much discussed by the English reading public for its vivid portrayal of revolutionary events in France.

Sometimes Louisa expressed herself in conventional childhood ways: 'I spell, read, write & cypher as well as most children' while in another entry she writes dutifully how she needed to defer to 'those who are older, wiser & better than myself' (Gleadle 2016:153–154). On other occasions she was enthusiastic about the carefree existence of the middle-class child: 'Why should not we be as merry & happy as we can, & be children as long as we can' (Gleadle 2018:154). Another time she recorded political experiments that led her to question the hierarchies of family life and society.

This last entry reflects the cultural and religious fields in which Louisa lived. Her own religious affiliation with the Quakers may have encouraged her 'radical' political sensibilities. The egalitarian views of Quakers evident in their disavowal of titles, opposition to hierarchy and support for the anti-slavery cause indicate their radicalizing possibilities. Thus it seems the city of Norwich supported its own enlightened 'public sphere' (Habermas 1989).[13] The city's progressive culture was dominated by young radicals which included a cohort in their late teens and early twenties, notably Thomas Starling Norgate (born. 1775), John Pitchford (born. 1772/3), Hudson Gurney (born. 1775; Louisa's cousin), Ollyett Woodhouse (born. 1769), Charles Marsh (born. 1774) and Thomas Amyot (born. 1775). These young men were leading contributors to the city's periodical *The Cabinet* (Gleadle 2016:159)

Louisa Gurney read the work of the late British scientific enlightenment, like Jacson's *Botanical Dialogues*, Goldsmith's work on natural history and Bonnycastle's *Introduction to Astronomy* as well as British history. She recorded that she read writers of the Scottish enlightenment like William Robertson's *History of America*. Louisa and her sisters also studied William Godwin, Jean-Jacques Rousseau and Thomas Paine, three important advocates for an egalitarian democracy. Godwin's *Political Justice* (first published in 1793), e.g., argued that by using our critical reasoning we can liberate ourselves from oppressive and hierarchical structures of society and the need for laws and institutions would disappear. It appears that the study of Godwin and Rousseau influenced the Gurney family's own approach to family life.

Finally as Gleadle notes, what is significant was not just the reading, but 'that these girls felt themselves to be part of a progressive constituency of youthful readers. The text they were studying was Livy's Roman History – a work that other young Norwich radicals were scrutinizing' (Gleadle 2018:165). The Gurney family were part of this network with Louisa, it seems, susceptible to what was later described as the 'contagion' of French radical philosophies that infected Norwich in the 1790s (Gleadle 2018:159). Louisa's sister, Kitty, recalled 'the literary young men of Norwich with whom we were acquainted' were known for their 'infidelity'. In this context infidelity was a synonym for the lack of religious piety that contemporaries associated with the politics and values of the French Revolution. It was something that highlights the fact that not everyone supported the new French experiment in popular sovereignty and democracy.

Responding to the new politics of the 'Rights of Man' after 1789, conservative English writers like Hannah More, 'scorned' the 'enlighteners' (Gleadle 2018:151). The reference was to enlightenment *philosophes* like Voltaire, Diderot and Rousseau and their English advocates. In 1799, More imagined that the next project by the likes of Tom Paine and Mary Wollstonecraft would be 'on the rights of youth, on the rights of children, on the rights of babies', warning of the current 'revolutionary spirit in families' (More 1799:147, Gleadle 2018:151).[14] As Gleade argues, More developed this theme in her novel *Cœlebs in Search of a Wife*, in which the conservative mother complained that:

> I know not … whether the increased insubordination of children is owing to the new school of philosophy and politics, but it seems to me to make part of the system… There certainly prevails a spirit of independence, a revolutionary spirit, a separation from the parent state. It is the children's world.
>
> *(Cited in Gleadle 2016:151)*

Moore's response highlights the influence of revolutionary thought on ideas about the family. As Eileen Hunt Botting argued, different accounts of the equalitarian family by enlightenment figures like Rousseau, Burke and Wollstonecraft shaped their political thinking. As each of these philosophers argued, the family was the primary site for corrupting the state, for regenerating the state and for instilling the moral dispositions that can create civic life (Botting 2006, Gleadle 2018:233).

As Gleadle noted, Mary Wollstonecraft's 'republican motherhood', in which she argued that women might achieve citizenship through childrearing, is the best known example of this view of the family as a site in of political action. 'Other Enlightened dissenters were insistent on recasting domestic relationships as part of political reform'. As the English poet Barbauld wrote 'Let public reformation prepare the way for private', adding a call for the 'abolition of domestic tyranny'. In France revolutionary principles led 'citizens' to adopt more egalitarian family structures, facilitating divorce and easing sibling distinctions by abolishing primogeniture (Gleadle 2018:233).

Yet children were not just politically active in ways that some today might find very surprising. This can be seen if we consider a quite different domain: children also played a role as military personnel. Today there is now universal condemnation of the practice of recruiting child soldiers. Then it was considered to be less of a problem.

In the Navy

While there is no discernible or credible research that would allow for confident generalizations about the recruitment of children into the eighteenth or early nineteenth century British army, there are glimpses of children enlisting as young as five and seven. There are archival notes, e.g., about Colour Sergeant John Murray, who at age five had enlisted as a drummer-boy in 1786 in the 50th Foot at Gibraltar. There was also James Wade, who at age seven enlisted as a drummer in the 9th Foot (The Royal Norfolk Regiment), and who served in the Peninsular Campaign under Wellington (The Army Children Archive 2020). What is known with more certainty is that the British navy recruited large numbers of boys and young men as sailors through the eighteenth century, and then during Britain's long naval struggle against France in the 1790s and 1800s.

From 1756 Britain's Royal Navy recruited children aged between 11 and 13. For some patronage ensured recruitment as teenage officers called midshipmen. One exemplary recruit was Horatio Nelson who as a 12-year-old went directly onto a ship. That midshipman became Admiral Nelson – England's 'greatest' naval officer. Others entered naval service through naval academies like the Portsmouth Naval Academy, established in 1729 advertising the fact that it was open to 'the Sons of Noblemen and Gentlemen, who shall not be under 13 years of age nor above 16 at the time of their admission' (Bennetts 2013). Two of Jane Austen's brothers attended the Portsmouth Academy. One of them, Francis, enrolled at aged 11 going to sea two years later. Charles went to sea also aged 11. Both brothers would become Admirals.

Samantha Cavell provides a perceptive ethnographic study of the recruitment practices, social backgrounds and naval experiences of a sample of more than 4,500 'young gentleman' midshipmen and quarterdeck boys recruited between 1761 and 1831 (2010). The age range of this cohort was large ranging from 7 to 58 years old, although most candidates fell between the ages of 13 and 22. Cavell adds that naval regulations stipulated that 'young gentlemen' were not to enter the service before the age of 13 or, if a naval officer's son, not before the age of 11. Pietsch also notes how the majority of the boys recruited by the Maritime Society were quite small: on average they were around four feet five inches short (2004).

The reference in naval regulations to a minimum age was frequently ignored. Commander James Anthony Gardner, e.g., began his naval career aboard *HMS Conqueror* at 5 years of age. Admiral Sir William Henry Dillon was approximately ten, when he entered the Saturn in 1790 and John William Bannister, who became a magistrate of Sierra Leone, was 'brought up to the navy', beginning his career at the age of seven, and becoming a midshipman by nine. This is not to deny that some distinctions were observed. A distinction was made between the ages of entry-level servants and volunteers, who tended to be younger (between 7 and 15 years), and the midshipmen, mates, and acting lieutenants, whose ages typically ranged from the mid-teens to mid-twenties (Cavell 2010:24).

This raises a question about how age and more pertinently the physical stature of child recruits was dealt with in practice on board the ships. Cavell answers this by pointing to the way 'young gentlemen' occupied an ambiguous status in the shipboard hierarchy. As officers-in-training they were granted the right to walk the quarterdeck and were expected to show the leadership qualities of an officer, even if they were too young and too inexperienced to perform the duties of one. Youth and inexperience 'reduced' young gentlemen subordinate to warrant officers. Young gentlemen were, in theory, superior in rank to standing officers although in practice, any sensible boy would subordinate himself to their skill and expertise. Midshipmen and masters' mates were also considered petty officers, alongside senior lower-deck men such as the warrant officers' mates, quarter masters, captains of the tops, the master at arms, sailmaker, captains' coxswain, and armorer, although their aspirations to commissioned rank rendered them superior in the shipboard community. The ambiguity of a young gentleman's situation aboard ship meant he hovered between the ranks and ratings. Midshipmen and quarterdeck boys of all ages generally were under the immediate supervision of a ship's lieutenants who served as professional and personal mentors. 'Youngsters' were kept busy with instruction in the art of seamanship and, if they were lucky, in some scholarly pursuits. As Cavell argues the diverse factors operating in Britain's navy in the eighteenth and nineteenth centuries make it difficult to generalise about the experiences of these child sailors.

What Cavell shows is that the presence of the children of the aristocracy and gentry among officer aspirants was directly affected, mainly by the state of war and peace and by the popularity of a naval career for the sons of well-born. Thus children of peers and the landed gentry were more prevalent in the peacetime service of 1771 and again after 1815, when the weight of social and political connections (i.e., patronage) again became determining factors in the selection of officer trainees.

Other 'kinds of boys' were recruited in different ways relying on social mechanisms other than patronage. Some boys went on board as captains' or other officers' servants, though their actual function is probably better described as trainee sailors. According to Pietsch, one key recruitment agency was the

Marine Society which kept records of the boys it recruited (2004). The Marine Society was founded in 1756, at the beginning of the Seven Years' War, by merchant and philanthropist Jonas Hanway and other London merchants, who were concerned about the British navy's problems of recruiting naval personnel at the time. The Marine Society's records reveal that between 1756 and 1762, the Society recruited and equipped over 4,500 boys for the navy. Their minutes record the way they worked:

> John Fielding having procured 24 boys for sea service, they were all clothed by the Society ... Order'd that 10 of said boys be sent to Admiral Broderick and 14 to Capt. Barber of the *Princess Royal* at the Nore and that each boy shall have a Testament, Common Prayer Book, Clasp Knife and a printed list of their Cloths.
>
> *(Bennetts 2013)*

Officially the Society's official minimum age was 14, but in practice many younger boys were accepted. Thus minimally 5% to 10% of the crew of an eighteenth-century warship were servants aged between 11 and 13 years of age. The actual percentage of boys on board is likely to have been higher, for it's likely there were also boys on board who were mustered as 'men' when they were not. Added to this were the occasional underaged sons of officers who were not kept on the muster lists.

Over half of the boys recruited by the Society had no father, and a fifth had no adult carer. The Society's philanthropic vision of the navy was as a surrogate family for 'deserted boys' which seems to have been a basis for their interventions. Thus while the boys recruited by the Marine Society were supposed to go to sea voluntarily, from the beginning the Society's scheme was also a way of policing 'poor' and 'delinquent' boys by sending them to sea. There is also evidence of delinquent and troublesome boys appearing at the Marine Society's office. The Marine Society also received complaints from the navy about boys deserting or being ill-disciplined, so it started an advertising campaign to remind parish overseers, parents and masters not to disregard the boys' personal liberty and to send only those who really wanted to go to sea. It is to be noted that since the beginning of the eighteenth century local authorities had the power to order parish children into a compulsory maritime apprenticeship. The Marine Society perhaps had itself to blame for receiving unwilling boys, since its own publications often promoted the undertaking as a form of crime prevention program that took care of troublesome and potentially dangerous youth.

Boy sailor as hero

The young maritime hero was a prominent figure in the British state's propaganda efforts. As Ronald documents 'late eighteen century writers made the young maritime hero a defining trope in modern patriotism' (Ronald 2015:6).

The 'boy sailor' became a valuable new myth epitomising particular characteristics sought after for Britain as an 'armed nation' facing the threat posed by the French revolution. It was a representation of boys and young men that owed much to a growing awareness of young people as a 'potent group with particular needs and distinctive qualities' (Ronald 2015:7).

Ronald is referring to the making of young heroes for the purpose of propaganda in a context were '…the search was on to define modern patriotism, the symbolic power of youth … acquired special usefulness and significance for the political sphere' (Ronald 2015:7). In this way '…the turning point for youth as a political construction came not when youth is conceived as a separate phase of life', nor when 'the individual finds his individuality.…' Rather, it was when a young person's 'self-identity' coincided with the events of Britain as an armed nation searching for new Britishness. That political identity was realized in 'the youthful Hero' at war (Ronald 2015:7). Thus the 'young maritime hero' became a 'tool' for war propaganda and 'modern patriotism' (Ronald 2015:5).

That image of the young hero was exactly what a nation and an empire under threat needed. The archetypal motif of the young male hero was of a strong and competent 'youth' able to overcome monsters of the dark and deliver military and economic victory a securing Britain's 'rightful' and superior place amongst all other nations. Replete with tales, poems and images of his amazing adventures, the representation of the young hero was projected into the newly emerging public sphere in Britain. Newspapers, political magazines and specialists periodicals provided a powerful medium for shaping and animating the popular imagination. *The Naval Chronicle (ca. 1799–1818)*, e.g., reported on the British Navy's encounters with the French navy during the Napoleonic wars, played a pivotal role in promoting this representation of the young boy hero and in doing so facilitated political communicative action.

The young hero motif was an important element in this 'turning point in Britain's history' and the propaganda campaigns that led to Britain's naval engagement against the combined forces of France and Spain during the Napoleonic wars. The young hero epitomized what many wanted and imagined could be Britain at that time: young and brave with an heroic spirit that could overcome what seemed to be enormous obstacles and achieve what 'everyone' wanted: the defence of Britain and confidence that Britain would return to its former maritime supremacy and economic power.

Conclusion

I began this chapter by drawing attention to the experience of eighteenth century figures such as King George III, Pitt, Nelson, Napoleon and Wellington. As quite young men, they were each given significant leadership roles in politics and military life in ways that today would be unthinkable. Were these the exceptions that prove the rule? I think not.

Representations of children and young people in the eighteenth century were very different to how they are now represented. In the eighteenth century, they were represented in fluid and diverse ways. Children and young people were expected to and indeed did exercise political judgement, and many took part in the public sphere and some assumed significant military responsibilities in what are now deemed child-free zones. There were no socially sanctioned attempts to remove them from 'adult activities' such as politics. In our time many people believe that adults have a duty to protect young people from their own developmental deficits and to prevent them from exercising freedom as described by Arendt. For promoting the freedom of young people is a 'dangerous idea' (Bessant 2014).

It is important to acknowledge the impact of the last decade of the eighteenth century dominated by the French Revolution (1789–1796). That Revolution was a central and defining political event. It shaped the lives of George III, Pitt, Nelson, Wellington, and Napoleon, as well as the lives of countless millions of Europeans at the end of the eighteenth century and into the nineteenth century.

The French Revolution matters in this book because it was initiated and led by young men and women, and was supported indirectly by young people all across Europe. Children and young people occupied and played visible, significant and formative roles in the fervent clamour for democracy promoted by the French revolutionaries. Young English Jacobins and democrats announced and provided support for republican virtue and the rights of man (and woman). Collectively, young people became significant players in various cultural and social movements that became vehicles for popular participation in political action and major change in Paris, in other French cities and in other European countries.

In Britain, boys and young men serving naval personnel also figured in Britain's naval political and propaganda exercises, represented as young heroes playing a central role in Britain's long military struggle against France. The visibility and explicitness of these cases of political processes involving young people highlights the changes that have occurred in the years since 1789.

The French Revolution helped create a new conception of revolution as a novel process of change. It linked an idea about being young with the idea of change. That affinity between the promises of the French Revolution and being young is reflected in William Wordsworth, Britain's poet Laureate who visited France in 1790 as a 20-year-old, recalled:

> Bliss was it in that dawn to be alive,
> But to be young was very heaven
>
> *(Wordsworth 1959:406)*

Yet not everyone was enamoured of the idea of change and novelty.

The French Revolution is also directly relevant to this book because opposing the French Revolution and all it stood for became the rallying point for all those who supported what the French called the 'old order'. That order rested on a reverence for monarchical and Church-based authority and for what was seen as a divinely-inspired natural hierarchy and social order. For those people the revolution was a hateful and catastrophic event that spread disorder, moral decay and terror.[15] It also created an association in the minds of many between the idea of democracy and equality, dangerous disorder and the destructive role played by young people. Soon that would lead to representations of young people as part of the 'dangerous classes'.

How and why did this change? How did young people come to be represented as unfit for entry to the public sphere and as not yet ready political responsibility? To these questions I now turn.

Notes

1 Hartley (1952) *The Go Between*, London: Hamish Hamilton.
2 Pitt was Prime Minister from 1783 to 1801, and then later served for two more years from 1804 before dying in office at the height of Britain's war with Napoleonic France.
3 Indeed closer to our own time, in 2012, journalists openly argued that Justin Trudeau then 40 years of age was 'too young' and had an 'age problem' to assume the Liberal party leadership (Hepburn 2012). At the age of 43 he went on to become the 23rd Prime minister of Canada. In the lead up to the 2015 election however his opponents used his young age and by implication his inexperience as reasons why he was unsuitable for that job. According to political opponents like the New Democratic Party (NDP) leader Thomas Mulcair, Trudeau did not qualify to be Prime Minister because 'Being Prime Minister isn't an entry level job...' (Mulcair 2014). On that occasion it seemed that not everyone agreed. Still at 43 he was considered young to lead a nation. In 2020 Peter Buttigeig a 37-year-old American presidential hopeful received the same treatment.
4 Napoleon became First Consul in the French republic at the age of 30 when he began waging war against Britain.
5 A systematic literature on 'the adolescent' did not exist in Britain or America before 1900. The word adolescence appeared rarely outside of scientific literature prior to the twentieth century (Kett 1971).
6 See authors like Thomas Boreman, John Newbery and Mary Cooper.
7 This remained so until the *Children and Young Person's Act* 1963 set the age of criminal responsibility at ten years.
8 In the first years of minority, i.e., 'Under seven years ... an infant cannot be guilty of felony; for then a felonious discretion is almost an impossibility in nature' (Blackmore 1807:23). The second stage from seven to fourteen was more complex. Children under fourteen were presumed to be *doli incapax*, so their felonies could be regarded as being the same as children under seven. Yet, wrote Blackstone, 'if it appear to the court and jury that he was *doli capax* ... he may be convicted and suffer death' (cited Magarey 1978:19). In the third stage, 'infants' were deemed to have reached the age of discretion and liable, on conviction of felony, to the same punishment as adults. But Blackstone argued:

> The capacity of doing ill ... is not so much measured by years and days, as by the strength of the delinquents' understanding and judgment ... in all such cases, the evidence of that malice which is to supply age, ought to be strong and clear beyond all doubt and contradiction.
>
> (Cited Magarey 1978:19)

88 Young people in the eighteenth century

9 This order was replicated across Europe. All rights and status flowed from the social institutions, divided into three orders: clergy, nobility and others (the Third Estate). Peasants had serf-like status and were excluded from this three estates arrangement.
10 In the eighteenth century a citizen was an inhabitant of a city. This is not to deny that some eighteenth-century writers like Boyer also used 'citizen' as a synonym for 'Bourgeois'.
11 In towns with over six thousand population, a 'citizen' had to own or rent a property with a revenue equal to the standard income for at least one hundred fifty or two hundred days of work. They were also required to have lived in their residence for at least a year. These criteria denied most French people the category of citizen.
12 Here I draw heavily on Gleadle including my reference to the 'Juvenile Enlightenment' (2016).
13 As Gleadle observed, the city also had a Natural History Society and a Botanical Society. The Norwich Public Library, founded in 1784, a project in which Louisa's family was involved, was a focal point for a various of cultural practices. In that space debating clubs like the Society of United Friars, the Speculative Society and the Tusculan School flourished. The Unitarian Octagon Chapel provided another focus for intellectual culture (Gleadle 2016:233).
14 Tom Paine wrote his *The Rights of Man* in 1791 after a year in France. It is said to have sold around a million copies.
15 Across Europe this pattern was replicated. All rights and status flowed from the social institutions, divided into three orders: clergy, nobility and others (the Third Estate). Peasants were effectively serfs and excluded from that three estates model.

4

CIVILISING LITTLE SAVAGES

Children and the dangerous classes

Forty-five people aged between 6 and 15 sat on a bench outside a meeting house in Dowagiac in the American state of Michigan on 1 October 1854. That day the house was operating as a Presbyterian Church. Dowagiac was a rural settlement established in 1848. Three weeks previously advertisements had been distributed by a New York organisation called the Children's Aid Society. The advertisements were asking families in Dowagiac to take in homeless boys and girls who would soon to arrive from New York City. They were described as the 'Little Ones of Christ' (O'Connor 2001:17). In the meeting hall that Sunday, one of the Children's Aid Society officials explained he was asking the 'kind men and women' of Dowagic to open their hearts and purses, and to select one of the children, take them home and raise them as their own. Within days most of the children were 'adopted', mainly by local farmers and craftsmen. The only criteria those adopting families needed to meet was to have a recommendation from a local pastor or a Justice of the Peace. This group of 45 children was the first of around 250,000 American children removed from big eastern cities.

This American muscular Christian philanthropic project owed much to the work of Charles Loring Brace, a protestant minister, pioneer social worker and one of America's best-known child-savers.[1]

Brace founded the New York *Children's Aid Society* in 1853 to help remedy 'the problem' of pauper and vagrant children. New York was a city experiencing growing pains. In 1852, over 175,000 immigrants arrived in America, rising to over 250,000 in 1854, and New York was the main point of entry. The oversupply of labourers meant reduced opportunities for children and adults to earn enough income to survive. Brace was also responsible for instigating the 'Orphan Trains' used to transport thousands of 'abandoned' and pauper street children of the 'dangerous classes' from American cities to rural settlements.

Brace was a Christian evangelical reformer and determined to remove the children of poor Catholics from crowded urban and family environments and put them in God-fearing Anglo-Protestant farming families. Brace and his peers considered Catholic parents naturally 'unworthy' even though the philosophy of child-saving privileged nurture over nature:

> Too many young people were tainted by poverty, urban overcrowding, and slums such that the streets of New York witnessed more acts of blood and riot [...] than is true of any other equal space of earth in the civilized world.
>
> *(Brace 1967:25)*

The 'Orphan Trains' relied on a simple system, and one misunderstanding. Few of the children fitted 'the profile of the homeless, neglected, or abused waifs' that Brace represented them to be chiefly it seems so he could solicit the sympathies of wealthy donors. In some cases families used the orphan trains to help cope in a context where few social services existed. Indeed the word 'orphan' implied the children had no parents, something that was generally untrue. Most of the children had families, but they were families of 'the wrong kind'. Large numbers of children, many children of Irish-Catholic immigrants worked and lived on the streets.

Considered a public nuisance, children as young as five years of age were regularly gathered by police and imprisoned with adult criminals (Patrick and Trickel 1997). This provided a key recruitment source for the *Children's Aid Society*. Children were removed from jails, orphanages and asylums or taken from the streets: sometimes they were surrendered by their parents who could no longer care for them (Cook 1995:186). Between 1854 and 1930 approximately 250,000 children from New York were sent by train to midwestern and western states and also to Canada and Mexico.

The 'Orphan Trains' bequeathed an unfortunate legacy. It was a model which was widely imitated. In America 45,000 children were sent to Catholic communities by the Sisters of Charity while organizations in Boston, Philadelphia and Chicago relocated thousands more (Graham and Gray 1995). Inspired by Brace's success, many European nations, including Britain, Germany, Norway and Sweden, introduced similar programs. In England, a program headed by Dr Thomas Barnardo relocated over 80,000 English 'slum children' throughout the British Commonwealth. Brace's legacy to modern welfare practice was to make it acceptable to intervene in the lives of low-income and disadvantaged families by claiming to protect their children as the prelude to removing them (Gish 1999:138, Pertman 2000).

In this way the 'Orphan Trains' highlights one way children and young people were represented to justify their removal or exclusion from social spaces which hitherto they had occupied comfortably, but had come to be deemed no longer 'child-friendly' spaces. In whose interest was it that these young people be represented as 'orphaned', 'abandoned', 'hapless' and 'in need of care and protection'? One answer is that they were representations specifically designed to allow for and indeed encourage, what Saskia Sassen refers to as the practice of expulsion (2014).

Sassen's focus is on the workings of the twenty-first century's political economy. She shows how whole neighbourhoods and communities have been dislocated and sometimes destroyed by mortgage foreclosures or by deindustrialization even when the larger macro-economy was booming can be understood as a process of expulsion. She refers to the vanishing of the industrial 'working-class' in America, Britain and Australia now living in regions where the category of 'working' has become redundant for most in those neighbourhoods. Expulsion is less spectacular process and more a slow, often somewhat hidden catastrophe, as waves of adversity crush people or move them on. Such processes add to the invisibility 'of those who are expelled from job and home' (Sassen 2014:13). In similar ways in the nineteenth century, large numbers of children were expelled from their families, neighbourhoods and regions as a result of repeated interventions by a growing welfare and child-saving industry claiming to be working in the 'best interests of the child'.

That practice and the underpinning representations of children and young people helps explain how the political and public engagement by young people that had once been accepted and expected in the late eighteenth century, were progressively negated through the nineteenth century. The 'discovery' that children and young people were 'immature', 'cognitively undeveloped', 'ethically irresponsible' and 'vulnerable' to adult manipulation and exploitation, would inform the evolving sciences of 'childhood' and 'adolescence' that was then used to justify the increasing confinement of children and young people in 'child-friendly' zones of exclusion.

This chapter considers how and why this happened. How was it that by the end of the nineteenth-century young people were disappearing from politics and from many other public spaces they had occupied in previous centuries? How was 'childhood' and 'youth' represented at the end of the nineteenth century? How can those diverse representations of children and young people be explained? How can the growing disposition to represent children and young people as members of the 'dangerous classes' be explained? Why were they represented as deficient when marked against 'the adult' and in ways that meant they were incapable of political activity and needing protected from such activity? How and why was 'childhood' and 'youth' assimilated into an apparently natural, evolutionary narrative.

One answer to these questions lies in the political legacy of the French Revolution. It was a legacy embodied in reactions against the democratic experiment generated by the *Declaration of the Rights of Man* of August 1789. That experiment was initially suppressed by the Thermidorean reaction of July 1794 and then more generally across Europe after 1815. It was an anti-democratic reaction committed to trying to restore the 'old order' and it would change how young people were represented across the nineteenth century, with effects that continue today.

The significance of the French Revolution

The concept of revolution originates from the Latin astronomical term *'revolution'*, signifying the rotation of celestial bodies. As such, revolution refers to a repetitious, turning over, or *endless return of the thing or place*. This idea of revolution implied an analogy between revolutionary movements and natural causality, a regular, consistent circular motion, independent of human action and governed by law-like principles. As Arendt argued:

> When the word first descended from the skies and was introduced to describe what happened on earth among mortal men, it appeared clearly as a metaphor, carrying over the notion of an eternal, irresistible, ever-recurring motion to the haphazard movements, the ups and' downs of human destiny, which have been likened to the rising and setting of sun, moon, and stars since times immemorial.
> *(Arendt 1990:42)*

An example of that understanding is seen in England's 'Glorious Revolution' of 1688–1689 which referred to the forced abdication of the Catholic James II in 1688 and his replacement by the protestant William III. The word 'revolution' applied here signified the 'restoration' or 'return' to a natural order.

The modern idea of revolution tends to be understood differently and this is due largely to the French Revolution. Arendt argued the French Revolution was a distinctly modern phenomenon. According to Arendt the French Revolution introduced the idea of revolution as radical novelty or *new beginnings*. Arendt saw in that idea of revolution confirmation of her idea of 'natality' as new beginnings, aimed at establishing a founding moment, a *constitutio libertatis* or a new set of republican political institutions. Freedom in such a Republic, she argued, was not identical with liberty understood as freedom from domination. Rather, freedom was what freely acting people enacted as they drew in improvisational ways on resources like a shared past or a common project to create new public spaces for future action and deliberation. In this way freedom could be used to create a stable space in which people continually realize their freedom through participation in 'public affairs'.

Yet ironically, Arendt was also antagonistic to the revolution which exemplified natality or newness. For while she agreed with the description of the French revolution as novel, she also thought that characterisation was problematic because she believed it descended too quickly into violence, which Arendt considered was the antithesis of politics. She was also critical of the idea of 'those who made the French revolution' that a government could be founded on a vision of human rights and natural equality based on the idea of human nature as inherently good (Arendt 1990).

Arendt says that those who made the Revolution actively pursued terror and domination, typified by the massacres of 'counter-revolutionary' prisoners in September 1792, a bloody civil war in the Vendée and the victory of the dictatorship of the Committee of Public Safety under Robespierre. In these cases the rights of man were suspended with tens of thousands imprisoned and guillotined (Arendt 1990).

Because she understood politics as public speech and action, Arendt warned against describing a revolution as the complete overthrowing of everything that went before and the establishment of a new regime of just violence to achieve its ends. This understanding would only reinforce the power of the state.

In the first half of the nineteenth century saw endless debates about the political significance of the French revolution. As we have seen the Thermidorean coup staged against the Jacobins in July 1794 brought the experiment in democracy by those advocating the use of terror to a bloody end. The Thermidor established a government by the Directorate enabling the French bourgeoisie to briefly stake a claim for citizenship status, until Napoleon Buonaparte came on to the scene after 1796–1797 and rejected that claim. Napoleon's conquest of Europe bought forth another political experiment as Napoleon implemented his legal and cultural Enlightenment agenda while also securing his own rule as Emperor. European allies led by Britain and Prussia crushed Napoleon's dream of Empire in 1815 while the Congress of Vienna encouraged attempts by a disparate group of aristocrats, Church leaders and the rising bourgeoisie to restore the old order under Louis XVIII and then Charles X. This was supposed to reinstate the old (i.e., aristocratic) order.

Yet the political field everywhere was slowly tilting in favour of the bourgeoisie, even as working-class, nationalist and democratic movements were becoming ever stronger and more confident. Later writers like Wallerstein saw this collapse of the 'old order' as a far-longer process that began when feudalism began collapsing in western Europe after the 1550s (Wallerstein 2007:4).

A sequence of political upheavals beginning with the Paris revolution of 1830 saw young people play a key role in a succession of 'world-revolutionary movements' in 1848.[2] In each case these movements were committed to dismantling the remnants of the feudal-monarchical order, and in some cases creating independent nation-states like Germany and Italy so as to promote liberal democratic reforms and to create representative liberal democracies (Wallerstein 2017:5).

In this flurry of revolutionary and counter-revolutionary politics, the novelty of the French revolution continued to inspire successive generations of young radicals, liberals and democrats, socialists, communists and anarchists. For many, the French revolution created a new tradition promising change and new beginnings. That is what Arendt described as 'natality': a novelty evident in the ways the *sans culottes* and Jacobins did not want to restore a past order, rather they wanted a novel political experiment that was without precedent.

The political significance and impact of the French Revolution was not just a discussion carried out in journals and pamphlets by intellectuals. As Hobsbawm observed, the nineteenth century was the 'age of revolutions' a time when political ideologies collided across the world.

The nineteenth century was characterised by agitation, marches and rallies, street politics, the creation of secret societies, international movements of various kinds in Britain, Europe, the United States and Europe's colonies. Sometimes it came in the form of mass democratic movements like England's Chartist movement (1836–1848). Sometimes it involved popular street action as the prelude to the overthrow of governments (e.g., France in 1830 and 1870–1871). Waves of revolutions again swept across European societies in 1848. Sometimes they included armed nationalist uprisings in southern and central Europe.[3] This is to say nothing of on-going cycles of working-class strikes, encouraged in part by the rise of social-democratic movements in Germany and Russia and late in the nineteenth century, anarchist violence across the northern hemisphere. Reactionary governments also made efforts to suppress the political ferment by keeping this dissent under surveillance while criminalising many forms of dissent, and pro-democracy and nationalist politics (Wallerstein 2017).

For those who were antagonistic to the French Revolution, this was a recurring nightmare, a source of disorder in France and across Europe. The tone of this conservative response was epitomised as early as October 1789 when the Anglo-Irish philosopher Edmund Burke wrote soon after the storming of the Bastille (14 July 1789) that the 'Elements which compose Human Society' seem all to be 'dissolved' in France, 'and a world of Monsters to be produc'd in the place of it – where Mirabeau presides as the Grand Anarch' (Burke 1967:29–30). A few months later Burke wrote his *Reflections on the Revolution in France*: his message clear: the revolution had destroyed the foundations of European civilisation. This was because the revolutionaries had not allowed a process of slow, organic change to occur in a social order grounded naturally in respect for tradition and hierarchical society (Burke 2001).

Later conservatives concurred, arguing the French Revolution was based on false and abstract ideas of liberty, democracy and human rights. For them the revolution was the result of a 'conspiracy against all the ancient institutions of Europe, civil, political, and religious' propagated by subversives like Voltaire, or authors like Diderot said to be devoid of moral principles and any sense of responsibility as well as 'licentious' German writings (Bowles 1798 cited in MacLeod 2013:382).

It was imperative that Revolutionary principles like liberty and democracy be decisively crushed by the counter-revolution in France and by a war waged by an alliance of Europe's monarchs if the threat to social order was to be quelled (MacLeod 2013:383).

This widespread anxiety experienced by European elites and conservatives about the 'future of civilisation', stability of Europe and fear of the threat posed by ideas of 'citizenship' and 'revolution' shaped nineteenth-century politics.

In early 1848 just before the first inklings of a renewal of revolutionary fervour in the 'February Revolution' in France, Alexis de Tocqueville spoke in the French Chamber of Deputies. De Tocqueville, claiming to belong to the left, came from an old aristocratic family in Normandy (Hansen 2009:3). He was a liberal who advocated for parliamentary government while being sceptical of what he saw as 'extre me democracy' promoted by the 'working classes' (Jaume 2013:6). De Tocqueville warned the French middle classes: 'We are sleeping on a volcano ... Do you not see that the earth trembles anew? A wind of revolution blows, the storm is on the horizon' (Cited Hobsbawm 1975:21).

This political ferment was actively promoted by young people. In the same ways that the key protagonists in the French Revolution (1789–1796) were young (in their early 20s and 30s), so too were the radicals who took to the streets in Sicily, Paris, Berlin, Copenhagen, Vienna, Munich, Prague and other European cities in 1848. Standout examples of political actions in which young people played important roles can be seen in Italy, Germany and Ireland.[4]

Young Italy, young Ireland and young Germany

The political movement *Young Italy* (*La Giovine Italia*) was a patriotic insurrectionary association established for Italian young people in 1831 by the then 26-year-old Giuseppe Mazzini. Its declared goal was to transform Italy into a unitary democratic republic committed to ideas of freedom, independence and unity, all of which entailed getting rid of all pre-unification states. Young Italy played a critical role in the struggle for Italian unification *Risorgimento*. Giuseppe Garibaldi was the best-known member of *Young Italy* and was part of a failed revolt led by Mazzini in the city of Piedmont.[5] Garibaldi went on to play a formative role in the nineteenth-century movement for Italian unification (*il Risorgimento*), that saw Count Cavour (Camillo Benso) establish the Kingdom of Italy in 1861 and become Prime Minister of Italy.[6]

In Ireland, the *Young Ireland* movement incorporated young men and women into struggles to overturn the Act of Union of 1801, a legislative agreement that brought Ireland into the United Kingdom. The origins of Young Ireland go back to the new College Historical Society, established on 29 March 1839. Founding members included 23-year-old Gavan Duffy, Jane Wilde (18), Thomas Meagher (16), Margaret Callan (22) and John Thomas Dillon (25) all involved in establishing a new national Irish newspaper, called *The Nation*. In July 1849 inspired by other European uprisings in 1848, William O'Brien, leader of the Young Ireland Party, staged a rebellion in response to the British introduction of martial law. He gathered together landlords and tenants with members of the Young Irelanders but the rebellion soon evaporated. Many of the rebellion leaders were tried for sedition and sentenced to penal transportation to Australia (Quinn 2017).

In Germany, networks of young writers and professionals established a liberal-democratic movement committed to republican democracy, rationalism, and for some socialism, created *Young Germany* (*Junges Deutschland*). It was supported by young German writers like Heinrich Heine and Thomas Buchner between 1830 and 1850. *Young Germany* advocated the separation of church and state, gender equality and the emancipation of the Jews (Lacquer 1984). Its members were also involved in developing radical working-class movements. Jürgen Schmidt documents how young teachers like Ernst Schüler (aged 23) settled in the town of Biel and established a 'reading society' in 1833 and a printing shop in 1835 (2019). Soon after Biel became the printed media centre of 'Young Germany'. In 1836 the 'Association of Craftsmen' (*Handwerkerverein*) of Biel centralised and coordinated different clubs and associations sympathetic to the republican ideas of 'Young Germany', and encouraged travelling apprentices and workers to initiate new clubs in other towns. In this way Biel became the centre of the 'Young Germany' movement. The young teacher Schüler identified the liberal concept informing this network:

> In Paris and other towns, as well as in Switzerland some people had the idea to communicate liberal principles to these journeymen who are sons of German parents so that once they return to Germany, they strengthen that party which is hostile to the princes.
>
> *(Cited Schmidt 2019:5)*

The degree to which these movements confirmed contemporary expectations of young people is unclear. Modern writers like Schindler argue that 'youth' had long been represented as 'a haven for disorder' (Schindler 1997:281). Luzzatto similarly observed how 'in every European country, throughout the nineteenth century, a heterogeneous but clear image emerges of a restless or rebellious youth' (cited in Ronald 2016). The idea that young people were inherently rebellious troublemakers helped shape representations of youth as a source of disorder, immorality and subversion. Given this it was not surprising that 'young people inspired fear throughout the nineteenth century' (Ronald 2015:7).

Discovering the 'dangerous classes' and the role of intellectuals

While the idea of the 'working classes' as dangerous can be traced to the fraught relations between the bourgeoisie and the *sans culottes* during the French revolution, it did not fully develop as a major idea until later. As Scheu argued, the idea of the 'dangerous classes' can be attributed to the work of Chief of Bureau of police in Paris Honore Fregier (1789–1860) who wrote an influential book '*Des classes Dangereuses De La Population*' (1840) (2011:117). Fregier's book helped shape the nineteenth-century bourgeoisie's collective fear of the lower classes as a dangerous lot who seemed to 'obey neither the law and or respect the naturally hierarchical order of society' (Scheu 2011:117). 'Good' (bourgeois) citizens of Paris became preoccupied with this 'mysterious class' (Fregier 1840:44).

As Foucault observed, representations of the dangerous classes involved discourses about the 'great fear of a [...] barbaric, immoral and outlaw class' (Foucault 1997:275). English writers also drew on this representation applying it to their own 'dangerous lower orders'. In Fregier's book he described modern cities as dangerous places that fostered crime, a view that mobilised people living in the country enjoyed. Charles Loring Brace (1872), mentioned earlier, wrote in parallel terms about the rise of the 'dangerous classes' in the large cities in his American bestseller called *The Dangerous Classes of New York*. Interventions by Fregier and Brace point directly to the role of intellectuals in the discovery of the 'dangerous classes'.

Representations are the work of intellectuals. As Moscovici and Bourdieu argued, those working in scholarly and professional fields constructed and reinforced powerful representations and social imaginaries focussing on a particular idealized symbolic order. Those people included professionals, intellectuals and symbolic occupations like journalists, writers, officials, scientists and academics (Hacking 1999, Isin 2002:215). This make-up of this heterogeneous intellectual order is partly why Bourdieu (1991) saw the 'intellectual' as having a paradoxical, bi-dimensional and unstable status *caught in an ambiguous relationship with politics and the state*.

Bourdieu argues that to be an intellectual, a cultural producer has to fulfil two conditions. One is that the intellectual needs to 'belong to an autonomous intellectual world (a field), that is, independent from religious, political, and economic powers (and so on), and must respect its specific law' (Bourdieu 1991:656).

However the intellectual must invest the competence and authority they acquired in the intellectual field in political action, which is carried out outside the intellectual field properly. He continued, the intellectual:

> ...has in it something unstable and unsettled, the consequence of which, as the to-and-fro movement observable in history attests, is that the holders of cultural capital can always 'regress' toward one or another of the positions designated by the pendulum of history, that is, toward the role of the 'pure' writer, artist, scientist, or toward the role of the simple political actor, journalist, politician, and so on.
>
> *(Bourdieu 1991:658)*

The criminologist Cohen argued in his 'moral panics' model that one way intellectuals intervene is as 'moral entrepreneurs' (1972). By this Cohen was referring to the ways some people make their careers from mobilizing public alarm about issues like crime, disease or disorder that arouse anxiety or fear and who then advocate reforms and solutions to those problem (1972). Others like Elizabeth Anderson refer to 'policy entrepreneurs' to describe a particular kind of institutional entrepreneur working in the policy field (Anderson 2018). They include government officials, elected legislators, non-governmental policy experts, interest group lobbyists, and civil society advocates. As Bourdieu and Wacquant argue, the policy field is a composite field comprising of the state and multilayered social spaces that incorporate different intersecting fields, including the intellectual field and various civil societies like philanthropic and charitable organizations (Bourdieu and Wacquant 1992). Significantly they are fields characterised by relations of competition and by relations of cooperation.

Networks of intellectuals, journalists, writers, scholars and officials in the 1830s and 1840s created an influential commentary on the 'social question' of poverty and 'connected' problems of depravity, degeneracy, and the crime said to plague industrial societies like Britain, France, Germany and other European societies. They were commentaries coming from social Catholics, positivists, monarchists, radicals, anarchists, socialists, communists, conservatives and bourgeois liberals each in their own ways addressing the 'social question' posed by the 'dangerous classes'.

Those who made up the 'dangerous classes', i.e., the working-class, the poor or the *la misere* were said to be characterised by a propensity to destitution, moral dysfunctions like crime, unemployment, homelessness, poverty, suicide, illiteracy, prostitution, begging and producing street children. In explaining the social problem many referred to the lack of moral discipline on the part of the new urban industrial proletariat and the poor (Lynch 1988, Cross 1989). Even Marx was unflattering in his depiction of the 'lumpenproletariat' (Marx 1990:75). Doubting that this class had any working-class virtues, Marx and Friedrich Engels warned that this 'passive decaying matter of the lowest layers of the old society', even when it is 'thrust into the movement by a proletarian revolution', was 'more likely to sell out to reactionary intrigues' (Marx and Engels 1967:92).

For English writers like Mayhew, Dickens, Miles and Chadwick, urban crime was the product of a 'criminal class', which included 'barbarians', 'savages', 'vagrants' and 'nomads'. They were the 'dregs of society' committed to crime not because of economic need or deprivation, but because they were lazy or lacked the good character for hard work. They were the 'enemy of society', the 'anonymous hordes', the inhabitants of the slums of big cities like London and the rapidly growing industrial cities 'pouring out of their hovels and into the wealthier areas to sack, plunder and kill' (Philips 2003:2).

In France the public economist and physician Louis Villermé (1840) wrote about the physical and moral condition of French textile workers. He described the wretchedness of workers' living conditions and their dirtiness, sexual immodesty, drunkenness and improvidence (Anderson 2018:190). Similarly manufacturer Jean-Jacques Bourcart of *Mulhouse Industrial Society* established by young industrialists, said 'society finds itself threatened by a weakly and degenerate population without principles' (cited in Anderson 2018:190). Likewise Eugene

Buret a French economist and journalist writing in 1840 'described' the problem as those:

> … Isolated from the nation, outlawed from the social and the political community, alone with their needs and miseries, they struggle to extricate themselves from this terrifying solitude, and like the barbarians to whom they have been compared, they are perhaps meditating invasion.
> *(Cited in Isin 2002:202)*

Such accounts reflect a growing anxiety and fear by elites experiencing increasing strikes and riots by workers reacting to the failure of governments to improve their situation in life.

The middle class in the mid-nineteenth century drew links between poverty and 'moral decay'. In our time scholars have pointed to a constitutive nexus between poverty, delinquency and criminality (Stallybrass 1990, Beirne 1993:65, Brantlinger and Ulin 1993, Geremek 1994). Beirne, who accepted the idea of a nexus between poverty and criminality, pointed to writers like Eugene Buret's study, *De la misere des classes laborieuses,* in which he argued 'The poor are the people outside of the society, outside of the law, they are outlaws, and almost all criminals come from their ranks' (Buret 1979:2).

The fear of civil strife and revolution by the 'crowd' or the 'mob' was ever present (Borch 2009, Brighenti 2010). As David Phillips argued:

> The image of the 'dangerous classes' united the threat to person and property of ordinary crime, with the wider threat posed to the whole society by a militant and possibly revolutionary working class.
> *(Phillips 2003:81)*

The figure of the 'dangerous classes' was used in a similar way to how contemporary representations of the 'terrorist' have been used to generate and mobilise alarm or panic in the minds of many.

'The crowd' or 'the mob' seemed to embody irrationality, excess and a tendency to collective violence, which as the history of the French revolution indicated could easily become revolutionary violence. That had been a central topic of discussion among conservatives from the revolution of 1789 and this fear of the crowd would never go away (McClelland 1989:138). Indeed it became central to the French multidisciplinary scholar Gustave Le Bon's (1895–2009) study of crowd psychology and modern urban 'civilization' in his *The Crowd: A Study of the Popular Mind (Psychologie des Foules)*. According to Le Bon, all civilisations have been created and directed by a small, intellectual aristocracy and never by crowds. That is because crowds are only capable of destruction.[7] Half a century later the writer Elias Canetti, a Jewish émigré from Vienna, offered a more nuanced account of crowds, describing the human psyche as impelled by a foundational instinct to gather together into crowds, an impulse moved by a universal fear or terror (Canetti 1962:75).

In this context characterised by an understanding of collective human action as dangerous and irrational, children and young people assumed a central role in the 'dangerous classes'.

Children, young people and the 'dangerous classes'

By the mid-nineteenth century children and young people came to be seen as an important component in the 'dangerous classes', an idea epitomised by representations of 'dangerous vagrant children', 'street urchins', 'juvenile delinquents', 'slum children' and 'hooligans' (Pearson 1983). It was a development explained in part by what some historians call the 'invention of juvenile delinquency' in mid-Victorian Britain (For Britain see May 1973, Gillis 1974, Gillis 1975, Pearson 1983, Bailey 1987, Shore 2011).[8] I argue later, it was more complicated than that.

In England and France, e.g., images of waves of juvenile delinquency threatening the existence of an orderly and civilised society had by the 1840s and 1850s become common. By 1850 'juvenile delinquency' was understood by many middle-class Britons as a critical national weakness. According to British professor of civil law J. S. More it was 'next to slavery … perhaps the greatest stain on our country' (cited Tobias 1967:52). Delinquency evoked a deep fear of 'a hostile power which has established itself within our citadel'. Juvenile delinquents were according to one investigator: a race sui generis, different from the rest of society, not only in Thought, Habits and Manners but even in appearance; possessing, moreover a Language exclusively their own' (cited in Tobias 1967:53).

Sometimes the link with the French Revolution and violence wrought by the 'juvenile dangerous classes' was made explicit. The children 'know very well', wrote the master of one of London's 'ragged schools' in 1850, '…that we are the representatives of beings with whom they have ever considered themselves at war' (cited in Magarey 1978:11).

The work of representing children and young people owed much the efforts of middle-class intellectuals in the 1850s and 1850s who created a fearful representation of uncivilised under-age 'hooligans' and 'street urchins' threatening an integrated, well-ordered society. In that imagined well-ordered society, a modern discourse of 'childhood' evolved which envisaged young people as in need of protection from physical danger, moral contamination and degeneration. Governing 'the young', understood as 'protecting their innocence' highlighted the ambiguity of childhood as dark representations of 'the delinquent' or 'little savage'. As Mary Carpenter, a well-known English 'child-saver' explained: the 'delinquent child' who '… exhibited in almost every respect qualities the very reverse of what we should desire to see in a child; we have beheld them independent, self-reliant, advanced in the knowledge of evil' (cited in Carpenter

1981:113). In practice, the delinquent child was a child who did what adults did. One thing that alarmed 'child-savers' like Carpenter was that many children worked for a living.

In the mid-nineteenth century the norm was for working-class children to work. Working-class families often relied on children as wage earners contributing 'between 28 and 46 percent of household income in two-parent families' (O'Connor 2001:98). From an early age when a child could hold a tool like a spinning card, they worked in the household. By age 12 or so most children were 'treated as adult producers' (Fass and Mason 2000:1).

This and the scale of 'juvenile delinquency' alarmed many middle classes people. One Sussex magistrate claimed in 1835 the 'Increase of juvenile Offenders has been arithmetical [sic] within the last Twenty Years'. In 1848 Anthony Ashley Cooper, 7th Earl of Shaftesbury, a Tory aristocrat and 'child-saver', estimated there were more than 30,000 'naked, filthy, roaming, lawless and deserted children' in London. In 1838, 9,686 young people under 17 were given prison sentences: by 1843 that rose to 11,720 (Magarey 1978:16).

However, as historians like Peter King and Heather Shore demonstrated, the mid-Victorian 'invention' of delinquency was well underway by the early nineteenth century.

King's statistical analysis of property offenders aged 10–17 using court records across Britain, found that an increase in juvenile prosecutions was happening well before the mid-nineteenth century (2006). That was confirmed by Shore's analysis of Middlesex offenders in the Criminal Registers after 1790 (1996). That work highlighted the issue of urban growth as central to the willingness of the courts to prosecute juvenile offenders.

In the shift to modernity and the emergence of the bourgeois family, young people and children were constituted as naive, vulnerable, innocent, natural and uncomplicated. Given that most working class children did not have a 'childhood' because they worked in factories, up chimneys, on the streets, drank and had sex, that idea of 'childhood' as innocent was used to justify various child-saving projects.

The 'child-savers' of the nineteenth century were also the predecessors to today's social workers, youth workers, teachers, probation officers, child protection workers, community workers, counsellors and psychologists. Through their work we saw the full flourishing of a 'civilizing offensive'.

Children, young people and the civilising offensive

German historical-sociologist Norbert Elias developed the idea of a 'civilizing process' to describe the thousand-year struggle by European elites and states to regulate and discipline certain anarchic biological and emotional instinctual life and libidinal energies (Elias 2012). Later writers developed Elias' idea of a 'civilizing process' to talk about a modern or bourgeois 'civilizing offensive' (Mitzman 1987, Verrips 1987, van Ginkel 1996, van Krieken 1999, Powell 2013).

The 'civilizing offensive' refers to deliberate attempts by powerful groups, who often worked in or for a paternalist state, to alter the conduct and the lives, of designated sections of the population. As Fletcher argued:

> Anything from trade to education, within which 'barbaric' practices could be discerned, came under the province of reform in the name of civilisation, involving the refinement of manners and the internal pacification of the country by the kings. This formed part and parcel of what has been described as a 'civilising offensive'.
>
> *(1997:9)*

As Isin observes, the 'civilizing offensive' took off after 1848, the year of revolutions (Isin 2002:202).

The civilising offensive was a large and wide-ranging project. As Mitzman notes, the project included suppressing many aspects of popular culture over the last four centuries like witchcraft, 'the festive violence of the young', 'irregular sexuality', excessive alcohol consumption, drunken fighting, sexual promiscuity said to be evident by the number of illegitimate births, lack of personal hygiene, crowded slum housing, the 'culture of worklessness' defined as an absence of a work ethic and unemployment. The civilising offensive would also involve 'medical-ethical' interventions relating to masturbation, prostitution, drug use, homosexuality and efforts to reform the 'incurable promiscuity' and 'vulgarity' of the lower-classes (Mitzman 1987:665).

The 'civilising offensive' focussed on the task of 'civilizing the savage'. It became a problem addressed by mountains of government and academic surveys, official and parliamentary inquiries, pamphlets, statistics, funded research and opinion pieces in papers in American, French, German, British and other European cities. Through the nineteenth century experts, social scientists and policy-makers turned their minds to the task of preventing the threat of disorder posed by growing numbers of people participating in social movements demanding democracy in the form of male suffrage, the liberal rule of law, social justice and recognition of national identity. By the end of the nineteenth century, that problem was increasingly being described in pseudo-biological terms which identified the 'dangerous classes' as 'racial degenerates' and 'racially inferior'.

It was a development that had major implications for children and young people.

Proponents of the 'civilizing offensive' drew on 'civilization' tropes that had already been used to 'describe' the 'barbarous' 'primitive savages' who had become subjects of various European colonies and empires. As Mitzman argued, authoritative institutions informed by ideas about what constituted 'civilized' behaviour, tried to regulate, suppress and eradicate retrograde elements deemed to be 'irrational', 'un-civilized' and 'primitive' (1987:663). While this took many forms, three interventions are directly relevant to this book: attempts to regulate or abolish child labour, increased attention to child-protection and the introduction of compulsory schooling.

Child labour

The modern regulatory welfare state in Europe and America introduced child labour laws in the 1830s and 1840s. European and American governments considered the control and later the abolition child labour essential (Anderson 2018:174). Industrialization, prospects of class-conflict, legal and policy development help explain the emergence of early child labour regulations in Britain, Prussia, France and America. As Anderson argues it also depend on interventions by policy entrepreneurs.

In England, one such entrepreneurial figure and famous child-saver was Lord Anthony Ashley-Cooper. As an evangelical Anglican Ashley-Cooper believed in the second coming of Christ, which seems to have animated his sense of urgency and determination to save children. Elected to Parliament at the age of 25, Lord Ashley introduced the *Ten Hours Act* into the Commons in 1833. It was a bill that stipulated children working in the cotton and woollen industries must be aged at least nine. Also no one under the age of 18 could work more than ten hours a day or eight hours on a Saturday and no one under 25 was to work at night.[9] The Act passed ensuring that no child under 13 worked more than 9 hours, it also required that they go to school and inspectors were appointed to enforce the law (Battiscombe 1974:88–91).

Another Bill supported by Ashley-Cooper was introduced into the Commons in 1840 outlawing the employment of boys as chimney sweeps, but it was unsuccessful. In these ways, Ashley-Cooper demonstrated his determination, finally persuading Parliament to pass the *Chimney Sweepers Act* in 1875 that saw the licensing of chimney sweeps and enforcement of the law by the police (Battiscombe 1974). In 1840, Lord Ashley headed a Commission of Inquiry into coal mines with a report published in May 1842 that was based on investigations into the conditions of workers (especially children) in the coal mines. The Report revealed that children as young as five or six worked as *trappers*, opening and shutting ventilation doors down the mine, before graduating to pushing and pulling coal tubs. Ashley-Cooper introduced the *Mines and Collieries Act 1842* which prohibited female labour and the employment of boys under ten years old in coal mines.

Inspired by Ashley-Cooper, Charles Dupin, an engineer in France, wrote a report in 1840 calling for the national regulation of child labour modelled on British and Prussian laws. Dupin's description of the child labour problem drew on the prevailing air of alarm highlighting the French working class's lack of morality and a patriotic discourse about needing to cultivate the nation's physical and mental capacities to restore France's military and economic might. Dupin's depiction of the child labour comprised of three components. The first component drew on statistics on Britain's industrial output before and after the passage of its child labour laws to show the new regulation was compatible with economic growth. Second, Dupin reported military statistics showing that disproportionately high numbers of French army recruits from industrial areas were rejected for being 'infirm' or 'deformed'. In this way Dupin connected child workers' poor health to national defense and economic prosperity, arguing that overwork caused 'individual suffering of the most afflicting kind', and rendered 'the country weak in military powers, and poor in all the occupations of peace' (*Annales du Parlement Français* 1840a:82). Thirdly, Dupin connected working children's lack of school attendance to the moral degeneration of the working class, calling for mandatory schooling to promote 'moral training'. His solution was embodied in legislation passed in 1840. It included a minimum employment age of eight, restrictions on children's working hours based on age and the requirement that children acquire two years of schooling before working or attend school while working (Weissbach 1989, Anderson 2018).

These developments were replicated across Europe, North America and in many colonies (e.g., Australia and Canada).

Criminalizing the child

Another component of the 'civilizing offensive' were moves to criminalise vagrant children and young people. In France, e.g., child vagrants were subject to prosecution. Foucault examined the case of a boy appearing before a French magistrate in 1840 on charges of vagrancy (1977:290–291). Foucault introduces the boy as Béasse, 'a child of thirteen, without home or family'. The following exchange occurs when interventions into families designed to 'rescue' children from 'neglect' were proceeding as part of a French 'civilizing offensive'.

The exchange between Béasse, and the magistrate follows:

Magistrate: One must sleep at home.
Béasse: Have I got a home?
Magistrate: You live in perpetual vagabondage.
Béasse: I work to earn my living.
Magistrate: What is your station in life?
Béasse: My station, to begin with, I'm thirty-six at least; I don't work for anybody. I've worked for myself for a long time now. I have my day station and my night station. In the day, for instance, I hand out leaflets free of charge to all the passers-by; I run after the stage coaches when they arrive and carry luggage for the passengers; I turn cart-wheels on the avenue at Neuilly; at night there are the shows; I open coach doors, I sell pass-out tickets; I've plenty to do.
Magistrate: It would be better for you to be put in a good house as an apprentice and learn a trade.
Béasse: Oh, a good house, an apprenticeship, it's too much trouble. And anyway, the bourgeois... always grumbling, no freedom.

Magistrate: Does not your father wish to reclaim you?
Béasse: Haven't got no father.
Magistrate: And your mother?
Béasse: No mother neither, no parents, no friends, free and independent.
(Foucault 1977:290)

This exchange is telling: it occurred in a very unequal relationship between a magistrate who represents the coercive powers of the French state and a boy with no property or civil status. Yet in that exchange Béasse had a voice and opted to address the magistrate not as a 'vagrant' should, but as someone talking about his life experience. While Foucault interprets the boy's stance as 'insolence', e.g., when the boy reformulates the offence of which he stands accused, his response is perhaps closer to what Arendt calls 'natality' – that is, speaking in the public sphere?

In France parental neglect was considered to be a major cause of 'delinquency' (which Béasse represented). The 'demoralising' influence of the home and streets could be countered by rescuing children and sending them to new institutions like France's Mettray penal colony. This reformatory for 'male delinquents' opened the same year that Béasse was sentenced (1840). Foucault described it as a curious blend of regiment, hospital, workshop, school and prison; a synthesis of inspection, training and punishment overseen by 'technicians of behaviour, engineers of conduct' (Foucault 1977:293). Mettray penal colony was a private reformatory, *without walls*. Its mission was to reform, through manual agricultural work and prayer, the young inmates many of whom had already been served sentences in traditional prisons. The heads of the boys were shaved, they wore prison uniforms and until to the age of 12 they spent most of the day studying arithmetic, writing and reading. Older boys had one hour of classes and the remainder of the day was spent working. Some were employed in trades, but the majority performed hard agricultural labour like digging and crushing stones for roads. It was closed in 1937.

In the decades following Béasse's appearance in court, reformatories in France and Britain were supplemented by other societies for child protection, the prevention of cruelty to children, school medical inspections and juvenile courts. They were initiatives that converged around a child-centric conception of vulnerability that constrained the agency of children while also defining childhood.

In England the shift was evident in the ways children were subjected to new policing and judicial practices. The British state was one of many states that criminalised children's activities using legislation like the *Vagrant Act* and the *Malicious Trespass Act*, passed in the 1820s and the subsequent *Metropolitan Police Act* of 1829. That act specified the 'offenders' a policeman might apprehend, without a warrant to include:

> ...all loose, idle and disorderly Persons whom he shall find disturbing the Public Peace, or whom he shall have just Cause to suspect of any evil

Designs, and all Persons whom he shall find between Sunset and the Hour of Eight in the Forenoon lying in any Highway, Yard, or other Place, or loitering therein, and not giving a satisfactory Account of themselves.

The *Metropolitan Police Act* enabled a wholesale onslaught on the poor and labouring classes and their leisure activities targeting London's street-children.

There were large numbers of idle or homeless children. Mayhew estimated the number of 'outcast boys and girls who sleep in and about the purlieus of Covent Garden-market each night' was 'upwards of 200' (Mayhew (1851 Vol 1): 476). The numbers of juveniles convicted under the Police Act rose from just over 2% of all convictions in that category in 1840 to just over 12% in 1843.[10] Along with the increase in policing went increases in the number of institutions used to 'treat' the poor, vagrant and criminal children.

In the 1790s, London's Philanthropic Society placed 'delinquent' boys in reformatories where they were provided with a moral and social education (Shore 2011:120). By the early nineteenth century children were committed to the reformatory by a 'dynamic interaction at ground level between philanthropists, Old Bailey justices, and the formal government authorities' (King 2006:161).

Once they were deemed 'sufficiently reformed' the children were transferred to work factories 'where they were taught practical skills' and sent to work. This division between the reformatory and factory would be reflected in the evolution of the industrial and reformatory schools. Thus reformatory schools were reserved for convicted offenders, while industrial schools took potential delinquent and neglected child (Shore 2011:121).[11] By the start of the First World War in England, 'there was a network of 208 schools: 43 reformatories, 132 industrial schools, 21 day industrial schools and 12 truant schools' (Radzinowicz and Hood 1986:182).

By then Britain had also introduced a number of Infant Life Protection Acts that led to the *Children's Act* of 1908 (or *Children's Charter*). Thus what began as child-saving, morphed into a discourse of 'child protection'. One consequence of that was the silencing of the child's voice. From then on in the emerging field of 'juvenile justice' marked by the introduction of Children's Courts across Europe, Britain, in many American cities concurrently and colonies, increasingly adults came to speak on behalf of the child.

Schooling

Compulsory schooling was the third element of the 'civilizing offensive' targeting children and young people (Gilliam and Gulløv 2014). It was a large scale project began with advocacy for 'ragged school' in places like Britain and elsewhere. That became part of a growing 'charitable' educational movement, committed to teaching children for free who were, 'too ragged, wretched, filthy and forlorn', to enter any other place of learning. By 1844, the Ragged School Union promoted the provision of free education, food, clothing, lodging and other services for poor children (Walvin 1982). Working in the poorest districts, teachers initially used stables, lofts and railway arches as classrooms. Most teachers were voluntary, although a small number were paid. The emphasis was on reading, writing, arithmetic and Bible study. The curriculum expanded into industrial and commercial subjects in many schools (Walvin 1982).

In 1846, eight years after his descriptions of masses of children scattered across London's landscape, the English novelist Charles Dickens recalled his visit to Field Lane Ragged School, opened in 1842. It was a school consisting of, 'two or three ... miserable rooms, upstairs in a miserable house', where children 'huddled together on a bench', while 'some flaring candles [were] stuck against the walls'. Not to be 'trusted with books' the children were taught 'orally' by a voluntary teacher, 'to look forward in a hymn ... to another life which would correct the miseries of this one' (Dickens 1846). Dickens understood evangelical Christianity as the heart of ragged schooling, that aimed to:

> Teach poor mothers how to clothe and bring up their offspring, to teach fathers their duties to their families and children their duty to their parents, to teach above all things that true wisdom is true religion and true religion supreme love to God.
>
> *(Ragged School Union 1857:26)*

Working in the poorest districts, teachers (who were often local working people) initially used stables, lofts, and railway arches for their classes. Most teachers were voluntary, although a small number were employed. The emphasis was on reading, writing, arithmetic and study of the Bible. The curriculum expanded into industrial and commercial subjects in many schools, and an estimated 300,000 children went through the London ragged schools between 1844 and 1881 (Walvin 1982).

By the last decades of the nineteenth century advocacy for schools for 'poor children' became per of a wider push advocating compulsory state education for all. It was a project that saw the passage of compulsory schooling legislation in Britain, Europe, America and the Australian colonies in the 1860s and 1870s.

One aspect of the evolution of compulsory schooling was the way it imported the cultural norms of the English, American or Australian middle classes into the respective national education systems. This was camouflaged by a discourse of meritocracy in which those class norms became objective 'measures' of intellectual or academic ability. Another effect, as White argued, was that education systems encouraged the division of the schooling system by social class into more or less academic schools (White 2006). Additionally we saw what Illich described as representations of childhood that were analogous to disability (or disease). In these ways it could be seen how the end purpose of public mass compulsory schooling was to managing children and young people (Illich 1972, Rose 1991).

By the early twentieth century, this 'civilizing offensive' had realized a number of its goals.

Yet it was not long before a new, different bio-political imaginary emerged in which young people became racial assets that needed to be protected and developed or else they risked being lost to the nation. From the 1880s older discussion about the 'dangerous classes' morphed into a 'new' discussion about children and young people preoccupied with countering 'degeneracy' and promoting 'racial fitness'. Based on the idea that children needed a 'childhood', guaranteed if necessary, by 'child-protection', the last decades of the nineteenth century and early twentieth century saw the rise of a new bio-political model. This bio-political imaginary can be seen, e.g., in evidence submitted by Shannon Millin in 1917 to the 'Statistical and Social Inquiry Society of Ireland'. Children he said must be 'protected' from the 'sordid greed' of predatory employers and from the neglect of 'idle, vicious and drunken parents, who utilise their children as wage-earning instruments' (Millin 1917: cited in Ryan 2018:10). It was an all-inclusive bio-political state project aimed at minimising 'the manufacture of criminals and paupers' and maximising the numbers equipped to 'serve the nation' into the future (Millin 1917:316). This was to be done by intervening directly into the human reproductive process itself.

It was a shift that owed much to Francis Galton's new 'science' of eugenics that claimed to link a developmental model of human life, intelligence and 'racial hygiene' in programs specifically designed to 'breed out' the racially inferior. In that project children and young people were central. The representation of youth-as-adolescence would be one of its key accomplishments.

Eugenics: progress and degeneracy

There are some ideas that have a powerful influence in bringing about change and influencing how we see the world. The idea of progress is one such idea. What Herbert Butterfield (1931) called the 'Whig view of history' argued that the flow of history was an inevitable progression towards individual freedoms and the rise of liberal-democracy, the triumph of reason in the age of enlightenment and the explosion of scientific knowledge. As the American sociologist Robert Nisbet (1980) observed, the western idea of progress pervaded the thinking of nineteenth-century social, political and scientific writers like Hegel, Jeremy Bentham, Comte, J.S. Mill, Saint Simon, Marx, Spencer and de Gobineau.[12] All agreed that the movement of history would always, and inevitably continue moving along in a gradual ascent towards improvement (Nisbet 1980). These writers referred to what they saw as an abundance of evidence to support this idea. Indeed the development of social sciences such as economics, sociology, psychology and anthropology in the nineteenth century was devoted to accumulating evidence about economic growth, the application of science and technology, and intellectual and moral development. The sociologist August Comte

(1798–1857), e.g., argued that human kind was compelled to evolve through three successive stages: the theological stage, the metaphysical stage and the positive stage. Supporting Comte's model of positivist science, J.S. Mill argued that this law meant 'we may hereafter succeed not only in looking far forward into the future history of the human race, but in determining what artificial means may be used ... to accelerate the natural progress...' (Mill 1846:587). Regardless of the truth or desirability of these ideas, they nonetheless had powerful effects that continue into our time.

One effect was how the language of 'race' was used in the new eugenic science of human development that did much to bring forth the idea of 'adolescence' as a natural 'stage of life'.

There were significant affinities between these late nineteenth-century representations of adolescence as a 'natural' stage in human development that represented adolescents as 'savages' and 'barbarians' and the popular white-racist view of colonialism as the necessary imposition of civilisation on 'savages' and 'natives'.

Civilising children, youth and 'coloured subjects' of the empires

Described as a set of governmental and scientific practices, the 'civilizing offensive' directed at children and young people, ran alongside a different 'civilizing offensive' that targeted the coloured subjects of the great European empires. Both these projects were political strategies developed by intellectuals, experts and policy-makers serving western states to prevent degeneracy and the decline of 'civilization' (Mitzman 1987:663–687, van Krieken 1999:297–315). Each produced similar interventions including regulating the use of language, and relying on schooling, and the incarceration of peoples in special protective reserves. In each case the justification was used that as immature, primitive and uncivilised, 'these people' needed protection from those who might manipulate or exploit or generally harm them. For children and young people, this meant their exclusion from various workplaces and streets which progressively became the domain of adult-only activities. For the colonized peoples it meant, amongst other things, being barred from entry into white-only housing, shops, occupations, buses and parks, and being confined to 'coloured' or 'native' reserves.

From 1492 and Columbus' 'discovery' of the Americas, European imperialism was justified by narratives that identified Europeans as the locus of progress and 'civilization' (Fernandez-Armesto 2004, Elias 2012). Eighteenth-century European social, anthropological and biological scientific inquiries were based on 'the need' to explain the obvious 'fact' that Europeans were wealthier, more civilised and more scientifically and technologically sophisticated than people elsewhere. The result was a narrative elaborated by theorists like Montesquieu, Condorcet, Miller, Fergusson, Hume, Steuart, Cordorcet, Kant and Smith.

These pseudo-social sciences drew on evolutionary and developmental metaphors that either highlighted or reworked traditional religious conceptions of a divine order. It was a story that declared everything in the cosmos either had a specific, god-ordained place in the 'great chain of being' and else relied on a new, secular but determinist idea that there was a natural hierarchy of civilisational progress. At the bottom of that natural hierarchy were primitive savage nomads (found, e.g., in Australia and South Africa) while the 'civilized' empires of white Europe were at the top.

This segued into a stadial narrative that referred to stages of 'racial' (human) development in which 'man' evolved from a 'state of nature' characterised as an anarchic, brutish, short and nasty 'war of all against all' into modern 'civilized man' living in 'civil society'. For many new social scientists (in anthropology, sociology and psychology) indigenous people were inferior and much lower down the hierarchical chain of order. Evidence for this was said to lay in their supposed inherent incapacity for abstract and logical thought and moral reasoning. Civilised societies comprised of 'individuals' who were superior to all others. Europeans, it was argued, were exemplars from which all others were evaluated and expected to emulate.

Through this European lens 'natives' were represented as childlike, undeveloped with all the deficiencies and charms of children. It was also anticipated that non-Europeans would sooner or later evolve, adopt civilised practices or 'fade away' (die out). It was a representation that formed part of a larger story to justify imperialist political ambitions and actions that necessitated the subordination of 'the colonised' (Fernandez-Armesto 1997:95). It was a developmental narrative used in a bid to legitimize colonial relationships of domination by mandating 'civilising processes' targeting the 'savage people' which 'enlightened western societies' had a God-given obligation to enact.

It is unclear if many people at the time saw the affinities between this imperialist and racist model of civilisation as a project to socialise 'the native peoples' of the world, and the life-cycle model of human development as it was applied to children and young people. Yet those similarities could be seen in various shared and pervasive metaphors. Children could be 'wild little savages': even today some talk about children and young people as 'digital natives'. At the same time indigenous people in colonial lands like Australia were commonly referred to as children also needing protection. In both cases indigenous people, children and young people needed to know their place and remain there.

Representations of the 'modern child' and later 'the adolescent' as 'lesser humans in the making' were used to validate claims about the intellectual and moral superiority of adults. It was a representation that shaped relations in which the young person was under the authority of adults. It was also a relationship secured through 'the spirit of the new discipline' that included confession, physical punishment and asking children to monitor each other and report on the transgressions and confessions that were used to arouse 'guilt in the hearts of little penitents' (Aries 1962:108). With schools and other child-youth specific sites came a clear divide between the child and adult. Central to this was the idea of children as subordinate in need of supervision and discipline.

For many mid-nineteenth-century intellectuals, the theory of evolution offered in Darwin's *The Origin of Species* (1859) provided the scientific basis for social and political progress. Indeed, the terms 'evolution' and 'progress' were used interchangeably in the nineteenth century (Nisbet 1980). Yet that idea of 'progress' was said to have been continually threatened, namely 'degeneracy'.

As Daniel Pick argued, fear of degeneracy was widespread by the late nineteenth century (1989). And like the older idea of the 'dangerous classes', it was the result of intellectuals working in the human sciences, in bureaucracies, writing literature and journalistic and official reports. Degeneracy was said to explain the continuing increase in everything threatening to 'us'. Moreover, degeneracy could be explained by reference to a biological defect within the individual evident by a weakening of the vital forces of its victim (Gelb 1995). It was also heritable.

Degeneracy was also seen to be based on the idea that lower-classes and inferior (non-white races) were naturally susceptible to neurological pathologies and mental illnesses due to their bad heredity. It was generally believed that these moral and physical pathologies would continue and proliferate across the generations because they were inherited. The eradication of this degeneracy was the key objective of Galton's eugenic project.

Racial fitness: Galton and Eugenics

Francis Galton (1822–1911) was a Quaker gentleman-scientist and cousin to Charles Darwin. He was also a statistician, anthropologist, sociologist, psychologist, geographer, meteorologist, inventor and the person who initiated a global eugenics movement. It was a movement committed to 'good breeding'. That movement, as Galton explained, was built on the:

> …science of improving stock, which is by no means confined to questions of judicious mating, but which, especially in the case of man, takes cognisance of all influences that tend in however remote a degree to give the more suitable races or strains of blood a better chance of prevailing speedily over the less suitable than they otherwise would have had.
>
> *(Galton 1883:25)*

For Galton eugenics was the solution to racial degeneracy. He believed his science of good breeding validated the prevailing race, class and social arrangements. It confirmed the superiority of elite ethnic groups, upper and middle classes, white men all said to be innately talented and biologically advanced. For Galton 'racial fitness' or 'civic worth' corresponded to one's position in the European class hierarchy, with the best genetic specimens found in the upper-middle class. Those considered well-born were nearly always upper-class and of Caucasian or Nordic descent (Black 2003:7). The characteristics that corresponded with what Galton meant by 'racial fitness' included intelligence, virility, sociality and morality. Intelligence was also critical as Galton was preoccupied with intellectual ability (Galton 1978).

Galton drew on Darwin's *The Origin of Species* (1859) to applying these evolutionary ideas to people. While he believed the evolution of our species would occur naturally, Galton thought we could speed and improve the process. Doing that, involved identifying and encouraging our finest stock to breed and discouraging 'degenerates' from reproducing. For eugenicists like Galton, the human race was characterised by innate and limiting differences in intellectual ability. While this was generally accepted by those working in this vector they faced a few scientific challenges: how to identify and then measure intelligence or its degenerate other 'feeblemindedness'.

Galton took on this challenge by initially developing a research project that tried to identify where talented scientists came from. He did this by comparing families, schools and nations. Galton believed individual differences in intellectual ability were biologically determined in exactly the same way that our physical features such as height were influenced (Galton 1978). Galton claimed he detected patterns that revealed a reality that was universal.

The development of research methods designed to collect data to make causal inferences about factors said to shape intellectual ability were in their infancy when Galton began his first investigations. Galton developed his own ways of identifying and measuring relations between certain characteristics of parents and offspring (Stigler 1986). This included amassing large data sets that he then used to develop his ideas. One such data set was a collection of evidence about the heights of parents and children (Galton 1890). He was so impressed with the way it described the distribution of height in England, France and Scotland, that he believed it could also be used to describe the measurement of intellectual ability. As he explained:

> ...if this be the case with stature, then it will be true as regards every other physical feature – as circumference of head, size of brain, weight of grey matter, number of brain fibres, &c. and thence, by a step on which no physiologist will hesitate, as regards mental capacity.
>
> *(Galton 1869:32–33).*

Other eugenic statisticians and psychologists would extend Galton's agenda, focussing on devising methods to prevent 'feeble-mindedness'. Some 'scientific research' also involved measuring the skulls of school children and documenting the facial asymmetry of criminals. Through the early 1900s eugenicists worked to refine what they saw as objective methods of measuring and quantifying valued traits, including intelligence. They did this to substantiate their hypothesis about the genetic advantage of whiteor Nordic people (Gould 1990:29). The English psychologist Charles Spearman published his influential paper that introduced the factor analysis model (1904). Building in part on Galton's early experiments, Spearman concluded that:

> All branches of intellectual activity have in common one fundamental function (or group of functions), whereas the remaining or specific elements of the activity seem in every case to be wholly different from that in all the others.
>
> *(Spearman 1904:284)*

While Spearman's work provided an important step, it was other work carried out in Europe and America that consolidated projects dedicated to constructing a metric of intelligence. The spread of eugenics in Europe, America and around the globe landed on fertile soil.

European social scientists were receptive to eugenics after a theory of progressive inherited degeneracy was first proposed by Morel in 1857 in his book, *Treatise on Degeneracy*. Morel claimed use of 'poisons' like hashish, alcohol and opium resulted in progressive physical and moral deterioration (feeblemindedness). This he argued could be passed across generations resulting in an unfit society. Degeneracy, he also argued, was also passed from generation to generation.

A few decades later the Italian criminologist Cesare Lombroso-Ferrero, 'demonstrated' links between 'degeneracy' and criminality. Lombroso argued that the 'criminal mind' was inherited and could thus be identified by physical features and defects. Lombroso also maintained that criminals were an evolutionary throwback. As Lombroso explained:

> The criminal is an atavistic being, a relic of a vanished race. This is by no means an uncommon occurrence in nature. Atavism, the reversion to a former state, is the first feeble indication of the reaction opposed by nature to the perturbing causes which seek to alter her delicate mechanism.
>
> *(Lombroso-Ferrero 1972:135)*

This theory of the 'hereditary criminal' gave eugenicists a scientific authority needed to control crime and criminals. The solution provided by most of the researchers doing these studies was to separate and halt the reproduction of these 'degenerate' lines, usually through sterilization for the betterment of society (Appleman 2018:425).

In France in 1909 Alfred Binet developed intelligence scale and thus we saw standardized intelligence testing, or 'intelligence testing' said to produce an IQ or 'intelligence quotient'. Binet's scale was said to identify children with developmental disabilities so they could receive extra help in school. The test assigned children a mental age based on a comparison of their skills with those of 'normally functioning' children. American eugenicists, like Henry Goddard and Lawrence Terman were keen to apply this method more generally. This was done in spite of Binet's warning that it was dangerous to extrapolate from his work, and use it to test 'normal' children and adults on a single, linear scale of intelligence, yet that is exactly what occurred (Gould 1990:184–189).

All this came in a context where American writers had already done genealogical studies of supposedly 'degenerate' groups of poor individuals, often falsely characterised as 'inbred' families (Whittaker 2002:41–42). By the early twentieth century American eugenicists were convinced of Galton's 'insights'. For experts like Lawrence Terman, professor at Stanford University, eugenics was good science:

> ...all the available facts that science has to offer support the Galtonian theory that mental abilities are chiefly a matter of original endowment... It is to the highest 25 percent of our population, and more especially to the top 5 percent, that we must look for the production of leaders who will advance science, art, government, education, and social welfare generally... The least intelligent 15 or 20 percent of our population ... are democracy's ballast, not always useless but always a potential liability.
> *(Terman 1922 paper, cited in Minton 1988:99)*

While being aware of Binet's work in France, prominent American psychologists Henry Goddard ignored his warnings against applying the test to normal children. Goddard translated them into English and promoted the widespread use of an amended version to rank 'the feebleminded' into degrees of mental deficiency.[13]

Eugenic ideas also strongly influenced late nineteenth- and early twentieth-century medical practitioners, child-savers, educators and people in the criminal justice and welfare systems. Many medical professionals believed eugenic measures were needed to ensure the survival of a fit population, one able to overcome problems associated with criminality, poverty, unemployment, illness and mental deficiency or 'feeble-mindedness'. It was a set of beliefs that had tragic results not only for many children and young people, but also for those all those people subject to forced sterilization and euthanasia, for people with disabilities, and for the millions of European Jews who were part of 'the final solution'.

Clyde Chitty has traced a link between Galton's eugenic mission and Cyril Burt's work on 'intelligence' and 'delinquency' between the 1920s and 1960s (Chitty 2007). Burt's work also informed the continuing popular belief in the twenty-first century that a child's 'innate intelligence' can be measured accurately.

It is likely that without the eugenics movement, the modern conception of adolescence would not have come into being.

Adolescence and Stanley Hall

As criminologists John Muncie argued, it was the late nineteenth century when the 'concept of adolescence began to affect the children of the working classes'

(Muncie 2009:66). Increasingly 'the adolescent' became associated with negative pathologies mainly because young people were considered to be undisciplined in their families or workplaces (Muncie 2009). Some decades earlier Gillis showed how such (alleged) adolescent attributes like trouble-making, laziness, insolence, and delinquency were regarded by early twentieth-century medical doctors and psychologists as 'natural' features of adolescence, and characteristics shared by all adolescents by virtue of their age (Gillis 1974:114).

For many scholars the idea of adolescence was predominantly an effect of compulsory education (Mucie 2009:67). Schindler had already argued that:

> If, at the start of the modern age, the boundaries between childhood and youth remained flexible, this was mainly because, for most of the population, school was not yet antithetical to the workplace – a contrast to the modern world. It was not until compulsory schooling was instituted in the early twentieth century that the cut off point at age fourteen was adopted....
>
> *(Schindler 1997:245)*

While compulsory schooling played its role in creating the concept of adolescence, so too did moves to regulate child labour, the continued growth of institutions for 'unmanageable working-class youth' and concerns about 'racial hygiene' and national efficiency. Representations of 'the adolescent' again reflect the continuing role of 'intellectuals' in elaborating a social science of urban industrial capitalist societies.

Since the 1970s we have seen a large body of research documenting the activities of intellectuals and allied institutions like schools and universities, the juvenile justice and criminal justice sectors and the welfare and charitable systems in the second half of the nineteenth century (Gillis 1974, 1975, Humphries 1981, Hendrick 1990, Griffin 1993, Davies 1998, 1999, Lesko 2001). That research has highlighted the many ways those intellectual networks were committed to eugenic ideas. One obvious example of this can be seen in the work of the pioneering American psychologist G. Stanley Hall (1905).[14]

Hall was a keen promoter of eugenic ideas and remained so throughout his life. In developing his 'scientific' model of adolescence Hall drew on eugenic theories of race, racial hygiene and evolution, all animated by 'the threat' of social and racial fitness and degeneration. This included his commitment to the belief, shared by many at the time, that whites were naturally superior. It included his support for a recapitulationist model of human development and his belief that class divisions were inherited. Its worldview helps explain his support for mental testing and belief that people should not only be:

> ...tested from childhood on, but assigned his grade, and be assured the place that allows the freest scope for doing the best that is in him... Ranks and classes are inherent in human nature ... and each must accept the

rating that consigns him his true and just place in the hierarchy of the world's work.

(Hall 1922:465)

Hall argued that the existence of 'racially unfit' people (the poor, racial minorities, immigrants) demonstrates to racially fit people (Nordic, wealthy, Whites) the value of recognising 'the problem' of the 'racially unfit' (1917).

While Hall's psychological-biological concept of adolescence had a powerful influence on thinking and practice at the time, his ideas continued to be influential and can be seen in modern psychological studies of adolescence and are prevalent in common-sense representations of adolescence as a risky, troublesome and angst-filled time (Arnett 2006). In short, Hall had a long-lasting influence on the representations of adolescence that continues today.

Hall emphasized the vulnerable and risky nature of a transition that all young people are said to make as they become adult. Adolescence is a stressful and difficult time for the young (male) person, for their family and community. For Hall adolescent development (understood occurring between the ages of 14 and 24) was inherently a time of 'storm and stress' (Lesko 2001). This was because 'the adolescent' had to negotiate the contradictions said to exist between very strong sexual impulses and the social control demanded by parents, churches, schools and broader community.

Hall developed a list of the difficulties and deficits said to be associated with being adolescent. He described it as a time of heightened sensation-seeking.

> At no time of life is the love of excitement so strong as during the season of the accelerated development of adolescence, which craves strong feelings and new sensations, when monotony, routine, and detail are intolerable.
>
> (Hall 1905 vol.1:368)

What today we call risky behaviour Hall saw as 'normal' in adolescence.

> Youth must have excitement, and if this be not at hand in the form of moral and intellectual enthusiasms, it is more prone ... to be sought for in sex or in drink'.
>
> (Hall 1905 vol.2: 74)

It was also a time when we can expect the adolescent to experience depression: 'The curve of despondency starts at eleven, rises steadily and rapidly till fifteen, then falls steadily till twenty three' (Hall 1905:vol. 2:77).

Adolescence was also a time when crime rates peak. 'In all civilized lands, criminal statistics show ... a marked increase in crime at the age of twelve to fourteen, not in crimes of one, but of all kinds, and that this increase continues for a number of years' (Hall 1905 vol. 1:325). Hall also represented 'the adolescent' as valuing their friends or peers more than family: 'some [adolescents] seem for a time to have no resource in themselves, but to be abjectly dependent for their happiness upon their mates' (1905 vol. 1:84). Given all this it is not surprising that Hall defined adolescence in terms of 'normal adolescent turmoil'.[15] As a devout eugenicist, he was particularly concerned about (male) masturbation because it was 'destructive of that perhaps most important thing in the world, the potency of good heredity' (Hall 1905 vol. 1:453).

Given this, strict practices of chastity reinforced and regulated by parents and other responsible adults, was needed to suppress expressions of sexuality, and masturbation in particular. As a good Victorian, Hall believed denial and diversion was required: 'The most rigid chastity of fancy, heart, and body is physiologically and psychologically as well as ethically imperative till maturity is complete on into the twenties' (Hall 1905 vol. 1:437). Promoting chastity required eternal vigilance and a lot of diversion:

> Work reduces temptation and so does early rising… Good music is a moral tonic … [C]old is one of the best of all checks… Cold washing without wiping has special advantages … Pockets should be placed well to the side and not too deep, … while habitually keeping the hands in the pockets should be discouraged … rooms …should not be kept too warm … Beds should be rather hard and the covering should be light.
> *(Hall 1905 vol. 1:465–469)*

Hall's idea was that if the adolescent's disposition to unregulated and immature emotional expression (e.g., sexual expression, anger, amorality, laziness or being seduced into drinking alcohol or smoking tobacco) were unregulated then the young person is unlikely to make a successful transition into adulthood. The key task was to identify markers that signified progress or regression along the risky rickety path to responsible adulthood.

This scientific model of 'the adolescent' also built on the foundations of earlier ideas of the child as vulnerable and needing protection. Adolescence was a transitional 'path' between the dependent, naïve, innocent state of childhood, and the independent, autonomous, rational disciplined and fully cognitively developed adulthood. Adolescence was an extension of childish dependence represented as intrinsically insecure, transitional, full of uncertainty, inherently risky and problematic. Much of this could be explained by the hormonal and sexual development said to make 'adolescence' an inherently agonistic and difficult time so much so it required continual vigilance, close observation and management (Hall 1905).

Recapitulation: transitions from barbarism to civilisation

For Hall adolescence could be explained by reference to the evolutionary history of humanity described by a theory of recapitulation. This idea of recapitulation was then a widespread scientific model among evolutionary theorists. Hall drew on nineteenth-century evolutionary thinkers including Ernst Haeckel and Francis Galton. This was the idea that the biological development of each individual recapitulates the history of the whole species. The theory of recapitulation proposed that the development of the embryo of an animal from conception to birth went through stages resembling, or representing successive adult stages in the evolution of the animal's remote ancestors.

Hall believed, 'The best of us carry a heavy handicap of biological sin from our ancestors' (Hall 1905 vol. 2:353). That is, because memories and experiences are inherited, we have remnants of the tiger, wolf, ape, and other beasts still in our nature. He believed that evolution provided us with the proper way of understanding how children and adolescents should be educated. Each 'stage' in individual's development was said to be a repeat a stage in the evolutionary drama. As the child, the adolescent and youth developed they passed through the same stages the entire race or species did, from primitive savages to civilised Europeans also meant young people, like 'natives' were 'naturally' close to nature. The infant corresponded to the animal with their inclinations towards hunting and shelter-building, play, corresponding in human evolution to the cave-dweller. The adolescent corresponded to human life in the "barbaric" stage of human history. The state of adulthood constituted evolution's latest normative achievement: civilised, i.e., white, Anglo-saxon or Nordic man.

This is why the dramatic biological and psychological changes of adolescence recapitulated an active and challenging period in the human past. For this reason it was a mistake to keep adolescents cooped up in a classroom all day. Rather they would learn best if their learning involved active engagement with their environment. Adolescents

> ...who have pets, till the soil, build, manufacture, use tools, and master elementary processes and skills, are most truly repeating the history of the race. This, too, lays the best foundation for intellectual careers.
> *(Hall 1905 vol. 1:174)*

Given all this the figure of the adolescent was seen as standing on the threshold of 'civilised' humanity represented by adults. Each new generation and each individual carried with them the task of making the transition from barbarism to civilisation. The 'adolescent stage' was particularly difficult, fraught with danger, as the barbarism that marked that 'phase' was overcome so the adolescent brought forth renewed hope for civilisation and regeneration (Hall 1905). In this way youth was (is) a figure of ambivalence: each young person is both the source of hope and regeneration and at the same time inherently mischievous and source of degeneration and loss of civilisation.

As a eugenicist Hall argued that the quality of a race could be improved by using a scientific approach to breeding and other social reforms. Racial fitness and racial decline were principal concerns. For these reasons the proper development of the child and adolescent was critical for those interested in securing a successful racial project. The child and youth-as-savage, with instinctive love of fishing, hunting and other outdoor activities raised questions for modern societies about how to direct their natural instincts for the greatest benefit of the young person, the race and society (Hall 1905:x–xi). Thus, they needed close governance to tame their 'primitive instincts' and to safely guide their transition along a rickety but clearly demarcated developmental path to civilisation and adulthood.

Conclusion

Representations of children ('childhood') and of young people ('youth') through the nineteenth century were shaped by on-going debates about the significance and meaning of the French revolution. The final defeat of Napoleon at Waterloo in 1814 triggered continuing attempts to restore the 'old order' in Europe. These efforts were a reaction against the original democratic conception of citizenship advocated by artisans, workers and peasant groups in Paris and gathered into the democratic program by the Jacobins.

Besides restoring monarchies and the authority of the church, the counter-revolution after 1815 was a victory that was achieved in part by middle-class intellectuals and professionals who consolidated their political, cultural and symbolic status around the theme of social order. In doing so they emphasised the threats to the 'natural' hierarchical social order and 'civilization' posed by the 'dangerous-classes'. Children of the 'dangerous classes' attracted much attention in the processes of 'discovering' the 'dangerous classes'. Yet the older idea that children and young people were also a threat and members of the dangerous classes because they were inherently little devils and depraved endured, themes developed and elaborated in a burgeoning literature on juvenile delinquents.

One result of all this was an on-going 'civilizing offensive' that targeted young people in general and in particular 'slum children', 'pauper children', 'delinquents' and 'juvenile offenders' (Mitzman 1987). It was a 'civilizing offensive' in which 'child-savers' and flourishing expert networks worked in slowly but continuously excluding young people from what became adult space by establishing child and youth only institutions like kindergartens, compulsory schools, reformatories and children's courts, child-specific, toys, literature and leisure activities. Progressively, governments across the globe introduced policies and legislation intended to deter and prevent children and young people from engaging in adult activities like paid labour and political life.

By the end of the nineteenth century a new hegemonic science of eugenics emerged. Galton's eugenic enterprise and Hall's representation of adolescence as a transitional agonistic and rebellious stage in the life-cycle became the new common sense for both conservative and progressive reformers, for public health, town planners and legal and medical experts across the globe. Galton and his colleagues developed influential research technologies or instruments to provide the 'objective' measures needed to define and measure things such as 'intelligence' and 'racial fitness' (Gould 1996).

That measurement-centred scientific account described the human 'life-cycle' with inevitable and unavoidable 'stages of development' was promoted by eugenicists like Galton, Binet, Burt and so forth contributed to a science of 'childhood' and 'adolescence'.

It secured and nourished a new consensus that 'childhood', 'youth' and 'adolescence' were distinct age-based stages in a universal model of human development. The main idea was that children or young people could be defined by what they were not (e.g., adults), or by what they lacked. Children, adolescents and youth shared in common the fact they were in different ways not fully developed and thus unable to make decisions about substantive matters and thus could not be taken seriously, amongst other things, as political actors.

The tropes used in representing children and young people were striking similar to dominant imperial and colonial narratives about 'race', 'savagery' and 'civilisation'. Parallels were drawn between the scientific racist anthropological narratives linking 'race' and 'civilization' (Stepan 1982, Loring 2005, Wardley 2019). The similarities imagined to exist between 'black savages' and 'juvenile savages' were seductive.

It was a view that was subsequently codified by modern sciences like developmental psychology, and some areas of education, youth studies and the sociology of youth. When represented as incompetent or deficient, children and young people were deemed to be naive and vulnerable, needing protection from 'the adult world'. Whether as innocents or as threats, children and young people needed close surveillance, discipline and regulation if they were to be tamed and prevented from harming themselves and others. As I demonstrate in the next chapter, this representation continued into the 1950s as many young people continued to push back.

Notes

1 As Holt notes, Brace did not invent this model. The practice of removing convicts and poor people from cities was not a new. Germany had a system known as 'The Friends in Need' that placed poor city children in the homes of rural families. The British system of 'transportation' also involved removal of these undesirables from Britain during the eighteenth century first to North America and later Australia (Holt 1992:44–45).
2 The 1830 uprising in Paris saw the left briefly seize central power. As Wallerstein argues, it was an uprising that '…was unexpected by most people – a happy surprise for the working class, and a serious danger from the point of view of the elites' (Wallerstein 2014:159). The resulting overthrow of King Louis-Philippe and a series of subsequent popular insurrection however culminated in the restoration of a kind of plebiscitary monarch, Napoleon III (1854–1870).
3 For example, by those wanting the unification of Germany and Italy or secession by Serbs, Czechs and the Irish.
4 Eyal also highlights the importance of the Young America movement in the USA (2007).

Civilising little savages and dangerous classes **121**

5   Garibaldi joined the movement around 1833.
6   While some historians represent the Risorgimento as the victory of liberalism, more recent historians see it as an aristocratic and bourgeois revolution that failed to include the masses. In di Lampedusa's Italian novel *The Leopard* the Prince of Lampedusa details the strategies designed to prevent change that were used by supporters of the Risorgimento, namely that 'everything must change so that nothing need change'.
7   Le Bon (2009: 7) argued that:

> History tells us, that from the moment when the moral forces on which a civilisation rested have lost their strength, its final dissolution is brought about by those unconscious and brutal crowds known, justifiably enough, as barbarians. Civilisations as yet have only been created and directed by a small intellectual aristocracy, never by crowds. Crowds are only powerful for destruction. Their rule is always tantamount to a barbarian phase. A civilisation involves fixed rules, discipline, a passing from the instinctive to the rational state, forethought for the future, an elevated degree of culture – all of them conditions that crowds, left to themselves, have invariably shown themselves incapable of realising. In consequence of the purely destructive nature of their power crowds act like those microbes which hasten the dissolution of enfeebled or dead bodies.

8   Heather Shore (2011) argues that Pearson's *Hooligan: A History of Respectable Fears* was the most important contribution to this idea of hooliganism as an invention linked to the notion of 'social fears', in terms articulated by Cohen's *Folk Devils and Moral Panics*.
9   The Whig government weakened this last provision by substituting 'thirteen in place of eighteen'.
10 The number convicted as 'known or reputed thieves' rose from 29% of all convictions in that category in 1838 to 36% in 1845 (Eade 1975:431).
11 This arrangement became systematic with the passage of the *Reformatory and Industrial Schools Acts* of 1854 which led to the establishment of many new reformatory schools.
12 This is not to deny the importance of nineteenth-century sceptics including Jacob Burckhardt, Friedrich Arthur Schopenhauer and Friedrich Nietzsche who rejected the Whig interpretation.
13 This included idiots (pre-verbal), imbeciles (illiterate) and morons (high-functioning), Morons, or those with mental ages of eight to twelve, presented the most serious eugenic threat because they could pass for being normal and reproduce. Goddard found morons everywhere: criminals, alcoholics, prostitutes and anyone 'incapable of adapting themselves to their environment and living up to the conventions of society or acting sensibly'. When New York City allowed Goddard to test thousands of public schools, he identified over 15,000 'feeble-minded' schoolchildren recommending their forced segregation and sterilization (Gould 196:191).
14 Hall is generally recognised as having established modern American psychology. He worked at Johns Hopkins University Hall and was the first president of the American Psychological Association and established the *American Journal of Psychology* in 1887 (Ludy 2007:66–68).
15 Added to this was the issue of sex, always a taboo subject when associated with young people. Hall accepted certain myths about masturbation like the idea it led to 'Neurasthenia … optical cramps … weak sluggishness of heart action … purple and dry skin … anaemic complexion, dry cough, and many digestive perversions can be attributed to this scourge of the human race' (Hall 1905 vol. 1:443). I Masturbation was also said to cause dwarfed and stunted growth. 'There are early physical signs of decrepitude and senescence. Gray hair, and baldness, a stooping and enfeebled gait…' (Hall 1905. vol. 1:444).

5

GIRLS POLITICS AND DELINQUENCY IN THE 1950S

A young man known as 'Graham' who lived in a working-class suburb of Melbourne Australia witnessed something in 1957 that he didn't expect to see. Graham who described himself as a bodgie, the Australian equivalent of an American 'zoot-suiter' or an English 'Teddy boy'. Some decades later he recalled that moment. It was the first time he saw some young girls who called themselves a 'widgie' in a full fight:

> ...they went in boots and all, knives, the whole flaming lot. There was nothing worse than seeing a couple of widgies into it, they really went at it hammer and tongs... Scratching and tearing at one another's faces with their nails. You've never seen anything like it in your life... It was really shocking.
>
> *(Graham W, Cited in Stratton: 1992:100)*

For Graham it was a 'discovery'. Given the repeated nature of such public spectacles, it was not surprising that many other Australians in the 1950s thought they were discovering a 'epidemic of juvenile delinquency' personified by these widgies and bodgies. The question is however what was exactly discovered? If we want a clear understanding of what is happening it helps to consider how such discovery processes come about and in whose interest in the discovery (Harrington 1962, Abel-Smith and Townsend 1965).

There are good reasons for scepticism about the long-dominant empiricist account of how such social problems are discovered. Without denying the existence of real social problems in the world, to which the attention of reformers, government officials and politicians are constantly being drawn by empirical researchers, we do not have to accept that a problem like 'delinquency' was only discovered in the 1950s: delinquency did not suddenly appear just or only then.

As I suggested in Chapter 1, there are real events and happenings taking place that provide the basis for accounts offered by experts and the professionally trained about what certain kinds of young people are doing and why. Those accounts rely on what Moscovici (1981) and Bourdieu (1984) referred to as representations. In Chapters 3 and 4, I argued the French revolution and the counter-revolution in Europe after 1815 helped set in motion a 'civilising offensive' that targeted young people deemed to be part of the 'dangerous classes'. The result was the expulsion of children and young people from what came to be adult-only settings and practices.

While the saying that the 'more things change, the more they stay the same' is true enough, we need to consider the new historical conjuncture emerging in the first half of the twentieth century. It was defined by experiences of war and extended economic disruption, reshaping how young people were represented in the second half of the twentieth century.

Young people and post-war affluence

The first half of the twentieth century was marked by two wars (1914–18 and 1939–45) waged with unprecedented intensity on an horrific scale. Added to this were numerous smaller civil and international conflicts in Russia (1919–21), Spain (1936–38), the Middle-East, China (1920–49) and Africa. The two 'great' wars were global in scale and resulted in an unprecedented scale of military and civilian bloodshed. By 1945, over 100 million people were killed, half of them civilians, while the destruction of cities, empires and ways of life took on a similarly epic quality (Leitenberg 2006:9). The two world wars were the result of antagonistic political imaginaries informed by illusions of national and 'racial' identity and by dreams of empire and imperial grandeur (Baker 2008, Macmillan 2013).

To this we can add the unprecedented economic and social disruption caused by the Great Depression which began in 1929 when global commodity prices crashed. Most governments slashed budgets, while employers laid off workers by the millions: mass unemployment and poverty disrupted the lives of tens of millions of workers and families around the world until the onset of total war restored full-employment after 1939 (Tooze 2015). This was because the onset of 'total war' after 1939 impelled governments everywhere to draw on the expertise of economists to design new, Keynesian-style forms of state intervention using mass income taxation to fund the extension of educational, health and welfare systems in what is conventionally referred to as the 'welfare state'. In the post-war period, the combination of new domestic policies, bottled-up consumer demand and novel forms of international co-operation, like the regulation of currencies and trade created the 'Long Boom' of 1945–75.

Because international relations in the late 1940s and 1950swere predominantly imagined as a conflict between democracy and communism, global politics was fraught, generating continuing military and diplomatic conflict especially in Asia and Africa as well as decades of 'Cold War'. Domestically, the post-war boom in countries like America, Britain, and Australia meant 'working people' enjoyed the fruits of full (male) employment. The emergent 'Fordist economy' facilitated by rising wages provided for many affordable housing, an increasing consumer goods and new forms of popular leisure (e.g., television, entertainment and sport) (Jessop 1992:48).[1]

As the post-war boom took off in the late 1940s, young people were among the many who enjoyed the benefits of what Kenneth Galbraith (1958) later called the 'Affluent Society'. During this period the figure of the 'teenager' also got traction in popular commentary and academic social science research (Frith 1986:9). Contemporary commentators argued that full-employment and regular wages meant young people had greater access to commodities and leisure like 'coffee and milk bars, fashion clothes and hairstyles, cosmetics, rock 'n roll, films and magazines, scooters and motorbikes, dancing and dance halls' (Abrams 1959). Subsequently scholars argued that a variety of socio-economic factors in the late 1940s and 1950s changed the expectations and patterns of consumption, previously out of reach for earlier generations of young people, especially working-class young people (Stratton 1992, Muggleton 2005, Savage 2007).

While the intention of sociologists or cultural studies scholars may have been to inquire into the lives of young people, our capacity to see what young people were doing and how they saw themselves is often obscured. Rather than offering 'thick' or 'rich descriptions' of how these young people (e.g., widgies and bodgies) were living, the interest of many scholars is in explaining them. As anthropologists like Geertz (1973) and Latour (1984, 2001) argue, the desire to 'explain' human activities typically relies on a process of reduction that involves moving away from the granular detail of the human action and context that actually characterise our lives.

Reductionism involves explaining a given phenomenon either by treating it as a subset of some larger reality or by explaining it as the result of some of its subcomponents.

We can take the 'going up' option by arguing that an event or a social practice (e.g., playing certain kinds of music) is best explained by reference to some larger entity. For example, the fact a young person is listening to music is 'explained' as the result of 'society', 'capitalism', 'or 'modernity'. It might, e.g., be argued that when that young person is playing music ona device, he is acting as any consumer acts in any capitalist economy. In this way, a large entity or 'structure' (capitalism) is used to explain certain smaller-scale actions or events like the young person listening to music on their iPhone.

Reductionism can also take a going 'down' form. If the young person is listening to some music, reductionism on the part of the researcher can be seen when they ask what elements in that particular young person's makeup explains why they are acting as they are. This explanatory reductionism involves identifying a smaller sub-element in the individual young person (or group) such as their genetic make up, or as an emotional impulse. In this case, it might be argued that Joe is being driven by an emotional impulse (e.g., excitement, happiness, or sadness).

This practice of reductionism is what academics and experts do when they represent young people by talking about 'youth culture', or particular 'sub-cultures' such as Australia's and New Zealand's widgies and bodgies, or England's 'Teddy boys'. The meaning is explained as something determined by 'structures' like class, gender, or ethnicity or from the attributes of historical periods like 'modernity' or macro-formations such as 'Fordist society' or 'capitalism'. This can be seen, e.g., when Stratton (1989) explains the relationship between bodgies and widgies and rock 'n roll:

> The linkage of pleasure and consumption is to be found in the articulation of youth as a new and active category during the post-war period... Youth ... displaced class in popular mythology. This displacement replicated the shift from a production economy to a consumption economy. The myth of youth was a generative moment in the articulation of consumerism. Youth was constituted as an alterity but was also embedded within the social order as part of it.
>
> *(Stratton 1989:43)*

The scholarly practice of reductionism involves using various theoretical approaches to interpret the life-worlds and experiences of young people in ways that have the effect of obscuring what is actually happening.

Either way of reducing, i.e., 'going up' or 'going down', takes us away from focussing on the particular qualities and complex existence of what is being studied (e.g., a young person listening to music). Either way the reductive process means many of the important elements of what is really going on are lost.

Paying attention to the lives of young people by providing 'thick descriptions' of what they are doing, who they are doing it with what they are doing it with and how their context is understood by that young person is likely to give us our best chance of understand what is actually happening.

We might discover, e.g., that the practice of listening to music involves, e.g., a prior historical process of learning what music is and finding out what kinds of music they like, something often done in the company of other people. It would also require access to and knowledge about how to operate the technologies of the day. It would also entail establishing how the person in question acquired and practised the skills needed to use the technologies and other complex abilities involved in listening to music, and how they acquired the capacity to enjoy the complex, embodied sensations and emotions evoked by music and activities such as dancing. Importantly paying attention to the details of human actions, to the context and how those who are being researched interpret what they are doing and their world, can provide valuable insight into their life-worlds. It can provide accounts of 'what is happening' that are quite different from those of the 'objective' observer-researcher.

The practice by researchers 'writing over' the experience and meaning of the people being studied, in this case, young people, has a long history. It can be seen in the ways many sociologists, social theorists and other social scientists work. We might think, e.g., of Parsons and Merton's structural-functionalist account of social order in which being young meant 'being deviant'. It is what happens when neo-Marxists like Stuart Hall, Tony Jefferson (1976) and Mike Brake (1980) from the Birmingham School of Cultural Studies treat working-class heroes and 'youth cultures' as 'resistance' to 'hegemonic' social control. And for some post-modernists this practice can mean that the life-world of young people completely disappear.

The case of Australia's widgies and bodgies of the 1940s and 1950s highlights the *gap* that exists between how young people have been represented and what they were actually doing, their lived experience, or how they interpreted their actions and the world around them. Widgies and Bodgies were real, especially to themselves, to their families and to their communities as they acted in ways that often challenged traditional established ways of living in long-established age- and gender-based relations. Widgies and bodgies were real but in quite different ways to how various experts and journalists who represented them as a particular kind of 'problem youth' (Bessant and Watts 1998:189–220).

So how can the lives of these young people best be understood? How were they variously represented in the late 1940s and early 1950s? Why were particular young women in Australia and New Zealand represented as evidence of an epidemic of 'juvenile delinquency' and a 'youth culture'?

In this chapter, I consider the experiences of young women known as 'widgies', how they represented themselves and how they were represented by others.

In doing this I note the difference or the gap that often exists between how researchers and experts represented young people and the lived experiences of those people and how they represented themselves. Why does that gap exist?

One answer is that scholars and experts are trained to think about the world and engage in research using what Danziger referred to as constructive schemes (1990). Constructive schemes use specialist vocabularies and rely on assumptions about the nature of reality and how we can know that reality. Specific questions, e.g., are asked which helps define 'sociology' or 'economics' and to demarcate boundaries between disciplines. Bourdieu made this observation when he referred to the scholarly habitus in particular fields of practice like political science, anthropology or sociology. It is likely that the habitus of a sociologist, which is different from the habitus of a psychologist or an anthropologist, will make a certain field of vision possible, one that only sees a small part of what happening because that is what being a sociologist is about, and is also what other sociologists expect. Other matters are best left to economists anthropologists or neurologists.

Another answer to why a gap exists between the ways researchers and experts represented young people and how they lived their lives, relates to what Heffernan describes 'wilful blindness' and what others call ignorance[2] (Sullivan and Tuana 2007, Heffernan 2013). According to these scholars 'wilful blindness' is more than an absence of knowledge. It is a deliberate preference not to know, a desire to be unaware, (or at least to claim to be) in the face of 'uncomfortable knowledge'. It is a strategy we often use to protect ourselves and certain interests when it is too difficult to acknowledge and see what is actuallygoing on in front of us. This also works to secure the privilege of certain social, political or economic groups and to keep certain people in subordinate positions. This disposition is implicated in reproducing the positional power and superior access to capitals like economic, symbolic and intellectual capital (Heffernan 2011, see also Taleb 2007).

In short while academics are meant to be experts in scholarship, research or constructing theories, they are, like all of us, likely to be wilfully blind. This can be seen, e.g., if we consider how some scholars represented young people as members of 'youth cultures'. In the 1950s in America and Britain those working in the social sciences tended to see 'youth' as central conceptual category in their respective disciplines, but did so in ways that ignored 'class', and as McRobbie noted later also being blind to gender.

Feminist scholars have argued, those working in the sociology of youth and 'youth culture' studies focussed almost exclusively on boys and young men and assumed 'youth cultures' essentially expressed male interests and needs (McRobbie 1980:37–49, 1991). As Stratton argued:

> In the history of working-class youth styles from the mid-nineteenth century on, it was always the males who formed the image. Both hooligan and larrikins were males.... McRobbie and Garber... point to the question of whether girls have really been absent from youth cultures or whether their presence has simply not been acknowledged... They go on to suggest that in later youth cultures girls occupy an increasingly large space though they have, nevertheless, remained invisible. This is correct.
>
> *(Stratton 1992:97)*

Thanks to McRobbie and other scholars like her, it is now generally acknowledged that key representations of 'the adolescent', 'the young criminal', 'the delinquent', 'the hooligan', or 'larrikin' presented a heavily masculine model.

While acknowledging all that, in writing this chapter I am presented with one problem.

I do not and will never have direct or immediate access to the actual lives of the widgies as they lived in the 1950s. Unlike ethnography, which involves researchers participating directly in the lives and activities of the people being researched (e.g., through participant observation, interviews and other experiential forms of research), historical ethnography of the kind offered here is quite different. It is an approach that draws on imperfect memory, sedimented into narratives, and supplemented by primary source materials like letters, photographs, and so on, as well as resources like newspaper reports or police and other official documents.[3]

This chapter attempts an inquiry into the lives of young women and girls and various representations of them. I identify particular gendered representations involved in the constitution of the 'widgie' represented by outsiders as young 'female delinquents' or as 'wayward girls'. I ask how some of those young women represented themselves, how they variously responded to representations of them coming from experts by, e.g., 'answering back' and resisting those depictions. I begin with a light sketch of the life-world of young widgies before considering how widgies and their male counterparts (bodgies), came to represent the problem of 'youthful delinquency' in Australia in the 1950s.

Widgies and bodgies

Widgies and bodgies were a phenomenon of the 1950s. It was a view exemplified when the South Australia Police Historical Society remembered 1953 as the year when:

> ...the Bodgie-Widgie cult hit South Australia ... [its members] indulging in acts of free groupie (sic) sex and perversion. Ages ranged between 13 and 17 years and members of gangs could be easily identified, with bodgies wearing very tight dark coloured stove pipe trousers, suede shoes, two-tone pullovers and long greasy hair. Widgies wore black tight skirts, skin-tight sweaters and had push back 'widgie' hair cuts. These gangs became known by names such as *The Saints, The Eagles, Vampires* and the *Black Dominoes* and based their behaviour on their American counterparts.
> *(South Australia Police Historical Society, 2005)*

While the widgies and bodgies did become increasingly visible in the 1950s, their origins can be traced back to Sydney, 1942 and especially to Kings Cross, an inner-urban part of Sydney.[4] There was a well-developed, vibrant street culture in King's Cross a space close to where American sailors docked during the Pacific war at Sydney wharves in Woolloomooloo. 'The Cross' had a reputation as a 'sordid' space where public displays of 'unconventionality' were the norm. In this way it was somewhat like London's Soho, Paris' Montmartre or New York's Greenwich Village- in that the lower than average cost of housing attracted both 'decent' working-class families, as well as sex workers, petty criminals, recently arrived immigrants and bohemian academics, writers and artists (Souter 1968:68). When Australia was swept into the Pacific war in late 1941 it was an easy walk for the newly-arrived American sailors to Sydney from the docks up to the milk bars, hamburger 'diners', brothels and bars at Kings Cross.

Large numbers of US servicemen who began arriving in 1942 enhanced the liveliness of Sydney's Kings Cross. Young local people began interacting with and often imitating American servicemen in the numerous bars and brothels or trading in the black market selling alcohol, tobacco or clothing that emerged to circumvent war-time rationing (Bessant and Watts 1998:189–220).

The widgie bodgie style took off in 1942 when some young locals realised that pretending to be American sailors when selling black market goods enhanced the marketability of those goods. John McDonald (1951) who wrote the first social scientific study of widgies and bodgies, recalled how in 1942 some young men formed groups like 'Burts' Boys' (named after a popular American milk-bar in King's Cross) and became 'Bodgie dealers'[5]:

> ...There was a great shortage of cloth during and after World War II; the gap was partly filled by a black market in textiles from America which could be bought around the Cross. These American materials fetched higher prices than the Australian article. So black-marketeers sold Australian cloth as American cloth and to add to the pretence, said they were American seamen. Since the Darlinghurst jargon for 'spurious, phoney, low quality and such' was 'bodgie' or 'bodger' these were called 'bodgie dealers'.
>
> (McDonald, 1951:4–5)[6]

By the late 1940s, bodgie and widgie groups also appeared on Sydney's famous beaches and cafes at North Bondi.

According to Clem Gorman, a bodgie living in Perth in the 1950s, the bodgie style was appropriated in the 1940s from African-American servicemen drawn to Kings Cross and Surry Hills (2015).[7] Young men like Val Squires, living in Sydney during the 1940s recalled going to dance halls, milk bars and private parties where black Americans joined in the fun and where jazz records were played. Young Sydney men purchased clothing, like drape jackets, from African-American servicemen on leave in Sydney (Gorman 2015). These young Australians also thought the African-American sailors and soldier's music, dance, clothes and the way they talked were 'cool' and worth emulating (Gorman 2015:7).

While this is some of what is known about bodgies, less is known of 'widgies' and where they came from. Sometime in the late 1940s girls who sometimes 'hung about' with bodgies became known as widgies.[8] The name 'widgie' may have had less pejorative origins than the bodgies association with black market. One possibility is that it was an abbreviation for 'wigeon' meaning girl or female teenager used in Australia in 1946 (Stratton 1992:71, 96). Another possibility is that it morphed from the words for 'ride' or 'horse' originating in Old English '*wig*', or '*wigge*', from Old English *wicġ*, or the Germanic '*wigją*', from Indo-European '*weģ*'- (to carry, move, transport, ride). This may imply a sexualised understanding of the widgie.

The following description by a local Sydney based police officer in 1955 gives a flavour of their dress style. A widgie, he explained:

> ...is generally dressed in a very tight blouse mostly without sleeves, and generally with a very deep plunging front. The blouse closely conforms to the lines of the body. In addition she has a very form fitting skirt which is very tight especially around the knees. The skirt flairs out a little below the knees and generally has a split at the side or at the rear to enable her to walk. A widgie wears a short-cropped haircut.
> (Sydney Morning Herald, *11 February 1955*)

For young women like Joy, being a widgie, which was how she described herself, was 'sexy and exciting' and entailed rejecting older 'yukky' styles of dress. She recalled her pleasure in being a widgie:

> It was a real opportunity I can tell you. We had all sorts of terribly twee skirts and dresses which my mother and her sister wanted me to wear and I wouldn't touch them... They were kind of Doris Day style ... Yuk!... the widgie gear was really exciting and a bit of a turn on. I felt really sexy in that gear.
> *(Joy Interview December 1992)*

The great excitement that came with flagrantly defying such dress standards was one of the most rewarding experiences for some widgies:

> Sometimes I went to dances and most young women would wear the big starched dresses. I was never into that. I always wanted to be the toughest of the roughest of the widgies.
> *(Bev Interview, March 1993)*

What seems clear is that widgies and bodgies began spreading slowly out of Kings Cross, Sydney after 1942–45 into similar precincts in other Australian cities like St Kilda in Melbourne or Northbridge in Perth. Their style became popular, especially in working-class suburbs. What is clear is that whatever widgies and bodgies were doing, or whatever they thought they were doing, seemed to matter much less than what others believed they were doing. By 1955–1956, the result of this was what Cohen would call a 'moral panic' about a 'bodgie and widgie epidemic' of 'juvenile delinquency' (Cohen 1979). Or more accurate we saw a 'moral panic' about the bodgies, in which widgies were nearly erased.

Moral panic and delinquents

Stanley Cohen's account of moral panics and folk devils involved an investigation into the sudden and intense way that Britain's media reported some violent clashes between groups of mods and rockers on a bank holiday in Brighton, England in 1964 (1972). Cohen examined newspaper coverage of the events identifying patterns of distorted facts, exaggeration, fabrication and misrepresentations.

Cohen's account of 'moral panics' showed how the press created representations of mods and rockers as 'folk devils'. This involves highlighting particular types of people and events engaging in 'deviant behaviour' (e.g., drug use, football hooliganism, vandalism, political demonstrations, or public violence) and on particular kinds of people or 'social types' – in his case the mods and rockers.

The process of representing folk devils involved practices like symbolisation where the 'folk devil' is portrayed using a single narrative, in which features like their appearance and identity are oversimplified so they can be easily recognized. It also involved exaggerating the facts of the event or even fabricating them.

In short, 'moral panics' involve much more than reporting an event: they are characterised by media exaggeration and 'over-reporting' a situation that then provides a reason for punitive responses that target the 'folk devil'. They are responses prompted by anxiety, fear and fantasies about 'folk devils'. According to Cohen, a 'moral panic' is what you get when the following happens:

> A condition, episode, person or groups of persons emerges to become defined as a threat to societal values and interests; its nature is presented in a stylised and stereotypical fashion by the mass media; the moral barricades are manned by editors, bishops, politicians and other right thinking people; socially accredited experts pronounce their diagnoses and solutions, ways of coping are evolved or more often resorted to; the condition then disappears, submerges or deteriorates and becomes more visible.
>
> *(Cohen 1972:30)*

Australian press reports on incidences of public violence by the bodgies and widgies and the introduction of American rock and roll in 1955–56 were the main ingredients in the 'moral panic' that emerged.

According to the Australia press, in the early 1950s, the bodgies and widgies were a barely recognizable or newsworthy. The frequency of newspaper reports about juvenile delinquency and bad behaviour by juveniles, was relatively low up to the mid-1950s, averaging one report every two weeks. The Melbourne *Herald* reported that St Kilda police issued a 'declaration of war' against a local 'bodgie gang' in December 1951 (Melbourne *Herald*, 4 December 1951). In November 1952, the Melbourne *Sun* reported on 200 bodgies and widgie clashes with police in a Swanston Street milk-bar (*Sun News-Pictorial*, 17 November 1952). Through 1950–1, one or two reports a week were published in crimes committed by young people, that involved theft, burglary, illegal use of cars, arson, knifings and gun-use, implicating young people. There were also some months when no such reports appeared.

Reference to clothes as a symbolic marker sometimes featured in reports on widgies and bodgies. In September 1951, the *Sun News-Pictorial* described 'two young men dressed as bodgies, bashed a Redfern doctor at his surgery ... and bound and robbed him' (*Sun News-Pictorial* 21 September 1952). One eyewitness reported the young men 'were well dressed but like American gangsters' (*Sun News-Pictorial* 21 September 1952). In November 1952, the *Sun News-Pictorial* reported how the Children's Court was told that Melbourne's 'estimated 150 bodgies and widgies' were 'not criminal types', and that 'the bodgie and widgie today were a mild form of exhibitionism' compared with the 'grey caps' and the 'crutchy gangs' of some years ago (*Sun News-Pictorial* 22 November 1952). To the extent that bodgies and widgies were acknowledged in the early 1950s, 'experts' seemed to place into the general category of delinquents. Thus G.S. Berrigan, a solicitor arguing on behalf of a young client charged with theft, claimed that- in spite of three prior convictions – the young man had never been 'in trouble until he got into the bad company of people of a quasi-criminal type – bodgies and widgies (*Sun News-Pictorial* 1 May 1952).

The tempo of reporting began to quicken in 1954–55. Through 1954 and the first months of 1955 the frequency of reports in Melbourne's largest selling newspaper (the *Sun News-Pictorial*) on teenage crime or young people and their tendency to be trouble-makers averaged eight reports per month. May–June 1955 saw an increase in the incidence of press reports about juvenile delinquency. By May–June 1955, the reporting increased significantly on average at one report per day. By the end of 1955, bodgies and widgies had been absorbed into the categories of 'teenage crime' and 'teenage anti-social' behaviours as readers were informed about how 'Bodgie gangs fought in Melbourne's streets' (*Sun News Pictorial*, 12 February 1955).

The Sydney press also ran with headlines like: 'Youth Delinquency Remains Grave Problem In Sydney', 'Bodgie Brawl', 'Gangs Of Bodgies In Crime Wave' and 'Bodgie Street Battle' (*Sydney Morning Herald* 18 January 1955, *Sun-Herald*, 18 January 1955; *Sunday Truth*, 29 April 1956; *Sunday Truth*, 17 June 1956 and 16 June 1957).

In April 1955, police and magistrates in South Australia declared they 'would stamp out bodgie gangs' (*Sun News Pictorial,* 9 April 1955). In December 1955 readers of the Sydney Daily Mirror read stories with the headline 'Bodgie "Saints" come Marching in', with dire reports warning of an impending 'epidemic of delinquency', from 'concerned professionals' predicting, 'a complete breakdown in the morals of those who come in contact with it'. The reason?

> [In Wagga Wagga] during the past few weeks representatives of a group of Sydney bodgies known as 'The Saints' have visited Wagga to recruit

members for a branch here. Some youths in the town claim bodgies have already initiated a number of Wagga girls in immoral rites.

(Sydney Daily Mirror, 16 December 1955)

Central to the construction of the bodgie and widgie panic were stereotypes and symbols used to simplify the representation of these young people's deviant status. The words 'bodgie' and 'widgie' themselves became linguistic markers, and identical with 'delinquency' itself and signifying membership in aggressive or violent gangs. As the *Sydney Morning Herald* put it: 'What is a bodgie? During the present wave of juvenile violence, the word has come to mean "juvenile delinquent"' (*Sydney Morning Herald*, 29 January 1956).

Particular objects and fashions like hairstyles, clothing and jewellery became symbolic markers of delinquency. The ducktail hairstyles for both sexes, bracelets, special cardigans, leather belts, jeans, zoot suits, stove pipe pants, blue suéde shoes and black shirts were symbols of delinquency (*Sydney Morning Herald*, 29 January 1956).

Their collective appearance made bodgies and widgies both visible and provocative to many older Australians. John McDonald reported in 1951 on the many negative stereotypes of bodgies. These included claims that they 'had low IQs', were 'criminally inclined', were homosexual, sexually deviant and promiscuous with women. They were also 'tall and skinny', came from 'bad homes', were working class, were 'Americanised', 'loafers' and politically deviant (McDonald 1951:3). These stereotypes soon became common sense. As one 14-year-old girl reported while she was walking in a crowd, a woman nudged a small boy and spoke to him before the boy cried, 'Go on get out of here, you widgie. We don't want widgies around here' *(Adelaide Advertiser, 15 April 1958)*.

In Adelaide the respectable citizens of that city knew what the immorality embodied by widgies and bodgies consisted of:

> At the [Adelaide] court hearing of charges against two girls this week, one of the girls, a trim 16 year old, admitted sleeping naked all night in a bed with a bodgie... The girl said she drank liquor when she was in a crowd of bodgies and widgies but had never been drunk.
>
> *(Truth, 10 April 1955)*

The people of Melbourne could read press reports in which:

> A senior police officer said that there had been many reports of sex orgies, vandalism, and demonstrations in recent weeks which police attributed to bodgies and widgies.
>
> *(Sun News Pictorial 17 May 1956)*

By mid-1956 one Melbourne police officer estimated there over than 1,000 members of the city's bodgie gangs, with more gangs in Geelong, Ballarat and

Bendigo (*Sun-Herald*, 17 June 1956). The threat bodgies and widgies posed seemed to be more than a moral danger. The personal safety of 'good citizens' were at peril from such lawlessness.

In addition to this narrative of physical violence was the cultural threat posed by American rock and roll. In August 1955, the Sydney *Sun-Herald* warned that the rock 'n roll 'dance music craze' that was sweeping America would soon reach Australia. Alerting readers to the 'hysterical ... abandon which characterize[d] its primitive rhythmic beat', the feature warned that the music was 'a contributing factor' to juvenile delinquency and had been banned by police in a number of American communities (*Sun-Herald*, 28 August 1955).

After the arrival of Bill Haley's *Rock around the Clock*, rock 'n roll swept across Australia. Newspaper reports of teenage delinquency escalated, especially when many bodgie and widgie gang members dressed to imitate rock and roll singers. In September 1956, just as Elvis Presley's *Heartbreak Hotel* reached the top of the hit parades, Sydney's first rock 'n roll riot occurred following the screening of *Rock around the Clock* in the Victory Theatre in George Street. This was accompanied by wild dancing in the street, with some defiantly dancing outside police headquarters who were then charged with offensive and indecent behaviour (*Melbourne Herald*, 22 September 1956). According to Australia's newspapers at the time, Elvis Presley was 'Satan personified', his 'erotic' gestures on stage were designed to corrupt the modesty of girls. When reviewing one overseas Elvis concert, Perth's *Daily News* complained that his performance was a 'frantic sex show', and under the headline 'Filth [and] eroticism', the same newspaper later advocated the banning of Presley's records (*Perth Daily News*, 14 November 1957).[9]

Significantly many of these press reports relied on expert representations of juvenile delinquency. We see here a shift away from the nineteenth century moralising representation of youthful 'viciousness', 'evil' or 'bad influences' and movement to s a medical model of delinquency.

The senior *Sun* journalist Douglas Wilkie published an article on the Children's Court in September 1953 highlighting this. He reported the idea, e.g., that it was the Court's job was 'to correct, not punish'. However Wilkie was critical of the Children's Court, saying it was unable to 'correct' because it was not funded to provide the modern services needed. He referred to 'advanced methods' that drew heavily on 'diagnosis' and 'treatment' approaches. As Wilkie observed, the Children's Court had a psychiatric clinic 'to diagnose the youthful offenders, to test his or her intelligence and to gauge the emotional problems present' (*Sun News Pictorial* 4 September 1953).

In another report on intelligence tests, referred to as 'mystery tests', the journalist Stewart Legge described the work of the 'psychology section' of the Education Department. Legge detailed the function of the IQ tests, the various interventions of the trained personnel and the role of the sociogram:

> When a child appears to be unhappy, unco-operative and maladjusted, the sociogram diagrams will show where the tensions are ... they enable the

teacher to understand the child and its behaviour against the pattern of its environment at school, and if necessary at home.

(Sun News Pictorial *14 August 1953*)[10]

Given these journalists report and what experts already 'knew' of these young people, there should be little surprise that the particular young men and women in the media gaze began attracting increasing attention by experts as 'moral entrepreneurs'.

The experts

As Cohen argued, a moral panic occurs when experts weigh into public debate and begin offering their diagnosis and solutions (1972). As Cohen demonstrated during these 'moral panics', moral entrepreneurs and governments alike launched a succession of 'civilising offensives' targeting 'youth gangs' and 'delinquents'. Through the 1950s, public concern in Australia about juvenile delinquency was maintained in similar ways that intellectuals had fuelled concern about the 'dangerous classes' and the problem of delinquency in the nineteenth century. As will become clear, the representation of the bodgie menace marginalised and rendered near-invisible the lives and public appearance of the widgies.

Experts, like the psychologist A.E. Manning, were not shy in using medical metaphors to declare that widgies and bodgies were:

> ...active boils on the body of Society, and the tragically unhappy ones of this generation. They are the ones who need friendly, skilled help.... Their wildness, their vandalism, and their immorality are revenge, at the unconscious level, a revenge for which, at the unconscious level, they will ultimately pay a tragic price in shattered lives.
>
> *(Manning 1958:89)*

Neither the form nor the content of the moral panic about widgies and bodgies-as-folk-devils was accidental or arbitrary. Modern representations heavily influenced by a convergence of eugenicist discourse and the idea of the 'troubled adolescent' was generally accepted as the most authoritative way to report on delinquency and the 'bodgie and widgie plague' in the mid-1950s.

Much of this media reporting focussed on adolescence as a necessary, but risky stage of human development, an account that sparked fears about young people 'going off the rails' and 'becoming delinquent'. Persuasive and seductive metaphors derived from biology and medicine relied on a eugenic medico-psychological vocabularies to explain juvenile delinquency. Delinquency was seen as akin to a disease or a 'plague' that 'infected' society. It did not require punishment of the young person, but rather it could be cured by skilled, technically proficient therapy.

From the first decade of the twentieth century and into the 1950s, a network of Australian psychologists, doctors, educationists, sociologists, criminologists and progressive intellectuals drew on the international eugenic literature to deal with the problem of 'maladjusted' children and adolescents (Bessant 1991:8–28). Their studies measuring intelligence, or establishing norms for literacy and numeracy began appearing in journals such as the *Australasian Journal of Psychology and Philosophy*, the *Australian Journal of Education* and Government education *Gazettes*. David McCallum shows how this research and government and policy were bent on establishing the best fit between an unequal economic and social order, and the regulation of the aspirations and abilities of the Australian schoolchildren so they could meet the 'needs' of 'industry' and the 'economy' while also securing 'social order' was maintained (McCallum 1985). After peace in 1945, social-liberal planners added new themes like 'adjustment' and 'democratic citizenship' (Rowse 1978). By the 1950s Australian adolescents became central figures in a range of eugenic projects. 'Adjustment' to adulthood and maturity was now the objective of everybody from responsible parents, through teachers to the community. This idea of adjustment was used to justify efforts to prevent the child and the adolescent, from having 'adult experiences' and relations, and toppling into delinquency something that required constant vigilance by adults.

By 1951 Kenneth Cunningham, perhaps the closest Australian equivalent to Stanley Hall or Cyril Burt, had been the Foundation Director of the Australian Council for Educational Research for 21 years. When the prestigious -and eugenicist- Carnegie Foundation decided to spend money to develop an Australian Council of Education Research (ACER) to promote the scientific study and measurement of intellectual and educational abilities and norms, Cunningham, was appointed as director in 1930 (Connell 1980). Cunningham was a a positivist psychologist, a secular rationalist and progressive eugenicist. He was deeply conversant with English and the American eugenicist psychologists such as Galton, Pearson, Terman, Thorndike, Cattrell, and Spearman. He remained faithful to their commitment to profiling the population's mental abilities as a prelude to state eugenic interventions. Under his leadership, the Australian Council of Education Research flourished and became -and continues in 2020 - to be the leading source of tests and educational norms for Australian students.

Cunningham's research on 'normal adolescent' competencies and abilities was based on hegemonic understandings of adolescence and 'normality'. Through his quantitative research adolescent competencies came to be understood and measured on a normative and numerical scale of standard, age-related competencies including reading, writing, numeracy and self-discipline.

This interest in maladjustment also helped with another issue. By the 1950s the long revered explanation of juvenile delinquency in education and fields like juvenile justice in Britain, America and Australia appeared to begin losing credibility. The argument was that delinquency was the result of poverty and economic, physical or emotional deprivation

Somewhat surprisingly, by the early 1950s affluence, and not poverty was now the problem. In western countries after the war mnay governments had committed themselves to full-employment, so there was plenty of permanent work, and workers had more disposable income than in living memory. Countries like the USA, England, Australia and many European nations also saw an expansion of affordable housing, extended schooling, health care and community resources. While poverty was certainly not abolished, many intellectuals and professionals were mystified about why young people continued to behave badly.

Many working-class 'teenagers' were worked and were relatively affluent (Abrams 1959). That relatively new affluence was used to buy new clothing, music and attend gatherings in city streets, milk-bars and dancehalls. It was an action that confirmed the longstanding disposition by experts and governments to emphasise the deviant and delinquent dispositions of young people. By the 1950s Australian psychologists were focussed on adjustment as the marker of normality, and maladjustment as the marker of 'delinquency'.

Their research provided the basis for a scientific identified bad behaviour and maladjustment as a psychological problem so all wayward youth were amenable to a therapeutic treatment. Cunningham's influential of adolescent adjustment relied on metaphors of growth and development, normality and pathology drawn from biology and medicine:

> The phrase 'adjustment of youth' is a brief way of referring to those processes by which young people of both sexes pass from the stage of dependence upon their elders to the stage of full participation in adult society... Each individual is of course called on to make 'adjustments' through the whole span of his life... But some stages call for more rapid and more thorough going adjustment that others. The commencement of schooling, and later the transition from school to work are amongst the chief of these.
> *(Cunningham 1951:1)*

Research on delinquency was also part of the Australian Council of Education Research's investigations into intellectual and academic skill norms. One pioneer researcher, Mary Tenison-Woods employed by the Council was part of the Australian eugenicist psychological network that included key Australian education psychologists like Cunningham, as well as Professor G.S. Browne and C.R. McCrae. Delinquency Tenison-Woods argued should not be seen as

> ...naughtiness, which much forthwith be punished, but as a symptom of some hidden and often apparently unconnected cause. In the majority of cases the cause can be dealt with and removed if the necessary steps be taken at the right time.
> *(Tenison Woods 1937:6)*

Tenison-Woods' view about the genetic and physical determinants of delinquency surfaced in her use of the metaphors 'naughtiness as sickness': 'As in the case of physical disease [treatment should begin] as soon as possible after the symptoms appear, before the young delinquent has time and opportunity to harden into the habitual criminal' (ibid).

A delinquent was the *alter ego* of the successfully 'adjusted adolescent'. Delinquents were maladjusted personalities with a disturbed character:

> ...frequently unaware of his strength and weakness, his motives and ambitions. He may rationalise his feelings and intentions thus deceiving himself and others. He may resort to undesirable activities to gain self-confidence, popularity or those attributes which he considers essential to impress his group favorably. *Lying, boasting, pretences, continuous protest, and juvenile delinquency* may be the results of maladjustment in young people.
>
> (Cunningham 1951:204)

The young psychologist McDonald used structural concepts like 'society' and 'culture' to explain what these 'structures' do to some young people:

> Becoming a Bodgie has provided a solution to the frustrating dilemmas in which youths, especially working class youths are placed in our society. Becoming a Bodgie has been much easier than upward social mobility, while becoming a Bodgie has been both much easier and faster than becoming an adult.
>
> (McDonald 1951:77)

Here becoming an adult was considered to be co-terminous with successfully completing the process of individual adjustment to the 'social order' and to what was seen as a single coherent moral consensus. That adjustment was synonymous with the conjunction of 'social integration' and psychological or personal equilibrium. Failing to achieve this equilibrium in the transition to becoming an adult was to be 'deviant'.

By claiming delinquency for psychology, experts like Cunningham and Tennison-Woods in Australia (like Burt in Britain) hoped to demonstrate that psychology offered the best chance of diagnosing and *treating* the delinquent. As Burt explained: '[Delinquency] is a mental symptom with a mental origin'. For delinquency to be effectively 'treated' its mental nature had to be verified. Once that was done appropriate psychological treatments could be developed. It seemed common sense to Cyril Burt and Cunningham that psychologists could 'cure' delinquency in the same ways doctors could 'cure' a patient of an illness, or how a teacher could teach a student new lessons. Here we see a coming together of medical and educational fields, courtesy of scientific metaphors used to support the view that:

> ...the best way to reform the potential offender is not merely to convict, birch and imprison him, but to catch him while young, to study him

individually as a unique human being, with a special history, a special constitution; special problems of his own, and to treat him not so much as a sinner to be punished outright, but rather as a pupil to be trained or a patient to be treated.

(Cunningham 1951:204)

Much of the discussion of 'delinquency' and the bodgies and widgies in the 1950s drew on these representations of delinquency as maladjustment. In 1956 the state government of Victoria established an expert committee headed by a Supreme Court judge J.V. Barry to give advice on the problem of juvenile delinquency and how to solve it.[11] The Barry Committee's members reiterated 30 years of scientific wisdom when they expressed:

…strong support for the idea that adolescence is a period of turmoil, a period of turbulent motion sometimes of disturbed behaviour when love, tolerance and imaginative understanding were never more in demand and yet never harder wholly to accept.

(Barry 1956:23)

'The youth problem', according to the Barry Committee were a consequence of the natural and animal instincts that any society had to conquer so as to be civilised: 'The acquisitive, aggressive sexual and escape tendencies that exist in all human beings in great or less degree underlie almost all delinquency' (Barry 1956:23).

In Australia through the 1950s, psychologists continued to shape how delinquency was seen and described. Psychologists gained popular acceptance for their claims about an interplay between heredity and the psychology of adjustment. In other words, delinquents were adolescents (or children) whose problems such as a lack of intellectual ability was a genetic problem. As those young people grew, they failed at various intervals to 'adjust' to the social requirements said to determine normality on the path to adulthood. As Manning argued, psycho-social adjustment and 'frustration' helped explain what was happening:

The greatest single factor in emotional disturbance is that of frustration. Every 'Bodgie' interviewed was a completely frustrated person, frustrated by focus operating in his own conscious mind, by the unrealised tensions and by his own inability to accept society.

(Manning 1958:25)

Like most experts, the Barry committee, agreed that 'aggression is a response to a situation of frustration' (Barry 1956:19) acknowledged the proposition that every bodgie was frustrated by the tensions in *his* conscious mind.

It was a story in which the widgies were largely blanked out or made invisible.

The Widgie fight back

Sydney's widgies and bodgies added colour to Sydney's inner-urban streetscapes and later to other Australian suburbs and capital cities. However, most of what we know about these young people is about the young men. Gender blindness kept the widgies in the shadows. One explanation for this was that most journalists who were reporting on this 'outrageous youthful' activity were men who emphasised the masculine features of the new style. This rendered both gender and women's experience invisible, evident, e.g., in the popularity of 'sexualised deviance' models (Cohen 1956). On rare occasions when widgies became a focus of public attention, they were represented as *female delinquency*: as *victims* of predatory male sexuality, as a vulnerable person who was, or is likely to be, 'in moral danger'. Or they were wayward, maladjusted and promiscuous girls unable to control their 'innate, seductive and powerful drives'.

The gendering of psychological and sociological discourses using a tacit norm based on male experiences of socialisation and on the male 'pathways' to successful 'social adjustment', was used as a normative frame for young women as well as men (Ausubel 1954, Friedenburg 1959).

When girls and women were acknowledged, it was often in terms of their 'sacred roles' as future mothers and wives: women were expected to be patient purveyors of children, care and civility. The dominant representations of women secured the prevailing gendered social order maintained a selective 'official' view of what was politics and indeed what was 'delinquency' that was counter to the actual experiences of widgies. The life worlds of widgies raise a number of political questions, some of which relate to sex and violence.

Sex and the widgie

According to official expert working groups, like the Barry Committee given the task of advising government, delinquency was: '… behaviour resulting from a failure of the individual to adapt himself to the demands of the society in which he live' (Barry 1956:19). Here we see experts emphaissing women's responsibility for the family and particularly to becoming mothers in families. Families were important because that was the first place where individuals learned to adjust, or where they failed to 'adjust' during the 'dangerous' 'time of transition'. Within the family they can learn in 'positive' ways about how to manage the 'storm and stress' said to characterise 'adolescent development'. When the family failed to ensure young people remained 'well adjusted' and stayed on track along that rickety developmental path, they became maladjusted:

> If the family is stable and there are no adverse or morbid conditions or influences, the possibilities of adjusting and harmonizing his nature self regarding impulses with the requirements of society are good.
>
> *(Barry 1956:19)*

While the clothing and hairstyles expressing the femininity of widgies, and the manliness of bodgies, were the subject of intense interest, widgies came in for special treatment (McDonald 1951:11–19). In understanding this reaction, it helps to bear in mind the context in which the convention of confining sexual expression within the constraints of marriage dominated. Widgies were a shadowy presence in McDonald's research: most of his respondents were men and they mostly talked about other young men. Only very occasionally did women figure in his work and when they did it was always in generalised stereotypical terms as nymphomaniacs, prostitutes or seductresses.

While it's clear what experts and the media reported, it is not so clear how the young, working-class widgies represented themselves. How did they see themselves, how did they describe their own experiences and what meanings did they give to their actions?

Some answers to these questions can be gained by my interviews with former widgies done in the early 1990s. There were no available insider accounts from widgies at the time. And when interviews were called for there was a clear reluctance on the part of many former widgies to come forward with stories and talk about their earlier lives? Significantly, for bodgies there was no such reluctance. Indeed it was seen as a chance for enjoyable nostalgic chat and opportunity to recall their youthful machismo.

Research, and my own experience, indicate that many women were reluctant to speak about their early lives as widgies largely because 'those girls' had a 'bad reputation'. A sense of shame and embarrassment was still felt by *some* of these women when looking back on those 'early days'. The stigma attached to being a widge limited the number of interviews and material I could access. Having said that, some women were happy to come forward and talk about their days as widgies. The results were illuminating.

The key message widgies received about who they were at the time, was one of disapproval and condemnation, based on normalising judgments that "they" were very different from other 'good' girls. Accounts of widgies 'immoral' behaviour and their exotic strangeness communicated a very clear message of what was desirable and undesirable when it came to femininity and what counted as a good, healthy young women or girl.

Disapproval of widgies was evident in the descriptions of them as: 'harlot' and 'street walker'. Priscilla recalled how 'being a widgie was equivalent to being a slut' (Interview, 'Priscilla', June 1992). Margaret also remembered the name calling.

> …adults used to call us, 'Sluts, sluts'!…We used to get called street walkers. That was the famous word for prostitute. That was a very strong word in those days. Sluts and harlots. Straight kids wouldn't dare say that because we would just lay into them.
>
> *(Interview 'Margaret', March 1993)*

Similarly, Trish recalled her the reaction of her parents to their discovery she was a widgie: My father said to mum once: '…oh isn't it dreadful babe, I never thought we'd have somebody like this [for a daughter]' (Trish May 1993). Alison also explained that being a widgie was not something she would want to tell every-one now (Alison April 1991).

These language categories were deliberately used to shame and spoil identities. Importantly there was no linguistic equivalent for men (Goffman 2009). Judgments or fantasies about widgies 'sexual promiscuity' evident in descriptors like 'tart', 'slut', 'whore' or 'mole' were used exclusively to describe particular kinds of girls or young women who, it was said, often behaved more like men. Indeed for a young man in Australia in the mid-1950s, being sexually assertive and 'successful' with one or more women was, in many quarters, valorised. It signalled being an 'alpha-male' or a 'stud', a high-status identity that communicated dominance and strength.

For a young woman in the 1950s, to challenge her feminine 'script' even in the mildest ways like wearing her hair 'differently' (short), or wearing a leather jacket, or admitting to have had sex and had liking it before marriage, was a clear sign of an irredeemably bad and 'fallen woman'. Even talking openly about such topics was taboo. Speaking about one's feelings and 'boys' was a private matter reserved for a private conversation in private spaces amongst themselves, as friends. It was definitely not for the ears of outsiders, and especially not for professional adults (Interview, Margaret, March 1993; see also 'Joan', April 1993).

This reluctance to talk about one's inner life was noted by experts at the time like the New Zealand psychologist Manning (1958) when he interviewed a number of widgies. Speaking about one 19-year-old widgie, Carol, he wrote:

> In certain moods she had no reticence [in speaking to me as a psychologists] ... and in other moods she would resist any question. .... The first four interviews were completely wasted time. At the fifth: 'Carol' said: 'Look, doc, I'm a perfect...
> Questioner: I am sorry. I am not a doctor'.
> Carole: I don't care a f---k what you are. You're like all the [f---g]--- doctors, wanting to look into people's insides. Alright, look into mine and see what good it does you.
>
> *(Manning 1958:40)*

Style, space and politics

Writing decades later, Angela McRobbie made a number of observations about space and gender, noting how girls and young women often use quiet private domestic spaces like their bedrooms and homes to 'hang out' and talk about their lived experiences (1984:130–161, 1991). This was the case for widgies like Margaret and her friends enjoyed spending time in each others' homes helping out with domestic tasks like child care (of younger siblings) and other 'house jobs' expected of them before they were allowed to go out (interview Margaret

March 1993). In that private space they designed and sewed some of their own new fashioned clothes, experimented with new outfits, hairstyles, language and music. It was where they sang, listened to music, read the few magazines then available and generally engaged in 'youth cultural' activities. This use of private space also explains in part their invisibility (Margaret interview March 1993, see also McRobbie 1980: 37–49, Johnson 1993, Walkerdine 1989). This private space was where widgies also aired their views about the prevailing cultural norms and what was expected of them as 'good' girls, wives and mothers to be (interview Margaret March 1993).

Yet while widgies shared time in these ways, they were also attracted to the fun and excitement of 'hanging out' with each other and with bodgies on the streets. In the mid-1950s however such action was considered highly inappropriate and indeed dangerous for young women. The social taboos around 'unaccompanied women' in public spaces like the streets reflected the dominant view that a 'woman's place' was 'naturally' 'in the home' performing 'home duties', and those who ventured beyond those boundaries were morally suspect.

Added to this was an interest in being defiant in daring to contest long-held gendered restrictions on the places they could rightfully be, how they could and couldn't act and how they could identify themselves. In making themselves visible in public spaces, by spending time on the street, widgies contested and challenged those powerful norms as well as those who represented and demonized them as 'street walkers' and 'wayward girls'. The political nature of being a widgie was evident in the ways they continued occupying public space challenging the the taboo of doing this. It was evident in the courageous ways they directly confronted censors by creating and wearing certain fashions like form-fitting and colourful clothes, by being bare-legged, or by smoking cigarettes (Featherstone 2011:262).

The political character of this was also evident in how widges dared to be 'outrageous' not just by occupying public space but by doing things like riding motorbikes. These actions by young women in the 1950s were acts of political dissent intended to create a little more space for them to be who they chose to be. As Lorraine explained, the attraction of being more free, of being bold, and breaking away from the gendered constraints of the 1950s was why she wanted to be a widgie: '...I was firstly attracted [to being a widgie] because I loved motorbikes' (Lorraine October 1992).

She continued:

> I [also] liked the ways the girls looked and at that time. We used to wear a skin tight black skirt with a slit up the back and very high heels and dark stockings, sometimes fishnet which was always very sexy, tight sweaters and I had my hair cut very short and a duck tail at the back and that was the hair style.

(Lorraine interview October 1992)

Widgies like Lorraine themselves seemed very well aware of what they were doing:

> I liked being defiant .... I have been in many other groups since, I think that sort of *sets the pattern for your life because you have been a rebel and you always will.*
>
> (Lorraine October 1992)

Rejecting traditional ideas of femininity and creating new ways of being, was overwhelmingly interpreted by many 'respectable people' as a direct challenge to the moral order and a serious threat to well-ordered social arrangements.

In defying conventional gendered norms in these ways, widgies were challenging oppressive representations and offering, courtesy of various forms of performativity, a new figure of girls and women. While widgies were interested in having fun, they also wanted greater equality between the sexes, including exercising certain rights. They were interested in exploring what was possible when opposing ethical worldviews come together. By identifying and questioning the consensus about traditional gendered roles and defying the status quo in the ways they did they were political activists well before anything like a feminist movement had evolved in Australia.

Widgies imagined, playfully entertained and enacted new ways of being feminine. They experimented with modern 'ultra feminine' identities by exercising positive freedom in ways that were typically conflictual. This was the case for \ Margaret, who thought traditional ideas of femininity ought to be wholeheartedly rejected. As she explained: 'we were fighting against the system. It was so bloody Victorian, it was ridiculous' (Margaret March 1993). That did not necessarily mean however a complete rejection of everything conventionally regarded as feminine. Rather the creation and embrace of 'new fashions' and 'different' ways of being a modern girl sometimes meant a modification or partial rejection of 'Victorian' protocols and ideas.

It wasn't just making new clothing styles and 'taking to the streets' that said what it meant to be a widgie. Girls who enjoyed the company of boys (especially 'wild boys'), as widgies did, defied traditional ideas of feminine virtue, something frowned on, if not prohibited. Figurations of gender and power in 1950s Australia and indeed in most countries at the time meant public and domestic authority was vested in men as politicians, bosses, professionals, fathers and husbands. Public and private roles and relations were characterised by sex-based segregation. It was also a time when domestic violence, in the form of 'wife bashing' was generally considered acceptable and when rape within a marriage was seen by many as exercising a husband's prerogative.

The power relations that informed such practices were also evident in public places like pubs where women were excluded from certain spaces like the public bar. Indeed the very presence of a woman in such a place meant she was not only defiant, but a disgrace. Her presence was an act of insolence or disobedience and against her nature. In this context girls and women who did not perform their 'proper role', who entered public space 'unaccompanied' by a male escort were deemed to be psychologically ill ('mad') or a prostitute. Social clubs were also imbued with the same ethos and segregated according to sex. Social occasions like birthdays, weddings or barbeques, e.g., followed a ritual in which men occupied one space typically around the beer keg and BBQ, while women filled a separate space where they prepared and served food and talked.

While widgies continued some traditional feminine 'roles' occupying a subordinate position in relation to boys-men, young women like Margaret were critical of many aspects of these customs. These young women had clear ideas about what they wanted and the limits to which they would go in assuming the traditional subordinate position to men in general and with bodgies in particular. This was most apparent when it came to the question of unwanted sexual activity:

> We used to have ... an animal instinct, or your antenna would go up. You could pick whether a bloke would want to have a go at you, or want to go to bed with you.... I remember one young bloke... He tried to rape me... I ended up getting a black eye, but I kicked him in the balls... I said to him... 'If you touch me, I will have you up for rape'. That stopped him. That was a criminal offence, the sentence was hard.
>
> *(Interview 'Margaret' March 1993)*

She continued:

> ...We wanted to be in control of ourselves. We had already rebelled against the system. So why should we come up against our own type [the bodgie] and have to rebel against them?
>
> *(Interview, 'Margaret' March 1993)*

In Manning's psychological study *The Bodgie*... which included a lengthy inquiry into widgies, he 'discovered' through his interviews that many widgies had 'unhealthy' attitudes to marriage. It was an attitude that included a desire for autonomy. As one young woman described by Manning as 'maladjusted' and 'neurotic' explained:

> If I get married I have to go without all the things I think are pleasant and I have to bear children whether I want to or not. I'd just be a slave. Once a man gets you, he forgets you. So long as I'm free he'll chase ... me.
>
> *(Manning 1958: 15)*

Similarly, for Lorraine becoming a widgie presented a chance to 'resist' an oppressed life she believed most women experienced. Being a widgie meant opportunities to pursue a more fulfilling life. It offered a 'way to protest' her ascribed female status, one marked by conformity with traditional gender roles. Lorraine's explanation about why she became a widgie had much to do with the repressive nature of the gender politics that pervaded the milieu in which she lived and grew up. She described why she decided to become a widgie after years of being a student in:

> ...a very strict Catholic school and living in convents ... I thought there was more to life than this. Being a rebel was just letting it all hang out after years of oppression and it was great.
>
> *(Interview Lorraine October 1992)*

For Lorraine being a widgie meant expressing her 'urge to rebel'. She rejected her identity as a good catholic school girl. To be a widgie was to be all that was forbidden. It was become the worst kind of 'wayward' girl.

Widgies 'undoing gender'

'Aggressive tendencies' were said to be a feature of 'the delinquent', indicating how the individual was 'frustrated' and 'maladjusted'. Such accounts rested on the therapeutic-functionalist premise that success as an individual required balancing 'biological drives' with the need for social control to produce people who were willing and able to develop and exercise self-control. As the Barry Report on delinquency explained, the challenge for 'the adolescent' is to reconcile 'conflicts' between certain 'fundamental' human 'biological impulses' like 'self-assertiveness' described as necessary for survival and sense of security and 'the demands of society' that require co-operation and compliance with social norms (Barry 1956:19).

It was normal for boys to 'play up' (get drunk, brawl and be 'rowdy'), and something they would 'naturally' (fingers crossed) grow out of as those 'boyish' behaviours mutated into an acceptable manly conduct and identity. However when girls did the same, when they 'acted out', became intoxicated, had sex, fought or simply hung out on the streets they were judged to be far worse than 'maladjusted.' When girls were defiant, rule breaking and engaging in 'immoral conduct' they highlighted how they were not just an immediate danger to themselves and society but more importantly a future danger. When widgies were at risk of losing 'what could never be replaced', their 'virginity' and 'reputation' and most importantly their capacity to be good women, wives, and especially as mothers to the next generation. The idea also that young women could be physically violent was unthinkable. Yet many widgies did just that.

Widgies actively engaged in physical fights, seen to be very unfeminine sight. Some carried weapons like flick knives and containers of pepper to throw in the eyes of any opponent. Joy recalled one 'big widgie fights' in the centre of Melbourne:

> I forget what it was that started it … within minutes there must have been twenty or more of us [widgies] going at it really hard. We used everything we had, feet, fists, fingernails, and things we had in our bags. I was using a nail-file at one stage. All of my clothes were in tatters at the end, but I really enjoyed it. I wasn't hurt too badly. I had some bruises and scratches…. It was great to let off steam and those bitches got what they deserved. The boys sure stayed clear of it all.
>
> *(Interview, Joy 1992)*

Stiletto-heeled shoes also came in handy during a fight as they could be quickly transformed from fashionable footwear to a lethal weapon (Interview, 'Margaret' March 1993). As Des, a bodgie, noted 'a lot of them [widgies] really loved fights, they used to get in them at parties' (Interview 'Des', October 1992, see also Dick 1965:188). Having a fight meant 'being tough' which was antithetical to being and feminine. It was not what nice girls did, but exactly what many widgies did.

In describing her introduction to becoming part of a widgie group, Margaret explained how being 'gutsy' and strong mattered:

> I left school at 13. I was working at 13. When I worked at Kinnears [rope factory] this fantastic girl, Miminda her name was… I was working with her on the spindles and I knew she was the head of the gang and I had to come up against her because I was a newy and I had to be tried out. She picked me and I thought of shit, either I m going to have to sock her one or I'm going to have to leave work. She picked me one day and I just went in and she said come outside…. I just turned around and gave her a king hit. I thought of shit this is it she is going to bloody hit me back and ill be dead. All the machinists stopped and looked around…. And she said are you going to have morning tea? And that was it – finished. I was in. I didn't back off. I was in.
>
> *(Margaret interview, March 1993)*

Margaret continued:

> I carried a knife, a couple of girls had flick knives, that was our protection. My favourite one was the pepper. And we had stiletto heels. If you had one of them in you you'd be crying for the rest of your life.
>
> *(Margaret interview March 1993)*

Lorraine account of fighting also revealed there was a lot more to a 'brawl' (fight) than its 'entertainment value'. Fighting she argued was also a powerful and effective way of demonstrating solidarity, loyalty and camaraderie:

> We were very loyal to each other and stood by each other. If somebody was in a fight, whether you could fight or not you were in there boots and all. If your boyfriend was getting bashed up, well my God! I had high heels. I didn't care where they got them from, but they got them. Yes, we were very supportive to our men, you didn't stand back and be feminine, you were in there, you were part of it.
>
> *(Lorraine interview 15 October 1992)*

In the context of the 1950s Australia, the actions of widgies were bold and defiant, which raised doubts about their capacity to be nurturant mothers and submissive wives who acknowledged their husbands as masters of the household. This was a big problem because, like it or not, as young women, widgies would also be the nation's future mothers and wives. To realise such expectations they needed to be soft, nurturing, and submissive not questioning of gender stereotypes and disruptive. When they resisted conventional dress codes, gendered scripts, entered public space and spoke out they were acting politically: action interpreted as highly disruptive to the symbolic order and a threat to the nation's future.

Experts armed with superior moral insight and the responsibility as guardians for the future, social justice, and social welfare called for remedies to what became a problem about moral welfare of the nation. Moral danger was the biggest risk a young women could face. This included being 'incorrigible', 'ungovernable', 'wayward' or 'uncontrollable'.

Conclusion

Like many other countries in the 1950s, Australia boasted an array of legally and socially reinforced gendered inequalities. They included paying women lower wages than men for work of equal value, and the imposition of a 'marriage bar' prohibiting the permanent employment of married women in the public services, education or hospitals. What the law did not enforce social convention did: the first female professor in a university was only appointed in 1974. Women were not permitted to drink in public bars. An unmarried woman who became pregnant was required to 'surrender' her child for adoption. Women could not buy property in their own right nor could they take out a personal bank loan. Once married they were expected to do unpaid domestic labour and child-care. Women also had little or no access to parliamentary politics, public life and extremely limited access to university education. For any *young* woman to transgress these social norms attracted considerable moral opprobrium.

In the late nineteenth and early twentieth centuries, the eugenic movement's 'racial hygiene' discourse generated a developmental narrative about 'adolescence'.

As we have seen eugenicists like Stanley Hall saw adolescence as a naturally turbulent, deviant 'stage' in the life-cycle. Such characterisations provide an enduring point of reference for the evolving industry of youth experts, social workers, criminologists, probation officers, psychologists and so forth across the twentieth century and into the twenty-first century. What was often not recognised was the extent to which notions of 'normal' child and adolescent development assumed a male or masculine model or norm.

As Carol Gilligan notes, when conventional accounts of human cognitive and moral development were developed in the middle decades of the twentieth century and applied to young people, they were conceived in overwhelmingly masculine terms. Gilligan observed, e.g., how women tended to score lower on Kohlberg's scale of moral judgement, because Kohlberg and other developmental theorists privileged rational thinking, independence, autonomy, and enlightened self-interest, and did so by framing these attributes in terms of male norms (Gilligan 1982). In this way, girls and women were effectively marginalized, if not rendered invisible.

This disposition may indicate why the presence of widgies in public places in Australian cities in the 1950s was such an alarming experience.

Widgies represented a visible assault on long-standing gendered social practices from everything from lady-like eating, the consumption of alcohol, to compliance with notions of respectable dress and codes of public conduct when public space was understood as the privileged preserve of men and boys. They also represented a challenge to the idea that chastity before marriage was a prerequisite if young women were to transition to the status of housewife and mother because that naturally represented the highest aspiration of any young woman.

Widgies directly subverted ideas about how girls should use their bodies. They did this when they spread their legs to ride a motorbike just as men did, or when they jumped on as pillion passengers hooking their arms around the waist of their bodgie rider. They did this as they wore tight-fitting clothes, cropped their hair short, smoked cigarettes 'like a man', occupied public spaces by attending rock 'n roll dances or the movies, or just hung out like boys in milk bars and public spaces. In all these ways they were both changing their gendered habitus and subverting dominant gender norms. When young women refused their 'proper feminine role', it signalled a challenge to the prevailing social arrangements and to an imagined social order (Carrington 1993). In the 1950s, concern about how girls and women fitted into the future of the country and the empire was hardly novel. The 'moral panic' triggered by the 'appearance' of the widgies had its antecedents.

The decades book-ended by the Boer War (1899–1902) and the Great War (1914–18) triggered widespread alarm about the degeneration of 'the (white) race' said to have been caused in part by the failure of many women to be good mothers, devoted wives and home-makers. Scandalously some became suffragettes protesting and demanding the vote for woman, or became eugenicists arguing for sex education, contraception and relaxed divorce laws (Dyhouse 1989). In the 1950s, we heard echoes of the Edwardian moral panic about the 'New Woman' and the threat they posed to future generations, social order and 'racial fitness' by the widgies.

When widgies defied gendered conventions they were denigrated, pitied and characterised as psychologically troubled or maladjusted. This translated into representations of them as psychologically troubled, difficult to control, as victims of broken or 'dysfunctional homes'. They were 'wilful' or 'wayward girls' and to that extent deserving of compassion. Rarely however were they held accountable for 'their offences' as was usually the case with boys. Such representations helped to ignore the deeply political nature of widgies action. Rather what their action was read as evidence of their maladjustment.

While outrage directed at widgies drew on their breaching of gendered developmental models it also served to ignore and misrepresent the political character of their interventions. Under the experts gaze widgies were the 'modern girls' who openly violated the clearly stipulated expectations of women and what it meant to be a 'good girl'. In this way widgies were a social movement *avant la lettre*.

Whether they knew it or not, they were challenging a hegemonic, gendered symbolic order and the fields of gendered power embedded in the state and its legal systems, the education and professional domains, the business sector, the organised working class and the media, all dominated by men.

As I argued in Chapter 2, such actions are generally not understood as political because they did not fit the conventional category of the political. These practices were not institutionalized, hierarchically organized, and they apparently lacked long-term goals as well as the capacity for 'new institution building' (Srnicek and Williams 2015). Yet politics takes many forms. It can take the form of collective and individual resistance and disobedience, or arguments made in this case about women's rights. Politics can take the form of acts of solidarity that disrupt and challenge traditional rules of the game manifested in individual and collective acts of defiance such as wearing certain kinds of clothes and the occupation of certain kinds of spaces.

In the 1950s, Australia's widgies were being political. Yet not surprisingly this was misrepresented in ways that denied the political character of what they did.

This mistake was not so easily made a decade and a half later. As I argue in the next chapter many more young people in the 1960s, lots of them in schools and universities, engaged in forms of political activism that left little doubt about their political intentions.

Notes

1 A Fordist economy refers to the confluence of mass production of old goods (food, clothing, automobiles) and new goods (household appliances, television, etc.) plus

mass media-based advertising and new retail outlets like malls, supermarkets and fast food outlets to encourage major increases in material affluence and commodified leisure.
2 It's a field of inquiry developed by feminist and critical scholars from the 1980s.
3 On this method see Berteaux (1981). My colleague Rob Watts, and I did 35 interviews with older Australians in the late 1990s who were widgies or bodgies in the 1950s. They were recruited when I appeared on radio shows in Melbourne to talk about the research project. This has been supplemented by other interviews carried out by other researchers including McDonald (1951), Stratton (1992) and Gorman (2015).
4 This has not always been acknowledged in standard works like Stratton (1992): see Gorman (2015).
5 Later the word "bodgie" was used to refer to people or a thing pretending to be something it was not (e.g., Australian people or products presented as American) (McDonald 1951:4–5).
6 John McDonald was a Sydney University Honours student, working under the supervision of Professor A. P. Elkin, Professor of Anthropology at Sydney University. He wrote an Honours thesis in 1951, based on participant observer research into the life-style and habitus of some of the 3,000–5,000 bodgies that McDonald estimated lived in Sydney. McDonald had some contact with the Bondi Pavilion bodgies and widgies since the summer of 1948–1949 (McDonald 1951:17). Between February and May 1951 McDonald records that he visited the Gaiety Dance Hall six times, the Jazz Concerts at the Sydney Town Hall six times, the Lots-O-Fun Penny Arcade 20 times and the Esplanade Dance Hall twice. As for the notorious Burt's Milk Bar, he visited that place over 30 times.
7 Gorman recalls that the style included 'big, loose-fitting jackets with brightly coloured shirts, and wore their pants tight at the ankles, while key-chains dangled from their belts. They wore suede shoes, often with crepe soles. Their hair [worn], long at the back and sides with curls cultured over their foreheads' (2015:1).
8 There are limitations with historical approach to the widgies. I relied on sparse documentary records and interviews undertaken two decades ago.
9 Many young people flocked to Elvis Presley's films ignoring the warning from the Sydney newspaper, *Sunday Truth*, that the Elvis movie *Jailhouse Rock* was 'sex-crazed and disgusting'. It depicted 'an unsavoury nauseating and muddy brew of delinquency, sentiment, bad taste and violence', the newspaper asserted (*Sunday Truth*, 9 February 1958). The city of Brisbane experienced its first rock and roll riot in November 1956. Following a Brisbane Stadium rock and roll concert, hundreds of young people began jiving in Albert Street. When police arrived, they abused officers. One fan reportedly threw a stone that hit a policeman's head and another smashed a bottle over a police car while another jumped onto the back of a detective while he was trying to arrest a demonstrator. The police charged two young women and six young men (*Courier-Mail*, 20 November 1956, 23 November 1956). Brisbane's citizens were divided on the issue. 'Old Timer' of Red Hill suggested 'the reintroduction of the birch rod for delinquents', while 'Perplexed' felt that youths involved did not deserve 'the bashing' that the police handed out to them (*Courier-Mail*, 23 November 1956, 27 November 1956, 29 November 1956). Newspapers repeatedly linked 'bodgie gang violence' with midnight screenings of rock and roll movies. In early January 1958, e.g., more than sixty police had intervened in street fights in Newtown in Sydney to move the participants on, but the 'gangs' had simply re-formed and armed with fence palings, fought in various locations throughout the night. (*Sunday Truth*, 26 January 1958).
10 'Difficulties' experienced by young people as school pupils was also said to be the consequence of 'problems in the relationship between the pupils psychology and

her or his social environment' – skilled professional intervention provided the answer.

> The psychologist finds out the root of the trouble and the social worker endeavours to remove it. Parents are very ready to co-operate when they are shown that some unfortunate home influence is the cause of a child's worries, fears or tensions. Disturbances in the home have been found to be the root of a child's problem, and in a good proportion of these, the social worker has been able to help the family while getting the child back on the right track.
>
> (*Sun News Pictorial* 14 August 1953)

11 The Barry Committee was eugenicist: two of its members Barry and Dr. Alan Stoller, from the Mental Hygiene Department were formal members of the Eugenics Society of Victoria.

6
REPRESENTING STUDENT POLITICS IN THE 1960S

Today when people think about student protest or student activism, there is a tendency to recall the 'long 1960s', the 'golden age' of student protest, epitomised by the global wave of student protest movements of 1968.[1] As Sarah Webster observes, this harking back to 1968 accurately reflects the international scale and scope of student protest in that year as young people took to the streets in Pakistan, Czechoslovakia, Australia, Germany, America, Poland, China, South Korea, France, Great Britain, Italy and Mexico (2015:14). There were many local and international causes espoused that included opposition to the elitist or authoritarian character of universities, support for democracy in Eastern Europe, for civil rights for Afro-Americans, or opposition to America's military intervention in Vietnam after 1965 (DeGroot 1998, 2008, Hanna 2013, Hoefferle 2013, Vinen 2018).

There is however value in being cautious about seeing the sixties as *the* modern example of young people's political action. As Webster argues, the uniqueness of the sixties' global student revolt has been overstated. She says that 'the dominant narrative', illustrated in Vinen's (2018) 'Long '68', emphasised the alleged 'exceptional and unprecedented status [of the 1960s] while overlooking evidence of campus unrest and activism before and since' (Webster 2015:14).

Revolutionary politics and dissent involving young people have a long history. As Chapter 3 demonstrated, children and young people played a central role in the French revolution.

Young people were also central to nineteenth-century liberal-democratic and/or nationalist movements like Young Ireland, Young Germany and Young Italy that swept across Europe during and after the 1848 revolutions (Jones 1991, Randers-Pehrson 1999). In Russia generations of young played critical roles in the 1905 and 1917 revolutions, and in the shift to socialism initiated by Stalin in the late 1920s (Morrissey 2000, Koenker 2001, Pujals 2005, Fürst 2010).

Young people in 1919 emerged as key actors in the Turkish revolution of 1919 – the 'Young Turks' – while Chinese students mobilised the May Fourth movement in 1919 that shaped years of struggle between the nationalist and communist movements until 1948 (Chen 1971). In Germany too the 'generation of 1914', those born in the years before the First World War, were identified as a distinct generation deeply affected by the experience of long-term unemployment in the last years of the Weimar Republic (Peukert 1987:188–189). They were not only drawn to the political parties of the left, but also to ultra-right groups including the Nazi party (Stachura 1975, 1981, Wohl 1979, Donson 2010, 2011).

While mindful of that long history, there are good reasons for looking more closely at young people's political action in the 1960s. This raises a question about how this can be done. An enormous volume of research on student movements reveals a tendency to employ certain kinds of theory to explain what is happening. This uses theories like collective protest or resource mobilisation, or larger narratives like Marxism, feminism or critical race theory. It can involve researchers trying to establish the role of structural variables like class, gender, race or dominant macro-formation like modernity, society or capitalism. In this way, the meanings of particular actions (e.g., writing manifestoes, designing anti-war banners, organising street marches or occupying university buildings as a form of protest) are often explained in terms that are quite different to those understood by the young people themselves. Whichever way, the end result is to obscure and block access to the young people and their political experiences.

Another reason to look more closely at student action in the 1960s relates to the tendency by many sociologists and historians to focus often exclusively, on university student action which tends to marginalise or make invisible the many and diverse forms of activism by much younger school students (De Groot 1998, Graham 2006). By taking a closer look as I do here, we can see the extensive and complex involvement of quite young secondary school students who initiated various movements for political and social change which have largely been forgotten.

In this chapter, I ask how were young people represented in the 1950s and 1960s by the social sciences, media and politicians? Why did some young people engage in politics in the 1960s and how they did they do that? While it was a global phenomenon, for pragmatic reasons I focus only on student action in America, Britain and Australia.[2] In what follows I start by considering how the social sciences represented student protest in the 1960s.

What the experts said: student protest as deviance

During the 1960s many experts, intellectuals and scholars represented student political action in negative and often pejorative ways. Saying this is not to deny there were scholars who were insightful about the waves of student politics.

Student politics in the 1960s 155

In America, e.g., we saw a number of perceptive contemporary accounts of the Berkeley Free Speech Movement (Draper 1965, Lipset and Wolin 1965, Savio 1965a, Heirich 1971). While I will draw on aspects of that scholarship later in this chapter, I begin with representations of 'young radical students' that were largely unsympathetic.

It seems that a combination of traditional ideas about social science and antipathy to the politics espoused by students worked to ensure negative representations of student protestors. That scholarship relied on particular scientific assumptions and methods, which it was believed, would explain student protest action. This often produced reductionist explanations that relied on assumptions that causal laws explained student dissent. It was an approach that tried to explain complex events like the 1960s anti-war movements by reducing them to an expression of a large phenomenon like intergenerational conflict or to contradictions in capitalism. Reductionist explanations also worked by reducing the phenomenon in question down to certain constituent parts like psycho-biological entity, or poor impulse control.

In the 1960s it was the vogue to represent student protest as a social or psychological pathology. As Gill and DeFronzo noite, many scholars in the sixties, and since, relied on social-psychological perspectives, in trying to explain the motivations of student activists by reference, e.g., to generational conflict (Gill and DeFronzo 2009:204).

For the sociologist Lewis Feuer America's student movement was the result of students inspired by unconscious psychological impulses 'which they try to explicate in a political ideology, and [are] moved by an emotional rebellion in which there is always present a disillusionment with and rejection of the older generation' (Feuer 1969:11). Feuer argued that student activists were taking out their parental hatreds against University administrators and faculty. He claimed that 'in 1964, a "generational complex" had become strong in Berkeley... A demonstration became a compulsive gesture ... [There] was a readiness to serve notice on the elders, to "confront" them' (1969:437). Feuer also argued that student leaders like Mario Savio were themselves 'in the throes of a personal generational rebellion' (1969:443). Feuer claimed to see how readily the University of California 'administration was defined in the activists' eyes as the Cruel, Heartless, Impersonal Father who aimed to destroy his sons' (1969:445).[3]

Robert Liebert (1971), a psychoanalyst at Columbia who wrote on the 1968 insurrection at Columbia concurred, using interviews, student term-papers and college records. He concluded that the 'attack' on the university was a symbolic 'murder' of a remote and authoritarian father, in which the students' unrealistic expectations of faculty intervention derived from the 'cognitive fusion' of parents *with* teachers, while the police action was interpreted as the sadistic, vengeful countenance of Big Daddy. Others like Bettelheim (1969) and Rubenstein and Levitt (1969) saw student protestors as 'amoral-and-neurotic rebels'.

Smelser, a psychoanalyst turned sociologist rejected one-sided psychological or biological reductionist, irrationalist anti-democratic accounts exemplified by Le Bon's (1960) account of the crowd in his account of student political activism. Smelser was a protege of Parsons and an advocate for a positivist model of social science that drew on the natural sciences. He wanted to find the broad explanatory principles that he assumed governed social life. Yet even as Smelser rejected Le Bon's crowd theory, he nonetheless argued that 'collective action was often irrational', suggesting that 'in all civilizations men have thrown themselves into episodes of dramatic behaviour such as the craze, the riot and the revolution involving ... distorted beliefs feelings of anxiety, fantasy, hostility' (Smelser 1968:11).

Others like Wilson saw student protests as a structural phenomenon that could be explained by referring to the dynamics of social control. Structural functionalist sociologists at that time defined 'social control' as the rational and normative reactions any 'society' has to deviance because deviance itself was defined as any infraction of a societal norm established by society (Gibbs 1972). Some also highlighted the role of permissive parenting (Parkin 1968:46). Orrin Klapp thought student protest in America could be understood by reference to theories of anomie or deviance which he believed show how young people with 'troubled identities' tried to resolve those feeling or alienation by taking part in collective action. Klapp also highlighted other characteristics he saw in American students such as being oversensitive, suffering from narcissism, or being excessively self-preoccupied (1969:11–13).

Robert Stout went further, arguing that radical student movements at universities like Columbia, Berkeley, Wisconsin, Ohio State and Kent were not in fact political (1970). Noting the prevalence of rebellious 'radical' acts on college campuses that lead to violence, Stout argued that this was all a product of psychological alienation. Stout considered alienation to be a serious pathological condition akin to a mental illness. Alienation apparently involved the separation from one's 'real self' or from other human beings with whom the individual interacts. Indeed so alienated is such a person that 'he' cannot grasp 'his' own identity as a person, let alone communicate effectively with other human beings. One clue to this pathology was the deviant appearance of these students: many were:

> ...unwashed and unkempt; their clothes are often drab and course. The males tend to wear clothing of the lower classes; their hair and beards may tend to be ungroomed and shaggy. Judged by middle or upper-middle class standards, the residences of many of these individuals are less than satisfactory.
>
> *(Stout 1970:37)*

Other psychiatrists like Walter Bromberg and Franck Simon suggested student protestors were suffering from a form of psychosis they called 'protest psychosis' (1968:155).

Social psychologists such as Wrightsman likewise emphasised the pathological character of student protestors. Wrightsman borrowed from G. Stanley Hall's account of adolescence as a transitional and inherently troubled state where young people, with young people trapped between childhood and adulthood:

> Many of the strange, disturbing, and even weird patterns of dress and behaviour of young students undoubtedly arise from the fact that in our society they are marginal persons, who, on the one hand are not accepted in the adult occupational and social world, and on the other hand are physically mature and thus are encouraged (at least biologically) to be independent of their elders.
>
> *(Wrightsman 1968:1)*

Some scholars emphasised what they saw as the effect of working-class student's arrival in what had always been a middle-upper class institution, the university (Rooke 1971). This produced representations of student action as expressions of frustrations experienced by upwardly mobile working-class students (Harman et al., 1968). Bereday was one who synthesised the Oedipal idea with this class-based representation:

> All universities train the elites. In all appear sons of the elite firmly and securely bound to follow their fathers. In all appear also some sons of the 'have-nots' aware that their talent will carry them into the ranks of the elite. Such students rarely riot. The activists are rather a coalition of the splinters of these groups: sons of the elite who for some reason or for the time being don't want to join in, who instead want 'to get even with their fathers'; and sons of the 'have-nots' whose prospects of absorption into the elite are not secure or not attractive and who instead of 'joining' elect to 'lick' it. The coalition of these two groups is usually unbeatable. The rebel sons of the elite supply the know-how of how to operate and to rock the establishment. The rebel 'have-nots' supply the fury and the determination to forge ahead which only those who have been 'left out' can muster.
>
> *(Bereday 1967:120)*[4]

Some political scientists focussed on more political-technical questions. In trying to understand the success with which student movements mobilized such large numbers of people writers like Oberschall (1973:246) looked at how students organized their campaigns or the tactics used (Turner and Killian 1972:159).

What the experts said: communist dupes

In the 1960s the desire to represent student protestors as radical extremists, draft resisters, unpatriotic or 'Fifth Column' for 'international communism' was popular amongst many university managers, mainstream journalists and opinion-makers. Campus-based political unrest was blamed on the unhealthy influence of small but toxic groups of 'extremists' and 'communists'. In the USA some of this drew on the idea that the children of communists and progressives born in the 1940s and 1950s were playing a disproportionate role as student leaders. They were referred to as 'Red Diaper Babies' (Shapiro 1985:3). (I return to this later in the chapter.) These representations involved a readiness to dismiss student protest as the harmful work of extremist revolutionary minorities.

Across the United States, governments, the media and many university administrators has been disposed to detect communist influence in schools and universities since the late 1940s. The suspicion that 'Communists' were subverting democracy became a central and institutionalised motif of the Cold War as early as March 1947 when US President Truman instituted his Loyalty Program. Truman signed *Executive Order 9385* requiring loyalty oaths and background investigations on those employed in the public service and universities suspected of communist sympathies or affiliations. This was followed in 1950 by state legislation like the Levering Act of 1950 introducing a local loyalty oath specifically targeting the University of California.

The appointment of anyone suspected of being a 'left-wing academic' to universities, or revelations of communist infiltration in universities was guaranteed to result in media coverage given the popular assumption that universities were 'hot beds' of student radicalism which needed to be explained.

In the USA, one explanation for student actions like the 'Free Speech movement' in Berkeley was that it was an organized communist conspiracy operating backstage to manipulate naïve students (Miller and Gilmore 1965). In the 1960s, the House Committee Un-American Activities (HUAC) continued its decades long investigation into communist influence issuing subpoenas to those it deemed to be subversives or communist agitators. By May 1960, a number of activists including teachers and students were subpoenaed to appear before a HUAC meeting. In response, Berkeley students staged a sit-in outside the hearing after being refused admission. In response, they were brutally moved on by police using batons and water cannon. HUAC then denounced the students calling them an 'angry mob' organised by 'communist agents and propagandists'. In late 1960, HUAC produced a documentary film (*Operation Abolition*) providing 'evidence' of communist influence and deception in the riot outside its hearing. The film's narrators, Francis E. Walter, Chairman of HUAC, and Fulton Lewis, son of a prominent anti-communist radio commentator, said the protesters were either members of or had been 'duped' by groups whose goal was to destroy the committee, weaken the FBI, and reduce the enforcement powers of the Federal government. Around 15 million people saw the film (Greenberg 1963).

By 1964 when the Free Speech Movement was actively pushing back against the university ban on any organised political activity or political speech, the FBI was using its agents to infiltrate, monitor and neutralize 'student subversives'. (Ironically, the President of Berkeley, Clark Kerr was himself under FBI surveillance because FBI Director, Edgar Hoover, considered him to be too soft on the subversives (Rosenfeld 2013:48–59).) Hoover's paranoia continued in spite of efforts by Kerr and other senior managers to suppress political activity on Berkeley. Ronald Reagan, then a rising conservative politician who became California's governor spent much 1964–1966 denouncing the Free Speech Movement as the 'work of beatniks, radicals and filthy speech advocates' (ibid).

In Australia, anti-intellectual stereotypes of the long-haired professor-subversive were used to 'explain' student protest while reinforcing the fear of communist subversion. In the early 1960s, Australian journalists complained about the:

> ...reasonable proportion of long-haired professors in teeming universities who ... are always on the side of the exotic enemy, and talking of the need for 'peace', but always the backers ... of Communist activities. These set the worst kind of example to their charges, whom they indoctrinate with their own 'academic' viewpoints.
>
> (Bulletin 30 June 1960:4)

They pointed to the lessons that should have been learned about the vulnerability of British university students in the 1930s, who were said to have been naive and susceptible to communist 'seduction' and manipulation. They were urged to:

> ...take time off from puerile demonstrations to study the careers of Burgess, Maclean and Philby... They were all seduced politically at Cambridge University by extremely clever communist dialectics... While we agree that youth should have a fling, we suggest that it might exercise more care as to what it is flinging.
>
> (Age, 7 May 1969)

As for evidence of secondary school protests, Sydney's *Daily Telegraph* warned, 'What these militant Billy Bunters and playground radicals don't seem to grasp is that they are being led by the nose by a handful of extremist political groups' (*Daily Telegraph* 5 July 1972).

In 1950 the Australian government attempted to outlaw the Communist Party and its members by passing the *Communist Party Dissolution Act* 1950 (Cth) ('*Dissolution Act*'). Declared unconstitutional by the High Court, the Menzies government then introduced a referendum to achieve the same thing but it was narrowly defeated. Anti-communist sentiment nontheless remained powerful. Known communists were no longer appointed to the public service. The proposed appointment of those considered to be left-wing academics like Dr Russel Ward or revelations of communist infiltration in Australian universities, sparked immediate media attention given that universities were said to be hot beds for fomenting student radicalism. Not surprisingly academic appointments had to be vetted (Douglas 2007:53). One account of an alleged 'communist cell' of academics in the University of Melbourne was provided by Dr Frank Knopfelmacher, a well-known conservative public intellectual at the time (*Bulletin*, 12

April 1961:44). This 'scandal' continued into the mid-1960s speaking years of official investigations, court cases and media-generated moral panics.

In this context, academics with communist affiliations were not likely to get academic jobs in Australia (Roberts 2008). As J. V. Stout another public intellectual explained how 'communists' were exceptionally dangerous (Stout 1965:55–72). For journalists employed by *The Bulletin,* communists were conspirators pledged to undermine universities, along with the rest of 'bourgeois society', willing to fake research, indoctrinate students, smear and intimidate their enemies, use their influence to get fellow-travellers into university positions and even to pass secrets on to foreign powers. 'Anyone now a member of the Communist party must be unfit for an academic job. And so, one must add, are fascists, gangsters, and members of the Ku Klux Klan' (*Bulletin,* 1961:9).

While affirming the right to protest, student protesters were subject to repeated warnings that their efforts were strengthening the hand of communist regimes in Hanoi and Peking. In Australia magazines like *The Bulletin* warned readers that Australian security was compromised by student protests which increased 'the effectiveness of [communism's] peaceful conquest of the world by internal subversion' (*Bulletin,* 30 June 1960:4). Visitors from overseas made the same point. In Brisbane at a gathering for 'a Coral Sea Week service' at Lyndon Johnson Place, the American Consul, Arthur Rosen warned that irrational student action 'posed a real danger to society akin to the evils of Nazism' (*Age,* 5 May 1969). Journalists continually argued that communists in China were saluting the revolutionary youth movements abroad pointing to reports from the 'Peking Communist Daily' to verify this 'fact'.

In Britain, the Director of the London School of Economics during the sit-in of 1967, blamed this on 'a small group of about 50 left-wing students who had enticed at most 200 of the school's total of 3,500 students to join them' (Caine 1967). From there it was a small step to claim that student protests were just one part of an international revolutionary conspiracy, and that it was a minority of "foreign students responsible for stirring up trouble. It was a quite negative representation insinuating they were 'merely copying' examples set by students in others and thus not moved by the political issues themselves but blindly mimicking others. It was a view shared by police or security agencies always alert to the security risk posed by communists and subversives.

In Britain, *The Times* warned that:

> ...the students who carry their intolerance to the borders of violence or anarchy are a very small proportion of the whole. That is doubtless true. But ... they have been able to impose their will on the majority, and in doing so are able to modify the character of their institutions.
>
> (*The Times, 1968, 8 May:11*)

In Britain, one Foreign Office report from 1968 described British student militants as 'frighteningly radical', maintaining that 'the threat to the west presented by student protest' was 'potentially dangerous'. A Cabinet committee was established to manage spying operations with particular attention given to international students, considered to be a potential source of dangerous radicalism (Lee 1998:312). The Special Demonstrations Squad, a covert Metropolitan Police unit was used to infiltrate activists groups like the national Radical Socialist Student Federation in the late 1960s.

In June 1968, Britain's Committee of Vice-Chancellors and Principals (CVCP) held a conference on the growing 'student menace' to formulate strategies to suppress the threat. Attendees expressed concern about manipulation of students highlighting the influence of left-wing staff, a view that justified one argument that it would be good to have a frequent police presence on campus. In 1973, British Vice-Chancellors and registrars discussed ways of dealing with student unrest. The Polytechnic of North London, e.g., offered an analysis that divided the student body into four categories: militants or 'wreckers', moderate activists who distrust the modern state, a passive majority and the right-wing 'back-lash' element (Lee 1998). Bristol's Vice-Chancellor preferred a tough line recommending various techniques for handling occupations which included:

> *Harass[ing]* the occupants by discontinuing Mains Service, cutting of telephones and by any other possible means try to keep the initiative. Try to breach their security while keeping strict security on the University side.
> *(Lee 1998:311)*

Apart from applying the communist tag to many people, media representations emphasised the offensive, violent behaviour and the unconventional appearance of student protestors. In Australia conflict between police and students became a daily staple of 'news' for television audiences, for those who read the newspapers or listened to radio from 1967. In Canberra in 1967, 'demonstrating youth' were arrested after pulling down a south Vietnamese flag from a hotel where Air Vice-Marshal Ky was attending a meeting. An ANU lecturer and a student were charged with offensive behaviour, resisting arrest and indecent language. 'Hostile demonstrators' many who were supporters of the National Liberation Front of South Vietnam were allegedly unsuccessfully trying to raise public support for their cause (*Age*, 20 January 1967).

On 4 July 1968 mounted police in the city of Melbourne charged into a group of approximately 2,000 anti-war demonstrators outside the American consulate generating press headlines like 'Troopers Ride Down Ant-war Rioters' *(Age*, 5 July 1968). The coverage included multiple images of 'wild mobs storming' the US consulate, 'savage street battles' in which 'razor wielding, bottle and can throwing students' were met by mounted police troopers who were ordered to "full canter into the crowds" (*Age*, 5 July 1968). In Sydney, police horses also charged into crowds of 'student demonstrators' who had gathered at the Armed Forces Recruiting Centre in York Street and at the Liberal Party headquarters in Ashe Street, Sydney (*Australian*, 5 July 1968). On 18 August 1968, police foiled an attempt to attack the Melbourne US Consulate with petrol bombs. Descriptions in the press of the 1969 May Day March through the city of Melbourne Australia estimated thousands of participants and included accounts of 'girls in jeans' and 'youths' collecting money for 'the enemy' -the Viet Cong and the National Liberation Front (NLF). 'Very pretty girls in boots, engrossed in long kisses', 'long haired and bearded students carrying yellow-starred NLF flags by the score' mixed in solidarity with politicians like Dr Jim Cairn and unionists as they made their way along the streets chanting: 'One, two, three, four – the Viet Cong will win the war' (*Age*, 5 May 1969).

Beside the violent clashes with police, student protestors also offended 'respectable' sensibilities. The deviant status of student protestors was regularly represented in visual ways highlighting how they were a 'long-haired scruffy looking lot', 'unkept and scraggy with ludicrous beards, long hair, slovenly, untidy in their dress, and even with bare and dirty feet' (*Age* 31 March 1967). One protest by students involved dragging Australian and American flags aboard their float and hurling rolls of toilet paper over them... which unfurled at the feet of the Lady Mayoress on the Town Hall stand': this *The Age* thundered, was a 'disgrace to their universities' (*Age*, 15 March 1967).

'Revolting, lewd, disgusting and indecent' was how Justice Newton of Victoria's Supreme Court described one edition of the University of Melbourne newspaper *Farrago* whose editor faced him on a number of charges. Justice Newton added, the article in question dealt with sex in ways that 'grossly offended community standards' (*Age*, 11 March 1967). Another student was gaoled in the late sixties for 'the printing of smutty literature' and his imprisonment was to set an example, to 'stir others to write decent article' (*Age*, 5 November 1968).

In the USA, the UK and Australia, the 'noise of solemn assemblies' generated by professionals, media workers, police and other agents of the state all working as 'moral entrepreneurs' tirelessly 'explained' the problem young people had become not only to their to parents but to the community and state. This made it made it difficult to acknowledge the politics of these representations.

Clearly, engaging in 'unconventional politics', meant student activists were easily represented as a threat to law and order, to democracy, the state and the West. These were not neutral or innocent representations: but deeply political. Young people were being made-up and subjected to what Foucault called forms of government, or what Bourdieu called symbolic violence. It was an expert commentary that failed to perceive the possibility that protesters could be protesting about issues that were important to them.

And many young people resisted theserepresentations. Student activists well understood the politics informing the uniformly negative representations of them as trouble makers or communist dupes. As one former Australian student at the time recalled, to be identified as:

> ...a radical student was to be identified as a ratbag at least, and possibly worse, a traitor or something that needed to be destroyed, or put down. If

we had initially been seen as a bit of a joke, that rapidly ceased to be the case by the late 1960s. I think there was quite a serious attempt to undermine the effectiveness of the student movement.

(Interview Neil Massey, 1991)

Even so, while the sounds of student politics were often drowned out by those hostile accounts of them, it was possible then, as it is now, to discern what they were saying and doing – and why they acted as they did. There was no mystery about why they took the action they did. They reacted then, as did their predecessors and as their successors have done in the twenty-first century for moral and political reasons as they responded in heartfelt ways to the major political issues of the day.

One thing that did characterise them was that most student activists were not interested in working on behalf of the Communist parties. As John Gray argues:

> 1968 represented a break with the Old Left, which for many protestors in France and America had become too involved in cold war struggles and, particularly in the US, too closely aligned with trade unions.
>
> *(Gray 2018:21)*

This is not to deny the relevance of connections between student activists and communist parties in the west or of their connections with trades unions, citizen based and other movements. There were significant relations between these groups on and off-campus. As Howard Becker argued 'we cannot understand a complex event involving many groups by analysing the origins and behaviour of just one of them' (Becker 1973:8–9). Writers like Bertrand Gordon have showed, e.g., how worker-student alliances formed during the 1968 student revolts in France, Italy and West Germany helped to shape student movements while acknowledging how anarchist, Trotskyist and Maoist groups also helped to shape student movements (1998:40).

The politics of student protest

Student protests of the 1960s involved a small, but active minority of students. In Britain, e.g., Thomas argues that if the 1960s were the 'halcyon age of revolutionary fervour', it only ever involved a small proportion of them (2002). One survey carried out at Warwick University in June 1968 found only 7% of students were politically active. Another survey at Leeds university in January 1969 suggested only 15% of students there were 'politically active'. Larger numbers were however said to be sympathetic to issues central to the student movement. A Gallup Poll survey carried out in May 1968 at Sussex University and Cambridge University found that 60% of students at Sussex and 43% at Cambridge were sympathetic to students who protested about the lack of student representation in university academic affairs. Only 16% and 32% were opposed, respectively. At Sussex, 67% of students believed 'that student protests and demonstrations serve a useful purpose', while only 8% regarded them as 'harmful'. In spite of this sympathy or support, most students did not participate in protest action. At Sussex University, 25% of students said they took part in demonstrations against the Vietnam War, the largest figure to protest on any single issue (Thomas 2002:282).

It was unusual in the 1960s to find scholars prepared to accept that student activists were morally and politically engaged with the leading political issues of the day. Fewer acknowledged what Ajunwa said in his study of black secondary school activists, namely that along with university students high school students were actively promoting policy change in the American education system (2011:5).

The psychologist, Kenneth Keniston was one scholar who did not denigrate America student activists (1965). In his study of young people, Keniston represented youth as a period between 'adolescence' and 'adulthood' as a time of change, freedom and ambivalence towards the world of adults (1965). It was a study based on interviews with only 12 young financially privileged male students at Harvard. It was an account of young people as alienated and experiencing despair, confusion and angst. This he argued was a result of their estrangement from the then dominant post-war American consumerist and materialist values, the privileging of technology and commitment to instrumental rationality. The young men in his student told Keniston they felt there was no compelling social imaginary that offered a conception of a good life. He also drew on a psychoanalytic model to emphasise how these young men were trapped in relations with their neurotic, possessive mothers while missing a close relationship with their fathers, who were usually absent. As he explained 'young Americans find themselves so distant from their parents that they can neither emulate nor rebel against them' (Keniston 1965:230).

Three years later Keniston modified his representations (1968). Based on interviews with 17 young privileged students involved in anti-war protests, Keniston still drew on the older idea that young people were still adolescents yet to transit to adulthood. The analysis was complicated by a recognition that the USA was going through a major process of social and technological change. He concluded there were now two types of young people, i.e., 'alienated Hippies' and 'committed New Left activists'. While the 'alienated Hippies' looked like his 1965 cohort, except they were now wearing brightly coloured clothes and took LSD or smoked cannabis, the 'committed activists' were quite different. They were 'personalistic', and often 'hostile' to traditional bureaucratic power and authority. Keniston maintained that his studies demonstrated that political leftists were rebellious, empathic, humanitarian, altruistic, and idealistic –even if they rejected traditional religion (1969, 1968a, 1968b).[5]

Keniston relied in part on Lawrence Kohlberg's (1963) theory of moral development. Keniston argued that research on Berkeley FSM activists revealed that most student activists exhibited high moral competence although 'even the highest levels of moral reasoning do not alone guarantee truly virtuous behaviour' (Keniston 1970:591). He also remained faithful to his psycho-analytic model arguing that the young activists' close maternal attachments explained their academic success, while their principled commitments to ideas of democracy or justice could be explained in terms of their relations with their fathers. Rather than representing student activists as deviants, delusional, and dangerous, Keniston highlighted their ordinary, well-adjusted disposition in which adherence to and identification with their parents' moral frames were apparent.

Having said this, like most of those offering more antagonistic representations of student activists Keniston did not engage with the specifically political moral issues that moved them to act. Keniston's preference was to speculate about 'explanatory factors' like the expansion of higher education exposing students to 'the sociology of knowledge, psychoanalysis, Marxism, philosophical analysis, cultural relativism, and a variety of other idea systems' to say nothing of the effect of alternate values encouraged by the spread of technologies like television (Keniston 1970:589).

A small number of other scholars like Seymour Lipset also accepted that student movements were informed by political-moral responses to what they considered unethical and unjust events (Lipset 1968:66–71). Merelman argued, e.g., that student activist's:

> ...sense of encouragement stems from the fact that youthful leftists appear to display a distinctive cognitive profile marked by unusually high levels of moral judgement.
>
> *(Merelman 1977:29–54)*

In Australia, observers like Ellery Hamilton-Smith, then the Development Officer of the Victorian Association of Youth Clubs, argued that young people had a commitment and assumed a considerable share of social responsibility:

> An interesting feature of the present protesting generation was that most of the protest was coupled with an ethical concern and practical concern for the well-being of people ... much of the protest focused on issues of ethics, and human suffering or injustice.
>
> *(Hamilton-Smith Mercury, Hobart 21 May 1969)*

This is recognition of the moral-political emotions that moved students to act is partly why academic Nick Thomas argued that the usual explanations for protest didn't seem applicable to student activism in the 1960s. Unlike the hunger marches by the unemployed in the 1930s, or most strike action by workers, student protests in the 1960s were not about jobs, wages or the economy (Thomas 2002:280). In this way, many student protests were about issues that had little to do with the immediate everyday lives of those who protested.

In Britain, e.g., students supporting the anti-apartheid movement founded in 1959 (Gurney 2000), or protesting the American war in Vietnam would not directly benefit from the consequences of their protest. Yet arguing that student action was inspired by altruism overlooks the ways that many issues that roused students also affected them directly whether it was how universities operated or the likelihood that they might become military conscripts. Paul Ginsborg writing about Italy's student movement argued that '[t]he year 1968 [...] was much more than a protest against poor conditions. It was an ethical revolt, a notable attempt to turn the tide against the predominant values of the time' (Ginsborg 1990:299). Similarly, surveys of English and European students activists in the 1960s, validated this judgement, showing they demonstrated the capacity to form more complex moral judgements when compared to the general student body (O'Connor 1974:53–79).

Student activists were more than willing to express the nature and strength of their moralcommitment. When it was announced that, e.g., the Australian government would establish an inquiry into how students were being manipulated by communists, students reacted strongly. They responded saying, they were not under the influence of communism, but rather they had 'the courage to think for themselves, and the desire to rouse others from their induced apathy.' In a letter to The *Age*, newspaper at the time Richard Hallworth, a student at University of Melbourne wrote:

> We need to know the real reasons why our youths must fight and die overseas before they are allowed to vote. We need an investigation into ASIO and their violations of personal privacy and the right of free speech in this country. I challenge the Federal Government to prove that students are being manipulated by anything other than their own conscience.
> (Age, 7 May 1969)

Perhaps the idea of habitus provides some insight into these representations and also how students saw and experienced themselves. Being young and progressive sometimes had much to do with being born into a left-wing family with strong attachments to leftist networks. Detailed accounts of the children of American leftists born in the 1940s and 1950s, the so-called 'Red Diaper Babies' suggest that children of left wing or progressive parents learned early how to interpret the world in particular ways. These young activists recalled that 'Politics was part of my life-blood [politics] was my mother's milk'. 'It never occurred to me not to be interested' (Braungart and Braungart 1990:260). As Lorena Shapiro explained:

> We were raised in opposition to – at best, in ambivalence to – a central tenet of American society: accumulation for private profit and personal upward mobility ... We were raised to value diversity in a sacred and ethically-bound society We were raised to value ideas in a society that is anti-intellectual We were raised to value collective action in a society that is desperately individualistic ... We were raised as fighters in a passive society.

> Born into a culture of struggle, our definition of being alive, adult, whole, is linked to fighting for social change.
>
> *(1985:4)*

In her study, McCurties described these children as a 'unique group of young Americans', primarily white, middle or working class, often Jewish with strong views 'about sexism, classism, and racism' that were formed when young (2011:6). Some of this reflected deliberate educational efforts by their elders. The American Communist Party, e.g., introduced their kind of politics to the next generation using special children's literature, youth programs and summer camps (Mischler 1999).

For the children of communist families 'persecution, secrecy, camaraderie, factionalism, and idealism' played a role in disposing them to be some of the first white, college-aged participants in the Student Non-violent Coordinating Committee (SNCC) and Congress of Racial Equality (CORE), and leaders in later movements like Students for a Democratic Society (SDS), The Free Speech Movement (FSM) and later the Weathermen (McCurties 2011:8).

Early exposure to the practices of dissent was normal in these families. While in grade school, Sharon Jeffrey, daughter of socialists, helped her parents canvass in support of Socialist Party candidate. Gail another 'Red Diaper Baby' said: 'I started marching when I was three. I was aware of being different' (McCurties 2011:6). Yet being born into a progressive family did not entail a straight forward process of socialisation or indoctrination: many young people explicitly rejected the ethos and commitments of the Old Left. Ron Ridenour was one who recalled why this meant he worked in the civil rights movement:

> I took the step... I needed to do something more tangible than be a member of the C[ommunist]P[arty]. It was too conservative and over-weighted with old people, who couldn't or wouldn't be activists. Through my civil rights work, I saw information about the upcoming Mississippi Summer Project. I had worked with CORE in Los Angeles. Now I took the big step to struggle in the lion's mouth.
>
> *(McCurties 2011:12)*

For this reason, it is important, particularly in the case of the American student movement of the sixties, to acknowledge how secondary school protestors also played a central role in shaping the political experience of those who went on to become university student activists.

Secondary school student activists

The American historian Steve Mintz made an insightful point when he wrote:

> The history of children is often treated as a marginal subject ... there is no question [the history of childhood] is especially difficult to write. Children

are rarely obvious historical actors. They leave fewer historical sources than adults, and their powerlessness makes them less visible than other social groups.

(Mintz 2006:1)

This is true of young student protestors. Ironically Mintz made this observation while overlooking the role of children in the 1950s civil rights protests, or the actions of high school students in educational reform campaigns, and free speech or anti-war protests in the 1960s. Now largely forgotten, America's school student movement in the late 1950s and 1960s played a notable role in these major political campaigns. In her study of young people's politics, Gael Graham documents the scale of secondary school student activism in the 1960s. In her account of the 1960s American secondary school activism, Graham highlights the fact that 59% of American high schools reported political disruption in 1969.[6]

According to Graham high school activists were inspired by the general climate of protest in the sixties while their struggles signified the awakening of a generation determined to reform schools and American society and to challenge how young people understood themselves. A series of major political issues interested and impassionate quite young people.

For Graham, the landmark 1954 *Brown vs. Board of Education* Supreme Court ruling placed high schools at the centre of the civil rights campaign aimed at recognising and protecting the rights of African-Americans students. In many cases, secondary school students from progressive or leftist families had their first experience of organising and participating in protest at their public schools in the 1950s. As Mitch recalled: 'I organized people in eighth grade to put peace buttons on in class'. Another high school student, Lisa recalled her involvement in school strikes:

> I was the only kid in my high school to go out on the picket line with the janitors. I refused to cross the picket line and I hung out in 20 degree 2 below weather. I went to marches. I wore black armbands.
>
> *(Cited in McCurties 2011:226)*

The result as Ajunwa argues was a determined effort by some high school students from late in the 1950s through to the 1970s, to engage in activism and educational reform (2011). That sometimes involved students forming groups to fight a particular school rule, to challenge dress codes, or protest grooming regulations that prohibited boys from having long hair (Graham 2006). From the late 1950s, many high school students also began advocating for major reforms seeking increased legal rights for students in schools and challenging the authority of school officials to make decisions without consulting them. Ajunwa documents how high school activists used underground newspapers to promote their educational agendas like reforming the curriculum, changing suspension policies and enlarging the rights and responsibilities of student councils (2011).

While the response from many adults to youthful challenge varied significantly, it tended predominantly to arouse alarm and often outrage from many parents, school officials and governments. Drawing largely on the recollections of former students, Graham documents responses to this mandate that range from enthusiastic collaboration, to resentful acquiescence, to overt and hostile resistance. Some progressive teachers tried to understand student politics and sometimes offer students a role in some decisions about their education. On the other hand, conservatives saw 'adolescent protest' as troubling and illegitimate, moving to suppress it whenever it arose and employing police services to do so. Many of the black and Chicano people Graham interviewed, remembered ostracism and hostility as 'minority' students in newly 'integrated schools'. Occasionally other students reacted violently. In the mid-1950s, David Horowitz then a secondary school student was surrounded by a group of older peers:

> Suddenly, the leader of the group grabbed my arm and shoved me against the wall, while another took the dangling cord of an auditorium drape and slipped it around my neck. Pulling the cord tight, he shouted, 'His father's a Red. String him up!' Another hissed: 'Send him back to Russia!' I struggled to free myself, but was too embarrassed to cry out. Nobody among the hundreds of people in the room seemed to be aware of my plight. Nobody cared ... It was the worst moment of the McCarthy era.
>
> *(1999:73)*

Notwithstanding outrage and opposition from many older people, teachers and governments, the sheer scale of the action sometimes ensured political success. One of the largest and successful strikes began on 5 March 1968, when 2,000 students from Garfield High School in East Los Angeles marched from school at midday, chanting 'Walk out' and *'Viva la revolución'*. They were mostly Chicano, protesting about the poor conditions of their schools. At the time, Mexican-Americans in Los Angeles had the highest dropout rate and lowest college attendance of any ethnic group. Members of a new community group calling themselves the 'Brown Berets' supported the students declaring that:

> For over 20 years, the Mexican American has suffered at the hands of the Anglo-establishment. He is discriminated against in schooling, housing, in employment and in every other phase of life. Because of this situation, the Mexican American has become the lowest achiever of any minority group in the entire Southwest.
>
> *(Timeline 2018)*

The walkout spread to other East L.A. schools with over 22,000 students participating. Local law enforcement performed undercover operations and arrested

13 activists. Charges were finally dropped, and the student-led protests produced change. In 1969, one year after the walkouts, the number of Mexican Americans enrolled at UCLA rose from 100 to 1,900.

In the second half of the sixties, opposition to the Vietnam war elicited increasing support from school students. Secondary school students not only took part in public demonstrations in school, but initiated discussions with peers and organised boycotts of companies involved in the war. Some high school students had started protesting against the Vietnam war. Mindy was one who said, 'When I got to high school, I did start getting involved. I was anti-Vietnam'. For many 'Red Diaper Babies' anti-war activism was always supported by their parents. As Jennifer remembered:

> I never had to rebel as a kid. My parents were so far ahead of me, I didn't have to say, 'I'm going to go down to Washington and protest the Vietnam War'. They were [already] teaching me what was wrong about it.
> *(Cited in McCurties 2011:227)*

Ira recalled: 'As early as ten or eleven … I did organizing work in sixth grade around the issue of the war. And of course, I went to a lot of anti-war demonstrations' (McCurties 2011:227).

While it is now largely forgotten and often overlooked by researchers, secondary school student protest in Australia had become a feature of the late 1960s and early 1970s.[7] A group of University of Sydney activists calling themselves *Resistance* began organising secondary school students and publishing a newspaper called *Student Underground*. One 1969 issue of *Student Underground* epitomised the politics of this exercise:

> To change the education system, the society which has created it must also be changed, since school is an important tool in creating the apathy that exists in Australian society… We, in the *Student Underground Movement*, intend to focus attention on this society in order to change it, and with it the abhorrent symptoms such as the Vietnam war, social injustice and the education system.
> *(Cited in Adamson 1998:2)*

By 1971, secondary school protests in Australia were becoming a mass phenomenon. Strikes, walkouts, demonstrations and other actions were taking place in all cities targeting the poor conditions of their schools (bad lighting, no heating, leaking roofs, etc.) and other local issues (Adamson 1998). On 19 April 1972, students at University High in Melbourne organised a demonstration of 500 students in the city.

On 20 September 1972, for the first time in Australia's history, tens of thousands of secondary students took direct action demanding their right to strike, to engage in school walkouts, and to hold meetings in schools and rallies after school. According to Adamson, around 10,000 students participated. In Sydney, thousands of students participated in over 100 schools. Based on the signatures collected for a petition, the composition of the rally was 7% year 8 students, 25% year 9, 19% year 10, 16% year 11 and 10% year 12. At Sydney's Penshurst Girls High, 400 students demonstrated on school grounds. Student demands included the liberalisation of school uniform regulations and 'no privileges for senior students: equal rights for all'. At Broadmeadow West Technical school in Melbourne, 200 male students protested outside their school on the day of the strike. In the city of Hobart, an after-school rally was attended by 300 in Franklin Square and in nearby Launceston, 200 Kingsmeadow High students demonstrating about the lack of a school gymnasium marched to Prospect High (Adamson 1998).

This action in Australia was paralleled in other cities around the world. In France in February 1971, over 10,000 secondary students defied government bans and successfully demonstrated for the release of a fellow student detained by police. In October 1971, 10,000 school students protested in Vancouver against the Amchitka atomic bomb test. In London, we saw protests against corporal punishment in 1972 (Adamson 1998). As in America, this action typically involved demands for the extension of human rights like freedom of expression and personal freedoms for young people. These movements were calling attention to the oppressive nature of schools and connect their struggles with wider national and global efforts for human rights (Ajunwa 2011:6). While this has yet to be documented conclusively it was action that informed and reflected the parallel development of university student activism.

University students politics

As with secondary students, the political issues of the day were central to the politics of university student activism. American university activists in the sixties, e.g., were moved to action by a series of political problems. The issues included white supremacist efforts to deny black civil rights, issues of democracy and free speech in universities, and opposition to America's war in Vietnam (Johnson and Feinberg 1980:173–174). In Britain, student discontent with universities segued into opposition to America's war in Vietnam, while in Australia the introduction of conscription to supply troops for military service in Vietnam created a major political rallying point for students. In each case, students asserted their political agency, typically against determined efforts by elites and experts maintaining they did not have the capacity or the right to act as they did.

In America university student activism initially engaged with the civil rights movements in the late 1950s. This mobilised thousands of largely white college students to engage in the "freedom marches" into the southern states. Between 1964 and 1966, while the scale of American student protest accelerated, the protest themes changed. While a freedom ride was completed in 1965 in Selma, it was followed soon after by 'the Watts riots'. By 1966, 'Freedom Now' was replaced with 'Black Power' and white students were purged from the Student Non-violent Coordinating Committee's (SNCC) (Johnson and Feinberg 1980:173–174). In 1966 the issues turned to America's increased involvement in Vietnam after the Tonkin Gulf Resolution as the draft becoming a major campus issue.

The free speech movement: Berkeley

Against a background of ongoing civil rights campaigns in the 1950s, it is generally agreed that university student action in America on the issue of free speech took off on 1 February 1960, when black college students staged a sit-in at a segregated lunch counter in Greensborough, North Carolina insisting that they be served (O'Brien 1972:33). The North Carolina sit-in triggered significant support by both black and white university students for the civil rights movement to enable more black voters to exercise their right to vote well into the mid-1960s (O'Brien 1972).[8] Between June–August 1964 the Student Non-violent Coordinating Committee, e.g., spearheaded a voting drive in Mississippi known as 'Freedom Summer' (McAdam 1988). This indirectly promoted the first major student movement focussing on the right to free speech in the university in Berkeley in the autumn of 1964.

The blend of recent experience in civil rights activism and a Students for a Democratic Society (SDS) campaign critical of the bureaucratic and authoritarian nature of American universities, turned out to be an incendiary combination at Berkeley in the autumn of 1964. Sixty Berkeley students participated in 'Freedom Summer' civil rights projects in Mississippi, Alabama and North Carolina in the summer months before returning to the new semester (Rorabaugh, 1989:19). When Berkeley students returned to campus in September, they created and joined new organizations that addressed civil rights, students' rights and the upcoming presidential election. The SDS chapter at Berkeley grew fast, while SNCC also established the first Berkeley chapter. And while these political commitments were central to what then happened, it was the university's attempt to ban political speech and activity on the campus that was the catalyst for the Free Speech Movement.

The 1962 SDS 'Port Huron Statement' encouraged students and other young people to become politically active and motivated many to join what became known as the 'New Left' and to organise the Free Speech Movement it was a 25,700-word statement drafted by Tom Hayden for the inaugural convention of Students for a Democratic Society in Port Huron, Michigan in mid-1962 which articulated 'the problems' of American society and set out a 'radical vision' for a 'better future'. Hayden was a 22-year-old university teacher who had already participated in a number of freedom rides in 1961 and served jail time.

Apart from rejecting what it called the 'older left perverted by Stalinism' the statement was a call for participatory democracy 'as a means and an end'. It advocated non-violent civil disobedience and argued that individual citizens should help make decisions that influence the quality and direction of their lives (SDS 1962). It also signalled the idea that universities become key sites for political action. The SDS argued for rallying support and to strengthen itself by looking to universities, which benefit from their 'social influence' and that are 'the only mainstream institution ... open to participation by individuals of nearly any viewpoint'. It looked to a national campaign directed towards achieving 'university reform by an alliance of students and faculty' who 'must wrest control of the educational process from the administrative bureaucracy', ally with groups outside the university, integrate 'public issues into the curriculum', and 'make debate'. In short, 'They must consciously build a base for their assault upon the loci of power' (SDS 1962).

In 1964, student political activity on the Berkeley campus was limited to a small 26 feet x 90 feet area on the corner of Bancroft and Telegraph, directly outside the main university entrance. Clark Kerr, the president of the University of California, claiming to be a liberal, seemed to have an illiberal view of on-campus political activity. Kerr's argued that 'Just like the University should not invade students' off-campus life ... so the students, individually or collectively, should not and cannot take the name of the University into ... political or other non-University facilities' (Heirich 1970:52). On 14 September 1964, Kerr, was concerned by evidence of overt political activities at Berkeley and directed Katherine Towle, the Dean of Students to issue a letter to all student organizations banning all political activities, fund-raising, and informational tables from the Bancroft and Telegraph area. The student response to Towle's memo was immediate and clear. Fourteen different political organizations, including SDS, SNCC, and the College Republicans, banded together to form the United Front.

Two days after they received Towle's letter, a number of United Front leaders petitioned the Dean, urging her to rescind her directive. In a meeting with the United Front, Towle agreed to allow tables at Bancroft but said that only informational literature could be distributed. Student leaders rejected the proposition. (Rosenbrier 1971:108). A key figure in this early process was Mario Savio, a 21-year-old, first-year philosophy student from New York who had spent several months in summer 1964 teaching young African-Americans as part of the Freedom Summer campaign in the South.

While student activists were committed to progressive political agendas focussing on civil rights, they were also able to rally support by identifying problems in the university itself. Mario Savio a key leader in the year-long process called the Free Speech Movement, made this clear in arguing for educational reform, in preference to more radical goals like the overthrow of capitalism, the ending of racism and sexism and the abolition of imperialism. According to Savio:

> In our free-speech fight at the University of California, we have come up against what may emerge as the greatest problem of our nation – a depersonalized, unresponsive bureaucracy.
>
> *(Savio 1965b:216)*

He was also critical too of what he saw as second-rate university education:

> If you are an undergraduate still taking non-major courses, at least one of your subjects will be a 'big' lecture in which, with field glasses and some good luck, you should be able, a few times a week, to glimpse that famous profile giving those four- or five-year-old lectures, which have been very conveniently written up for sale by the Fybate Company anyway. The lectures in the flesh will not contain much more than is already in the Fybate notes, and generally no more than will be necessary to do well on the examinations.
>
> *(Savio 1965a:4)*

From September 21 to the first week in October 1964, the United Front organised protests and vigils across the campus. After a week of student protests, the Berkeley Chancellor Edward Strong issued a statement allowing political literature to be distributed at the Bancroft and Telegraph entrance but kept the ban on demonstrations and fund-raising. On September 29, the students bypassed Chancellor Strong's ban on fundraising. As one student said later: 'We decided to set up the tables, express our right to collect money on the campus because the campus – in our view – was public property … We wanted to establish the right to collect money on any piece of public property' (cited in Rosenbrier 1971:110).

On 30 September 1964, Berkeley chapters of SNCC and the Congress on Racial Equality (CORE) again set up tables on campus to collect donations. Representatives from the dean of student's office immediately turned up and took the names of five student organizers and required them to appear before the dean. The students complied but were followed to the Dean's office by 500 other United Front members, led by Savio and Goldberg. Chancellor Stroing of Berkeley ordered the dean to suspend the five student activists. In solidarity, Savio and the 500 other students called for their suspension too. Savio then coordinated a sit-in at Sproul Hall, which included the dean's office and threatened to remain until Strong and Towle lifted the five suspensions or suspended all United Front members. Savio addressed the sit-in crowd arguing the university administration 'manipulates the university … to suppress the vast, virtually powerless majority' (cited in Ritchie 1973:102). He continued saying that no longer saw the crisis as a small campus issue but as a broad question of students' rights to freedom of speech and the First Amendment. The United Front morphed into the Free Speech Movement.

In early October 1964, following the first sit-in students again set up tables at the same Bancroft and Telegraph locations and continued to solicit funds. Representatives from the dean's office, accompanied by campus police, again approached the students and told them to cease and desist. The students refused. One graduate student, Jack Weinberg, was arrested for trespassing and escorted to a police car. Hundreds of passing students then sat around the police car and blocked exit routes. The crowd caused a great commotion and within minutes, several hundred more students placed themselves around the car. Savio removed his shoes and climbed to the roof of the car and began calling for Weinberg's release. Savio quickly turned the stand-off into a forum calling for free speech. 'We are being denied our rights by them. We will stand around this police car until they negotiate with us' (Ritchie 1973:106). On 2 December, between 1,500 and 4,000 students occupied Sproul Hall as a last bid to re-open negotiations with university administration on restrictions on political speech and action on campus. The authorities had had enough. Shortly after 2 a.m. on 4 December 1964, police encircled the building, and at 3:30 a.m. they began arresting around 800 students. Many charges of police brutality resulted (Lipset and Wolin, 1965).

Support for the Movement's goals grew dramatically. Before police intervention, approximately 2,500 students supported the FSM (*Report*, 1970). It seemed that police intervention backfired. FSM's meetings and rallies began attracting large crowds of 7,000 or more (Lipset and Wolin, 1965). In a survey done after October 2, over 50% of the student body approved the goals and tactics of the FSM leadership (Heirich 1971:169). The semester-long dispute expanded drawing members of the state legislature, the governor, alumni and the faculty (Lipset and Wolin, 1965). Such a crisis developed, that classes and other academic activities were cancelled. Eventually, in January 1965, the Free Speech Movement achieved its primary goal. The university lifted its restrictions on political activities.

Leeds University sit-in, 1968

In Britain, though there were campaigns to ban nuclear weapons that encouraged small numbers of students to demonstrate in the early sixties, there were no major political issues engaging large number of students in the way America's civil-rights campaigns against white racism had done there.[9]

If Britain was understood in the sixties to be a somewhat traditional society with a hereditary monarch, a regard for an aristocratic hierarchical order and a somewhat rigid class system, all that was challenged in 1968 as British universities experienced a wave of student protest on campus. The issues that sparked this were initially local, relating to student housing, and student participation in university governance and decision-making. Resentment, an important moral emotion, was engaged as students rejected being treated as irresponsible and too young to know what they were talking about. In March 1968, for example, one Cambridge University student objected the idea that universities should regard their students *in loco parentis* observing:

> 'what we object to is our sub-adult status' adding that 'my parents have no responsibility for me ... so why should the college'.
>
> *(Thomas 1996:158)*

In 1969, a survey of 529 students at Leeds University discovered that 70 percent opposed the University's position of *in loco parentis* (Thomas 1996:158). It became an issue that impelled many students to protest against university restrictions on visiting hours in halls, in off-campus accommodation and rules about 'fornication'.

We also see the influence of the Students for a Democratic Society (SDS) 'The Port Huron statement', a political manifesto drafted in 1962 by the American SDS offering new ways of thinking about democracy, how to pursue a 'more authentic, concrete form of democracy in the economic, political and social realms' (Klimke and Scharloth 2008:129). Like their Berkeley Free Speech Movement peers, British activists used similar political tactics including demonstrations and rallies which were usually followed by student occupations of university administrative offices. These waves of protests swept over the London School of Economics and universities in Leeds, Birmingham, Manchester, Liverpool, Bristol, Keele and Leicester universities in 1968 (Thomas 2002:284–288).

While these student actions did not fit into a neat tidy pattern, most were initially small protest actions eliciting a disproportionate response by university authorities. This allowed some students to represent the management response as excessive, undemocratic and unjust. Based on that account those students were then able to mobilise the support of far larger numbers of normally indifferent students. It was a 'pattern' exemplified in the Leeds University occupation that saw around 400 students continuously occupy the Chancellery between 25 June and 27 June 1968. The occupation began with a student demonstration protesting a visit by Patrick Wall, a right-wing Conservative MP to address the Conservative Association in the Students' Union at Leeds University on 3 May 1968. Like Enoch Powell, Wall was known for his 'outspoken views' on race and immigration. Hundreds of protestors rallied, and according to reports, Mr Wall was spat on as he left the meeting. His wife, Sheila, reported that when she was leaving 'a student wearing brown trousers kicked me with both feet (sic) and I went down on my back on the steps …I was trampled on by several students'. She added that she put the incident down to 'pre-exam nerves and damned bad manners' (cited in Hanna 2013:43).

After the incident, the university established a disciplinary committee to discipline students involved in the violence. On this occasion, university managers pre-empted one possible critique by co-opting six students onto the disciplinary committee. In spite of efforts by the National Union of Students to promote student participation in academic governance, it was not the normal practice in the 1960s (Thomas 2002:284). That exclusion normally enabled students to highlight a breach of natural justice as the university seemed to allow the prosecutors to 'try and convict' accused students. At Leeds, six staff members and the Vice-Chancellor, (Sir Roger Stevens), who had the casting vote were added to the disciplinary committee. Undeterred by the apparent concession, the student movement formed a 3rd May Committee. This group's concern was that the co-option of student members to the disciplinary committee not democratic because there was no election. They also claimed there had been politically motivated investigations by the university's security service. The 3rd May Committee called for the abolition of security files, the abolition of the unrepresentative disciplinary committee and the dismissal of the heads of the security service. They also demanded the Vice-Chancellor's resignation and further sit-ins if their demands were not met.

By 20 June the disciplinary committee had deliberated and decided to fine five students a total of £16.10s. At the same time, the Leeds Student Union had made investigated the allegations against the security service. It was said evidence was uncovered suggesting the allegations against the security service might be true. The Vice-Chancellor then made statements that allowed the conclusion to be drawn that the allegations were true. Soon after at a student Union General Meeting (21 June), calls were made for an inquiry, and the threat made that more sit-ins would be organised if the inquiring was not forthcoming. By 25 June, the Union had received no reply from the Vice-Chancellor. That day, around 400 students occupied the administrative offices housed in the Parkinson building, including the Vice-Chancellor's and the Registrar's offices.

This action came with support from the Student Union and seemed also to enjoy considerable support on campus. Six months after the sit-in the Student Union newspaper *Union News* surveyed some 546 Leeds University students. They found only 15.5% of students described themselves as politically active. It also found that 86% described Union politics as boring and 63% did not agree with the earlier demonstration against the visit by a right-wing Conservative MP Patrick Wall, with only 22% supporting it. In respect to political allegiances, 22.5% supported Labour, 35% supported the Conservatives, 16% supported the Liberals, 20% were 'don't knows' and only 3.5% identified with 'the left'. Even at Leeds where most students were politically inactive, some students were still able to prompt large numbers of those moderate students to participate in serious challenges to the authority of the administration (Thomas 2002).

On the evening of 25 June, the Vice-Chancellor issued a statement breaking off all negotiations until the sit-in was ended. This proved to be a standard response by British university authorities. Refusing to talk meant that students had to put up with a significant level of physical hardship. Those engaged in the occupation were supported by other students throughout the sit-in by the temporary participation of much larger groups of students. The sit-in continued for several days and nights. Security, food and entertainment was organised by the students. The Leeds Trades Union Council sent its support, and speakers arrived from other UK universities and even from France. The conditions for the occupying students were pithily summed up by one participant in the Birmingham University sit-in of December 1968, who said 'when you're sitting in, what can you do about changing your socks? After three days in the same pair they not only have a very distinctive odour ... but they also change their original texture and become closely akin to wire mesh' (Thomas 2002:285).

On this occasion, the occupation was not immediately successful. Faced with the practical difficulties associated with in sleeping arrangements, the supply of food and maintaining hygiene, those involved in the occupation could only continue for a limited time. On 27 June 1968, students at Leeds sent a letter to the Vice-Chancellor asking for a public inquiry, and when the Vice-Chancellor refused, students ended the occupation. No inquiry was held. At the end of 1968, however, a committee was established by the university to consider proposals for new disciplinary procedures and for new forms of student involvement in university government. In this way, the student occupations at Leeds and other universities helped to persuade university administrators to begin including students in their governance structures.

Monash University 1968

While Australia was a much smaller country than the US or Britain, many of the new Australian universities established after 1961 saw a considerable degree of activism.[10] The focus here is on Monash University established in 1961.[11]

Like Britain, a small number of public issues like capital punishment, censorship and the White Australia policy attracted university student interest in the early 1960s.

The Australian government's decision to send troops to the Vietnam War and the introduction of a selective conscription scheme in late 1964 also encourage significant student activism. In early 1965, two students Pete Steedman and Phillip Frazer became the editors of the Monash student newspaper, *Lot's Wife* (Russell 1999:115). That student newspaper commented on events in Berkeley. It published, e.g., a review of Lipset and Wolin's (1965) book on the university and highlighted the 'bleak' undergraduate experience at Berkeley, the huge class sizes, the bureaucracy and the absence of an authentic education, all features familiar to Australian students (Murphy 2015:259). *Lot's Wife* also published articles on the war in Vietnam (Wood 2017).[12] After the first Australian university teach-in (at ANU), a committee of Monash student representatives organised a teach-in on the war in Vietnam in July 1965, which attracted around 2,000 staff and students. The Victorian government, alarmed by these developments amended the Police Offences Act and the Summary Offences Act giving police the power to enter university campuses (Russell 1999:110).

In March 1966, the Australian government announced increases in troop numbers in Vietnam which meant more conscripts were needed. This triggered waves of anti-conscription protests across capital cities. In August 1965, a Vietnam Action Committee pamphlet titled *American Atrocities in Vietnam* funded by the Monash SRC, was seized by police who described it as an obscene item, with one police officer declaring that 'there is an undesirable trend towards the protection of what are called loosely civil liberties' (Russell 1999:114). That year the Monash Labor Club hitherto affiliated with the ALP, began shifting to the left (Ockenden, 1985:8). Dave Nadel, President of the Labor Club in 1967 recalled that 'the reason that we went left was because of the Vietnam War and conscription. And a little bit because of Berkeley' (Murphy 2015:260).

In 1966–1967 the Labor Club assumed the role of revolutionary vanguard. Key leaders of the Labor Club like Michael Hyde, who had direct experience at Berkeley in 1965–1966, and Darce Cassidy who was involved with the SDS branch at Sydney university, understood the dynamics operating in American university protest.[13] Both guessed accurately, there was a likelihood that the general student body, while politically indifferent, could be politicised if exposed to demonstrations and other direct action. And if university managers overreacted, as they tended to in the past, that too would cause students to react (Hyde 2010:21, 32–33). Meanwhile, the pace of protest accelerated especially after President Johnson visited Australia in October 1966: in Melbourne, Monash students were among protestors who splashed the presidential car with paint. *The Bulletin* magazine declared the government should stop funding universities until the 'left-wing minorities in them have been silenced or rendered impotent' (Russell 1999:117).

In July 1967 the Monash Labor Club, emulating tactics used by students elsewhere (e.g., Cornell University in 1965 and at Sydney University in March 1967), voted to collect donations to support the National Liberation Front (NLF) in Vietnam (York 1983:143–144). In response, the Australian parliament passed the *Defence Forces Protection Act* (1967) making it an offence to aid to Vietnam's NLF. The Vice-Chancellor of Monash, Louis Matheson, directed that no collections for the NLF were to be made on campus (Matheson 1980:132). Soon after, the university charged three Labor Club members with misconduct. A general student meeting refused to disassociate the general student body from the Labor Club action upholding the right of the group to collect for any cause it chose. As Nadel recalled, while much of the student protest in Australia and overseas was about the Vietnam war, 'the actual issues that ended up with buildings being occupied and students being expelled ... were in fact the universities trying to discipline the students. It was a question of free speech' (Murphy 2015:262).

As Matheson observes, many University administrators believed the issue of discipline was the central cause of the student unrest. It is what was promoting 'the same kind of disorder as was then occurring in universities all over the world' (Matheson 1980:116). As tensions rose on the Monash campus Vice-Chancellor Matheson established a committee to revise the university's disciplinary statutes.

In May 1968 a protest meeting of over 2,000, students responded to a press article about the new statutes with 400 students staging the first occupation of the Administration building. The key issue was the so-called 'double jeopardy' provision, which allowed the university to discipline or exclude students convicted of an offence off-campus. The occupation did not deter the Vice-Chancellor from disciplining key students leaders, including Nadel and Langer, who were charged with misconduct over their involvement in the occupation. As the two students left the Council Chamber they sang the second verse of American protest singer Phil Ochs' song 'I'm Going to Say It Now':

> Oh you've given me a number and you've taken off my name
> To get around this campus why you almost need a plane
> And you're supporting Chang Kai-Shek, while I'm supporting Mao
> So when I've got something to say, sir, I'm gonna say it now.
> *(Murphy 2015:264)*

While Monash students later mobilised other occupations student action had peaked in 1967–1968. In 1970, students occupied the 'Careers and Appointments' office at Monash protesting against the recruitment of students by corporations profiting from the Vietnam War. That action resulted in 32 students appearing before the Discipline Committee. Matheson later declared an amnesty for those students. When, in late 1974, another student occupation resulted in several students occupying the administration offices for over a week, and breaking into private offices at night, Matheson called in the police. That was the first time the police had been called onto the campus. The students were taken away, but the following morning Matheson dropped all charges.

Conclusion

Confronted by successions of protests by young people during the sixties, governments and many experts countered by arguing that student protestors were variously under-socialised deviants, troublemakers, impulsive, infantile or the dupes of extremists and communists. The authority of science understood to be 'value free' and objective was used to back such claims while denying the deeply political nature of student activism. These narratives ignored the deeply political character of student action (Brocklehurst 2006, Bessant 2014:138–153, Watts 2021). These representations of young people were intended to emphasise their cognitive and developmental deficits while denying them any legitimacy as political actors. On this occasion, these young people simply and persistently rejected these long-standing representations of them.

We can debate *ad nauseaum* the many consequences – or failures – attributed to the student politics of the 1960s. Student protestors in many countries challenged decisions made by those in authority. They played a key role in informing debate and changing policies as well as enlarging the capacity of democratic institutions. They both reflected and helped change social values and practices. They also effectively pushed back against the negative representations of young people and the predominantly hostile responses that their activism provoked. They demonstrated that young people were very well able to engage in continuing creative and well-organised political practices.

Yet as Thomas argues, their novelty can be easily overstated (2002:296). He argues that the 1960s protest movements were 'not an exceptional and failed attempt at revolution by an extremist minority, nor were they, consequently, a novelty or curiosity'. In ways that are directly relevant to the rest of this book, he added that 'attempts in subsequent decades by the right to dismiss the protests of the 1960s, or to blame the 1960s for the complex social problems of later years, must be examined afresh' (Thomas 2002:297). To that task, I turn in Chapter 7.

Notes

1 Arthur Marwick's (1998) discussion of the 'long sixties' refers to a period of cultural and political change beginning from around 1958 and ending around 1974.
2 Likewise, I do not consider the articulation of non-conformity by 'the counter-culture' in which mainly young people developed and explored alternate lifestyles and cultural meanings. This saw themes like illicit drugs, 'sexual promiscuity' and the 'hippie' movement loom large in the popular imagination. Referred to as 'the Great Refusal' (Marcuse 1964) many young people did reject traditional family arrangements, suburban life-styles, and wage labour. I also draw in part on interviews done in the early 1990s with people who were student activists in the sixties in Melbourne, Australia.
3 Some left-wing commentators also referred to the Oedipal struggle thesis. Herbert Marcuse, e.g., claimed the capacity for Oedipal struggle only applied to those who were not yet embedded in the 'repressive tolerance' of consumer capitalism and 'technological rationality' (Marcuse 1967). For others like the Australian philosopher Max Charlesworth, 'the generational struggle' cold be understood as a natural disposition that existed between the generations (1969:391–397). Charlesworth thought there was something wrong if 'the young' were not revolting.
4 Other scholars highlighted the middle-class and what some described the elite provenance of student activists. Altbach, e.g., emphasised how activist leaders came from more affluent families than the general student population (1989). Once more the effect of these accounts was to ignore or downplay the moral-political dispositions that moved students to act while at the same time promoting a misconception that being middle class somehow explained a minority disposition being an activist.
5 Keniston provided summaries in his bibliography of hundreds of empirical studies (1973). He argued that most of those studies revealed student radicals were well adjusted (1973). He also said they had a higher moral sense than their uninvolved compeers because they were committed to acting out their values.
6 America produced a number of important studies of young student activism. It refer, e.g., to Ian Hany-Lopez study of Mexican-American high school students in East Los Angeles in the 1950s who protested about their school's appalling conditions, and to Lorena Oropeza's (2005) research on Chicano student anti-war protest in the sixties in California and New Mexico. For studies of black secondary school activism in the fifties and sixties see Franklin 2000, 2004, Franklin 2003, Wright 2003, Rury and Hill 2012, 2013).
7 Besides Adamson (1998), whose account relied on in the following paragraphs, there seem to be no substantial research addressing Australian secondary school activism in this period.
8 O'Brien noted however that the largest demonstration during the period 1960–1963 was at Ohio State University when 5,000 students marched to protest the university's rejection of a bid for the football team to play in the Rose Bowl (1972).
9 British student protests seem to have received little scholarly attention. Writers like Sylvia Ellis argue that British student movement was less violent and radical and more easily controlled in comparison with 'the drama and the passion of protest in the USA and continental Europe' (Ellis 1998:68, Marwick 1998).

10 There is a significant body of Australian scholarship on the student movement of the sixties: see Gordon 1970, Alomes 1983, York 1983, Rootes 1988, Gerster and Bassett 1991, Beer 1996, Docker 1998, Scalmer 2002, Evans and Ferrier 2004, O'Hanlon and Luckins 2005, Robins 2005, Barcan 2011, Trometter 2013.
11 See Russel 1999 for a general account of protest in Australia (1965–1968).
12 Steedman was also an editor of Melbourne University's student newspaper *Farrago* (1967–1968) and was targeted by security forces as a person guilty of sedition (Steedman 2019).
13 Albert Langer the other key Labour Club leader was one of the few student leaders in Australia who was also a member of the Maoist Communist Party.

7
THE GREAT TRANSFORMATION
The young precariat and young entrepreneur

If the 1960s promised the dawn of a new society in the minds of many young activists, the following decades did deliver on that promise of change, but not in the way most of the young activists of the sixties had imagined.

When the Second World War ended in 1945, most western countries enjoyed a long economic boom characterised by full employment and economic growth which lasted until the early 1970s. The relative prosperity of that period owed much to the commitment of governments to securing full employment. It was a period of extended economic growth that was made possible by governments pursuing a neo-Keynesian policy of investing in public works and social infrastructure projects, tariff protection, managed currencies and progressive income taxation systems (Marglin and Schor 1992, Judt 2006). The years from 1945 to 1975 were marked by unprecedented rates of employment and increasing income equality as capital lost its share of national income to wage earners. Each of these successes would be gradually dismantled after 1980 as governments changed policy tack (Piketty and Zucman 2013, Piketty 2020, Bengtsson and Waldenström 2015).

More ominously the long boom also marked the period when the dramatic increase in the emissions of CO_2, and the production of coal, oil, plastic, concrete, plutonium, and aluminium confirmed the arrival of the Anthropocene a new geological era marked by increasing global warming (Waters et al. 2016). These trends have not been dismantled by government action, with effects that will be documented in Chapter 8.

The long post-war boom started coming to an end around the same time in many western countries in the 1970s. While the details of what happened will be outlined later, the end of the long boom was especially problematic for successive cohorts of young people born since the 1970s. Those problems included the destruction of the full-time youth labour market, increasing under-employment and an increase in casualised and precarious jobs for many young people, the last feature now referred to as the rise of the 'gig economy'. These trends were becoming obvious by the 1990s (McDonald and Giazitzoglu 2019). The restructuring of the labour market encouraged a significant expansion in the length of time many, although not all, young people spent in schools and post-secondary education. This in turn changed the experience of being young in a number of important material, cultural and symbolic ways. The end of the 'long boom' and the acknowledgement that we now live in the Anthropocene era has challenged the long-standing belief held by many intellectuals, policy-makers, governments and citizens that everyone was benefitting from an unrelenting historical process of socio-economic, technological and intellectual progress.

By 2015 many western politicians, policy-makers and journalists such as Larry Elliot were slowly coming to acknowledge that something unprecedented was occurring:

> Perpetual progress has been at the heart of western society for the past 150 years or more. The idea has been simple: each generation should be better off than their parents ... *The idea that each generation would be more fortunate than the last no longer applies.*
>
> (Elliott 2016) (My emphasis)

Elliott made two observations in justifying his claim that young people were now more likely to be worse off *as a generation* than their parents. First, many young people were now struggling to earn a decent wage in an increasingly insecure and casualised labour market. Second, the 'millennial' generation (i.e., those born since 1980) were on average 26% points less likely to own their own home than the 'baby boomer' generation (people born in the 1930s and 1940s).

In trying to understand how these changes influenced the ways young people were represented the concept of generation is helpful, if used thoughtfully. I have in mind an approach that draws on Karl Mannheim's socio-historical conception of 'generation' that involves recognising the actual diversity that characterises the lives of people born into certain periods. Many young people now feel the burden of being less well off than their parents and grandparents (Mannheim 1952, Woodman and Wyn 2014, Bessant et al. 2017).[1] This changing context has had a significant influence on the experiences of being young, and on how young people represent themselves and how they are represented by others.

Steven Threadgold drew attention to some figures of youth generated by experts, politicians and commentators. As he argues:

> Just as politicians or business advisors create versions of young people as rhetorical devices to obfuscate social and economic problems or to blame for the decline of western civilisation, social scientists construct their own

heuristic versions of youth, depending upon their orientation towards them.

(Threadgold 2019:2)

To this Threadgold adds: 'Figures of youth can illustrate how one thing can be used as a stereotype, cliché, meme, target, scapegoat, folk devil, stigma, discourse, and signifier. A figure can be all these things, sometimes at once' (Threadgold 2019:3).

While there are many ways of thematising how experts created different 'versions of youth', one dominant representation involved a response to questions about the 'future of work'. This problem was discovered or constituted some time ago by writers like Jones (1982), Gorz (1987), Reich (1992) and Rifkin (1995). More recently it has been articulated by writers like Brynjolfsson and McAfee (2014:215), Frey and Osbourne (2017) along with a plethora of governments, global consultancies and think-tanks all asking questions like: do we face a future in which paid employment will be displaced or augmented by automation, digital technologies, autonomous vehicles and AI-based robotic processing? Are '...utonomous vehicles, self-service kiosks, warehouse robots, and supercomputers the harbingers of a wave of technological progress that will sweep humans out of the economy'? (Brynjolfsson and McAfee 2015:1). Will technology augment existing work and create new jobs (Susskind, and Susskind 2015).

Questions about the 'future of work' promoted various representations of young people. Of these two stand out. One drew on Standing's (2011) account of a 'precariat' in which a 'new youth precariat' is identified (Woodman 2012, Imhonopi and Urim 2015). The other identifies 'the young entrepreneur' (Roxburgh 2018). Robert McDonald and Andreas Giazitzoglu highlighted the juxtaposition of these two narratives in their work on Britain's 'gig economy' and young people (2019:1–17). In what follows I consider the 'young precariat' and 'young entrepreneur' narratives.

Specifically I ask what happened to the youth labour market after 1975? How can those changes be explained? How were young people been represented in that context? Are the arguments and evidence used to support certain representations of young people credible (e.g., that young people have skill deficits, inadequate education or lack the motivation to work hard, factors that make them unemployable)? Do those arguments explain the increasing levels of youth unemployment? How can these representations be understood politically? As I argued throughout this book, there is value in recognising the politics that shaped those representations. I begin by asking what happened to labour markets in many western countries in the early 1980s?

What happened to the youth labour market after 1975?

Several things occurred around the same time in 'the developed' world in the 1980s. One was the realisation that the prevailing political-policy and socio-economic arrangements in place were not providing full-time employment to all those who wanted a job. This became particularly obvious as unemployment and underemployment steadily increased. While this change affected many groups, it had a particularly adverse impact on young people. Governments of all colours expressed alarm and urged young people to remain in school and enrol in universities and colleges. At the same time educational reforms were called for to help ensure young people received the skills, knowledge and qualifications they needed to make them 'job-ready'. The assumption was that young unemployed people lacked job-relevant skills or capacities, deficiencies that pointed to both deficits in young people themselves and to failures in the education systems. From the 1980s, many governments began talking up the positive role education could play in ensuring young people could get a job and opportunities that allowed them to become responsible adults.

In some ways, this may seem like a continuity in policy aimed at encouraging investment in human capital, but from the early 1980s, there was a significant difference. The difference was that beginning in the mid-1940s, governments went much further than just providing education and training, they were also committed to ensuring there was work.In the 1980s that commitment to ensuring there was work evapourated.

While it is true that young people (15–24) have long been particularly vulnerable to unemployment (e.g., Junankar 2015:2), it is an observation that needs to be understood in its historical context.

Young people in many countries between 1945 and 1975 benefited from government policies designed to ensure the availability of full-time work. That in turn helped provide a continual and fairly predictable 'transition' to responsible adulthood. The years from 1945 to 1975 were marked by the longest period of consistent economic growth in world history. For many, it was also a time characterised by low unemployment, increased access to affordable housing and consumer goods, increasing rates of educational achievement, health, longevity and optimism about the future (Cuervo and Wyn 2011:8, Sukarieh and Tannock 2016:1281–1289).

While pent-up demand for consumer goods and services developed during the years of austerity that characterised the second war (1939–1945) might partly explain the boom, it was more the result of government and international policy. That policy involved, e.g., national pledges to full employment and international policy like the 1944 Bretton Woods agreement.[2] While this cannot be explained as the result of any one factor, the work of the British economist John Maynard Keynes played a significant role in shaping government economic policy especially after 1945. In the depth of the 1930s Depression J.M. Keynes (1935) delivered an influential critique of economic policy arguing that if left to its own devices a free market would generate unemployment. He also outlined a new macroeconomic model in which governments played a lead role in managing economies to deliver full employment.

This new policy was adopted after 1941 by countries such as Britain, the USA, Canada and Australia. It was an approach that used Keynesian ideas of manpower planning, capital investment in production and taxation to control war-time inflation. In 1944–1945, many governments issued formal policy statements like Australia's *White Paper on Full Employment in Australia,* declaring that henceforth full employment would be the primary policy objective of governments. This also involved linking welfare provision to labour market engagement positioned the nascent welfare state as a 'safety net' for those outside the labour market (Watts 1987:123–140).

In many 'liberal welfare-state regimes' (Esping-Andersen 1990), including America, Canada, Britain and Australia, the 'welfare state' was based on the idea that governments should maintain full employment, whilst at the same time, providing a universal safety net for those unable to participate in the labour market (Watts 1987:147). In the early to mid-1940s many western states adopted the Keynesian paradigm, ensuring the process of post-war reconstruction was rapid, with world industrial production returning to its pre-war levels by 1947–1948. Countries whose production capacities were not destroyed by saw their production levels rise above pre-war levels by 1947. They included the United States, Canada, European countries that had remained neutral, Turkey, countries of the Middle East and Latin America and India.

Full employment was bolstered by major public works programs that harnessed enormous levels of public investment in infrastructure or in the case of the USA by massive spending on post-war defence forces. This also required governments to build an economic and political consensus and to invest in the welfare and economic infrastructure. It included relying on widespread tariff protection, and highly regulated currency, banking, and financial systems. In many cases, it also involved large post-war immigration and refugee resettlement schemes that bought millions of 'new people' to countries as immigrants.

One result of all this was that countries like Australia doubled their population between 1945 and 1975 from 7½ million to 13 million. By the 1960s average annual growth rates among developed market economies were around 5% between 1961 and 1970, while in developing countries it was 5.5% for the same period. Given these policies, it was not surprising that the unemployment rates in most western countries from 1945 to 1975 remained historically low. Unemployment fluctuated on average between 2% and 3% (1963). The average length of any unemployment to the mid-1970s was relatively short (Jones 1983:196).

Even in this context, most young people did not experience the same access to jobs as their parents (and especially their fathers) during the long boom. In the 1950s and 1960s, the youth unemployment rate was continuously higher in places like the USA, Britain and Australia sitting between 5% in Australia and going as high as 15% in the USA in the 1960s. As O'Higgins observed, youth unemployment was always higher than adult unemployment in most countries for which figures are available, and this is the case whether aggregate unemployment in a country is high or low (2001:13).

Yet job security for most young people became the normal expectation from the 1950s to the mid-1970s. In the USA, e.g., young people (aged 16–19) had a lower labour force participation rate and employment-population ratio than young adults aged 20–24. These two indicators for 'teenagers' fluctuated between the 1950s to the 1990s, before declining in the 1990s (Fernandes-Alcantara 2018:12–14). The labour force participation rate and employment-population ratio for young adults (20–24) mostly followed an upward trajectory after the Second World War. This was the result of increases in labour force participation and employment especially among young women (Fernandes-Alcantara 2018:12–14). In Australia, e.g., in the 1970s about 86% of young Australians left school at age 15–16 to become full-time workers and earn a living wage.

This income gave many young people the opportunity to leave the parental home and establish their own families. For many young men, it meant the beginning of a working life that usually continued until the age of 65 when they retired. For most young women the experience was different: it normally meant a short spell in the workforce, followed by marriage, unpaid domestic labour and child-care and possibly part-time work once the children commenced school. Once a young person got their preferred employment, the usual expectation was upward mobility in the workplace (Cuervo and Wyn 2011:7). It provided a 'pathway' from adolescence into adulthood young people especially in western countries could take.

This full-employment economic regime began collapsing in the second half of the 1970s a collapse that sped up in the 1980s and through the 1990s. In the years after the first 'oil shock 'of 1973 which saw dramatic increases in oil prices, the rate of economic growth slowed dramatically in ways that began affecting the creation of new jobs. It was clear then that youth unemployment was linked to the general unemployment situation, implying that solutions developed to address youth unemployment could not be separated from the general political and economic context.

The relative novelty of increased unemployment in the 1970s provoked considerable policy analysis, controversy and public commentary, with much of it centred on youth unemployment. While young people were affected it wasn't until the early 1990s that the full effect of changes to the labour market became apparent. Life for many young people became particularly difficult after the first serious post-war recession in the late 1980s. By the late 1990s, the International Labour Organisation (ILO) estimated at least 60 million young people were without work and that average youth unemployment rates were three times as high as adult rates (ILO 1998). In member states of the Organisation for Economic Co-operation and Development (OECD), approximately 10 million young people were unemployed in the OECD countries. The unemployment rate for the 15–24 age group in 1998 was 12.9%, more than double the figure for adults, which was 5.7% (O'Higgins 2001:9). Some countries experienced higher youth unemployment rates than others. While OECD members like Germany (5%), the Netherlands (8.8%) and Austria (8.8%) had low rates, some had higher rates like the USA (16.6%), Britain (16.7%), Australia (23%) and Canada (22%), others had even higher rates like Belgium (45.7%) and Finland (50%) (O'Higgins 2001:20).[3]

Mindful of the diversity of economic conditions in the OECD, a pattern emerged that was common to member countries. What took place in Australia illustrates that general trend. While nearly two-thirds of young Australians aged 15–19 were in full-time work in 1988, a decade later, just a third were in full-time employment. The recession of 1992–1995 produced a steep increase in youth unemployment that hit 25% in 1994 (Cuervo and Wyn 2011). By the mid-1990s the destruction of Australia's youth labour market was obvious. In 1995 full-time employment of young people was equivalent to one-third of full-time employment in 1966 (Wooden 1996:149). Similarly in 1995 part-time employment accounted for 36% of all youth employment while for 'teenagers' it accounted for 51% of male employment and 72% of female employment. That compared with 5% in the 1960s. As research by Wooden demonstrated, by the mid-1990s the full-time youth (15–24) youth labour market collapsed with disproportionate levels of youth unemployment and/or part-time employment (1996:137).[4]

Since then the proportion of young Australian in full-time employment has declined from 40% of all young people aged between 15 and 24 in 1995 to 29% in 2015. In contrast, part-time employment for young people increased from 20% in 1995 to 30% in 2015 (Bowman et al. 2015). The cohort of young people during this time also came to be defined by the precariousness they experienced in the labour market. Now young people are the visible face of insecure and non-standard employment which has become a new-old norm in the modern 'flexible', deregulated economy (Standing 2011, Bessant 2018:780–798).

Representing youth unemployment after 1975

By the late 1970s, western governments had rejected the full-employment policy objectives and the mechanisms adopted by many governments in the mid-1940s (Whitwell 1986, Ewer et al. 1991).

In its place, most governments subscribed to a new orthodoxy. The new task of government was to develop policies that would encourage markets to generate economic growth. That in turn it was said would generate jobs. This was the new goal to be accomplished 'over time' (Accord 1983 cited in Wilson, Thomson and McMahon 1996:30, Commonwealth Australian Government 1994:i). The new policy was fighting 'inflation first'.

From the 1930s most governments had come to depend on economists to establish their economic policy (Burchall 1998:194–196). From the late 1970s many governments, along with their economic policy communities began developing a 'new' discursive context or 'scientific revolution' that ushered in a new period of 'normal policy' (Kuhn [1969] 2012). It was a shift characterised by considerable bi-partisan policy consensus about the problem being faced and the range of options that policy-makers had. Economics as a discipline also experienced a major paradigm shift in the 1960s and 1970s. It was a development that led to the resurrection of neo-classical ideas that had been partly displaced during the period influenced by a neo-Keynesian neo-classical synthesis (Whitwell 1986).

It was a paradigm shift prompted in part by a discovery made by most western economies in the mid-1960s, and especially after the 1973–1974 OPEC oil shock, that they were experiencing historically high unemployment in conjunction with increasing inflation. While the early signs of this were hard to identify, full employment began declining in the early 1970s as young workers especially began to find it difficult to get full-time employment. This, in part, was a consequence of certain policy changes that were bringing to an end the long post-war boom period in the global north.

Internationally it was a consequence decision like that taken by the US Nixon administration to end the Bretton Woods agreement, to take the USA off the gold standards and to create a free market in currency and capital flows (Garber 1991).[5] That action was critical in triggering the dramatic growth in the 'financialization' of many developed economies which involved, among other things, a decline in manufacturing in the late 1970s and 1980s. (I return to later in this chapter.) The destruction of Bretton Woods also prompted dramatic OPEC oil price increases (1973–4) and a surge in inflation. This led to the popularisation of monetarist policies that argued increasing inflation and unemployment (stagflation) were a consequence of an oversupply of money caused by government deficits and high wages (Barratt-Brown 1989:72).

Neo-classical economics was based on two assumptions. One was that economic growth and particularly productivity increases caused employment growth (i.e., if Gross Domestic Product increased so did employment). Secondly, all free markets generate a 'natural rate of unemployment': if an excessive labour supply existed (too many unemployed people) then wages would automatically decline. If there were more jobs than there were workers, then wages would rise to attract more people to the labour market. Monetarists and conservative governments argued that the 1960s and 1970s saw large real wage increases that created a spiralling inflation, that in turn priced labour out of jobs causing employers to replace labour with new more capital intensive technologies.

Underlying this thinking was the claim that an efficient and rational free marketplace prevented unemployment from occurring. Thus for proponents of this view something was distorting the free market. It was clear who the culprits were.

Monetarists blamed state interference especially 'excessively high' income tax and wealth tax rates. This combined with overly generous state income support benefits is what created a 'passive' welfare system.

This, so the argument went, rewarded the unemployed and encouraged them to seek an income while doing no productive labour and thus remain unemployed. In short, the unemployed were to blame for their plight: too many of them lacked relevant skills and motivational attitudes and this is what thwarted policy-makers who were trying to fix the unemployment problem (Crosby and Olekalns 1997).

These factors, it was argued, had negative effects on the labour market in attaining maximum allocative efficiency and growth. What was needed to fix this were 'tough policies' that 'freed the market' so it could 'naturally' correct itself without undue 'interference' from governments and unions. Dropping wage rates and reducing government expenditure and tax revenues were needed to promote non-inflationary real economic growth and increase employment. The first governments to adopt this new approach included Chile under the Pinochet regime (1976), Thatcher's conservative government (1979–1992) in Britain, Reagan's administration in the USA (1981–1988), and the Labor governments in Australia (1983–1996) and New Zealand (1983–1988). In this context the OECD unveiled its 'active society model' in 1986.

The active society

In 1988 the OECD officially approved this new policy regime, recommending that member states adopt an 'active society' model (Gass 1988). Kjell Eide, a key OECD official recalled how unemployment, and especially youth unemployment, had become a major problem in the 1980s (Eide 1990). This encouraged many to blame increasing youth unemployment on the education system. They could not get work, it was argued because the education they received failed to prepare them for the needs of the labour market. The OECD developed projects ostensibly aimed at securing the 'transition' of young people from education to work.

Concern was also expressed that on-going payments of unemployment benefits adversely affected labour market performance. It was argued that receiving income support eroded the moral character of those in receipt of such payments because it made them 'passive' and 'dependent', encouraging the view they could 'get an income for doing nothing'. In short, the OECD suggested that 'overly generous' unemployment benefits actually increased unemployment because it discouraged the job-search activities of the unemployed and reduced their interest in accepting job offers (OECD 2006:54). The OECD recommended that all governments review their benefit systems to determine whether they were too generous and should be cut.[6]

The OECD 'active society model' advised governments not to pursue full-employment policies. Instead what they needed were polices that encouraged deregulation and a freeing up of the market so 'it' could increase growth and productivity. The advice also included 'a shift away from measures that generate dependency on income transfers to those that mobilise labour supply and foster economic opportunity, improve the efficiency of labour market matching, and develop employment-related skills' (OECD 2012).

The aim of the new agenda was to mobilise, discipline and when necessary, punish the unemployed *because they were the problem*. As explained in an OECD communique that came after a meeting of social security ministers:

> ...social policy should be guided by orientations that contribute to society as well as to market efficiency by facilitating employment, rather than perpetuating reliance on public income support alone through active labour market measures which stress the development of human potential through opportunities for learning and skill upgrading.
>
> *(OECD 1992:4)*

The OECD's 'active society' model reinforced concern about the 'insufficient effort' made by the unemployed to find work. From the late 1980s employment policy in many countries came to be preoccupied with the unemployed. It was an approach reliant on a deficit model of the 'unemployed', one that identified 'their' alleged lack of skills, job readiness, flexibility and motivation as the problems for which labour market programs were the appropriate response.

Such advice fell on receptive ears. The Australian experience is indicative of what happened 'on the ground' in many countries as this kind of advice was implemented. In 1988 a new approach to income support was developed, one more consistent with general policy pronouncements made by the OECD (OECD 1988a, 1988b). The key message was clear: governments should not invest in job creation.

In Australia, a review of the national income support system was established in 1986. By 1988 that Review accepted the idea that 'welfare recipients' were 'demoralised' and reduced courtesy of unemployed benefits that caused them to become 'dependent'. Welfare policies it was argued encouraged 'passivity', while the new 'Active Society' approach promoted the power of markets, 'participation' and 'activity'. It was an approach that linked 'work' and 'welfare' in a new-old way (with its origins in English New Poor Law).[7] Individual 'deficiencies' like 'dependence' and 'demoralisation' needed to be tackled by 'labour market programs', and if people wanted income support they would be required to pass 'activity tests'. It was an approach that significantly increased stigmatising representations of unemployed people along with an increasingly punitive approach to the income support system.

Governments began developing new policies that promoted punitive strategies to 'deal with' unemployed people young and old. In Britain, Australia and the USA, e.g., the old idea of a "youth underclass" was recycled. As writers like Ball (et al. 2000) and McDonald (2008) note, by the 1990s a plethora of normative labels enjoyed widespread currency in policy and academic circles like 'the disaffected', 'disengaged' and 'disconnected', the 'hard to reach' and 'the hard to help', 'the socially excluded', 'the youth or juvenile underclass' and more recently 'NEET' (i.e., those 'not in education, employment and training').

In each case the message was clear: the young people being referred to were best characterised by what they lacked. 'Deficit models' that focussed on the supply-side of the labour market – on what aspirant job seekers workers lacked – have a long history. By the 1990s in the UK the Blair Labour government's Social Exclusion Unit used 'social exclusion' as '…a shorthand label for what can happen when individuals or areas suffer from a combination of linked problems such as unemployment, poor skills, low incomes, poor housing, high crime environments, bad health and family breakdown' (SEU 1998:1). Describing the cause of youth unemployment as an absence of education skills, job readiness and motivation was a time-honoured practice (e.g., Mizen 2003, Pohl and Walther 2007).

In many cases, this kind of representation worked to encourage the idea that the unemployed needed "labour market programs" (Stretton and Chapman 1990:3). The intention of these programs was not to create jobs but to try to keep the motivation to work on the part of the unemployed intact as long-term unemployment for many became permanent.

The provision of 'labour market programs' was also closely aligned with monetarist macro-economic policy in the 1980s. It gave authority to the official line that the unemployment problem and its continuance was a 'problem with the unemployed'. Informing these labour market programmes was the assumption that unemployed and especially the long-term unemployed young people, were different from 'normal' working people. The preference for Labour Market Programs for the unemployed also helped camouflage the refusal by governments to develop job creation policies which by then were being labelled as "socialist".

All this however was not new. The metaphor of the 'underclass' and now the 'youth underclass' had many historical resonances with the 'dangerous classes' of the 1840s and 1850s (Bessant 1995:32–48, see also Chapter 3). Government and tabloid media constructed moral panics about the long-term unemployed youth, represented as drug addicts, homeless, irresponsible, lazy, or criminal (Gordon 2018). Typifying this tendency Australia's claimed that 'the most deeply disadvantaged' have 'poor living skills', as well as 'a history of substance abuse, insecure housing, recent criminal records.

This belief that the most disadvantaged were jobless and destitute and had poor living and work skills 'along with a history of substance abuse, insecure housing, criminal records became a staple part of many government announcements about 'welfare dependency' (e.g., Australian Task Force on Employment Opportunities, 1994:ii). Workers in the social and community services industry were also able and willing to add their own ideas to this. Others including social scientists were also producing 'objective scales' of 'youth at risk" so to validate what was a discursive fiction – albeit one with real consequences (Rutter et al. 1998).

This story however had a major flaw: it clashed with the fact that youth unemployment and unemployment generally were explained by the fact there were not enough jobs available for all those wanting work. It had nothing to do with the perceived characteristics or deficiencies of jobless people, and more to do with the reality there were not enough jobs to satisfy the demand for jobs.[8] This

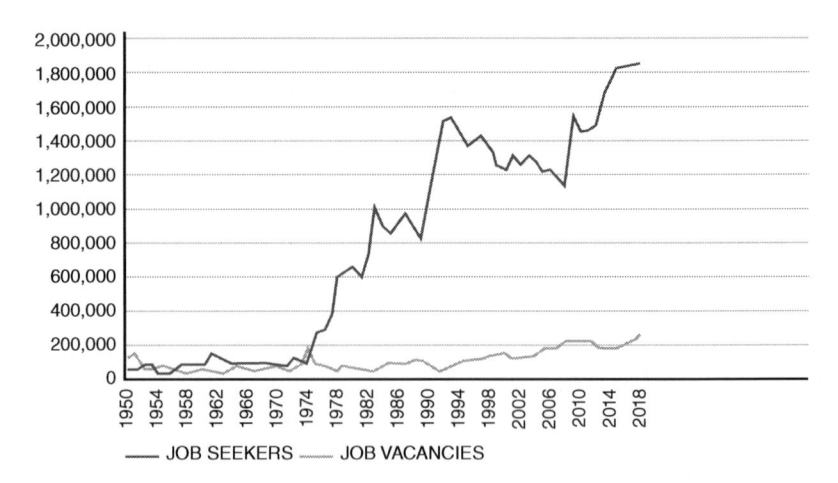

FIGURE 7.1 The number of job seekers and job vacancies (marginally attached not included) 1958–2018.

Source: ABS and CES (cited in Bennet et al. 2018: 68).

is evident in the table below which identifies the relationship between unemployment and job vacancies. As can be seen from 1974 to 2019, there were many unemployed people for each job vacancy. This compares with over 20 people for every vacancy in the early 1990s recession. In the twenty-first century, this problem continued: in 2014, there were still five job seekers for every vacancy. While this is an Australian example, it is a development that was evident globally (Figure 7.1).

However describing the absence of jobs is one thing, explaining it is another.

Three explanations for rising joblessness: neoliberalism, financialisation and the digital revolution

Three key political-economic developments shaped the 'creative destruction,'of western labour markets one effect of which was the destruction of the old full-time youth labour market.

Those developments are the rise of a neoliberal political consensus, financialisation and 'the digital revolution'. From the early 1980s, the imbrication of these three dynamic processes proved problematic for successive generations of young people. To start with, the near-global adoption of the neoliberal worldview had immediate and dramatic effects.

Neoliberalism

By the late 1970s, the neo-Keynesian economic policy that was so influential in the post-war boom was considered obsolete. From the early 1980s, governments and parties of all political persuasions (conservative, republican, democrat and labour) began adopting the key principles of neoliberalism. It was a political enterprise that reneged on earlier commitments by governments in 1944–1945 to secure full employment.

Governments began cutting tariff protection to industry, making welfare more difficult to access and more punitive, reducing income taxes, privatising public services, deregulating the financial and labour markets. Added to this was a greater reliance on market mechanisms like user-pays and values like individualism and competition to produce a 'good society' reconceptualised as a market society (Real Democracy Movement 2020). This produced an overall decline in the quality of public services, shrinking growth in productivity and a dramatic increase in the unequal distribution of wealth and income (Picketty 2014).

Neoliberalism, is a worldview that steadily if unevenly spread across the globe. For social scientists like Brown, this 'new' political imaginary encouraged us to see everything in terms of its economic value. As she argued, under the reign of neoliberalism we are '…all converted into 'market actors', and where all fields become 'markets', and all public and private entities, every person, commercial practice, or state is 'governed as a firm' (Brown 2015:1). David Harvey correctly notes that neoliberalism is a political project *promoted by the state*. It 'proposes that human well-being can best be advanced by liberating individual entrepreneurial freedoms and skills within an institutional framework characterised by strong private property rights, free markets, and free trade' (Harvey 2005:3).

Paradoxically while proponents of neoliberalism promoted what they saw as the value of an unrestrained free market and a smaller state, government policy-making is critical to neoliberalism, including policies offering tax cuts, industry subsidies, privatisation of civil infrastructure, and interventions that favour for-profit business entities. It is a worldview directed towards achieving economic growth courtesy of hyper-competition, economic deregulation and policies favouring business, which courtesy of the 'trickle-down effect' will benefit everyone. What it has actually done however is produce stagnant productivity growth, unemployment, massive private (household) debt, seep economic inequality, financial crises and ecological disaster (Harvey 2005, Brown 2015).

By the late 1960s and 1970s, employers in many countries were expressing dissatisfaction with the existing opportunities for variation in wages and conditions and began demanding greater opportunities for variation. In pursuing this they also demanded a 'relaxing' or the removal of protective regulatory measures because they caused 'rigidities' and inhibited 'individual enterprise'. They also called for a re-instatement of the principles of 'freedom of contract' and 'managerial prerogative'. This employer demands fuelled the push towards *labour market deregulation* as a new line of policy.

'Labour flexibility' became a key metaphor in the neoliberal drive for labour market deregulation in the 1980s. Protective regulation in its various forms[9] was identified as 'rigidities' that needed to be eradicated in order to create greater 'labour market flexibility' (Siebert 1997:37–54). This call for greater flexibility concept received the imprimatur of the OECD (1988a) and helped set new policy directions that loosen or removed 'restrictions' on the individual and business enterprise with respect to retrenchments, approaches toward wage determination, working-time arrangements, recruitment, non-standard employment and practices for consulting with employees.

Talk of labour flexibility dominated discussion about the labour market in places like Europe, where it was also linked to analyses of the poor record of job creation in EU countries (Giersch 1985, Commission of the European Communities 1993, Blank and Freeman 1994, Siebert 1997). Labour market deregulation was directed to removing 'external constraints' on enterprise autonomy, opposing external protective regulation and weakened system of industrial relations and the trade unions. Its proponents also supported 'contractualization' that would restore the individualised contracts of employment characteristic of an earlier period (Humphreys 2018).

In short, since its introduction from the late 1970s and early 1980s, neoliberalism affected most economies globally (Sawyer 2013–2014). As Zuboff argues, neoliberalism 'presided over the erosion of major regulatory institutions and policies designed over the first seven decades of the twentieth century to mitigate the worst aspects of the free market's normal tendency to sponsor social inequality and economic injustice' (Zuboff 2019:39). This meant that major institutions originally developed to promote the public good were privatised, corporatised or abolished.

Given these features of the neoliberalism, it is not surprising it has been linked to financialisation by many authors (Wallerstein et al. 2013, Streeck 2016, Mirowski 2019).

Financialisation

Financialisation is the process that saw 'financial markets, financial institutions, and financial elites gain greater influence over economic policy and economic outcomes' (Palley 2007:2). As Epstein argued, financialisation is a new stage in the history of capitalism characterised by 'the increasing importance of financial markets, financial motives, financial institutions, and financial elites in the operation of the economy and its governing institutions, both at the national and international level' (2005:1).

It involves a 'pattern of accumulation in which profit making occurs increasingly through financial channels rather than through trade and commodity production' (Krippner 2005, Fasianos et al. 2012:8–9). One measure of financialisation is the growth in the scale of financial transactions in US equity (stock) markets. This grew from $US136.0 billion (or 13.1% of US GDP) in 1970 to $US1.671 trillion (or 28.8% of U.S. GDP) in 1990. By 2000, trading in US equity markets was worth $US14.222 trillion or 145% of US

GDP. By 2018 this trebled to US33.02 trillion or nearly half of the world's total trade of $US68 trillion (World Bank 2019). Another measurement of financialisation is the increase in the American market for derivatives or futures contracts on interest rates, foreign currencies, Treasury bonds, etc., reached $US1,200 trillion in 2006 when US GDP in 2006 was just $12.4 trillion. It is also worth stating the obvious here: the financial services sector is not a major employer.

Financialisation represents a significant shift towards a 'shareholder value orientation'. This is the idea that companies which historically pursued a strategy for reproducing capital growth, shifted away from a 'retain and invest' strategy and to a 'downsize and distribute' strategy (Lazonick and O'Sullivan 2000). In this way as Dallery argues, the profit rate has become 'an end in itself' (2008). Unlike managers who typically aim for long-run growth of the firm, shareholders pursue a short-term orientation with respect to firms' profits because their goal is higher dividend payments and higher stock prices. As Hein observed that shareholder pressure on managers to increase rates of profit and capital growth can be measured using the rate of mergers and acquisitions (2009). The world saw an explosion of mergers and acquisitions after 1990.

In other words, financialisation in conjunction with neoliberalism promoted a major shift away from productive economic activity in many of the advanced or developed capitalist economies. Zuboff emphasised how '[F]inancial carrots and sticks persuaded executives to dismember and shrink their companies, and the logic of capitalism shifted from the profitable production of good and services to increasing forms of market speculation' (Zuboff 2019:40–41). Over the last three decades, we saw a growing asymmetry between the production of goods and services for profit, and non-productive and highly speculative activity that did not produce goods or services, but which did return a profit (Lapavitsas 2013:792).

This had a major effect on the creation of new jobs. As the OECD acknowledged, employment in the manufacturing sector has declined by 20% in the past two decades contributing to labour market polarisation: the shares of low-skilled and particularly high-skilled jobs have increased, while middle-skill level jobs began disappearing (2009).

One index of this is the disappearance of publicly-listed companies. The listing of public companies on a stock market characterised western capitalism for several centuries. It enabled enterprises to raise money from investors. In America in 1996, e.g., US listings reached a record high of over 8,000 domestically incorporated companies. By 2003, there were only 5,295 domestic US-listed companies. After the 2008 financial crisis, the number of domestic US-listed companies briefly stabilised again, ranging between 4,100 and 4,400. By the end of 2018, only 3,383 firms were listed on U.S. stock exchanges down more than half from 1997 (Brorsen 2017, Statista 2019).[10] New businesses have been offering shares to the public at half the rate of the 1980s and 1990s. Mergers and acquisitions eliminated hundreds more.[11]

Another key aspect of financialisation has been the enormous increase in household or private debt that allowed large numbers of people to borrow money to fund the consumption of housing, food, clothing and leisure. From the 1980s, this became a central characteristic of many economies (Palley 1994). Australia, e.g., saw a doubling of household debt between 2003 and 2019. In 2019, total household debt was estimated to be $AU2.46 trillion and as a ratio to total disposable income was sitting at 199.7%. Australia was behind Switzerland (213%), Norway (231%), the Netherlands (270%) and Denmark (290%).

Many governments also moved to funding mass university education by requiring students to borrow the cost of tuition in part or in whole. In Australia, e.g., by 2015–16 around 2,468,939 Australians were education debtors owing a total of $AU47 billion with the burden falling disproportionately on those born in the 1980s to the mid-1990s (Ey 2018). Thus in a context where labour markets emphasised increasingly flexible employment practice epitomised by the 'Gig economy' we saw a steady move away from stable welfare provisions and or the 'democratisation' of debt (Erturk et al. 2007, Lapavitsas 2013).

Another important marker of financialisation is financial innovation. In this case, the growth of debt highlighted above, is directly linked to 'innovative' packaging up of debt and associated risks and selling these packages in new markets. This can quickly become a criminal enterprise. In short, the growth of debt (i.e., giving credit to low-income households) saw the creation of new kinds of financial assets designed to facilitate financial speculation and protect capital from any risks in doing this. From the 1970s and 1980s, new kinds of financial assets were created that could be traded to ensure that profit and capital growth continued (Phillips 1996, Bhaduri 2011).

Financialisation propelled by the invention and increased the use and sale of new financial 'assets' like packages of debt credit default swaps, and the betting on interest rate changes, i.e., interest rate derivatives. The derivatives market quickly became the largest segment of the global financial market after 1970. In December 2008, the global derivatives market was worth an estimated €471 trillion in notional terms. In 2008, the derivatives market was then more than five times larger than the global equity and bond markets combined – and it has grown consistently. The size of the market increased by approximately 25% per year between December 1998 and June 2008 (Deutsche Boerse Group 2009:10–11). In 2018 the notional value of outstanding derivatives had increased from $US532 trillion (2017) to $US595 trillion by June 2018. This is 6.7 times larger than the estimated total global GDP ($US88 trillion) (BIS 2018).[12]

Financialisation not only increased private debt to unprecedented levels but has created a significant inequality (Graeber 2011, Picketty 2014). We now see a return to patterns of inequality in most advanced economies not seen since the 1890s (Hein and Mundt 2013, Picketty 2014).

In many OECD countries, more people now experience low and erratic wages, precarious employment, inadequate and increasingly conditional welfare payments and escalating living costs all of which make life financially insecure for increasing numbers of people in the advanced economies. Non-standard work i s no longer a minor problem[13] (Mastercard 2019:5, OECD 2019:66). Casual workers are 40–50% p less likely to receive any income support when they are out of work than standard employees. For those who do receive support, out-of-work income assistance is often significantly less than it is for standard employees. This represents a major break with the long-term trajectory of capitalism. It also has implications for how the labour market now works and for the relations between labour and capital.

The digital revolution

The expansion of financial speculation could not have occurred without digital technologies which are noiw a key feature of contemporary economies (Hein and Mundt 2013). Technology and financialisation also have major implications for future demands for labour, a topic that has prompted a renewed interest in the future of work.

Reduced demands for labour in this context points to what some economists call the 'productivity paradox', and others call the 'Solow paradox' (Turban et al. 2007:720). It refers to the ways information and communication technologies have not delivered on the promise of growth in the number of jobs, wage growth and increased productivity, that neo-classical economics predicted would occur (Solow 1957, David 1990).

In spite of the significant investment in computer equipment tied to new products and methods of production, productivity has not increased. Technological innovation has not been the circuit breaker that would kick start productivity growth and expansions of labour market as it was over the previous two centuries (Brynjolfsson 1993:66–77, Wallerstein et al. 2013).[14] Generally productive sectors in most developed economies enjoyed mediocre growth with profit rates hovering around or below the 1950s–1960s levels, while unemployment and under-employment rates barely moved. The expected benefits for workers did not materialise and real wages did not increase in a sustained way, a problem exacerbated for young workers typically on lower wages and less secure income (Lapavitsas 2013). Thus despite expectations the digital economy would produce increased wage growth in response to higher productivity, for most workers wage growth remained flat and for many people job prospects remained low (OECD 2017).

This rapid growth of the financial sector from the early 1970s was made possible by the neoliberal deregulation of the financial and industrial sectors which also relied on the advent of fast, high powered computers and increasingly sophisticated software (Lapavitsas 2013).

The confluence of financialisation and digital technologies that some call 'fintech', transformed the advanced economies. According to the international 'Financial Stability Board', Fintech is:

> ...technologically enabled financial innovation that could result in new business models, applications, processes or products with an associated material effect on financial markets and institutions and the provision of financial services.
>
> *(Financial Stability Board 2019)*

Fintech promoted a new information economy that was reliant on the increased speed and intensity of information exchange. Demands for increased speed, scale and intensity to survey markets (for signs like rising or falling interest rates, data about sales of goods or prices of currency and commodities) vital for speculative financial trading were met by high-speed digital analytics and fast connection speeds.

An iconic example of the financialisation project is high-frequency trading which dispenses with financial brokers and used algorithms and powerful computers to buy and sell financial assets in nano-seconds across the globe. High-frequency trading involves the use of algorithms and data to make money from placing vast amounts of orders to earn thin margins. High-frequency trading is thought to have been responsible for as much as 75% of trading volume in the United States in 2009 though this has declined somewhat since then (Linton and Mahmoodzadeh 2018:237). In 2018 over half of all trade in equities in the US was done by supercomputers capable of placing millions of orders each day and gaining an advantage by buying or selling milliseconds before the competition (Warner 2018). In Europe, high-frequency trading is responsible for about 40% of the trading volume in European equity markets (Gerig 2015). While some claimed to see benefits in high-frequency trading there is some concern that high-frequency trading makes the financial system as a whole more fragile (Gerig 2012:1). These concerns were epitomised by events like the Flash Crash of 6th May 2010 and the bond market flash event of 15th October 2014 indicate. In the former event, nearly $1 trillion temporarily evaporated in minutes (Linton and Mahmoodzadeh 2018:238).

As capital became dependent on digital technology especially in banking and financial transactions it freed itself from labour. In this way, *capital can be accumulated and reproduced without human work* (Wallerstein et al. 2013).

A prime example of the confluence of financialisation and digital technologies and its impact on the demand for labour can be seen with the evolution of a new kind of capital. Zubov describes this as 'surveillance capital' (Zuboff 2019:93–94). Facebook provides one of many examples of the symbiosis between the financialisation process and the digital project. Facebook and similar platforms have become marketing platforms for generating 'surveillance capital'. As Zubov notes, unlike most forms of capital, surveillance capital does not rely on human labour (2019). In this way, labour has been displaced by algorithms that track the behaviour of social media users to analyse and predict their behaviours and then on-sell that predictive data to advertisers. This is how money is made. In this way, social media sites, search engines and technology companies (Amazon, Google, etc.) provide real-time surveillance of consumer behaviour that is then used to make predictions about consumer-user and is then sold to advertisers who precisely target individual consumers when they are using various sites.

Significantly also, Facebook employs around 35,000 people set against a current market valuation of $US479 billion. As Zubov notes this compares with General Motors, an automobile manufacture, that dominated the old industrial order with a market capitalisation of $US225 billion in the 1950s and which employed around 735,000 workers (2019:500).

Against this backdrop two key representations of young people as the 'young precariat' and as 'young entrepreneur' emerged. In what follows I focus on these two representations and explain how they connect to the key theme of the book, namely the central place of young people in politics especially in periods of crisis and major change.

Representing young people

It is generally agreed that we are now experiencing a period of unprecedented change in the labour market, in our personal and social lives, in the economy, in politics and how we experience and know the world. How the 'future of work' is described acknowledges the ways new and emerging technologies are generating major changes in the economy, in work and society more generally. Some argue that the capitalist market economy is in trouble and even in terminal decline (Collins 2010, Streeck 2016, Collier 2018).

The figure of the young precariat emerged from this narrative.

The young precariat

In 2011, the British economist Guy Standing argued we are witnessing the development of a new class, 'the precariat'. He located the 'new precariat' at the bottom of a seven-class system (Standing 2011, 2014:12–15). At the top is a small, elite, rich group using their extraordinary wealth to influence governments and other decision makers. Then come the 'salariat' working in large corporations and government administration enjoying stable full-time employment, pensions and paid holidays. Beneath them are skilled 'proficians', highly rewarded consultants and specialists. Then in descending order is what remains of the 'working class', the 'precariat', the unemployed and finally the lowest class of all – the 'socially ill misfits' (2011:10). The precariat can be found in existing classes and even within the professions. The legal profession, e.g., have silks at the top, below them are salariat lawyers and beneath them para-legals constituting a kind of legal precariat without any clear career path. It is a pattern repeated in medicine and academia (Standing 2011). While acknowledging the precariat included many groups, young people are an important component of this new class.

Standing defined the precariat by reference to a lack of security of income, security of employment, and protection against illness and accident. He argued that this insecurity of income and identity was creating a 'dangerous new class'. For Standing the rise of the precariat was a consequence of a deregulated labour market and demands by employers for more 'flexible' labour markets which undermined the standard full-time working week as the norm. The result was a significant rise in casualised labour. He also focused on the role of neoliberal policy-makers:

> The central plank of the neoliberal model was that growth and development depended on market competitiveness; everything should be done to maximise competitiveness, and to allow market principles to permeate all aspects of life (2011:1).

Standing's intervention soon got traction in the fields like youth studies, sociology and political studies and related policy groups. Typically the precariat is seen as the 'Twentysomethings and thirtysomethings' working on short-term contracts and temporarily or permanently jobless. These insecure, 'unsafe, abusive, no-future jobs are the hard reality of young people's lives in the late 2010s' (Foti 2017:9). Academics like Furlong drew on Standing to argue that young people were part of a new and 'dangerous class' a 'globalised precariat' characterised by anxiety, anomie and alienation that emerged from the 2008 global recession (2015a:26). Furlong warned this wasn't a 'temporary aberration', but a long-term feature of 'the economy in the late modernity'. He also criticised Standing, arguing that he 'over-simplifies contemporary contexts and misrepresented the dynamics of social class in a way that privileges middle-class insecurities while helping to obscure the suffering of marginalized groups' (2015b:3). For Shildrick and Rucell however, Standing's work offered a helpful theoretical contribution especially given Standing's emphasis on neoliberal policy (2016:30–31). For Woodman young people are among those most likely to find themselves part of this 'emerging class' (2012).

The life of the 'young precariat' is characterised by income and social insecurity and uncertain future prospects. They are positioned as victims of economic crises and of liberalised markets bought about by the 'Washington consensus', part of a distinct global class in which they are subjected to market forces. As such their complex non-standard 'transition' from school to work or 'journey' to adulthood, a status ostensibly marked by a reliable income needed for independent adulthood is thwarted. Woodman (2009) and Woodman and Wyn (2014) argue that while many tried to develop theoretical and empirical ways of representing insecure and fragmented precarious work forms, few tried to link the new conditions to broader processes of change, and identify relations between structural change and new forms of consciousness (Woodman and Wyn 2014). Standing's work reflects the legacy of sociology's continuing interest in 'structural factors', which as Boden observed, has not always been beneficent:

> The ... solidness and separateness attributed to structure has had ... extraordinary consequences in ... sociology, effectively driving a wedge between action and both its causes and its consequences.
>
> *(1994:2–3)*

Underlying these representations of the precariat is the longstanding expert disposition to represent young people as victims of 'structural forces'. This effect is heightened when these young people morph into threats (as well as victims) of the kind represented in the figure of 'youth-as-folk-devils' (Cohen 1972). Standing himself acknowledges that while his 'book emphasises the victim side' of this story, the book's sub-title, 'a new dangerous class', underscores the popular idea that 'unless the precariat is understood, its emergence could lead society towards a politics of inferno. This is not a prediction. It is a disturbing possibility' (Standing 2011:vi).

This representation of the 'young precariat' highlights the value of identifying the larger 'structural' processes that took place from the 1970s, such as the confluence of neoliberal policy, financialisation and digital disruption. Paying attention to these developments helps explain what was happening socially, politically culturally and economically. They are developments that brought about the contemporary 'future of work' problem, especially as it is now experienced and navigated by young people. It also sheds light on the politics that informs representations like 'the young precariat'. The 'young precariat' acknowledges some of the negative effects on young people of the transformation now taking place, a more 'optimistic' casting comes from another dominant narrative about the transformation now taking place. Proponents of this account argue we are moving to a fourth industrial revolution, and from this emerges the young entrepreneur-hero.

The 'young entrepreneur' and 'Industry 4.0'

Neoliberal governments, international financial agencies like the International Monetary Fund and major think-tanks like the OECD and the World Economic Forum offer a more upbeat and reassuring story of the transformation taking place. Their story is that we are moving from a 'third industrial era' to a 'Fourth Industrial Revolution', sometimes referred to as 'Industry 4.0.' or 'Industrial revolution 4.0' (Schwab 2016). European think-tanks like Germany's Friedrich-Ebert-Stiftung, suggest we are on the brink of a 'technological revolution', that will be much like previous technological revolutions implying that we don't need to worry (Schroeder 2016:2).

This 'Industry 4.0' account relies on the assumption that 'general purpose technologies' have continually triggered technological revolutions that ultimately benefit all of humanity (Durlauf and Blume 2010). 'General purpose technologies' include everything from the domestication of plants and animals that drove the Neolithic revolution (around 10,000 BCE), cognitive technologies like writing (3,000 BCE) and mechanical printing (1480 CE), or contemporary electronic and digital technologies that endlessly created wealth and promoted human progress (Pinker 2018). As one United Nations report suggested '…throughout history, technological innovations have *enhanced* the productivity of workers and created new products and markets…' (UN 2017:1). An Australian Senate report on the 'future of work' concurred arguing that the:

> …automation of workplace tasks has not historically speaking resulted in an upward trend in unemployment' and this next fourth industrial revolution will see 'new technology' 'create more jobs than put jobs at risk.
> *(Australian Senate 2018:36–37)*

Underpinning this narrative is the idea developed in 1943 by Joseph Schumpeter of 'creative destruction'. Schumpeter appropriated the idea of 'creative destruction' which entered the western philosophical discussion in the late nineteenth century courtesy of Nietzsche's account of the *Übermensch* (literally the 'above man' or 'superman'). In this account, Nietszche highlighted the need for a new generation of human beings willing to develop new kinds of post-Christian values in world after the death of God. Schumpeter took this idea and giving it an economic twist. Schumpeter used the metaphor of 'creative destruction' to emphasise its importance for when a market economy falls into a kind of equilliubrium in which productivity and growth seizes up. For Schumpeter, entrepreneurial figures like James Watt, Alexander Bell, or Thomas Edison were heroic figures whose inventions (i.e., the steam engine, telephone or electrical generation) produced by their audacity and passion for innovation, endlessly revivify capitalism. Schumpeter claimed 'creative destruction' described how 'markets' incessantly destroy parts of themselves to regenerate. It is only through 'creative destruction' that any economy maintains its vitality and health (Schumpeter 1943). It is only because there are entrepreneurs willing to take a risk that this can happen.

Today Schumpeter's ideas are being channelled in representations of 'high level' young entrepreneurs, the creative agents, motivated by 'their dreams', prepared to take risks as they disorganise and destroy the old to create new industries and initiate major change in the economy. In contemporary representations of 'the young entrepreneur' the emphasis is on the youthful figure regenerating new modes of production, creating new products and saving the economy, and in some instances fighting for and saving democracy (Clinton 2012).

In a context where neoliberal stories about the self-made 'man' are exemplified by figures like Zuckerberg, Gates, Jobs and Musk, it is no coincidence that the figure of the 'young entrepreneur' has gained traction. The young entrepreneur has become a central figure in the creative destruction story, who are what

Kerr and colleagues call: '…the founders behind … ventures [that] are in vogue everywhere' (Kerr et al. 2017). According to Zuboff 'the cult' of the entrepreneur has achieved 'mythic prominence' replacing 'second modernity' designed for the 'glorification of competitive cunning, dominance and wealth' (Zuboff 2019:41).

Today governments, business leaders, international agencies, youth peaks and educational institutions regularly promote the argument we need more young entrepreneurs (Green OECD 2013). From the neoliberal perspective, the young entrepreneur reproduces the long-standing human capital investment claim that more education creates economic growth, promotes social mobility and enhances individual income. It is assumed as fact that young people are naturally equipped and culturally disposed to be creative and part of 'accelerators', 'incubator cultures', 'showcase innovation booths' and 'start-ups'. All that is needed is to change the curriculum in schools and universities to ensure students have 'the right entrepreneurial skills', and a better understanding of the private sector. Accordingly, these skills include 'soft skills', 'problem-solving, self-reliance, initiative, risk taking, flexibility, [and] creativity' (Scott-Kemmis 2017:16, see also Daniel and Kent 2005).

The 'young precariat' (and associated representations of 'unemployed youth', or NEET's (Not in Education or Training) *and* the 'young entrepreneur', are not objective or innocent descriptions. They were made-up in the middle of an unprecedented transformative process.

How can we understand the emergence of these two divergent representations of young people in the context of a historic transformation? More specifically how can we understand their coming into being in the context of political crisis about the future of work that also has implications for economy and the welfare state?

Both the 'young precariat' and the 'young entrepreneur' are representations shaped by political worldviews and specific political-economic interests. The young precariat representation highlights how many young people are the victims or 'casualties' of dramatic new socio-economic processes. Many young people are now being screwed in an economy where the options for secure work are drying up, where young people are the main source of labour in a 'gig economy' capable only of providing minimal or no job security.

The politics of this representation of the young precariat, cannot be disguised by talking about the benefits of 'flexibility' and misleading promises about what 'self-employment' and 'individual enterprise' can do (Shildrick et al. 2012, Burrows 2013:38–96, McDonald and Giazitzoglu 2019:723–740). At the same time, the 'young precariat' also implies a threat, as disenchanted and unemployed they are said to be prone to the youthful vicissitudes and dangers constituted by idle youth who as we know, are a menace to society due to their propensity to engage in drug use, juvenile crime, graffiti and gang violence (Eckersley 1993).

The 'young entrepreneur' is a more optimistic representation of the hero-saviour. It's a representation embedded in 'Fourth Revolution' or 'industry 4.0' narratives. It is a story intended to assuage anxiety, and reassure us everything is fine. While there may be a few bumps on the way, the capitalist economy will continue to thrive. Just as oil revived and sustained the older industrial order, so 'data as the new oil' will secure the future of capitalism (Schwab 2016). In short, we are simply transitioning from a third industrial age to a fourth industrial age.

While the 'Industry 4.0' narrative pays attention to the effects of digital disruption on employment patterns, it fails to acknowledge the confluence of neoliberal policies and financialisation. It does not account for the decline of full-time employment or long term stagnant productivity or halting wage growth. It is for this reason instructive to link actual political and economic processes that are reshaping modern labour markets to broader processes of change (Woodman and Wyn 2014, Bessant et al. 2017).

Critical to such a political-economic account are the sweeping changes affecting key structural features of the relationship of capital to labour. Writers like Wallerstein et al. (2013), Streeck (2016) and Collier (2018) go so far as to suggest that these changes signal the end of capitalism.

Conclusion

Stephen Threadgold is right in highlighting how a diverse range of representations of young people function politically. He sees those representations as figures of struggle positioned between injunctions based on various government promises such as 'study hard, work hard' and 'the meritocracy will see you prevail' contrasting with the 'everyday reality of precarious labour markets, political upheaval lead by conservative and reactionary forces, and global risks such as climate change' (Threadgold 2019:5).

This chapter inquired into how governments, economic actors and experts described and tried to explain the far-reaching changes in the economy and the shape of the labour markets that began in the 1970s and 1980s and how certain representations of young people came out of those accounts. It identified the key gaps between those accounts and what was actually happening.

They were gaps partly created from the political drive by governments and financial capital to redesign capitalist economies in the advanced developed world so as to restore what was deemed to be the right and natural dominance of capital over labour. One emerging aspect of this was the recognition that labour could be eased out the market courtesy of digital displacement. This transformation had major consequences for certain groups and their ability to access jobs. The expulsion of young people from the full-time labour market became especially apparent from the 1990s.

The misleading stories about what was happening played a critical role in shaping representations of young people. They also provided a way that the change process that was taking place could be managed and legitimated. For many leaders of the day acknowledging that 'the economy' was no longer generating enough jobs was too much to admit. Acknowledging such an uncomfortable truth would have raised questions about the legitimation processes preferred by elites to manage advanced capitalist societies. They needed to encourage the belief that most people would benefit from the way things were.

Translating the problem of unemployment into a problem of the unemployed and of young unemployed in particular, by arguing that their inability to get work was due to their deficiencies of skill, poor education, experience or lack of motivation was a misleading way of representing this key sign of major transformation.

Another strategy adopted from 1986 on, saw many western countries designing a new 'active society' model of welfare, reliant on a combination of stigmatising and punitive practices that disciplined and regulated the lives of the millions of workers now expelled from the full-time labour markets. Young people were one of the first in the firing line and typically had a tenuous footing in the labour market. Moreover, as everyone knows, young people are inherently troublesome and if left to their own devices would prove idle and likely to descend into delinquency and criminality.

Among the many representations of young people references to the 'young dole bludger' (in Australia) or the 'youth underclass' in Britain and the USA was useful for a while (McDonald 1997, Cieslik and Simpson 2013). But even then as Threadgold notes, these representations were a kaleidoscope of contradictions and inconsistencies where young people were represented as 'active and passive', cultural dupes but economically valuable, risky but in need of protection, echoing one's past while representing the future' (Threadgold 2019:6).

The larger significance of this major change in the labour market is yet to be revealed, signalled by the apparent absence of young people themselves as political actors from this chapter. This however should not be taken as inferring that the decades of change described here saw no evidence of political pushback by young people. Far from it. To document the political responses of young people is the task of Chapter 8.

Notes

1 This includes 'Gen-Xers' (born 1965–1980), 'Millennials' (born 1980 to the late 1990s) and 'Gen Z' (born 1995–2010).
2 As John Quiggin argues, an important feature of international policy was the 1944 Bretton Woods agreement (Quiggin 1999:240–259). The aim of that agreement was to control capital flows in ways that allowed for fixed currency exchange rates and sufficient domestic flexibility to secure full employment. The objective of the system was to expand trade in goods and to ensure that fluctuations in exchange markets did not create instability like that had brought on the Great Depression of the 1930s. The Bretton Woods system established two international institutions, the International Monetary Fund and the International Bank for Reconstruction and Development now the World Bank. The IMF provided short-term assistance to countries experiencing balance-of-payments problems. The World Bank was to provide long-term finance for development projects.

3 There are many complexities with these figures that cannot be discussed here. They include, e.g., the differential rates of unemployment shaped by gender, region, ethnicity, level of education and more general issues about how to conceptualise and measure the youth labour market and what are the best ways to describe unemployment, underemployment, part-time and casual employment, etc.

4 This turned out to be a permanent change. Young people had a lower share of the labour force – around 15%, compared with around 25% in the early 1980s (reflecting in part a decline in the participation rate of younger workers). Young people's employment has also changed in noticeable ways; over half were then in work part time, an increase from around 15% in the early 1980s (Dillon and Cassidy 2018). Overall, around 55% of younger workers were in casual employment in 2017. The decrease in labour force participation and increased prevalence of part-time work for younger Australians is partly related to the increase in the share of 15–24 year olds who are studying full time. However, in recent years there has been a marked increase in the share of 20–24 year olds working part-time who are *not* studying full time (Dillon and Cassidy 2018).

5 Garber documents how that the Nixon Administration erred in taking America off the gold standard (1991). This made the US dollar the default global unit of exchange:

After 1968, the system was, as it was before 1968, fundamentally a dollar standard, with little chance that foreign official claimants would ever get their hands on the remaining U.S. gold stock. Yet foreign monetary authorities valued the system to the extent of absorbing up to $70 billion in dollar claims, most of which was subject to exchange risk, to defend it. They had to go to these lengths because the inflationary policy of the US administration made a speculative attack inevitable. If the administration had been committed to less inflationary monetary policies, the basic Bretton Woods system would have remained intact' (Garber 1991:486).

6 In 2006 the OECD was still concerned that unemployment benefits were too generous (OECD 2006:58). It was argued that evidence from cross-country panel regression models substantiated claims that generous benefits raise the equilibrium level of unemployment and that the econometric studies confirm that higher benefit levels are associated with more unemployment and that generous unemployment benefits significantly increase unemployment durations (OECD 2006:60).

7 According to the OECD an 'active society' would cure 'welfare dependency'. This could be done by moving away from 'passive welfare' that generated 'dependency' on income transfers to 'those that mobilize labour supply and foster economic opportunity, improve the efficiency of labour market matching and develop employment-related skills' (1988b).

8 For exceptions to this see, e.g., Mitchell and Muysken (2002) who pointed to evidence that continuing unemployment was a problem of demand deficiency.

9 Examples include minimum wage requirements, sick leave requirements, unfair dismal laws, environment protection laws, health and safety standards, etc.

10 Equally public companies grew in size. The average market capitalization of a US-listed company was $7.3b, and the median was $832m for a typical domestic-listed company in 2017 (Brorsen 2017).

11 In the US of the Fortune 500 companies in 1955 like American Motors, Brown Shoe, Studebaker, Collins Radio, Detroit Steel, Zenith Electronics, and National Sugar Refining, none were in the Fortune 550 list in 2014. Nearly 88% of the companies from 1955 either went bankrupt, merged, or still exist but have fallen from the top Fortune 500 companies (ranked by total revenues) (Perry 2017). In the US by the second decade in the twenty-first century public listed companies were employing fewer half as many Americans as they did in the 1970s (Zuboff 2019:41).

12 Arrighi (1994) and Krippner (2005) document the financial innovations shaped by the 'shareholder value orientation'. Sometimes we saw, e.g., productive firms turn to

financial activities: e.g., automobile producers started offering credit to car-buyers. This is because the expected profit in the financial market was higher than the profit in the traded goods market (e.g., a car), and/or because the conditions associated with the need to pay shareholders high dividend payments forced firms to pursue capital growth in the financial market.
13 Non-standard workers can be independent contractors working alone, self-employed workers potentially employing other people, dependent employees working part-time, workers on temporary contracts, casual workers, platform workers and other workers who are not in standard employment, i.e., working full-time and on open-ended contracts for a single employer.
14 As Acemoglu et al. argue 'by 2009, there [was] no net relative productivity gain in IT-intensive industries' (2014:396).

8

MAKING THE WAVES

Contemporary youth action

By June 2020, the COVID-19 pandemic had infected over 11 million people and killed at least 530,000 people. Most governments responded by imposing extended and large-scale restrictions on social, economic and cultural activities in a bid to control the viral epidemic. Schools and universities went on-line, and scores of businesses and organisations either closed or instructed their workers to work from home. The unprecedented lock-down engendered confusion and disorder in many communities as businesses closed, stock markets plunged, credit dried up, and jobless rates soared to levels not seen since the 1930s depression. Governments of all political persuasions reacted with 'stimulus packages' totalling trillions of dollars to stave off the collapse of their economies.

In the move to lock down and impose social distancing, politics did not disappear. The measures taken by governments to try and control the pandemic, and their efforts to mitigate the negative economic and social effects of those measures, generated new waves of political contest and controversy. In dozens of countries alt-right and conservative groups angered by what they saw as arbitrary restrictions of their rights to freedom of movement and association, linked the COVID-19 virus, 'deep state' conspiracy theories, anti-Vaxx and anti-Semitic memes when they took to the streets in mid-2020. When Derek Chauvin, a white police officer killed George Floyd, an African-American on 25 May 2020, a wave of 'Black Lives Matter' protests also erupted first across the USA and then globally. In Hong Kong, pro-democracy marches defied police to continue their campaigns even after China passed new national security laws prohibiting, amongst other things, criticism of China's governing Communist Party. Not surprisingly children and young people played key roles in these last two waves of protests.

It is a time when in spite of decades of neoliberal politics, disastrous economic crisis, austerity regimes and repeated assaults by authoritarian governments and the security state on human rights and democratic practices, political life seems to be operating at a more heightened level than it has for some time. As Charles Dickens said: we are in '…the worst of times and the best of times'.[1]

According to researchers at Cambridge's Centre for the Future of Democracy, 2019 saw 'the highest level of democratic discontent' since 1995 when the centre first began assessing people's view of democracy (Foa et al. 2020).[2] Researchers at the Centre concluded that globally democracy was in a state of malaise. In the mid-1990s, most citizens in North America, Latin America, Europe, Africa, the Middle East, Asia and Australasia reported they were satisfied with the performance of their democracies. Since then, the share of individuals 'dissatisfied' with democracy rose by around 10%, from 47.9% to 57.5%. The year 2005, said to mark the beginning of the so-called 'global democratic recession' was also the high point for global satisfaction with democracy, with just 38.7% of citizens dissatisfied in that year. Since then, the proportion of 'dissatisfied' citizens increased by almost one-fifth of the population (18.8%). As the Centre notes this dissatisfaction with democracy is in large part a response to objective circumstances and events like economic shocks, corruption scandals and policy crises that 'have an immediately observable effect upon average levels of civic dissatisfaction' (Foa et al. 2020:2).

Out of all those 'objective circumstances', the 2008 Recession was the catalyst that shifted popular opinion against 'normal' politics. This was evident in the rise of anti-austerity movements, pro-democracy protests, and the re-emergence of various forms of left and right-wing populism (Müller 2016). Public trust in political institutions like parliaments, government departments, the courts and political parties and some religious orders went through the floor. Voter attendance at polls 'declined across the established democracies of North America and Western Europe' (Foa and Mounk 2016:6). Even the World Economic Forum (WEF), warned that 'The crisis of democratic legitimacy extends across a much wider set of indicators than previously appreciated' (WEF 2017:7). The WEF argued there was evidence 'of a growing backlash against elements of the domestic and international status quo that was threatening the liberal political consensus' (WEF 2017a:12). Declining participation in formal politics and increasing engagement in alternative or 'anti-establishment politics' was said to be particularly problematic among the young and those who 'feel left behind in their own countries' (WEF 2017a:13).

Yet in this we saw conspicuous evidence of a healthy democracy in the political actions of many young people around the world from 2000.[3] One question implicit in Chapter 7, that can be addressed here is the extent to which this political action reflects the changed circumstances of young people born since the 1990s.

Many writers argue that 'millennials', (born between 1985 and 1995) and 'Generation Z' (those born between 1996 and 2010) do not enjoy a better standard of living than their parents. Laura Gardiner, argues that in contrast with the assumption that each new generation will do better than the previous one, a typical 'millennial' earned £UK8,000 less during their twenties than those in the preceding generation – generation X' (Gardiner 2016:5). In the USA Angela Morabito reported that American 'millennials' had 'less opportunity than any previous generation currently alive today' experiencing 'lower incomes, fewer job opportunities, and less likely to own homes and cars' (Morabito 2016). Researchers at the Pew Research Centre argued that European 'millennials' also had a negative outlook about prospects for the next generation. When asked whether they thought children in their country would be better off financially than their parents once they grew up, only 38% of young British, 37% of young Germans and 15% of young French were optimistic (Stokes 2015). In countries like Spain and France persistently high levels of youth (15–24) unemployment may, in part, explain the pessimism. In Australia, Jennifer Rayner argued that her generation was the first in more than 80 years to go backwards in work, wealth and well-being. She presented evidence that Australian 'millennials' were doing badly, with the number of young people working casually jumping from 32% in 1992 to 50% in 2013. At the same time, while wage growth more than doubled for 50 to 54 year olds between 1990 and 2013, the 20–24 age group were only earning 25% more than in 1990 (Rayner 2016:15).

This evidence and commentary points to the tectonic shifts taking place in the socio-economic orders of advanced societies that are connected to increasing expressions of social protest, especially by young people. Various movements like Spain's Indignados, UK Uncut, the Occupy movement, France and #Nuit Debout look to be responses to the Recession of 2008 and other moves by governments to impose neoliberal austerity policies (Pontusson and Raess 2012, Gitlin 2013, Hutterb and Kriesi 2013, Kriesi 2013, Milkman et al. 2013, Sukarieh and Tannock 2014, Pickard and Bessant 2018). Yet it is important not to read this action by so many young people simply as an economic spasm.

This is nowhere better demonstrated than by the third Global Climate Strike campaign, staged in the last week of September 2019, the largest climate protest ever staged. In that week between 4 million and 7.6 million people, many of them schoolchildren and students, took part in around 6,000 protest events in 185 countries around the globe (Barclay and Reznick 2019). Significantly it was school students, many of them quite young, who initiated, organised and participated in these waves of climate action (De Moor et al. 2020:2). We saw large numbers of young people moved by high levels of 'ethical energy' taking various kinds of political action including street protests across the globe from London, Lebanon, through Barcelona and California to Hong Kong and Sudan. Research in Europe and Australia shows how these young people were galvanised by powerful moral emotions like hope, disillusionment and righteous anger, responses to a variety of 'situated injustices' (Wahlström et al. 2019, Collins et al. 2020). Some commentators described events as 'a youth-led revolution [that] is coming alive':

> Around the world, young people are becoming a power in their own right. Millions of young people are now engaged in what has become the civil-rights struggle of our time – the fight for every child's right to go to school, and to do so in safety.
>
> *(Brown 2018)*

Similarly, a *Lancet* editorial in 2019 opened with the following:

> We are living in the midst of a wave of worldwide cultural change. Peaceful global activism led by young people is gaining momentum, challenging power structures at every level of society. ... Cultural change led by young people is sweeping across society and young activists are becoming legitimised.
>
> *(Lancet Editorial 2019)*

Yet there is more to those expressions of young people's political action than these observations capture. Such political action is also not a novel or unique.

Young people including children have been politically engaged at least since the end of the eighteenth century. A century and a half ago school students in Britain engaged in waves of school strikes. These began in September and October 1889, when students from two Board schools in Hawick 'went on strike, marched in processional order ... causing considerable commotion'. During the ensuing three-week school strike the children demanded 'shorter hours, fewer and easier lessons, and better teachers' (Cunningham and Lavallette 2002:172). *The Times* complained about the 'breakdown in discipline' and the 'very shocking' demands presented by the children while blaming militant trade union parents. In 1911, another set of school strikes occurred affecting schools in over 60 cities and towns across Britain. Students demanded the abolition of corporal punishment, an end to home lessons, an extra half-day holiday and the payment of monitors (Cunningham and Lavallette 2002:174).

As we saw in Chapter Six secondary school students were significantly engaged in anti-Vietnam war politics in America in the 1960s (Graham 2006:4). In 1972 the London-based Schools Action Union, founded in January 1969 by a group of London schoolboys, inspired by the success of student unrest in France, staged a series of one-day strikes throughout Britain. They demanded rights drafted into a formal school children's 'charter' which included an end to corporal punishment and detentions, more participation by students in the running of schools, the abolition of school uniforms, better school meals and the reintroduction of free school milk abolished by Margaret Thatcher when she was Education Secretary (Cunningham and Lavallette 2002:179). Decades later British school-children were again involved in the mass mobilisation of street marches protesting the Blair government's decision to take Britain into the Iraq war in 2003 (Such et al. 2005).

This history highlights the value of acknowledging children's and young people's role as *political actors*, capable of understanding and engaging with the social and political world. This history also indicates the importance of questioning conventional views of children that see them as *passive objects*, or as 'incomplete adults', incapable of rational judgment or thoughtful participation in politics.

In this chapter, I ask what are some of the dominant ways children and young people have been represented over the past few decades? My focus is on the relationship between certain representations of children and young people, and how politics has been understood. I then consider how children and young people engaged as political actors.

I begin with a brief survey of the contradictory ways children and young people continue being represented in the scholarly literature. Attention is also given to the ways children and young people represented themselves as political actors. While contemporary social movements involving children and young people have a global reach, I survey a few prominent campaigns in a few countries.

Representing children and young people

I have taken some time and effort to refute the idea that it is possible and desirable to produce a definitive and literal definition of categories like 'child' or 'young person'. Needless to say constructing definitions or ideal types is considered to be an important, if not indispensable methodological step that continues to be done in the conventional social sciences in spite of critiques of this practice from various perspectives (Latour 1999, Bourdieu 1992a, 1993a; Caputo 2018, Harman 2018).

I also drew on accounts of representations developed by Moscovici (1981, 1982, 1984a) and Bourdieu (1992). Recall how Moscovici suggests how we think of:

> ...social representations ... almost as material objects, in so far as they are the products of our actions and communications. They are in fact the product of a professional activity: I am referring to those pedagogues, ideologues, popularizers of science, cultures and priests, that is the representatives of science, culture and religions whose task it is, is to create and transmit them, often, alas, without either knowing or wishing it.
> *(Moscovici 2000:27)*

While Bourdieu goes some way on this with Moscovici, he does not assume that experts, scholars or scientists provide a single set of social representations.

According to Bourdieu, we are involved in classificatory struggles in the scholarly field and in broader cultural fields. Bourdieu argues that the modern sciences natural and social are involved in a:

> ...game whose stake is the power of governing the sacred frontiers, that is, the quasi-divine power over the vision of the world, and in which one has no choice, if one seeks to exercise it (rather than submit to it), other than to mystify or demystify.
>
> *(Bourdieu 1992:228)*

For Bourdieu, all classifications of age groups such as 'child', 'adolescent' or 'young adult' are arbitrary and subject to struggle. These are not naïve, natural objects or categories. As Bourdieu explains:

> ...groups are not found ready-made in reality. And even when they present themselves with this air of eternity that is the hallmark of naturalized history, they are always the product of a complex historical work of construction'.
>
> *(Bourdieu 1987:8)*

As Bourdieu argues these groups are part of the politics of classification. In terms of 'age cohorts':

> One is always somebody's senior or junior. That is why the divisions, whether into age-groups or into generations, are entirely variable and subject to manipulation... My point is simply that youth and age are not self-evident data but are socially constructed, in the struggle between the young and the old.
>
> *(Bourdieu 1993:95)*

This is why it is important to acknowledge the contested representations of children and young people.

Perhaps the proverb 'the more things change, the more they stay the same' applies, at least to some degree, to how we continue representing children and young people. There is a continuity evident in recent surveys of scholarship on children and young people. Tghius scholarship highlights the persistence of generally negative and often contradictory representations of children and young people (Cockburn 1998, Prout 2000, Forrester 2002, Such et al. 2003, Sorin and Galloway 2006, Smith 2011, Zhao 2011, Hartung 2017),

One set of representations identify essential differences between 'children' and 'adults'. Childhood is the opposite, or 'Other' of adulthood (Mayall 2002). In this way, childhood is represented as a time of innocence, and playfulness because children are free from the pressures and cares of adult status (Higonnet 1998). Yet alongside this exists a parallel set of representations that refer to differences between childhood and adulthood focussing on qualities like frailty, vulnerability, limited autonomy and effects like anxiety and depression (Prager and Donovan 2013, Thapar et al. 2012, Wilson and Lyons 2012). This framing emphasises a need for care and protection, for learning and support that adults are expected to provide (Jenks 1996). In some cases, this is used as justification for arguing that children and young people should be protected from participating in decision-making about substantive matters and from political activity more generally (Arendt 1959, Sen 1999, 2009, Nussbaum 2011).

As demonstrated in previous chapters these themes are central to a long-running story about 'childhood' or 'youth', understood as 'stages' in the 'human life-cycle'. The history of this approach was documented by Phillipe Aries (1962) in his groundbreaking history of changing representations of childhood an approach subsequently adumbrated by Mitterauer (1992) and Griffin (1993). The idea that there are discrete stages of development, generated a vast scholarship theoretical and professional in fields like psychology, child development, legal studies, education, youth studies and social history (Griffin 1993, Zaff et al. 2003, Melkman 2017, Haggman-Laitila et al. 2019).

The stadial frame supports a number of approaches and emphases. One tradition that generated much research focussed on youth transitions. Beginning in the 1970s, we saw the appearance of scholarship interested in 'youth transitions' in 'advanced capitalist societies' represented as an increasingly complex, risky and protracted process of transition (McDowell 2002, Furlong and Cartmel 2007, Thompson 2011, Sanderson 2019:1). Drawing on this body of work some scholars claim the stage of 'youth' has been extended, becoming a form of 'adulthood arrested' (Côté 2000, du Bois-Reymond 2009: cf. Côté 2014).

In these ways, childhood and youth are represented as preparatory stages on the road to adulthood, whereby children and young people are incomplete, half-adults trapped in a state of becoming, as distinct from being (Jenks 1988). As I argued in Chapter 7, representations of young people whether as 'unemployed youth', 'delinquents' or 'wayward girls' or more recently as 'Gen Y', 'millennials' or 'the young precariat' are all age-based representations constituted predominantly by experts of various kinds and governments. Not surprisingly they are representations in which young people themselves had little, if any involvement in creating.

We also see a repetitive tendency in popular cultural discourses and expert or scholarly research to construct children as problematic by emphasising their troubled even deviant nature (Pearson 1983). They are variously dysfunctional, deficient, deviant, or more recently at risk, and therefore unable to take part constructively in political processes without close supervision (Goldson 2001, Bessant et al. 2017). This representation comes to the fore in the idea of 'adolescence' or 'youth' framed as the 'transition from childhood' to adulthood, a time that references many significant legal or civic milestones on the rickety road to 'adulthood' (e.g., the age of criminal responsibility, the age of consent, the end of compulsory education and the age of majority) (Griffin 1993).

While acknowledging this diversity of representations, there is one common factor, namely, older people tend to use their superior symbolic capital to produce these accounts. As Zhao explains, these representations signify how children and young people have been 'used for different social, cultural, economic, and political purposes' (Zhao 2011:242). Sometimes 'adult power' has been misused and children abused or worse.[4] In the modern era, we can generalise to some extent and say that 'adult power' has increasingly been applied to talk about the 'best interests of the child' – an attitude ostensibly informed by narratives about sensitive adult–child power-sharing (Powell et al. 2016). Yet as Prout (2000) observes, while claiming to prioritise the future of the child and society over the child's present well-being, adults still practise a control, which many scholars see as a distinguishing feature of modernity (Freeman 2000).

Further, regardless of the form these representations take, any idea that a child or young person can and/or should participate in political life or activities has generally been opposed or resisted. As Helen Brocklehurst argues, this is the result of 'representing children as un-political and, male or female, developing, innocent, and passive, is to downplay their politics or agency' (Brocklehurst 2020:89). The idea they can or should participate politically, conflicts with representations of 'the child' and 'youth' as incomplete, not fully rational or adult. It can also mean that other considerations take priority, like the idea that adults are obliged to protect children from a dangerous world:

> …[children] either need to be better protected (better policed from the evils of the adult world) or better controlled (because of the failure of certain families to police properly their children).
>
> *(Roche 1999:477)*

Even Hannah Arendt, whose emphasis on the 'politics of natality' might be read as implying that children should be involved politically, recoiled from any suggestion that children should be exposed to what she called 'the dangers of political life' (Bray and Nakata 2020:6–8). In Arendt's famous essay on the civil rights protests at Little Rock in 1957, she addressed the question of the relation of children and politics.

Arendt thought it was wrong to use children in a political fight like the civil rights campaign in which, among other considerations, there was a real possibility of violence. Arendt thought 'the child requires special protection and care so that nothing destructive may happen to him from the world' (Arendt 2006:182).

In short, a series of overlapping representations exist which cohere around the idea that children and young people should not be allowed to take part in political activity because they are variously:

- vulnerable, frail, naïve, or emotionally troubled, 'dysfunctional', 'deviant' 'trouble-makers' and need protection, or

- they lack the requisite cognitive, ethical emotional skills and experience to participate in political life which requires them to know things or exercise judgement of which they are incapable.

Having said that, a small number of writers do acknowledge that children and young people are political animals.

The child's construction of politics

In the late 1960s, Raewyn Connell described how children understood politics (1971). She rejected the structural-functionalist socialisation model then used by mainstream sociologists. Connell drew on Piaget and other cognitive theorists to interpret the 119 interviews she did with young children aged 5–16. The interviews made up much of the text, and offer a rich, complex picture of children's political thinking.

Connell presents a two-dimensional account of political learning. The first identifies four age-graded categories that involve intuitive thinking, primitive realism, construction of the political order and ideological thinking (Connell 1971:231). In parallel with this cognitive development, was a more affective and moral kind of thinking, or what Connell called 'stances'. One stance was that politics is non-problematic and the children's judgments random, unqualified even ad hoc. In the second stance, politics is recognised as problematic. Preferences are evident, alternatives are advanced, the interconnected nature of stances is often recognised, and the problematic nature of the child's own political behaviour is identified. Connell understood that notwithstanding efforts by many parents and schools to shape the political identity of children, that children were also actively constructing their own political thinking:

> The children selectively appropriate the material provided by schools, by mass media, by parents and build of them individual structures ... the theories of 'political socialization have produced distorted accounts of the development because they have failed to recognize and account for the conscious creative activity of the children themselves.
> *(Connell 1971:233)*

This was why Connell acknowledged that young, and not-so-young children '...not only show evidence of "socialization", but of surprisingly outspoken, idiosyncratic, blunt, and imaginative political opinions. They can poke fun at the self-important... and wryly take on subjects the rest of us have learned to skirt, or get at indirectly' (Connell 1971:235).

The French philosopher Henri Lefebvre presented a similar view, arguing that children experience and try to understand social events in complex ways because there are different political frameworks available to evaluate their everyday experiences (1991). He said children are navigating politicised landscapes that include a 'cacophony of voices' about right, wrong and how things might be changed (Lefebvre 1991:45). In research that drew on interviews with adults about their childhood, Dorothy Moss, observes how political engagement can have a powerful emotional dimension: children's political understanding develops in relation to experiences, fears and caring connections with others typically in their family or community (Moss 2013:33). She tells how 17-year-old, 'Martin' remembered Enoch Powell's infamous 'Rivers of Blood' speech (1968) raging against the flood of coloured immigrants into Britain. While Martin lived a privileged life in England his father taught him not to discriminate and introduced him to Kenyan colleagues:

> There was a lot of anti-immigration feeling... I was probably fairly politically naive ... but I was certainly of the view that these people were actually contributing to British society and they had every right to be here as we did...
>
> *(Moss 2013:30)*

Moss also wrote about 'James', growing up in conflict-ridden Ulster in the 1970s who experienced electricity power cuts in the 1970s due to strikes organised by the Ulster Workers' Council. James explained how they went on:

> ... for three years... wiping out the whole of the city lights, for days... lots and lots of times, sitting with candles and having meals... there's somebody out there that's doing this and they are very, very scary people that control to such an extent as that, but at the same time, knowing it was sort of on the same religious side, there was no fear.
>
> *(Moss 2013:29)*

Like Moss, Mary Nolan notes how these experiences indicate how children 'have to negotiate their agency through social spaces of their own changing times' (Nolan 2001:310).

These writers also highlighted how certain interpretative frames inhibit our capacity to see what children are doing and experiencing. Nolan, e.g., argued that children's political engagement has been underestimated when social scientists define politics in ways that rely on 'narrowly defined concepts of civil society and socio-political participation at the macro level' (Nolan 2001:308). Similarly, Cockburn argues that if political activity is framed narrowly in terms of a young person's engagement with formal organisations, then it will be underestimated, enabling 'media and government continue to portray children and young people... as "politically apathetic" and disinterested in politics and the life around them' (Cockburn 2007:446).

Sometimes as writers like American academic Victoria Grieve (2018) note, representing children as innocent, vulnerable and apolitical and thus unable to engage in politics can produce some paradoxical and unpredictable consequences.

Grieve documents how images of childhood innocence and vulnerability, did not prevent the United States government in the 1950s from using that innocence in ways that 'constituted the basis for their political activities on behalf of the state' (Grieve 2018:7). Notwithstanding the claim that 'children in the Soviet Union were being "brainwashed" by state propaganda' the US government did the same thing, creating a domestic 'public information campaign'.

In conjunction with consumer advertising, the government produced public information campaigns to sell the Cold War to Americans at home and to foreign audiences by using children as 'symbols of the virtues of democratic capitalism and of the nation's vulnerability to Soviet communism' (Grieve 2018:128). Here once more we see young people represented as warriors, this time as 'little cold war warriors' who were assigned a political role as saviours of democracy. As Grieve demonstrates, while much of what happened in schools and other sites during the 1950s supported the agenda of America's national security state, some students and teachers questioned and resisted the anti-communist line, promoting instead a foreign policy ethos that emphasised 'world friendship and international understanding' (Grieve 2018:169).

Zhao notes that historically this surplus of 'adult power' has often been misused, resulting in children being abused or worse.[5] In the modern era while that eventuality cannot be dismissed – as the history of sexual crimes committed against children by religious personnel attests – adult symbolic power has generally been applied in ways that many adults to talk about, in terms of pursuing the 'best interests of the child'. That is, the ostensible point of the *UN Convention of the Rights of the Child*. This has been associated with many narratives proposing the increased participation of young people and more 'sensitive adult-child power sharing' (Powell et al. 2016). However, as Prout argues, when adults claim to prioritise the future of the child and society over the child's present well-being, adults are exercising their power, which is a distinguishing feature of modernity (2000, also Freeman 2000). It is this presumption of an adult right to direct the lives of young people, that young people who take part in various kinds of political action challenge.

Young people's politics

The most obvious way many young people have rejected representations of them as developmentally immature or politically ignorant, and so incapable of political action, has been to take direct and highly public political action. In this way they have demonstrated a capacity both personally and collectively, to be both well informed and to know something of what is happening around them, to accept responsibility, and then to act on matters they judge are important locally nationally, or even globally. I illustrate this with several cases from Britain and Australia that highlight the capacity of sometimes quite young people to engage politically and effectively with complex issues. In what follows I illustrate this with cases from Britain and Australia that highlight the capacity of sometimes quite young people to engage politically and effectively with complex issues.

From the beginning of the twenty-first century, we witnessed major waves of protest in which young people played a key role. Some were against the American-led invasion of Iraq in 2003; others were opposed to neoliberal policies applied to public universities and other civic institutions, while more recently we saw major campaigns urging governments to act on climate change.

Anti-war protests

In 2003, quite young people demonstrated their capacity as articulate participants in campaigns of school-based protest against Britain going to war in Iraq. It involved students leaving school during school hours and taking part in street marches. The British students were not alone. Tens of thousands of American schoolchildren marched out of classes, calling for 'books not bombs'. In Switzerland students left their classes carrying rainbow flags for peace, along with their classmates in Greece, Denmark, Sweden, Germany, Italy, Spain, Australia and Britain (Phipps 2003). As Brooks reports:

> This spring, in the first days of war with Iraq, the country was witness to a new kind of protest. In the most significant child-led campaign for a century, schoolchildren as young as 10 walked out of their classrooms to attend what were, for most, their first political demonstrations ... These young people were organising and leading their own protests, leafleting at school gates, organising e-mail networks and expertly working the media. Their determination to be heard was palpable. The results were awesome.
> *(Brooks 2003:41)*

In Britain young people catalysed by an ethical energy involving political emotions like moral outrage and hope, opposed what became one of the most disastrous wars in modern history. Olivia (aged 10) was concerned about the children of Iraq: 'Bush and Blair will kill thousands of Iraqi children, just like me and my friends. My teachers told me I was too young to protest, but if I'm too young to protest, they're too young to be killed' (cited Cunningham and Lavattelle 2004:261). Clare (aged 16) explained how she and two hundred children had walked out of school to demonstrate at the city's war memorial because they wanted to send a message to Prime Minister Blair:

> We all feel strongly that war is wrong. There is no valid reason for war on Iraq, dropping bombs will solve nothing and innocent lives will be lost. Young people have a voice and Tony Blair needs to listen to us.
> *(Cited Cunningham and Lavattelle 2004:262)*

Jaswinder (aged 13) explained that he and 350 students walked out of school because they believed that 'innocent people shouldn't die so George Bush and Tony Blair get their oil' (cited in Cunningham and Lavattelle 2004).

They were also organisationally adept. Kenny (aged 17) identified some elements of 'self-conscious leadership' that some of the young people displayed:

> I went to the 15 February demo ... There were 70 of us from our school who went on the train organized by the local Stop the War Coalition. On the way back, some of us got together and had a meeting. We decided that on the Monday morning [17 February 2003], we would meet in the city centre and march into school. We borrowed the coalition banner, met at 8.45 and off we went. The following week, I organized a room and we set up School Students Against the War ... We talked about getting organized and having a school strike. We made pledge sheets for people to sign. They signed them guaranteeing that they would strike. Some people signed them easily, some we had to convince, but this was a great way of committing people. On 5 and 6 March, we managed to get loads of students out on strike, we sat down on the road, demonstrated and really felt our voice was being heard. It was great.
>
> *(Cited in Cunningham and Lavattelle 2004:262–263)*

Anti-austerity campaigns

Seven years later in 2010, another student campaign occurred this time directed against the British Cameron government's higher education 'reforms'. The polices were detailed in a Higher Education White Paper and followed by government moves to increase tuition fees for English university students from £3,290 to £9,000 per year while cutting the higher education teaching budget by 40% in 2014/2015. The National Union of Students (NUS) announced that a national demonstration would take place in London on 10 November 2010. The march attracted around 52,000 students from over 100 universities (Hensby 2014:93). At one point a small group of students broke away from the main march moving to the Conservative Party's campaign headquarters in the Millbank Tower. Students smashed the building's front windows while some 200 protesters rushed inside. This led to clashes between protesters and police, in which 14 people, including police and activists, were injured while around 50 protesters were arrested. Yet as the NUS distanced itself from the breakaway protestors, it also announced another 'National Walkout and Day of Action' for 24 November. This time around 150,000 college and university students participated in protests across Britain (Solomon and Palmieri, 2011:15). It provided a springboard for student occupations of campus buildings, with approximately 50 individual occupations taking place between November and December (Solomon and Palmieri, 2011:60).

One year later in November 2011, several thousand students once more marched across London to protest against the Cameron government's higher education policies. This time as Hensby reported, they faced extraordinary security measures (2017:3). Scotland Yard warned the marchers they would use rubber bullets and water cannons. Students were greeted by an estimated 4,000 police officers. During the four-hour march, police used their large numbers to kettle or herd protestors so as to isolate them into smaller groups before arresting them (Pickard 2019). Those police tactics effectively ended the protest.

In Chapter 6, I argued that children of politically active parents are likely to be disposed to having an early interest in public affairs and a will to participate in political activities. Nick Crossley drew on that research in conjunction with Bourdieu's relational practice approach, to argue that becoming politically active is part of a relational process. People become politically active by developing an 'activist habitus' drawing on certain cultural capitals needed to be politically effective. As Crossley argues, this is done in the context of sustained engagement with others in fields of activism (2002:168). Attention to the process of becoming politically active reveals how people do not become politically active just by choosing to be so. Rather it requires acquiring distinct forms of political knowledge, certain kinds of social and cultural capital that generate opportunities to participate and the practical skills and experience developed through participation.

Alex Hensby's research on the 2010–2011 student protests in Britain documents how and why some young people became politically active, while others kept well away from such action. The result is a detailed account of the many paths into protest.[6] Many students interviewed were at school during the 2003 anti-Iraq War protests. For some, their school experience encouraged them to become politically engaged. They had opportunities to study politics at school and were influenced by other students who were already active. For those students, their early experiences of the protests had a profound effect on their self-identification as 'activists'. One student 'Damon' recalled how:

> ...the Iraq War had a big influence on me. As a school kid I was 14 and spent two weeks organising and taking part in walkouts. That was radical, and it felt invigorating [...] My school was very left-wing, certainly liberal. The head teacher gathered the whole school for an assembly and said 'I know that some of you may be thinking about walking out – I don't really mind'.

Another student Andrew remembered:

> The first real form of activism I took was when I was in the sixth form the English Defence League had one of their first marches was in Manchester, so I mobilised a group of students from my sixth form to go down to the Unite Against Fascism demo... It was quite a terrifying experience because it was the first time I'd ever actually done something with my politics apart from read about it.

Not surprisingly being at university provided student activists with a field for involvement. Many of those involved in the 2010–2011 campaigns joined political clubs and societies, or the student union. Many already knew in advance what clubs and societies they wanted to join. 'Raphael' remembered how he 're-searched it and found out exactly what I wanted to do before I even came here. I found this little group, so I made contact with them, probably in the first week of being here, or so, and then joined in at that point' (Hensby 2014:97).

Hensby also discovered that while political activists often pointed to parental influence and spoke of their family's political heritage, most thought there was little overlap between 'political upbringing' and their political activism. Instead those students pointed to how their own politics developed with time. Most recalled 'discussing politics around the dinner table' and acquiring political knowledge and insights from the media. A small number were taken to demonstrations by their parents. Angie remembered growing up being aware that:

> ...when [my parents] were students they went on protests and that kind of thing. Protest has always been something that is kind of like, 'that's what we did'. I know that my mum was at Greenham Common for a while.
> *(Cited in Hensby 2014:96–97)*

Yet as Hensby discovered, family background, could also produce political apathy: As one non-participant called 'Sharon' explained:

> The main reason people vote the way they do is because that's what their parents voted, and I make no pretence that I'm not active because I'm just copying them [...] We're political in that we complain a lot, but there's never been any kind of 'let's go and make a difference, let's go and protest'. We wouldn't write a letter to our MP or anything like that.
> *(Cited in Hensby 2014:97)*

Like Connell, Hensby understands that notwithstanding efforts by parents, schools, the state and various private interests to restrict, deny or shape the political identities and affiliations of children and young people, they have been actively constructing their own political identities and commitments. And since the 1990s we can now add they have also been also reshaping the way politics can be done.

Digital politics

While many young people continue to engage politically using time-honoured repertoires like rallies in city squares, street marches, or occupying spaces like university administration blocks or disused buildings, the invention and spread of the internet, smartphones and the rise of social media platforms (e.g., Facebook and Twitter) transformed the many ways young people are political. Since writers like Bennett (2008) identified how the digital age was promoting new forms of citizenship especially for young people, the past few decades have seen a flourishing of new-old forms of political action as young people use this technology to exchange information, recruit, mobilise and organise in entirely new ways (Vromen 2007:48–68, Vromen and Collins 2010:97–112, Bessant 2014, Barrett et al. 2018, 2019, Boulianne and Theocharis 2018).

Digital media has been central to recent movements from the anti-Austerity campaigns in Europe (2008–), the global Occupy movement (2009–) and pro-democracy movements such as the 'Arab Spring' (2010–2012) and the 'Umbrella revolution' in Hong Kong (2013–).

As one ongoing research process indicates, movements like Black Lives Matter rely on digital news feeds as well as platforms like Twitter. These were used to inform and mobilise around 4,134 protests over nearly six years of action (Elephrame 2020).

Recent research emphasises how the affordance of new technologies has changed the form of political practices. Contemporary digital media are fundamentally different from previous kinds of broadcast, print, or cinematic media. They enable a degree of agency previously impossible, allowing activists to reach an 'audience' by allowing young people to develop a participatory culture as they create, remix and remake cultural products directly. Equally the same digital platforms also allow this material to be distributed across internet networks in a peer-to-peer flow (as opposed to a centralised mode of cultural production characteristic of TV stations or newspapers and do so on a potentially vast scale) (Jenkins et al. 2016).

Some girls are now using digital technologies in continuing challenges to enduring ideas about appropriate gendered dress codes and conduct. In 2020, eight-year-old Mariam Scott was sent home from school in Michigan on the day school photos were to be taken: her crime was wearing red hair extensions. This was a reprise of action Widgies (Chapter 5) took some 70 years earlier on the other side of the Pacific. This time however when Mariam Scott responded, she had technology at hand, giving her far more reach and the capacity for greater impact. In response to her treatment, Scott posted a short video photo shot of herself on Twitter showing off her stylish hair along with commentary about being excluded from the school. The message received 2.2k 'likes', 544 retweets, and was accompanied by reams of commentary. It ignited public debate about school discipline and the value of girls and women having freedom in how they dress (@nowthisnew 2020).

These new political practices, are less focussed on forms of 'dutiful' citizenship like voting, and more a form of personalized politics of expressive engagement involving digital networking, self-expression, protest and volunteerism (Bennett and Segerberg 2011:770–799, 2010:394). As one 2018 survey across 14 countries concluded, young people aged 18 to 29 are more likely to participate in online political discussions than older adults. The same study found that the use of social network sites – which typically implicates younger and more educated people – was strongly associated with the likelihood that these young people would not just talk about the issues, but would also take political action related to those issues (Wike and Castillo 2018).

This highlights why new or non-conventional 'objects' and practices need to be included in our understanding of digital politics. This can involve the creation and distribution of photos, memes, videos, political songs, music, comedy routines and satire to networks (Keller 2012). Video-sharing platforms like the Snap Chat and TikTok[7] have become popular among young people, supplanting Twitter and Facebook.

TikTok is used to create and distribute short-form music videos, comedy skits and satire. It was the most downloaded app in the Apple store in 2018–2019 and has been download 2 billion times. Cassidy Taylor a17-year old who has attracted 16 million TikTok followers since late 2019, says TikTok has become the 'go to destination' and 'first stop for youth activism (Taylor cited by McLymore and Wang 2020). TikTok was also used to intervene politically in direct and novel ways. It has been used to disrupt President Donald Trump's 2020 re-election campaign. In the midst of a global pandemic and an official count of 2.8 million infected and 130,000 fatalities (early July 2020), Trump was encouraging as many as possible to attend one of his first rallies in Oklahoma. Based on formal responses to his call to rally, President Trump boasted that he expected the attendance of large number – indeed an 'overflow'. Yet it seems that many of those requesting tickets for that first rally were young pranksters registering to attend the rally online but without any intention of turning up. Footage of the rally revealed many empty seats. The effectiveness of this was not lost on US politicians like Democratic Representative, Alexandria Ocasio-Cortez who tweeted:

> Actually you just got ROCKED by teens on TikTok who flooded the Trump campaign w/ fake ticket reservations & tricked you into believing a million people wanted your white supremacist open mic enough to pack an arena during COVID.
>
> *(Ocasio-Cortes 2020a, 2020b)*

The Republican strategist Steve Schmit agreed, tweeting 'The teens of America have struck a savage blow against @realDonaldTrump. All across America, teens ordered tickets to this event. The fools on the campaign bragged about a million tickets. lol' (Schmidt, cited in O'sullivan 2020).

In late 2019, 17-year-old Feroza Aziz, from New Jersey in the United States posted a short video to TikTok which called attention to the Chinese state's campaign of terror targeting Uighur Muslims. Aziz spoke directly to the camera: 'Hi guys, I'm going to teach you guys how to get long lashes.' After a few seconds of using an eyelash curler, Aziz then said, 'Use your phone that you're using right now to search up what's happening in China, how they're getting concentration camps, throwing innocent Muslims in there.' The video attracted almost 500,000 'likes' on the platform before TikTok temporarily suspended her account. Aziz, who never stopped curling her lashes as she talked, used visual and auditory dissociation to confound censors using visual scanning technology without audio was a low-tech way of 'hacking' TikTok while evading state surveillance. This highlights young peoples' capacity to use this technology with skill and aplomb (Zhong 2019).

This is confirmed when considering other ways the digital provides opportunities for new-old forms of practice such as virtual sit-ins or virtual occupations of spaces called distributed denial of service activism and for digital satire. In what follows I briefly survey both forms of action.

Distributed Denial of Service action

Popular among some young people (as well as governments and corporations), are distributed denial of service attacks (DDoS), used to crash a website or a network of computers temporarily or indefinitely. Distributed denial of service action can involve thousands, even millions of people flooding websites, disrupting services sometimes forcing them to close. It involves mobilising many computers to target a website at a set time so that the site is inundated with traffic until it reaches its maximum capacity after which it cannot process requests, or if it can, it does so slowly.

As a form of protest, it is the digital equivalent of traditional forms of protests like sit-ins or occupations that flood a site and disrupt or deny access to it (Bessant 2016:921–937). One of the first such cases occurred in 1996 when Panix, the third oldest Internet Service Provider was attacked, bringing down its services for several days. On 5 March 2018, an unnamed customer of the US-based service provider Arbor Networks fell victim to the largest distributed denial of service in history, reaching a peak of about 1.7 terabits per second (Goodin 2018).

Another early classic attack involved young people using the website 4chan to protests against the Church of Scientology. On 10 May 2008, a 15-year-old boy peacefully protested in front of a London Church of Scientology carrying a sign that read: 'Scientology is not a religion, it is a dangerous cult'. The police instructed him to take the placard down but he refused. In reply to the police referred to a 1984 United Kingdom High Court ruling by Justice Latey in which the Judge described Scientology as a 'cult' that was 'corrupt, sinister and dangerous'. The police then seized the placard and issued the boy with a court summons referring to Section Five of the United Kingdom's *Public Order Act* 1986. This boy was part of a global campaign against Scientology launched by the political 'collective' Anonymous in January 2008 (Gleick 2014).

The campaign, mostly involving young people, included using distributed denial of service interventions, targeting Scientology websites. Social media was also used to mobilise traditional forms of street-based protest activity against Scientology. In London it seemed that describing Scientology as a 'cult' was 'threatening' – and illegal. Police action against the boy provoked the ire of groups concerned about free speech and encouraged the collective Anonymous to protest further in support of free speech (Chakrabarti cited in Dawar 2008).

Police subsequently abandoned their prosecution of the boy. The case of the 15-year-old highlights the evolution of new forms of dissent which created by young people using the affordances of the new digital media.

Besides the anti-church of scientiology campaign, distributed denial of service action has been used to target government sites in the USA, Israel, Australia, Tunisia, Uganda, Tunisia, Egypt, Libya and Yemen have been subject to DDoS as part of anti-government protests. DDoS have been used in protests against the CIA and against gaming companies like Sony and Nintendo. LulzSec,[8] Anonymous and other collectives have targeted credit and payment companies like PayPal and MasterCard in retaliation to their decision to suspended the processes of payments to the whistle-blowing site WikiLeaks after WikiLeaks disclosed 'classified documents' to the public. According to Coleman, each of these actions was motivated by an interest in securing liberal-democratic values like public accountability, freedom of information, speech, and the right to privacy (Coleman 2014).

Distributed denial of service action was used in America when Congress attempted to enact the *Stop Online Piracy* (SOPA) Bill in 2011–2012. If that legislation had passed it would have expanded the powers of law enforcement by criminalising certain online activities backed by penalties of up to five years imprisonment. The use of distributed denial of service activism helped persuade Congress to drop the legislation. They were also part of a mass demonstration by an estimated 9,000 people who targeted government departments like the FBI and Department of Justice supportive of the legislation (Bessant 2014). There are also closely related activities like DNS Zone transfers, which re-direct users from one site to another (Moses and Gardiner 2011). An example of this took place in 2011 in the wake of the UK News Corporation phone-hacking scandal which saw activists hack into the British tabloid's website. *Sun-Herald* readers were directed away from the newspaper's website to a mock site that carried a fake front-page headline announcing generated a lot of disruption and led to the temporary closure of the websites for *The Sun, The Times,* BSkyB and *News International*. LulzSec was also said to have stolen information from the site, including user names and passwords (Moses and Gardiner 2011).

Actions like these often spill off-line and onto the streets. 'Zombie flash mobs', e.g., were part of the anti-Scientology campaign run by Anonymous that saw thousands of people dressed as ghoulish zombies walking or roller-skating along the streets of New York City to occupy the front of the scientology Church on a monthly basis.

Those participating in distributed denial of service actions have often been represented as criminals, 'the enemy' and even as 'militant Islamic jihadists' (Coleman 2014). Yet conflating distributed denial of service with war and 'cyber-terrorism' and trying to frame the problem in terms of national security, only works to thwart clear-sighted public discussion (Gjelten 2011, Amoroso 2013).[9]

When asked about their own motivations, those involved pointed to a number of political reasons. Some referred to the fun involved (the 'lulz') and the thrill of transgression that comes from 'straddling serious political protest and carnivalesque shenanigans' (Bakhtin 1984, Coleman 2014). Their live actions were intended, as Bakhtin argued in respect to manifestations of the *carnivalesque* in earlier periods in European history, to expose and subvert the core assumptions and practices of the dominant culture by combining absurdity, jesting and chaos (Bakhtin 1984). According to Coleman, many participants in this action could be best described as political provocateurs and saboteurs committed to exposing shoddy security systems while foregrounding problems such as racism, and anti-democratic regimes (Coleman 2014).

This particular technological affordance has however a double-edged sword. The new technology is also available to states and other interests wanting to identify those involved in such action and to repress even criminalising their action. Governments have used existing legislation or introduced new legislation to sanction or criminalise Distributed Denial of Service action: DDoS actions are now a criminal offence in most countries. Yet specifying how the criminalisation processes used is not easy. While a jurisdiction may have laws that can be applied to those participating in direct digital action like DDoS, determining what a person is to be charged with depends on the particularities of the case, the nature of the actions involved, whether intent can be demonstrated, the nature of the evidence gathered, who is involved and to what degree they participated in the action. Much also depends on the jurisdiction. As Slobbe and Verberkt observe:

> As the digital world is much larger than country borders prescribe, it is difficult to cope with cases where the national legislation of two countries differ. At the same time, world wide legislation is not easily made not even to mention enforcement.
>
> *(2012:5)*

Clearly in the hands of some young people, digital technology has been used to create and build solidarities and alliances, and there have been responses to their actions from the state and other interests. The technology has also been used to create and exacerbate divisions and polarise. It has also been used not only for progressive democratically inclined political action, but also fascist, 'alt-right', white supremacist and populist right politics.

Digital political satire

Satire and humour generally have long been integral to politics. With the popularisation of digital media we have seen a burgeoning of political comedy of all forms, using a variety of platforms sometimes in combination with more traditional forms of media like television, and. Unsurprisingly many young people have taken to these platforms with gusto. Equally unsurprisingly their use of humour and satire has not always been well received.

In late 2014, Facu Diaz, a 23-year-old Catalonian comedian decided to create and broadcast a three-minute-long satire called 'The Popular Party is Dissolved' on the Spanish 'Tuerka' television news program (Bessant 2017:204–221). It was then uploaded on to the internet. It was a simple comedy routine that generated major national and international controversy and provoked a swift legal reaction. Diaz's short comedy sketch began with him sitting behind a desk, pretending to be a spokesperson-news reader with his face covered by the iconic black balaclava worn by the Basque separatists. Behind him on the wall were logos made to resemble those of the ruling conservative Christian 'Popular Party' (PP). In front of Diaz was a photo of Francisco Granados, former Minister of the Presidency, Justice and Home Affairs in Spain's governing Popular Party government. In October 2014, Granados was sentenced to prison for high-level corruption for accepting lucrative kickbacks of 2–3% on government contracts worth 250 million Euros. It was a highly sensitive issue.

The statement Diaz's read as part of his skit referred to widespread political corruption which he declared had left the 'People's Party' on the brink of collapse and disbandment. While still pretending to be a spokesperson for the 'Peoples party' Diaz asked for a 'ceasefire from far left-wing political group', a reference to the new and increasingly popular leftist party 'Podemos' ('We Can') (Global Voices 2015). He used re-mixed announcements calling for the 'Popular Party corrupt prisoners' to be relocated closer to places '…where the food is good', a barbed reference to ETA's earlier demands that their imprisoned members be repatriated to their Basque homeland.

Diaz then switched genres performing a mock interview with himself, asking (himself) what he would do in the future as a comedian if the 'Popular Party' collapsed under the weight of the series of corruption scandals. He answered he would lose a rich source of inspiration for his satirical work. He continued the jibing, announcing that several members of 'Popular Party' would be 'integrated' back into political life through the new right-wing Christian 'Popular Party', a breakaway party 'VOX' ('Voice') and the anti-separatist UPyD ('Union Progress Y Democracia').

Diaz's critique of government corruption went viral. The satire worked as a lightning rod for Spanish popular anger and indignation directed at political fraud and a government seemingly more concerned about the health of major banks and the well-being of financiers than their citizens. It was a situation made more difficult in a context where so many people were suffering from the harsh austerity policies which the government claimed were necessary in order to make savings and to demonstrate the state's fiscal responsibility to international creditors.

One Spanish conservative group *Dignity and Justice* immediately initiated criminal proceedings, claiming Diaz contravened Spain's anti-terrorist legislation by 'glorifying terrorism'.[10]

Diaz was summonsed to appear before the Spanish High Court on charges of 'glorifying terrorism' where he was required to answer for his 'mocking tone', offences that carried the prospect of imprisonment for two years. At that point Diaz voiced his suspicion that the legal challenge was really prompted by his support for the then progressive popular politician Pablo Iglesia, founder of what was then Spain's new left 'Podemos' political party (March 2014). At that time Podemos had become an increasingly popular opposition party born out of the anti-austerity *Movimiento 15-M* and the *Indignados* protests against inequality and corruption (Global Voices 2015).

These were Spanish expressions of a global youth movement that came into being in the wake of the international economic crisis of 2008, out of concern primarily by young people about their future prospects, high unemployment, and cuts to the public sector. The Supreme Court case was subsequently dropped.

Diaz was not alone in taking such actions. The young Spanish rapper 'Cesar Strawberry' was one of many arrested in 2016 during police campaigns against young people using Facebook and Twitter for allegedly committing the crime of glorifying terrorism. Police claimed the rapper praised the Anti-Fascist Resistance Group left and the Basque separatist group ETA.

Alfonso Lazaro de la Fuente and Raul Garcia Perez two young puppeteers from the theatre group 'Puppets From Below' (Títeres Desde Abajo) were arrested in 2016 after a puppet show and were charged with the same offence (making comments supportive of ETA).

As the mass mobilisation of millions of young people globally, calling on governments to take action to prevent a climate catastrophe also drew on the affordances of digital politics as well as more traditional political practices.

Climate action: Arendt Meets Thunberg

While environmental politics has a long and rich history, by 2018 it had become a dominant feature on the international political landscape, igniting global action by millions of young people (Carter 2007). It was a global movement recharged in late 2018 when Greta Thunberg, a 15 year-old school student absented herself from school on Fridays and instead sat in solitary protest outside the Swedish Parliament. That was the beginning of the 'SchoolStrike4Climate' movement (*Skolstrejk för klimatet*) also variously known as 'Fridays for Future' (FFF), 'Youth for Climate', 'Climate Strike' and 'Youth Strike for Climate'.

To use Arendt's vocabulary, what we saw was a mixture of 'speaking and doing' by young people as they 'inserted themselves' into the public world. It was action that directly challenged dominant representations of children and young people as incapable of political action. Thunberg herself developed a well-deserved reputation as a leader with the rare capacity to inspire others through her political speech and action.

This skill was in evident when she spoke to the French parliament in mid-2019, telling legislators they needed to 'unite behind the science' of climate change, observing that, 'You don't have to listen to us, but you do have to listen to the science' (Thunberg 2019a). It was a skill evident in her speech to the 2019 United Nations Climate action Summit when Thunberg chastised world leaders while directly challenging representations that she and other young people were just 'playing at politics'. As she explained:

> This is all wrong. I shouldn't be up here. I should be back in school on the other side of the ocean. Yet you all come to us young people for hope. How dare you! You have stolen my dreams and my childhood with your empty words. And yet I'm one of the lucky ones. People are suffering. People are dying. Entire ecosystems are collapsing. We are in the beginning of a mass extinction, and all you can talk about is money and fairy tales of eternal economic growth. How dare you! ...The eyes of all future generations are upon you. And if you choose to fail us, I say: We will never forgive you. We will not let you get away with this. Right here, right now is where we draw the line. The world is waking up. And change is coming, whether you like it or not.
>
> *(Thunberg 2019a)*

In terms that resonate with speeches of other formidable leaders like Churchill who through his words galvanised the British people in 1940 in a time of crisis, so too Thunberg has moved large numbers of young people to action. The ensuing campaign framed as a 'school strikes for climate' movement mobilised millions of schoolchildren. Her initiative 'set something in motion' which in solidarity with similar initiatives by other young leaders, rallied millions of young people, and their elders to join in collective action. As Arendt argued, natality is an 'impulse' that 'springs' from the beginning 'something new on our own initiative' (Arendt 1958).

The globally coordinated protest on 15 March 2019 also attracted many older participants. Encouraged by that success the young Fridays For Future campaigners organised a third Global Climate Strike, with thousands of protest events around the world in September 2019[11] (van Stekelenburg and Teodora Gaidyte 2019, Wahlström, Kocyba, De Vydt and de Moor 2019).

The September 2019 protests saw a broadening of the support base beyond school-children to include many of their elders. The event became the largest climate protest to date with action taking place in 185 countries with over 6,000 events and 7.6 million participants (Chase-Dunn and Almeida 2020).

It also involved young people choosing their own forms and levels of engagement. For some that meant organising participatory campaigns, running climate campaign workshops, training students and an organising local and networked online and offline action (Collins et al. 2020). Schools Strike for Action or FFF, and #SchoolStrike4Climate movement were spontaneous school-student led movements organised by young people. In places like Australia, #SchoolStrike4Climate was initiated by school students in rural and regional areas, producing highly organised mass mobilisations across the nation in September 20–27, 2019 (Collins and Matthews 2021).

The young Fridays For Future campaigners demonstrated a capacity to use traditional techniques like marches and rallies, along with digital technology to build networks and consensus building, as well as to exchange information and ideas. The value of the new digital politics became apparent with the advent of the COVID pandemic in early to mid-2020. That disruption to large protest gatherings by the global pandemic provided an added incentive for finding new ways of being political on-line which included making and posting of placards on Twitter, Facebook, TikTok, etc. We also saw 'digital strikes' that involved participants making images and messages about climate change then posting them each Friday. It included local and international on-line via Zoom meetings, regular webinar meetings in which scientists and other experts were invited to 'talk about the future' extended by live streaming to showcase and profile young political actors across the world. Protestors also created 'Twitter storms' a variation on Distributed Denial of Service', (DDofS) action that involved the co-ordination of large numbers of people sending Tweets at a set time to flood particular politicians, government departments and companies.

In March 2020, e.g., two groups 'FFF Digital' and the 'Polluters Out'[12] joined forces 'to target Shell and Adani a global coal mining company, demanding they keep fossils fuel in the ground (@fffdigital 30 March 2020 https://twitter.com/fff_digital/status/1244358022882877441).

While new technology is changing the political landscape it is important to recognise how young people are also using more traditional resources available to them. Since 1990 over 1,300 legal challenges have been lodged in courts against governmental inaction on global warming across the world. While not all those cases were brought by young people, many were. As Parker notes this is part of a global legal movement to compel governments to acknowledge raising the constitutional recognition of the fundamental right to live in a healthy environment (Parker 2019).

The right to a healthy environment is now considered legally established in many places around the world. It is enshrined in the constitutions of more than 100 nations, and has been incorporated in legislation, treaties or in other documents of at least 155 nations.

Both the United States and Australia however have yet to endorse this legal principle.

Of the court cases based on a constitutional right to a healthy environment, the majority are winning. This includes cases like an action taken in 2018 by young Dutch people who sued their government for inaction on climate change, winning their case when the court ordered the government to curb carbon emissions by 25% by 2019. In 2019, 25 young people won their lawsuit against the Columbian government for failing to protect the Colombian Amazon rainforest. The court concluded that deforestation violated the rights of young people and the rainforest and ordered the government to reduce it to net zero by 2020.

A seven-year-old girl in Pakistan established her legal right to proceed with her climate change lawsuit on its merits—establishing, in a first for Pakistan, the rights of a minor to sue in court.

In Australia a 23-year-old student Katta O'Donnell highlights how some young people are now using legal strategies to challenge governments and fossils fuel corporations, by playing them at their own game. In what is likely to be a landmark trial, O'Donnell filed her case in the Federal Court of Australia alleging the Government, and two government officials, had failed in their duty to disclose how global warming would impact on the value of superannuation and other investments. O'Donnell is bringing a class action on behalf of current and future investors in government bonds tradable on the Australian Securities Exchange. The case links the failure to halt global warming to the financial risks this creates for investors. O'Donnell is not seeking damages. What she wants is a court judgment that the Government, the Secretary to the Department of Treasury and the chief executive of the Australian Office of Financial Management breached their fiduciary duty. She also wants an injunction that compels the government to stop endorsing its bonds until it makes a full disclosure about the risk of global warming. This is likely to be the first of many similar kinds of litigation as drought, bushfires, floods and rising tides expose the government and companies to increased financial risk (Slezak and Sadler 2020).

In the United States, a similar case brought by young people was dismissed by the courts in January 2020 on the grounds that global warming was not their responsibility. According to lawyer Brendan Sydes 'such cases, which pit young people … against government or big business, can play a role in making the injustices of global warming that will be suffered by young people clear – even if they lose' (cited in Stanton 2019). He continued: 'The idea in some of the "youth versus government" cases in the US is to not only ensure a credible legal case and to try and develop new legal doctrine around the public trust concept, but also to use … that case to draw attention to the issue' (cited in Stanton 2019).

Conclusion

In ways that are evocative of the 1960s, children and young people are again at the centre of major waves of political action. It may be that unlike the activism of the 1960s, which seemed to have served, at least in part, as a precursor to the revival of neoliberal politics, this time around we may be witnessing the emergence of a new kind of politics. Latour argues that we have entered a political landscape he calls a 'New Climactic Regime' (2018). He uses this idea to refer to the simultaneous:

> …explosion of inequalities, the scope of [neoliberal] deregulation, the critique of globalization, [and] the panicky desire to return to the old

protections of the nation-state a desire that is identified, quite inaccurately with the rise of populism.

(Latour 2018:2)

This also highlights how agonistic politics continues to mark the political landscape. Clearly also these latest waves of political actions by children and young people have not been welcomed by all. They pose challenges to long-standing normative ideas about children and young people which have aroused strong reactions. The substance of their messages to governments and elites that we can no longer ignore the dangers of global warming, the dramatic increases in social inequality, and the costs of the headlong rush to maximise profit while abandoning any ethical commitment to 'ordinary people' will become increasingly difficult to ignore. Above all these most recent waves of political action by young people has directly challenged the authority and symbolic legitimacy of parents, teachers, the state and the symbolic principles and representations of what is deemed normal and desirable.

In Chapter 9, I turn to this question about the politics of recognition of young people as political actors.

Notes

1 The whole quote by Dickens which opens his *A Tale of Two Cities* is more interesting than the usual snippet:

> It was the best of times, it was the worst of times, it was the age of wisdom, it was the age of foolishness, it was the epoch of belief, it was the epoch of incredulity, it was the season of Light, it was the season of Darkness, it was the spring of hope, it was the winter of despair, we had everything before us, we had nothing before us, we were all going direct to Heaven, we were all going direct the other way….

2 The centre uses a dataset that combine 25 data sources, based on 3,500 country surveys, and a data base of some 4 million respondents who between 1973 and 2020 were asked whether as citizens they were satisfied or dissatisfied with democracy in their countries.
3 This assessment relies on the premise that democracy goes beyond the formal political institutions of democracy like voting turnout, party affiliations or surveys of people's level of trust in their political representatives.
4 Eisenberg reports, e.g., how infanticide was 'an accepted procedure for disposing not only of deformed or sickly infants, but of all such newborns as might strain the resources of the individual family or the larger community' (Eisenberg 1981:300) Tort reports that '10–15% of all children ever been born have been killed by their parents: an astounding seven billion victims' (Tort 2008:187).
5 Eisenberg reports, e.g., how infanticide 'has been an accepted procedure for disposing not only of deformed or sickly infants, but of all such newborns as might strain the resources of the individual family or the larger community' (Eisenberg 1981:300) Tort reports that '10–15% of all children ever been born have been killed by their parents: an astounding seven billion victims' (Tort 2008:187).
6 Hensby interviewed 41 students who as participants or non-participants engaged with the 2010–2011 student protests. They were drawn from four British universities – Warwick, Edinburgh, Cambridge and University College London.

7 TikTok is owned by the Chinese company ByteDance Technology. In the context of growing tensions between the USA and China and a number of other countries, TikTok has become the source of claims that it is being used by China to censor political content and surveil users. As I noted earlier in this book in discussions about surveillance capitalism this claim is also made of a number of other big tech companies.
8 LulzCew is a hacktivist group established in 2012.
9 Confusing DDoS with hacking also underscores the criminal label. As the FBI's Deputy Assistant Director, Steven Chabinsky argued even if 'hackers can be believed to have social causes', their actions are unlawful and unacceptable (Chabinsky cited in Gjelten 2011). It is worth noting here the reference to political motivation by the FBI which distinguishes DDoS users from criminals and terrorist, but does not exempt them from prosecution. This is an important distinction because as criminals or enemies-terrorists the state is justified in prosecuting because they are said to have broken the law or breached the social contract. Those participating in DDoS are exercising their citizen rights to protest for a cause (Coleman 2014).
10 *Dignity and Justice*, is a conservative group claiming to represent victims of terrorism association', an organization closely associated with absolutist and extreme members of the ruling Popular Party.
11 These campaigns ran in parallel with other new movements like Extinction Rebellion and the US-based Sunrise Movement.
12 'Polluters Out (Defend the Defenders)' is an; International youth led coalition dedicated to kicking the fossil fuel industry out of indigenous lands, governments, banks, universities (@pollutersout https://twitter.com/pollutersout).

9
ANSWERING BACK AND THE POLITICS OF RECOGNITION

Young people's politics is a subject that is generating contradictions and often confusion. Elizabeth Such and her colleagues highlighted the confusion that characterised British public commentary in 2002–2003 about the anti-Iraq war protests:

> ...about what role young people below the age of majority should play in community and political life. This confusion is evident in legislation and policy and not surprisingly, in the media discourse that both reflects and helps to construct policy debates.
>
> *(Such et al. 2005:301)*

As I argue, such misunderstandings reflect the uncertainties produced by the numerous and varied ways many young people have rejected the conventional ways they have long been represented. This includes, as I demonstrate here, often hostile responses to the very idea that children should ever be engaged politically.

Writers like Jenks (1996), Prout (2000) and Hartung (2017) identified some of the contradictions that orbit around the figure of the child over the last century or more. In part this relates to what it means to be modern and to associated ideas about endless progress and representations of children and youth as the future. As Jenks argued: 'The modern family enabled the modern state to invest in "futures" as the ideology of care both lubricated and legitimised the investment of economic and cultural capital in the "promise" of childhood' (Jenks 1996:15).

Considering this claim in terms of relations the family-state relation can be seen as mutually constitutive. As Bray and Nakata argue, the various contradictions in the ways children and politics are represented reflects how, in spite of what is said about keeping them out of politics, this has never actually been possible (Bray and Nakata 2020:1). Children have always been caught up in political controversies.

Today this is evident in debates about marriage equality, child poverty, child sexual abuse and domestic violence. This is to say nothing of how they figure in political crises like the various asylum-seeking tragedies in which the bodies of children are pictured drowned on beaches, or when they are separated from their families and put in detention after being trapped on the US-Mexico border after the US President Trump imposed his 'zero tolerance' immigration policy (Davis and Shear 2018). As Bray and Nakata argue, in such cases 'we are being compelled to consider a representation of children made for political purposes, with important constitutive effects on the terrain of political contestation' (2020:2). So while many experts debate whether children should, or should not be, part of political processes and discuss issues like lowering the voting age, the fact is that children and young people are already political whether as political objects, as political subjects or as political agents. This indicates there are more substantive normative and theoretical issues in question.

Given the general unease about matters like giving people under 18 the vote (Bessant 2020), and given that voting has been seen by many as a threshold for citizenship, this raises questions about how citizenship and political activity are understood.

Public debates and scholarly commentary about how children and young people are embedded in political processes and practices raise important political-conceptual issues about citizenship. They also raise larger questions, namely how we understand the political and citizenship.

In his account of schooling as a technique of 'government', the contemporary American scholar Friedrich noted that, 'The formation of the citizen has been at the heart of schooling's concerns since the emergence of institutionalized modern school systems at the end of the nineteenth century' (Friedrich 2010:649).[1] Yet as Hartung observed, given that 'nobody is monitored and managed more closely' than children and young people, we surely need to ask 'what does it mean and what can it mean for children and young people to participate as citizens in the twenty first century?' (Hartung 2017:xi). The question of citizenship is relevant to the question of politics and young people because, as I demonstrated in Chapter 1, there is a long tradition in the western political theory of seeing politics as coterminous with being a citizen (i.e., a member of a political space or social body or 'city-state' (*polis*) united in law.

Determining who is a citizen is a political process that involves *saying who is not*. As Hartung argues, recent debates about young people and citizenship have been contextualised by a wider neoliberal agenda that emphasizes the figure of the responsible and rational young citizen, while reproducing and reinforcing inequalities that disadvantage many and exclude them from valued social resources (Hartung 2017:80). Brocklehurst reformulates this idea saying that the 'political world is not separate from children but is constitutive of children's roles and presence [because] they have a political capacity as agents and actors' (Brocklehurst 2003:79, Brocklehurst 2015). In effect the political field is, in part, sustained and reproduced through particular representations of the child and youth which are themselves political (Bourdieu and Wacquant 1992). Exploring this can be done by attempting to address questions like the following.

What this chapter is about

How have political elites (e.g., politicians, policy-makers and mainstream media workers) represented children and young people when they demonstrated their capacity to be political?

What reactions or dialogues ensued as young people responded to and 'answered back', as they contested those accounts? What do their representations of themselves, and the challenges made to dominant ways of depicting young people say about our own more general ways of understanding of politics and justice?[2]

I begin by documenting some responses to the political actions of young people from the media, governments and others. I argue there is value in appreciating Charles Taylor's idea of the 'politics of recognition' and how that involves a 'politics of misrecognition'. I ask what the implications of that are for how young people and their actions are represented (1994). I do this while being mindful that young people have long been subject to negative representations (Bessant et al. 2017). I begin with a cursory survey of how children and young people have been represented.

'Respectable fears': reactions to climate change action

Arendt argued that when people take political action, they act and speak in the presence of others, and in doing so display who they are. They make a public appearance to which others respond (Arendt 1958).

What does Arendt's thinking suggest if we apply it to children and young people who act politically?

When young people entered the public sphere to speak and act, they sometimes had the support and blessings of their elders (parents, teachers, scientists and some political leaders). This however is not typically the case. The political action by large numbers of young people examined in the previous chapter was generally not welcomed or accepted by political elites. When children and young people challenge the authority of their elders and social institutions by going on strike, by staging occupations, or speaking in national and international forums they are engaging in political action. They are also disturbing or destabilizing a symbolic order which represents them in terms of 'age appropriate behaviour' (Bourdieu 1998).

In her 1992 speech to the UN 12-year-old Severn Cullis-Suzuki called for action on climate change reprimanding the world's leaders for their inaction. In similar fashion in 2018 Emma Gonzalez when she advocated for effective gun control admonished America's political leaders saying that: 'To every politician who is taking donations from the NRA, shame on you!'

These young women were not just negotiating with or defying their elders, they were engaging in a major role reversal: they were 'the responsible ones', the adults scolding wayward children. In this way, they were destabilizing a 'naturally' ordained hierarchy upsetting the subordinate position that children and young people were supposed to occupy within an age-class hierarchy.

The political character of popular and official responses to interventions of this kind, to people such as Greta Thunberg, or Emma Gonzalez and to other less well-known young leaders like Germany's Luisa Neubauer, Ghana's Patience Alifo, Puerto Rico's Salvador Gómez-Colón or Zambia's Natasha Mwansa is apparent.

For many, the very idea that a child, or young person can have a political consciousness, and be capable of giving expression to that is a difficult, if not abhorrent idea.

Critiques of young people acting politically are typically grounded in human development theory using metaphors of 'stages' of cognitive and moral development. They can also rely on metaphors of the kind George Lakoff investigated in his study of moral politics and American conservative's commitment to a natural dominance hierarchy overseen by a strict father morality (1999).

Representing young people who engage in political action as disobedient, precocious or spoilt brats is to represent them in ways that resonate directly with conservative traditional values (Lakoff 1999). This is because 'conservative political thought is governed by a very specific hierarchy' (Lakoff 2019). It is a traditional way of thinking in which the status or ranking of young people and children is naturally and always lower and adults are always on the upper reaches of that order. As such children and young people are and ought to be subject to adult authority because young people are naturally inferior to and must always be recognised as subservient to adults.

As Lakoff argues those committed to a conservative moral hierarchy experience a kind of existential challenge when they encounter young people who are being political. This helps explain certain reactions to young people who engage politically:

> So, the sight of young people raising their voices to call for change is an existential threat to the conservative moral hierarchy –just as the sight of women, people of colour, or LGBTQ people standing up for their rights is always met with fear and derision by conservatives.
>
> *(Lakoff 2018)*

Those working within a conservative moral frame are likely to be persuaded by representations that resonate with conservative values. As Lakoff argued, this is why student anti-gun protests in the USA that occurred after that mass shooting in Parkland, Florida were so outraged:

> Radical conservatives have found a new target for their anger, scorn, and ridicule: children. Conservative attack dogs have made a point of specifically berating, harassing and insulting the young victims of the school shooting in Parkland, Florida.
>
> *(Lakoff 2018)*

Representing young people who act in political ways as naughty or disobedient affirms the traditional conservative worldview in which they are naturally and rightfully meant to be dutiful and obedient. If they are not quick to obey or to submit to authority then they are spoilt, ill-disciplined or wayward. In such cases, it is the duty of any responsible adult to punish and correct them so they learn obedience and accept their proper place in the age-based order. It is morally right and in accord with 'proper standards' that young people respect authority, do not speak out, exercise freedom, 'give cheek' or argue back against their elders. Thus whatever it is that young people are doing, it can never fit the category of politics. For many in established positions, this is convenient, as it means the actions and claims of young people, no matter how serious, can be disregarded and treated as the trivial actions of naughty, ill-disciplined children deserving of punishment.

Thus when conservatives attack anti-gun student protestors like Emma and David, 'they aren't just attacking them because they disagree with their stance on gun massacres. They're also attacking them because conservatives don't believe children have a right to raise their voices, period' (Lakoff 1999). When young people speak truth to power, power doesn't like 'being spoken to in that way'.

Although I say more about this later, one effective way of ignoring or disregarding a message is to misrecognise those delivering it. In what follows I consider media responses to the political actions of young people and then turn to more overt authoritarian responses by the state.

Media reactions

It is not new to point to the ways mainstream media engage in and promote\ 'moral panics' targeting young people (Cohen 1979). The tabloid media in the west has long represented young people as deviant or delinquent, by emphasising their disposition to street violence, anti-social behaviour, hooliganism, illicit drug-taking and gang thuggery (Lumley 1998, West 1999, Gordon 2018).

The 2011 student anti-austerity campaigns were not the only expressions of discontent that year in Britain by young people. What began as a peaceful protest after the shooting by police of Mark Duggan a 29-year-old black man on 6 August 2011, turned into a series of riots across England as thousands of people looted and burnt shops and buildings over five days leaving five dead. This provided a rationale for many working in mainstream media to fill the public airways with stock phrases and clichés that affirmed conventional modes of thought. Although some 3,000 people who were arrested and brought before the courts were not young people, the events were framed as a 'youth revolt' (Riots Communities and Victims Panel 2012). According to the press, 'British Youth' are 'The Most Unpleasant and Violent in the World' (Moran and Hall 2011) Commentators claimed that 'Years of Liberal Dogma have Spawned a Generation of Amoral, Uneducated, Brutalised Youngsters' (Hastings 2011) while 'feral kids with no jobs (were running) amok' (Riddell 2011, Farthing nd).

As Hier 2011 and Critcher argued the 2011 riots presented a chance for 'political elites' to highlight and reinforce existing representations of young people as uncivilised savages (2009). The power of the media was used to impose particular interpretations of events by drawing on pre-formed ideas of youth as uncivil, deficient in citizenship qualities, impulsive and most importantly not properly British (Hier 2008, David et al. 2011:216). Several studies revealed how these pre-existing beliefs and assumptions about young people provided content for Britain's newspaper reports on the political action of school and university students. This was particularly evident in media reports on protests against British involvement in the US-led illegal invasion of Iraq launched in March 2003.

Describing school protestors as deviant is a long-standing journalistic trope. In Britain in 2002–2003, journalists drew on a rich vocabulary featuring youth as disobedient, disruptive, and violent who were inciting unrest and harassing motorists and causing criminal damage. Some reporters spoke of the negative examples these 'irresponsible' students were setting, with claims they were risking self-harm and injury to 'innocent' bystanders. One obvious sign of this deviancy was their truancy.

Such and her colleagues observed how the word truancy is most often used in critical commentary. Truancy, a pupil's equivalent to strike action, slipped from description to criticism (Such et al. 2005). On 23 March 2003, the *Daily Telegraph* reported that 'the mass walkout [the day before had been] organised by the Stop the War Coalition, [and] was joined by pupils all over the country despite head teachers threatening sanctions for truancy' (Such et al. 2005:318). The general tenor of much reporting was epitomized by the *Daily Telegraph* when it reported that:

> ...thousands of children played truant ... to join protests against war ... all over the country' including 'an estimated 5,000' in Birmingham, 3000 each in Manchester and Edinburgh, 300 in Swansea and '20 pupils at

Cape Cornwall School at St Just [who] were suspended for taking part in a rally'.

(Such et al. 2005:312)

The theme of 'playing truant' was readily associated with the other theme of manipulative adults said to be pulling the strings of vulnerable and immature young people. The *Daily Telegraph* on 20 March 2003 reported: 'There is something creepy in the anti-war movement's mobilisation of school children behind a political cause' and that the organizers should be 'ashamed'. Letters to the editor repeated this theme:

It saddens us to see young people being encouraged to leave their studies and join these protests. Many are not well-informed and they are merely following the crowd and joining the hysteria for a chance to play truant.

(Such et al. 2005:318)

The theme of the natural immaturity and incompetence of children was also a familiar motif: Miriam Stoppard, writing in the *Daily Mirror*, argued children were simply incapable of the moral compromise necessary in politics:

Many of us are convinced the war is wrong and not surprisingly, so are our children. The difference is adults can work out why we are at war and why we now support Tony Blair and our forces fighting in Iraq. Our children can't. Such is a child's sense of justice and just as uncompromising sense of wrong-doing, they can't make the moral compromises some of us are prepared to

(Cited Such et al. 2005:316)

Other political commentators referred to the 'adolescent brain'. American conservative David Pellowe was one of the many who argued that:

Their developing brains aren't mature enough to weigh the balance of evidence, consider all the consequences and make objectively rational decisions. They can barely cross the road safely or wear clothes properly. They are important, but they are children – undeveloped clumps of cells if you prefer.

(Pellowe 2019)[3]

Another characteristic of responses to youthful activism has been the use of a binary: children or young people acting up politically are either 'brats' or 'dupes'. The vocabulary of 'brat' and synonyms like 'little emperor syndrome', 'princess disease', 'snowflakes', the 'me-me generation' and 'coddled', explicitly and exclusively signify children and young people. The implication is that their characters have been ruined or spoilt because they have been over-indulged. Quin Hillyer, editor of *National Review online* was one who used this language in responding to young people who participated in #Black Lives Matters protests, arguing they should not be arrested because such a response would give them too much legitimacy:

> They are acting like spoiled brats. What they and others like them really need is to be spanked and sent to bed without supper… That so many college administrators have kowtowed to these pathetically juvenile delinquents is worrisome.
>
> *(Hillyer 2015)*

In 2019 at John Hopkins University in Baltimore USA students staged an extended occupation of the university's main administration building in protest against the university's plan to create its own private police department and contracts with the US Immigration and Customs. For journalists like Rosalind Ellis, the student occupation revealed one thing '…we have created a generation of spoiled brats'. For These 'snowflakes' are too 'stupid to appreciate the value of police protection'. She continued: '…what truly sickens me is that these over-privileged, self-indulged, helicopter-parented students will receive no punishment' (Ellis 2019).

Pellowe joined the chorus construing the 'evidence' to confirm pre-existing explanations. Young activists we were told are notorious for their 'furious little feet stamping'. Their political actions will 'achieve absolutely nothing but the squealing delight of the overwhelming majority to be free of classes for a few precious hours and maybe get on TV' (Pellowe, 2019). In Australia critics similarly lambasted climate strikers as 'pampered', 'chauffeur driven kids'. Their parents 'create road congestion' at peak hour driving them to and from school. They are the 'same kids' who:

> …have become truly insufferable, posing as climate martyrs and lionised by the Fairfax/ABC media and renewables lobbyists. Kids unwilling to unstack the dishwasher after dinner are now condemning their parents for climate criminality
>
> *(Thomas 2018)*

Greta Thunberg was not 'spared the rod' for she was an ideal candidate for such characterisations. In an open letter to Thunberg, American Professor Jason Hill referred to her 'smug generation' who were too precious to:

> …work up to forty hours per week without being chronically depressed and anxious. Its members cannot even decide if they want to be a boy or a girl, or both, or neither, or a 'they.' They cannot eat meat without crying. I might add that your generation needs "trigger warnings' and 'safe spaces',

as pre-conditions for learning in school. Its members have a pathological need to be coddled and protected from the challenging realities of life.

(Hill 2019)

Hill continued, referring to Thunberg and her generation as '…attention-deficit children who spout bromides, platitudes and slogans…' (Hill 2019).

In 2019 President Trump joined the fray tweeting about what he saw as her impulsivity and immaturity. Trump tweeted: 'she seems like a very happy young girl looking forward to a wonderful future. So nice to see!' (@realDonaldTrump). Drawing on long-standing developmental narratives of youth as 'impulsive' and 'at risk' he added: 'So ridiculous. Greta must work on her anger management problem, then go to a good old fashioned movie with a friend! Chill Greta, Chill!' (Trump 2019).[4]

If they are not privileged brats, then they are vulnerable dupes, a trope that also relies on claims about the developmental defects of young people. As helpless and hapless victims, youth are susceptible to predatory adults. This is another common representation used to deny the political agency of young people and to ignore the content of the issues raised. Thunberg has been endlessly subjected to this kind of reaction. As American conservative commentator Michael Knowles 'explained' on FoxNews, Thunberg is 'a mentally ill Swedish child being manipulated by her parents and by the international left' (Knowles 2019). In another example of this, conservative commentator Dinesh D'Souza claimed Greta Thunberg was being manipulated, and that her image used in ways in the same way Goebbels had used images of Nordic children:

> Children-notably Nordic white girls with braids and red cheeks—were often used in Nazi propaganda. An old Goebbels technique! Looks like today's progressive Left is still learning its game from an earlier Left in the 1930s.
>
> *(D'Souza 2019)*

Sebastian Gorka, another American conservative radio commentator –and former Assistant to - President Trump, also tweeted:

> …this performance by @Greta Thunberg is disturbingly redolent of a victim of Maoists 're-education' camp. The adults who brainwashed this autistic child should be brought up on child abuse charges.
>
> *(Gorka 2019)*

In Australia, the journalist Gemma Tognini drew on a different well-worn historical analogy claiming that leftist teachers were recruiting students to fight the 'climate wars'. Like Joseph Stalin, she claimed, teachers recognise 'the power of education and how it can be used to manipulate' (Tognini 2019). This theme of indoctrination has been popular with other journalists and was continued in

Australia on social media with New South Wales Senator Concetta Fierravanti-Wells tweeting 'Kids shouldn't be brainwashed but if they really want to protest, let it be on their own time' (Fierravanti-Wells 2019).

As academics Rob White and Johanna Wyn argue, this is a familiar allegation: if young people are politically engaged they must be doing so at the behest of manipulative adults because they are not capable of their own autonomous substantive decisions:

> ...a common critique voiced in the media and by mainstream political leaders was that these young people were being "duped" by left-wing organizations, who were manipulating the young people for their own ends.
>
> *(White and Wyn 2011:110)*

Political responses

The fact that young people cannot think for themselves is evidence they are brainwashed or indoctrinated by the schools, teachers and parents and 'the left'. Responding to 'SchoolStrike4Climate' protests in 2018, the Australian MP Matt Canavan and then Federal Resources Minister, used his office to declare that students should not protest. Their proper place is in school which is where they need to return so they can learn how to build mines and do geology, how to drill for oil and gas. This 'is one of the most remarkable science exploits in the world'. Protesting can only equip them for 'join[ing] the dole queue' (Canavan 2018). A politician like Canavan was not a lone voice. In the lead-up to the student climate strike on 26 November 2018, the Australian Prime Minister Scott Morrison chimed in, using the Australian Parliament to communicate his disapproval:

> We do not support our schools being turned into Parliaments [...] We think kids should be in school learning [...] What we want is more learning in schools and less activism in schools.
>
> *(Morrison 2018)*

To this Thunberg replied: 'Sorry Mr Scott Morrison, we are unable to comply' (Thunberg, 2018).

These responses by political elites are part of a long-running 'culture war' in which it has long been standard line run by conservatives that teachers and schools are all 'left-wingers' or 'anarchists' using 'bootcamps' run by 'seasoned activists' to train high school student leaders" to become climate activists' (Tehan, Australian federal Minister for Education minister 2019 cited in Bye 2019) committed to indoctrinating 'the young'.

It is a view regularly echoed in the mainstream news:

> Taxpayer-funded eco-worriers are coaching children to skip school again next month, giving them detailed instructions on how to play truant, make posters and organise "marshals" for a climate change protest march.
>
> *(Bye 2019)*

Given this, whatever it is that students say can be readily dismissed because they are really just dupes or puppets of 'the left' (Canavan 2018). For others like the Australian conservative Tony Thomas writing for the far-right journal *Quadrant*, young protesters had their heads filled with 'green mush'. Thomas drew analogies between the 'School Strike 4 Climate' and the Children's Crusade of the early thirteenth century. Like their medieval predecessors recruited as soldiers to win back the Holy Land, today's students will end up as ideological slaves: 'Today's kids would know as much if their brainwashers, also known as "teachers", focused on fact rather than getting them into the streets to demonstrate against nasty weather' (Thomas 2018). It seemed, said Thomas that even 'Five-year-olds are exhorted by adult trainers to dump pre-school and go on strike' (Thomas 2018).

Students in the USA protesting against gun violence in schools were similarly represented as the 'puppets' of adults covertly working behind the scenes. According to the websites Infowars and *The Daily Signal* (Paris 2018) we saw a 'surge of left-wing high school student activism that grew out of the mass shooting …' In Florida it was encouraged by 'the far-left …' (Paris 2018). It was 'professional community-organizer left and the gun-control lobby – and not the 16- and 17-year-olds – did most of the heavy lifting in organizing the so-called March for Our Lives anti-gun rally in Washington on March 24 …' (Paris 2018, see also Hill 2019). Yet not all such responses however offensive are always so benign.

Naughty Truants

Representing school student protests as forms of 'truancy' is not just the preserve of certain journalists. A dominant response to the 2002–2003 protests in Britain coming from the education establishment was that the action was actually an 'unruly' excuse to be truant (Cunningham and Lavalette 2004:259). As Chris Woodhead, former Chief Inspector of Schools for England, 'explained' he was 'concerned about truancy, whatever the motivation for truancy because I see a slippery path towards anarchy and kids being in school at all' (Woodhead, BBC News 2003). Woodhead resorted to the archetype of the 'immature and naïve child' when he went on to say he was worried about:

> …encouraging young people to articulate judgements and feelings, however strongly they are held, when they haven't got the evidence, they haven't got the experience to really understand the full ramifications of what they are talking about.
>
> *(Woodhead, BBC News 2003)*

While Bob Carstairs, assistant general secretary to the 'Secondary Heads Association' (SHA) was reportedly 'dismayed' by the expertise and organisational skills of the students, he was 'alarmed' at the speed with which the protests spread:

> It seems to have escalated each day … Children are getting blanket text messages telling them to join in. In other cases, one child will get a message

which refers them to an e-mail site. That's how it's spreading. This is the biggest event I can remember in 30-odd years in teaching.

(Cited Cunningham and Lavalette 2004:260)

School was where these young people needed to be, so any protest in school time was unacceptable: as Bob Carstairs said: 'Our advice is not to allow this, but to treat it as normal truancy and take appropriate action. If pupils wish to demonstrate they are perfectly free to do so outside of school hours' (cited in Such et al. 2005:315). According to *the Guardian*, The Secondary Heads' Association reported that 'absences should be treated like normal truancy and schools had a responsibility not to let younger pupils take to the streets' (Brooks 2003).

In schools across America, many students were punished for joining sit-ins and other 'March for our Lives' actions. At one Missouri High School students were locked out of their classrooms after striking to protest against gun violence in schools. At Pennridge High School in Pennsylvania, students who participated in the National School walk-out in protest against gun violence in school were all given detention (Boccella 2018). In New Jersey, a principal threatened to cancel prom night if students protested. 'When a handful of teens began to protest at 10 a.m., most students were directed to an assembly while school staff and police officers physically blocked the exits' (Hernandez and Sacks 2018, see also Boccella 2018). In some cases, strike action was declared prohibited like the Baldwin County Public Schools in Alabama students were suspended. As the district's superintendent Eddie Tyler declared:

Being disrespectful and ignoring authority that is seeking to protect you is not the way to accomplish the good that needs to come from this…

(Tyler cited in Hernandez and Sacks 2018)

According to Kevin Ciak, President of the Sayreville Board of Education, New Jersey the national student walkout that took place after the Florida school shooting was simply an example of 'wilful disobedience'. The student action was a clear 'failure to follow administrative directions' and for these reasons they required punishment (cited in Perez 2018). Likewise in Britain, instead of acknowledging the Strike4Climate action taken by students who walked out of school across the country calling on the government to declare a climate emergency, conservative MP Andrea Leadsom insisted it was not political action or a strike: 'it's called truancy, not a strike' (@andrealeadsom 16 February 2019).

In Australia, when a nine-year-old girl Harper Nielsen, who had been active in campaigns supportive of indigenous rights, refused to sing the national anthem, she was threatened with suspension by school authorities for 'defying instructions'. Nielsen and had long been marginalised and disrespected by a song that glorifies white Australia in its declaration that we 'are young and free' (Tavan 2018). The intensity of reactions to this event, tells us a lot about the strength of feeling some Australians have about traditional (white) patriotic rites and ceremonies. While some praised the girl's courage for taking this position, others including Tony Abbott, a former prime minister of Australia described it as discourteous and bad-mannered (Abbott 2018). Joining the chorus of opprobrium Queensland's shadow minister for Education, Jarrod Bleijie tweeted:

> Shame on her parents for using her as a political pawn. Stop the silly protest and stand and sing proudly your National Anthem. Refusing to stand disrespects our country and our veterans. Suspension should follow if she continues to act like a brat.
>
> *(Bleijie 2018)*

Australian One Nation Senator Pauline Hanson went further, though she couldn't work out whether physical punishment or expulsion was good enough when thinking about the right and proper response to the girl's disobedient refusal to stand for the national anthem:

> It's about who we are as a nation, it's part of us ... Here we have a kid who's been brainwashed and I'll tell you what, I'd give her a kick up the backside. ... This kid is headed down the wrong path and I blame the parents for it, for encouraging this. No. Take her out of school.
>
> *(Hanson 2018)*

The evidence indicates that when children and young people take political action they face intimidation, discipline (in many cases physical or threat of physical assault), suspension from school and even arrest. These repressive responses reflect the seriousness with which strikes by young people have been viewed by many states.

In 1972, for example, Edward Heath as Prime Minister of the United Kingdom was so concerned about pupils protesting about the authoritarian nature of state schooling that he instructed his private secretary to write to the director-general of the National Security Service (MI5) for an intelligence briefing about the demonstrations. MI5 reported it identified two schoolboy organisers, Heath then wrote to Margaret Thatcher, then Education Minister, telling her the solution 'may require special action at particular schools to isolate the ringleaders' (Cunningham and Lavalette 2004:264). For cases that ended up in the courts, we saw recourse to the denigration of protestors as 'immature children'. The judge who banned Elena Grice 15-year-old from school for 30 days for organising a demonstration of 200 protestors in an anti-war rally, described her as 'a very silly girl' (Brooks 2003:41).

Here the significance of Prout's point can be seen: given the natural and thus 'legitimate' imbalance in power relations between children, young people and their elders, it is the adult who needs to determine what is in a young people's best interests. For this to happen, children and young people must always be subject to the control of 'grown-ups' for their own present and longer-term good (Prout 2000). Yet many young people are not impressed with how they are represented and responded to. This they are engaged in struggles for recognition.

The politics of misrecognition

Canadian philosopher Charles Taylor points to the potential of those in subordinate relations, like young people, to defend themselves against depreciating representations that deny their capacity and cause harm (Taylor 1994:25). However while some young people may internalise representational claims about their inferior or apolitical status some of the time, many do not and reject them. In what follows I point to the ways many young people are rejecting how they are being represented and engage in debates to contest how they are named. In doing so they affirm their political status and directly question the authority of those offering those accounts of them.

Charles Taylor's account of the 'politics of recognition' draws attention to and examines these established practices of exclusion that focus on the damage and distortion that misrecognition can cause to the identities of minority groups and to society (1994). As Taylor explains: 'A number of strands in contemporary politics turn on the need, sometimes the demand, for recognition'. While his emphasis is on women, gendered identities and ethnic communities, it is an approach that also applies to children and young people. As he argues:

> ...our identity is partly shaped by recognition or its absence, often by the misrecognition of others, and so a person or group of people can suffer real damage, real distortion, if the people or society around them mirror back to them a confining or demeaning or contemptible picture of themselves.
>
> *(Taylor 1994:25)*

Taylor builds his thesis in opposition to the dominance of the individualisation narrative in modern (European) social and political theory. He does this by arguing that identity formation has a 'fundamentally dialogical character' (1994). As he explains:

> ...my discovering my own identity doesn't mean that I work it out in isolation, but that I negotiate it through dialogue, partly overt, partly internal, with others. That is why the development of an ideal of inwardly generated identity gives a new importance to recognition. My own identity crucially depends on my dialogical relations with others.
>
> *(Taylor 1994:34)*

Focussing on multiculturalism, while acknowledging connections to other liberation movements, Taylor argues for the need for equal recognition in democratic societies. Taylor argues that:

> Equal recognition is not just the appropriate mode for a healthy democratic society. Its refusal can inflict damage on those who are denied it, according to a widespread mod ern view, as I indicated at the outset. The projection of an inferior or demeaning image on another can actually distort and oppress, to the extent that the image is internalized. Not only contemporary feminism but also race relations and discussions of multiculturalism are undergirded by the premise that the withholding of recognition can be a form of oppression.
>
> *(Taylor 1994:36)*

Taylor draws on Hegel's discussion of the master–slave relationship in conversation with Rousseau, to emphasise the interdependent relationship between those with power and those without, arguing that in this relationship both 'master' and 'slave' can corrupt the other.

I apply this framework to the dialogue between young people engaged in political action and political elites to identify the harms of misrecognition to those young people and democracy. There is also evidence of young people attempting, as Taylor describes, to 'purge themselves of (…) depreciating self-images' (Taylor 1994:65). The dialogical nature of mis-recognition includes the possibility of young people both accepting and resisting the degrading images projected onto them. It's a process that has implications for the nature and quality of democratic dialogue. This is why today those young people who resist dominant representations of them as 'immature', 'ignorant', 'apathetic', 'impulsive brats' or 'dupes' of leftists or lacking political nous have chosen to answer back (Bessant and Lohmeyer 2021).

In 2018, 46 students at Pennridge High School, in Pennsylvania, who had taken part in the 'National School Walk out Day' to support gun control as part of the 'March for Our Lives' movement were punished. They were given a two-hour weekend detention by school officials for 'violating school rules'. Students used that detention as an opportunity to publicly reject official accounts of them as simply naughty and disobedient and to highlight the political nature of their action. They did this by turning the detention into another public expression of their politics. The students turned up for the detention with placards in hand that displayed the names of students killed in the Parkland school massacre. They then all proceeded to sit on the floor arm-in-arm in silent protest. While the student within the school detention remained silent, other students, parents and others in solidarity with them congregated outside voicing their objections to the detention until police were called and they were required to leave.

As 17-year-old student Anna Sophie Tinneny commented: 'They tell us in announcements every day to be the change you want to see in the world … And then when we tried to do it, they told us we couldn't. That's hypocrisy of the highest order' (Tinney in Boccella 2018). A video of the detention protest was made, posted and it went viral (Pennridge 225 @NeverAgainPenn 18 March 2018). Reportedly it was viewed over 3 million times, 'mostly on Twitter, where it's been re-tweeted more than 32,000 times – and turned the Bucks students, now calling themselves the #Pennridge225, into icons of a growing youth movement going into Saturday's March for our lives in Washington' (Boccella 2018). This response fuelled increased national debate. Some conservative school board members wanted to chastise the students while one survivor of the Parkland massacre, Lauren Hoggs tweeted:

> Yes!! You guys are on the right side of history. It's like a modern Breakfast Club except you guys are making a change in the world.
>
> *(Hogg, L @lauren_hoggs)*

Another 18-year-old student leader at Pennridge school leader Sean Jenkins said: 'We were so surprised to see this many people come out and support us ... The Parkland shooting and student activists have really changed the narrative' (cited in Boccella 2018).

Many other young people also contested representations using mainstream media platforms. David Hogg and Cameron Kasky two student 'March for Our Lives' leaders appeared with Bill Maher as hosts of HBO's talk show 'Real Time'. Hogg and Kasky challenged the popular narrative that because they were young they 'lacked the expertise' needed to enter debates about such important matters as gun control. They used the TV interview to highlight their expertise pointing to their experience as eye-witnesses of the school massacre. This they argued gave them direct first-hand knowledge of what they were talking about. Its knowledge and experience that Maher and many other 'experts' lacked. As Hogg and Kasky argued: 'We've seen our friends text their parents goodbye. We are the experts'. They went on to identify themselves as the 'grown-ups' and 'responsible' and the ones who have been left with the burden of a violent legacy bought about by their 'irresponsible elders'. They continued: we can and indeed will 'rebuild the world that you fucked up' (Hogg and Kasky 2018).

In Australia students who organised major rallies across the country calling on governments to address the climate crisis, responded to critics who told them to stay in school. As one Sydney student Siniva Esera said:

> Our prime minister thinks we should be in school right now, and maybe we should.... But how can I just sit by and not do anything to protect the future of this planet and as my family on the islands worry about the rising sea level?
>
> *(Cited in Costin and Staff Writers 2018)*

Lucie Atkin-Bolton the school Captain at Forest Lodge Primary school added:

> I wish I didn't have to be here today ... I'm the school captain at my primary school. We've been taught what it means to be a leader. You have to think about other people. .... When kids make a mess, adults tell us to clean it up and that's fair. But when our leaders make a mess, they're leaving it to us to clean up.
>
> *(Cited in Zhou 2018)*

Some replied quite candidly: 'we'll be less activist if you will be less shit', referring to the Australian Prime Minister Morrison's call for 'less activism in schools' (Morrison 2018). These examples of *answering back* highlight how many young people rejected representations of them as incapable of political thought and action and as inferior when it came to responsible leadership. Placards carried messages like: 'If you don't act like adults, we will!' and 'schools have to be parliament when parliament is a schoolyard' or 'I've seen smarter cabinets at IKEA' (Sweet 2018).

Conclusion

In 1992, a 12-year-old Canadian girl Severn Cullis-Suzuki, was invited to speak at the 1992 Rio de Janeiro Earth Summit. She spoke on behalf of an organisation she had established called the 'Environmental Children's Organisation' with her friends when she was nine-year-old. Her message was clear and articulate: leaders are failing to safeguard the environment and she called for immediate action so the chances for a good life for future generations were not ruined (Cullis-Suzuki 1992). She caused a brief media-refracted stir after which not much happened. Fast forward to 2019 and Greta Thunberg's appearance before the United Nations and other international gatherings galvanised a major global political campaign.

Why did Severn Cullis-Suzuki's intervention involving an articulate, impassioned 12-year-old speaking publicly in 1992 about the climate crisis, not take-off in the way Greta Thunberg's intervention did years later in 2018? In Suzuki's case, the urgency of the issue was significant and her capacity to communicate or carry the message as capable as Thunberg's. Perhaps there is one obvious difference. By 2018, increasing numbers of young people were able to use new communication technology in ways that have changed politics. One reason why these two similar actions in two different points in time were so different in their reach and in their capacity to recruit and organise compared to earlier actions like Tiananmen square or protests of the 1960s is because since the 1990s increasing numbers of young people have immediate access information, recruit, mobilise locate the whereabouts of police or militia, update and communicate their strategies and respond to what was happening in real time as the events unfolded.

This is not to overlook the capacity of the state and others to use the same technologies to surveil and repress social action. With this in mind this technology still enlarges young people's political agency and capacity in ways hitherto not possible before the popularisation of digital media. By 2020 young people had plenty of experience either of their own, or on the part of other young people on which to draw.

Yet technology is not the only consideration in understanding changes in political action in the last few decades. The changing context is also directly relevant, e.g., increased financialisation, declining demand for human labour, increased danger posed by climate change etc. Also the sheer number of young people increased globally as their prospect of a good life diminished, their access to information about what was happening and political awareness increased. So too did the refusal on the part of many to be represented as minors without the interest or capacity to think and act in ways that could make a difference.

Since 2000 a raft of protests taking place across the globe relied heavily on new media to inform, recruit, mobilise and respond to reactions from others. Events in the Middle East and north Africa provide other examples of how young people with mobile phones in hand played a central role in pro-democracy action like that which led to the Arab Spring of 2010–2011. They were uprisings that spread quickly, in large part due to social media, and soon led to the toppling of governments in Tunisia, Egypt, Libya, and Yemen. News and details of events spread immediately courtesy of new communication technology inspiring similar movements around the globe.

What also strikes me most about the past few decades of protest action is that while each of these actions had many different characteristics, all participants shared an interest in moving beyond established arrangements towards something better, and although it may sound a little clichéd, to 'create a different and better world'. Evident in these actions is a shared interest in creating more equitable socio-economic institutions as opposed to being complicitous in never-ending change processes designed to ensure nothing substantive happens. They shared a common recognition that in spite of all the prevailing talk about freedom, many people across the globe were experiencing diminished forms of political, socio-economic freedoms. They shared in responding to calls to move beyond the narrow notion of freedom as 'free markets', 'free enterprise', 'freedom of speech' and 'free trade' which mean challenging those who benefit from the prevailing inequitable arrangements and who want to preserve their privileges.

Another feature of these decades marked by rising political action is how those who shaped these dominant representations rarely if ever invited young people to the table as legitimate 'grown-up' participants. More rarely were the spaces that young people occupied and where they acted recognised or visited by the authors of those representations.

What voice young people were 'given' was typically subdued, located in the frame of formal non-spontaneous 'youth participation', initiated and managed by the relevant specialist agencies and governments. Young people by virtue of their age and minimal access to capitals (e.g., economic, social, cultural or symbolic) compared to their elders, rarely set political agendas or shaped dominant and official representations of them. Young people's more recent political actions however suggest something else is now underway.

This time there are indications we might witnessing challenges to the ease with which those representations were made historically. There is evidence we may be witnessing challenges to the allure of representations like the 'young precariat' and 'young entrepreneur'. We are also seeing young people articulating new ways of shaping our future.

This can be seen in way millions of young people have taken a seat at the table, sometimes invited, oftentimes not, but who have nonetheless made their presence felt as they have begun articulating clear representations of who they are. As Roberto Unger argued, articulating an alternate social imaginary is the first task in a creating reconstructing our economic and political institutions when informed by an appreciation of the momentous changes taking place (2014:339).

Young people's politics in the twenty-first century are distinctive. Some used metaphors like a 'youth quake', 'youth rising' or 'political awakening' to talk about what saw evolving (Pickard 2017, Sloam Henn 2018). It bids fair to lead to the creation of new politics, to new kinds of people and consciousness. Yet all this did not arise out of nothing, from a vacuum (*ex nihilo*). Although this seems to have been subjected to social amnesia, children and young people actually have a long history of political action and of being present in the political field. Remembering that history also needs to involve a recognition of the ways children and young people have been ignored, misrecognised or mis-represented by many of their elder and more specifically various social and political elites.

Notes

1 Friedrich uses 'government' in its Foucauldian sense to refer to all the efforts aimed at shaping, guiding and directing the conduct of others in a multiplicity of institutional spaces, as well as those endeavours that aspire to conduct one's own behaviour (Foucault 1997:219).
2 For a more comprehensive collection of studies of student protest that surveys many countries see Bessant et al. (2021).
3 For a counter to this argument, see Bessant (2008:347–360).
4 Some commentators read Trumps Tweets as payback to Thunberg who had 'beat him for *Time's* person of the year.' (HuffPost 2019, see also Trump @realDonaldTrump 12th December 2019). In reply to these Tweets Thunberg: 'A teenager working on her anger management problem. Currently chilling and watching a good old fashioned movie with a friend' @greatThunberg).

CONCLUSION

Young people have long been and continue to be central to politics especially in times of crisis or major change whether this be as political actors, or as objects of state regulation, policy-making or government propaganda. This fact is rarely acknowledged today in dominant representations of children and young people. It is a widely held view that young people are not capable of political action, something attributed to their immaturity, lack of experience, deficient rationality and incomplete moral development.

These representations have much to do with the ways modern social and life-sciences have produced influential narratives about the human life-cycle. They are narratives that emphasise the inevitability of stages of development as the infant becomes a child, who then passes into adolescence and youth before 'transitioning' to adulthood. However, rather than being a natural process, being or becoming a certain kind of human being is the result of complex historical and social constitutive processes as writers like Mary Poovey (2004), Ian Hacking (1999) or Deidre McCloskey (2006) demonstrated.

In this way, we can refer to the different kinds of young people have been and continue to be made-up through intellectual, research and policy-making practices by experts, writers and government officials drawing on the authority of social and natural sciences. These representations can also be explained in part by the limited conceptions of politics that the social sciences and popular opinion take for granted.

The reliance on representations also helps explain why most experts and lay-people alike are committed to the view that children and young people should only participate in limited forms of political participation or decision-making in which their subordinate and deferential position is accepted without question. After all, as children or youth, they cannot exercise good judgement and for that reason they will harm themselves and the community in which they live if they seek to participate in 'adult matters' before they are ready to do so.

Such representations also reflect, in part, the desire of governing elites to secure and protect their own interests and power. Young people by virtue of their age and limited access to economic, social, cultural or symbolic capitals or resources when compared to their elders, rarely get to set political agendas or influence dominant and official representations of them. This can be changed and it is changing.

While governments and expert opinion acknowledge the value of young people learning about democratic processes and talk about promoting youth participation, this is typically allowed for only on strictly limited grounds. This constrained participation is again justified by reference to the limited or non-existent political capacities of children and young people and by the need to protect them and the prevailing social arrangements from their inherent impulsiveness and ill-considered political precocity. What voice young people are 'given' is typically subdued, initiated and closely managed by the relevant specialist agencies and governments.

For some time, young people have been actively contesting these representations by engaging in a politics of contention. They have also pushed back against those political leaders and social commentators who denigrate them as childlike, mentally unwell or as dupes of manipulative adults.

The wave of recent political action by young people also indicates something else is also happening. They are experimenting with new possibilities and forms of political practice, offering new ways of understanding politics that challenge and supersede conventional politics.

Significantly, this is occurring in the context of major social and technological transformation in how humans experience and understand our world. We are changing the basic conditions of living in bounded time and space.

We are now living in a historical moment at least as profound and far-reaching as the Axial age (800–200 BCE), a period that saw the emergence of philosophy, ethics, theology and sciences such as physics, astronomy and mathematics simultaneously across China, India, the Middle East, and Greece. That earlier axial age involved a pivotal shift that changed human consciousness and how humans experienced and understood their world. It drew on our relationship with new technologies such as writing, libraries and scientific instruments that enlarged human cognitive, intellectual and spiritual capacities ushering in new economic political and religious institutions (Bessant 2018a).

Our relationship with new and emerging technologies is literally changing our minds, enlarging individual and cultural or collective consciousness, enhancing our cognitive capacities. We are dis-embedding important aspects of human activity (intellectual, physical, emotional) and consciousness and reconfiguring them in algorithmic codes and neural machine learning networks and autonomous machines. Again, we are transforming what intelligence means and how we think *and* act. We are also changing our bodies as we transform our biological and physiological architecture redesigning the processes of our bodies and the practices involved in re-producing human life itself. We are transforming most basic human experiences from conception, birth, growing, feeling, our cognitive capacity, desires, illness, conflict and death. We are changing the human condition, and the *very nature of reality and human consciousness*.

All this is revolutionising our social relations. Young people do not need to wait until certain embodied processes of cognitive or emotional development have occurred before engaging in the public sphere. They have the demonstrated capacity to act in complex and sophisticated political practices.

All these observations highlight certain ethical issues and questions. In acknowledging how children and young people are demonstrating the capacity to engage in political life, I am not making a *laissez-faire* or libertarian argument that young people can and ought to be left to their own devices and be given all the freedom they like to engage politically – or indeed do anything they like. On the contrary, older people have a responsibility to work with young people to exercise good judgement, to help establish what it is that children or young people want to be or do and to provide the relevant intellectual, social and material support to allow them to achieve what it is they chose to be or do.

This raises the question: at what age can and should a young person engage politically (which includes voting)? I would say it is *at the age they express an interest in doing so*. When a young person expresses an interest in being political is precisely when their elders, whether they are educators, parents, or policy-makers, need to encourage that interest, to educate where necessary by offering relevant information about the viable options and to assist them in making good judgements. This involves determining the desirable 'golden mean' between denying freedom outright (by assuming an overly paternalistic position) and a libertarian free-for-all approach. It is also a relationship that is reciprocal. Older people as teachers or parents or politicians may discover opportunities to learn about the politics young people are involved in and to discover new forms of political action.

The fact that we now face a crisis also needs to be recognised. By 'crisis', I mean that we are at a cross-roads where we need to choose a direction. Michel Serres used the metaphor of two tectonic plates converging to illustrate the nature of this crisis (2015). There is nothing riskier than living across such a gap that 'strangely resembles the tension between two tectonic plates'. He also used a medical metaphor to talk about 'the crisis' we face, describing it as a critical condition, the point at which the body itself takes a decision unless there is an intervention (2015: xii). We are at the start of the demise of a 400-year-old industrial, work-based social and economic order. This change process is driven by recent developments in artificial intelligence, the internet, new bio-technology. As Serres observes, once that critical point is reached, we can never go back to the previous state, because doing so requires us returning to that critical situation (Serres 2015: xii–xiii).

All this connects to questions about how we can use the very technological affordances that are rendering the old industrial order and associated institutions redundant to better use?

We have the technological affordances to create higher forms of cooperation that connect 'people regardless of their place in the scheme of social divisions and hierarchy' while also enabling cooperative alliances and competition to combine (Benkler 2013: 288–307, Unger 2014). The architecture of distributed innovation technology, e.g., can subvert traditional expert status and power hierarchies. This can be done in ways that enable young people and other non-experts to access the domains of deliberation, to open up space to think, deliberate, speak, edit and create alternate policies and practices and social imaginary. These design features of new and emerging technologies also encourage forbearance as they weaken distinctions long used to mark conventional power relationship and responsibilities between those who define tasks (the politicians, business elites, managers) and those who implement them (the obedient youth, the drone, the automaton, or the worker) (Unger 2014).

While the prevailing crisis or transformation is difficult, it is also a rare opportunity for new possibilities in which young people assume a key role and a seat at the table the inner sanctum of decision-making forums while also opening up and filling new political spaces. It is a chance not only to address issues at the heart of the old order and social imaginary, but also to encourage the *possibility* of a new social imaginary and the creation of new social arrangements (Castoriadis 1987).

BIBLIOGRAPHY

@fffdigital 2020, 30 March, https://twitter.com/fff_digital/status/1244358022882877441.
@nowthisnew, 4 June 2020, https://twitter.com/nowthisnews/status/1268438083743203329.
Abbott, 2018, Fordham, B., Radio 2GB, 12th September, https://www.2gb.com/she-should-be-courteous-tony-abbott-on-Abbott%202018%20Fordham,%20B.,%20radiostudents-national-anthem-boycott/.
ABC News, 2020, 3 June, https://www.youtube.com/watch?v=jxvxYoATF2E.
Abel-Smith, B., and Townsend, P., 1965, *The Poor and the Poorest, A New Analysis of the Ministry of Labour's Family Expenditure Surveys of 1953–54 and 1960*, London: G.Bell & Sons.
Abrams, M., 1959, *The Teenage Consumer*, London: Routledge and Kegan Paul.
ABS and CES, Cited in Bennet, O., Dawson, E., Lewis, A., O'Halloran, D., and Smith, W., 2018, *Working It Out: Employment Services in Australia*, Per Capita and Australian Unemployed Workers Union, 68, https://percapita.org.au/wp-content/uploads/2018/09/Working-It-Out-FINAL.pdf.
Acemoglu, D., Autor, D., Dorn, D., Hanson, G., and Price, B., 2014, 'Return of the Solow Paradox? IT, Productivity, and Employment in US Manufacturing', *American Economic Review* 104(5): 394–399.
Acton, W., 1862, *The Functions and Disorders of the Reproductive Organs in Youth, Adults and Old Age, and Advanced Life, Considered in Their Physiological, Social, and Psychological Relations* (3rd ed.), London: Chapman and Hall.
Adamson, G., 1998, 'A Proud History of Secondary Student Activism', *GreenLeft*, 20 September, https://www.greenleft.org.au/content/proud-history-secondary-student-activism.
Adcock, R., 2014, *Liberalism and the Emergence of American Political Science: A Transatlantic Tale*, Oxford: Oxford University Press.
Adelman, C., 1972, *Generations: A Collage on Youthcults*, Ringwood: Pelican Books.
Ajunwa, K., 2011, 'It's Our School Too: Youth Activism as Educational Reform, 1951–1979', Ph.D thesis, Philadelphia: Temple University.
Allen, D., 2001, 'Law's Necessary Forcefulness: Ralph Ellison vs. Hannah Arendt on the Battle of Little Rock', *Oklahoma City University Law Review* 26: 857–895.

Bibliography

Almond, G., and Verba, S., 1963, *The Civic Culture: Political Attitudes and Democracy in Five Nations*, Princeton, NJ: Princeton University Press.

Alomes, S., 1983, 'Cultural Radicalism in the Sixties', *Arena* 62: 28–54.

Altbach, P., 1989, 'Perspectives on Student Political Activism', *Comparative Education* 25(1): 97–110.

Altbach, P., 1997, *Student Politics in America*, New Brunswick, NJ: Transaction.

Amoroso, E., 2013, *Cyber Attacks: Protecting National Infrastructure*, Boston, MA: Elsevier.

Anderson, E., 2018, 'Policy Entrepreneurs and the Origins of the Regulatory Welfare State: Child Labor Reform in Nineteenth-Century Europe', *American Sociological Review* 83(1): 173–211.

Anderson, G., 2018, *The Realness of Things Past: Ancient Greece and Ontological History*, New York: Oxford University Press.

Anderson, M., and Jiang, J., 2018, 'Teens, Social Media & Technology', Retrieved 7 June 2020, from Pew Research Center: Internet & Technology website: https://www.pewinternet.org/2018/05/31/teens-social-media-technology-2018/.

Anonymous, 2008, *Chanology Begins 1*, January 15, 2008, http://picasaweb.google.com/uvalbtn/Thesis#5518978926519882610.

Anonymous, 2010, http://www.p2pnet.net/story/48649.

Appleman, L., 2018, 'Deviancy, Dependency, and Disability: The Forgotten History of Eugenics and Mass Incarceration', *Duke Law Review* 658(3): 417–478.

Archer, J., and Maddox, G., 1975, 'The 1975 Constitutional Crisis in Australia', *The Journal of Commonwealth and Comparative Politics* 14(2): 141–157.

Archer, J., and Maddox, G., 1976, 'The Concept of 'Politics' in Australian Politics', *Politics* 11: 7–12.

Arendt, H., 1958, *The Human Condition*, Chicago, IL: University of Chicago.

Arendt, H., 1959, 'Reflections on Little Rock', *Dissent* 6(1): 45–56.

Arendt, H., 1990, *On Revolution*, London: Penguin Books.

Arendt, H., 2006, 'The Crisis in Education', in Arendt, H., (ed.), *Between Past and Future*, London: Penguin Books, 170–193.

Aries, P., 1962, *Centuries of Childhood: A Social History of Family Life*, trans. Black, R., New York: Alfred Knopf.

Aristotle, 350 BC, trans. Ross, W., *Nicomachean Ethics*, http://classics.mit.edu/Aristotle/nicomachaen.1.i.html.

Arnett, J., 2006, 'G. Stanley Hall's Adolescence: Brilliance and Nonsense', *History of Psychology* 9(3): 186–197.

Arrighi, G., 1994, *The Long Twentieth Century: Money, Power and the Origins of Our Times*, London: Verso.

Arrighi, G., Terence, K., Hopkins, T., and Wallerstein, I., 1989, *Antisystemic Movements*, London: Verso.

Australian Senate, 2018, *Select Committee on the Future of Work and Workers*, Canberra: Commonwealth of Australia.

Ausubel, D., 1954, *Theory and Problems of Adolescent Development*, New York: Grune and Stratton.

Bäck, E., Bäck, H., Fredén, A., and Gustafsson, N., 2019, 'A Social Safety Net? Rejection Sensitivity and Political Opinion Sharing among Young People in Social Media', *New Media & Society* 21(2): 298–316.

Bailey, V., 1987, *Delinquency and Citizenship: Reclaiming the Young Offender, 1914–1948*, Oxford: Clarendon Press.

Baker, N., 2008, *Human Smoke: The Beginnings of World War II, the End of Civilization*, New York: Simon and Schuster.

Bibliography 263

Bakhtin, M., 1984, *Rabelais and His World*. Trans. Iswolsky, H., Bloomington: Indiana University Press.

Bakhtin, M., 1993, *The Philosophy of the Act*, trans. Liapunov, V., Austin: Texas University Press.

Ball, S., Maguire, M., and Macrae, S., 2000, *Choice, Pathways and Transitions Post-16: New Youth, New Economies in the Global City*, London: Routledge/ Falmer.

Bang, H., 2004, *Everyday Makers and Expert Citizens: Building Political not Social Capital*, Canberra: Australian National University,

Barcan, A., 2011, *From New Left to Factional Left: Fifty Years of Student Activism at Sydney University*, Melbourne: Australian Scholarly Publishing.

Barclay, E., and Amaria, K., 2019, Photos: Kids in 123 Countries Went on Strike to Protect the Climate', *Vox*, 17 March, Retrieved from https://www.vox.com/energy-and-environment/2019/3/15/18267156/ youth-climate-strike-march-15-photos.

Barclay, E., and Reznick, B., 2019, 'How Big Was the Global Climate Strike?' *Vox*, 22 September, https://www.vox.com/energy-and-environment/2019/9/20/20876143/climate-strike-2019-september-20-crowd-estimate.

Barker, C., 2008, 'Some Reflections on Student Movements of the 1960s and Early 1970s', *Revista Crítica de Ciências Sociais*, http://journals.openedition.org/rccs/646; DOI:10.4000/rccs.646.

Barratt-Brown, M., 1989, *Models in Political Economy*, Harmondsworth: Penguin.

Barrett, M., and Pachi, D., 2019, *Youth Civic and Political Engagement*, London: Routledge.

Barry, J., 1956, *Report of the Juvenile Delinquency Advisory Committee to the Honourable A.G. Rylah, MLA, Chief Secretary of Victoria 17 July 1956*, Victorian Parliamentary Papers, 1956–1957.

Battiscombe, G., 1974, *Shaftesbury: A Biography of the Seventh Earl. 1801–1885*, London: Constable.

BBC News, 2003, 'Head Teachers Are Being Warned They Should Take Firm Action against Pupils Who Stage Anti-war Protests or Leave School to Take Part in Demonstrations', 20 March, http://news.bbc.co.uk/.

Becker, H., (ed.), 1973, *Campus Power Struggle*, Atlantic City: Transaction Books.

Becker, G., 1976, *The Economic Approach to Human Behavior*. Chicago: University of Chicago Press.

Beer, D., 1996, 'Doing a Van Winkle? Student Activism and Attitudes at the University of New England, 1964–69', *History of Education Review* 25(2): 34–36.

Beier, J., 2015, 'Children, Childhoods, and Security Studies: An Introduction', *Critical Studies on Security* 3(1): 1–3.

Beirne, P., 1993, *Inventing Criminology: Essays on the Rise of Homo Criminals*, New York: State University of New York Press.

Benedicto, J., 2012, 'The Political Cultures of Young People: An Uncertain and Unstable Combinatorial Logic', *Journal of Youth Studies* 16(6): 712–729.

Bengtsson, E., and Waldenström, D., 2015, *Capital Shares and Income Inequality: Evidence from the Long Run*, Discussion Paper No. 9581 Bonn: Institute for the Study of Labor (IZA).

Bennett, L., and Alexandra Segerberg A., 2011, 'Digital Media and the Personalization of Collective Action', *Information, Communication & Society* 14(6): 770–799.

Bennett, W., 2008, 'Changing Citizenship in the Digital Age', in Bennett, W.L. (ed.), *Civic Life Online: Learning How Digital Media Can Engage Youth*, Cambridge, MA: MIT Press, 1–24.

Bennetts, M., 2013, 'Boy Sailors during the Age of Nelson and Napoleon', English Historical Fiction Authors, https://englishhistoryauthors.blogspot.com/2013/05/boy-sailors-during-age-of-nelson-and.html.

Benzaquen, A., 2004, 'Childhood, Identity and Human Science in the Enlightenment', *History Workshop Journal* 31(57): 69–95.

Bereday, G., 1966, 'Student Unrest on Four Continents: Montreal, Ibadan, Warsaw, and Rangoon', *Comparative Education Review* 10 June: 188–204.

Berger, P., and Luckmann, H., 1967, *The Social Construction of Reality*, New York: Anchor Books.

Berlant, L., 2011, *Cruel Optimism*, Durham, NC: Duke University Press.

Berman, H., 1992, 'The Impact of the Enlightenment on American Constitutional Law', *Yale Journal of Law and Humanities* 4(2): 311–334.

Berrerda, L., 2015, cited in 'The PP Criticized the Support of the Comedian Facu Pable Iglesiuas Diaz: Not Anything Goes', *ABC*, https://translate.google.com.au/translate?hl=en&sl=es&u=http://www.abc.es/espana/20150110/abci-iglesias-facu-diaz-201501091656.html&prev=search 10 January.

Berteaux, D. (ed.), 1981, *Biography and Society: The Life History Approach in the Social Sciences*, Beverly Hills, CA: Sage.

Bessant, J., 1991, 'Described, Measured and Labelled: Eugenics, Youth Policy and Moral Panic in Victoria in the 1950s', in Wilson, B., and White, R., (eds.), *For Their Own Good: Young People and State Intervention in Australia*, Special Issue of *Journal of Australian Studies*, La Trobe University Press, 8–28.

Bessant, J., 1995, 'The Discovery of an Australian 'Juvenile Underclass', *Australian New Zealand Journal of Sociology* 31(1), March: 32–48.

Bessant, J., 2004, 'Mixed Messages: Youth Participation and Democratic Practice', *Australian Journal of Political Science* 39(2): 387–404.

Bessant, J., 2008, 'Hard Wired for Risk: Neurological Science, 'The Adolescent Brain and Developmental Theory', *Journal of Youth Studies* 11(3): 347–360.

Bessant, J., 2014a, 'A Dangerous Idea? Freedom, Children and the Capability Approach to Education', *Critical Issues in Education* 55(2): 138–153.

Bessant, J., 2014b, *Democracy Bytes: New Media, New Politics and Generational Change*, London: Palgrave-Macmillan.

Bessant, J., 2016, 'Democracy Denied: Youth Participation and Criminalizing Digital Dissent', *Journal of Youth Studies* 19(7): 921–937.

Bessant, J., 2017, 'Digital Humour, Gag Laws and the Liberal Security State', in Baarda, R., and Luppicini, R., (eds.), *Digital Media Integration for Participatory Democracy*, Hershey, PA: IGI Global Publishers, 204–221.

Bessant, J., 2018a, *The Great Transformation, History for a Techno-Human Future*, London: Routledge.

Bessant, J., 2018b, 'Young Precariat and a New Work Order? A Case for Historical Sociology', *Journal of Youth Studies* 21: 780–798.

Bessant, J., 2020, 'From Denizen to Citizen: Contesting Representations of Young People and the Voting Age', *Journal of Applied Youth Studies*, doi: 10.1007/s43151-020-00014-4; https://link.springer.com/article/10.1007/s43151-020-00014.

Bessant, J., and Grasso, M., 2019, 'Security and the Liberal-Democratic State: Criminalizing Young People's Politics', Special Issue: Security and the Liberal-Democratic State: Criminalizing Young People's Politics, *Revista Internacional de Sociología* 77(4): 1–12.

Bessant, J., and Hil, R. (eds.), 1997, *Youth, Crime and the Media: Media Representation of and Reaction to Young People in Relation to Law and Order*, Hobart: National Clearing House on Youth.

Bessant, J., and Lohmeyer, S., 2021, 'Politics of Recognition When Students Protest', in Bessant, J., Mejia Mesinas, A., Pickard, S., (eds.), 2020, *When Students Protest* (Volume 2)

Global Unrest and Anti-Neoliberalism (Volume 3) *Civil Rights and Social Politics*, London: Rowman and Littlefield, in press.

Bessant, J., and Watts, R., 1998, 'Explorations in the Ethnography of Masculinity and Violence amongst the Bodgies 1948–1958', in Hazelhurst, K., and Hazelhurst, C., (eds.), *Justice and Reform*, Piscataway, NJ: Transaction Publishers, 189–220.

Bessant, J., Farthing, R., and Watts, R., 2017, *The Precarious Generation: A Political Economy of Young People*, London: Routledge.

Bessant, J., Mejia Mesinas, A., and Pickard, S., 2021, *When Students Protest* (Volume 1) *Education Matters* (Volume 2) *Global Unrest and Anti-Neoliberalism* and (Volume 3) *Civil Rights and Social Politics*, London: Rowman and Littlefield, in press.

Bessant, J., Pickard, S., and Watts, R., 2019, 'Translating Bourdieu into Youth Studies', *Journal of Youth Studies* 23(1): 76–92.

Bettelheim, B., 1969, 'Obsolete Youth', *Encounter* 23(3): 29–42.

Bhaduri, A., 2011, 'Financialization in the Light of Keynesian Theory', *PSL Quarterly Review* 64(256): 7–21.

BIS, 2018, 'OTC Derivatives Statistics at End-June 2018', https://www.bis.org/publ/otc_hy1810.htm.

Black, E., 2003, *War against the Weak: Eugenics and America's Campaign to Create a Master Race*, New York: Thunder's Mouth Press/Avalon Publishing Group.

Blackmore, W., 1807, *Commentaries on the Laws of England: In Four Books* (Volume 4), Portland: Thomas B Wait and Co.

Blank, R., and Freeman, R., 1993, Evaluating the Connection between Social Protection and Economic Flexibility NBER Working Paper 4338. Cambridge: NBER.

Bleijie, J., 2018, 'Jarrod Bleijie ✓@JarrodBleijieMP' #qldpol http://www.couriermail.com.au/news/queensland/news-story/4368e8e72309376d9e6ae0eee994c06f …).

Blenker, Y., 2013, 'Distributed Innovation and Creativity, Peer Production, and Commons in Networked Economy', in Gonzales, F., (ed.), *Change: 9 Key Essays on How the Internet Is Changing Our Lives*, Bilbao: BBVA Publisher, 1–29.

Boccella, K., 2018, 'Punished for Walkout, Bucks Students Turned Detention into Viral Gun Protest', *The Washington Post*, 21 March, https://www.inquirer.com/philly/education/national-school-walkout-detention-viral-gun-protest-students-pennridge-high-school-pennsylvania-20180321.html.

Boden, D., 1994, *The Business of Talk: Organisations in Action*, Cambridge: Polity Press.

Boggs, C., 1995, 'Rethinking the Sixties Legacy: From New Left to New Social Movements', in Lyman S.M., (eds.), *Social Movements. Main Trends of the Modern World*, London: Palgrave Macmillan, 331–355.

Bon, F., and Schemeil, Y., 1980, 'La rationalisation de l'inconduite: comprendre le statut du politique chez Pierre Bourdieu', *Revue française de science politique* 30(6): 1198–1228.

Boniolo, G., 2007, *On Scientific Representations: From Kant to a New Philosophy of Science*, London: Palgrave Macmillan.

Borch, C., 2009, 'Body to Body: On the Political Anatomy of Crowds', *Sociological Theory* 27(3): 271–290.

Boulianne, S., and Theocharis, Y., 2018, 'Young People, Digital Media, and Engagement: A Meta-Analysis of Research', *Social Science Computer Review* 38(2): 111–127.

Bourdieu, P., 1984, *Distinction: A Social Critique of the Judgement of Taste*, trans. Nice, R., Cambridge, MA: Harvard University Press.

Bourdieu, P., 1987, Keynote Address to the Dean's Symposium on *Gender, Age, Ethnicity and Class: Analytical Constructs or Folk Categories?* at The University of Chicago, April 9–10, trans. Wacquant, Loic J.D., and Young, D., https://edisciplinas.usp.br/

pluginfile.php/2290040/mod_resource/content/1/Bourdieu%20-%20What%20 makes%20a%20social%20class.pdf.
Bourdieu, P., 1990a, *The Logic of Practice*, Cambridge: Polity Press.
Bourdieu, P., 1990b, 'The Scholastic Point of View', *Cultural Anthropology* 5: 380–391.
Bourdieu, P., 1991a, 'Fourth Lecture: Universal Corporatism: The Role of Intellectuals in the Modern World', *Poetics Today: National Literatures/Social Spaces* (Winter) 12(4): 655–669.
Bourdieu, P., 1991b, *Language and Symbolic Power*, ed. Thompson, J., trans. Raymond, G., and Adamson, M., Cambridge: Polity.
Bourdieu, P., 1992a, *Outline of a Theory of Practice*, London: Cambridge Press.
Bourdieu, P., 1992b, *Identity and Representation: Elements for a Critical Reflection on the Idea of Region in Language and Symbolic Power*, Cambridge, MA: Harvard University Press, 220–226.
Bourdieu, P., 1993a, ''Youth' Is Just a Word', in Bourdieu, P., (ed.), *Sociology in Question*, Thousand Oaks: Sage, 94–102.
Bourdieu, P., 1993b, *The Field of Cultural Production: Essays on Art and Literature*, New York: Columbia University Press.
Bourdieu, P., 1998, *Practical Reason: On the Theory of Action*, Cambridge: Polity Press.
Bourdieu, P., 2014, *On the State: Lectures at the College de France 1989–1992*, ed. Champagne, P., Lenoir, R., Poupeau, F., and Riviere, M., trans. Fernbach, D., Cambridge: Polity Press.
Bourdieu, P., and Wacquant, L., 1992a, *An Invitation to Reflexive Sociology*, Chicago, IL: University of Chicago.
Bourdieu, P., and Wacquant, L., 1992b, *Towards a Reflexive Sociology*, Stanford: Stanford University Press. Published in French as Bourdieu, Pierre and Wacquant, Loïc. 2014, *Invitation à la sociologie réflexive*, Paris: Le Seuil.
Bowles, J., 1798, *Letters of the Ghost of Alfred, Addressed to the Hon. Thomas Erskine, and the Hon. Charles James Fox, on the Occasion of the State Trials at the Close of the Year 1794, and the Beginning of the Year 1795*, London: J. Wright.
Bowman, D., Borlagdan, J., and Bond, S., 2015, *Making Sense of Youth Transitions from Education to Work*, Melbourne: Brotherhood of St Laurence.
Brace, C.L., 1967, *The Dangerous Classes of New York and Twenty Years' Work Among Them*, New York: Elibron.
Brace, C.L., 1872/2011, *The Dangerous Classes of New York and Twenty Years' Work among Them*, Montclair: Patterson Smith.
Brake, M., 1980, *The Sociology of Youth Culture and Youth Sub Cultures*, London: Routledge and Kegan Paul.
Brantlinger, P., and Ulin, D., 1993, 'Policing Nomads: Discourse and Social Control in Early Victorian England', *Cultural Critique* 25: 33–63.
Braungart, M., and Braungart, R., 1990, 'The Life-Course Development of Left Wing and Right Wing Youth Activist Leaders from the 1960s', *Political Psychology* 11(2): 254–268.
Braunstein, P., and Doyle, M., 2002, 'Introduction: Historicizing the American Counterculture of the 1960s and '70s', in Braunstein, P., and Doyle, M., (eds.), *Imagine Nation: The American Counterculture of the 1960s and '70*, New York: Routledge 5–14.
Bray, D., and Nakata, S., 2020, 'The Fgure of the Child in Democratic Politics', *Contemporary Political Theory* 19: 20–37.
Brewer, H., 2007, *By Birth or Consent: Children, Law, and the Anglo-American Revolution in Authority*, Chapel Hill: The Omohundro Institute of Early American History and the University of North Carolina Press, 2007.

Brewster, 1968, The Age, 2 August.
Brighenti, A., 2010, 'Tarde, Canetti, and Deleuze on Crowds and Packs', *Journal of Classical Sociology* 10(4): 291–314.
Brocklehurst, H., 2003, 'Kids 'R' Us? Children as Political Bodies', *International Journal of Politics and Ethics* 3(1): 79–92.
Brocklehurst, H., 2006, *Who's Afraid of Children? Children, Conflict and International Relations,* Hampshire: Ashgate.
Brocklehurst, H., 2015, 'Educating Britain? Political Literacy and the Construction of National History', *Journal of Common Market Studies* 53(1): 52–70.
Brocklehurst, H., 2020, 'Doing IR: Securing Children', in Beier, J., (ed.), *Discovering: 89-Childhood in International Relations,* London: Palgrave Macmillan, 89–113.
Bromberg, W., and Simon, F., 1968, 'The 'Protest' Psychosis-A Special Type of Reactive Psychosis', *Archives of General Psychiatry* 19: 155.
Brooks, L., 2003, 'Kid Power', *Guardian Weekend,* 26 April, 40–44.
Brorsen, L., 2017, 'Looking Behind the Declining Number of Public Companies', *Harvard Law School Forum on Corporate Governance,* 18 May, https://corpgov.law.harvard.edu/2017/05/18/looking-behind-the-declining-number-of-public-companies.
Brown, C., and Diehl, P., 2019, 'Diehl 2019 Conceptualising the Political Imaginary: An Introduction to the Special Issue', *Social Epistemology* 33(5): 393–397.
Brown, G., 2018, 'The Global Youth Movement Is Gaining Momentum', *World Economic Forum,* https://www.weforum.org/agenda/2018/04/the-new-global-youth-movement.
Brown, M., 1994, 'The Work of City Politics: Citizenship through Employment in the Local Response to AIDS', *Environment and Planning A* 26(6): 873–894.
Brown, T., 2009, '1968' East and West: Divided Germany as a Case Study in Transnational History', *American Historical Review* 114(1): 69–96.
Brown, T., 2013, *West Germany in the Global Sixties: The Anti-Authoritarian Revolt, 1962–1978,* Cambridge: Cambridge University Press.
Brown, W., 2015, *Undoing the Demos: Neoliberalism's Stealth Revolution,* Cambridge: Zone.
Brynjolfsson, E., 1993, 'The Productivity Paradox of Information Technology', *Communications of the ACM* 36(12): 66–77.
Brynjolfsson, E., and McAfee, A., 2014, *The Second Machine Age: Work, Progress, and Prosperity in a Time of Brilliant Technologies,* New York: WW Norton.
Brynjolfsson, E., and McAfee, A., 2015, 'Will Humans Go the Way of Horses?' *Foreign Affairs,* https://www.foreignaffairs.com/articles/2015-06-16/will-humans-go-way-horses.
Bucholtz, M., 2002, 'Youth and Cultural Practice', *Annual Review of Anthropology* 31: 525–552.
Bulletin, 13 January 1960:4.
Bulletin, 1961, 'Communists in the Universities', *Bulletin,* 15 March, Rosenfeld, S., 2013, https://nla.gov.au/nla.obj-684300631/view?sectionId=nla.obj-700235731&partId=nla.obj-684465398#page/n7/mode/1up.
Burchall, D., 1998, 'The Mutable Minds of Particular Men: The Emergence of 'Economic Science' and Contemporary Economic Policy', in Dean, M., and Hindess, B., (eds.), *Governing Australia,* Melbourne: Cambridge University Press, 194–209.
Buret, E., 1979–1840, *De la misere des classes laborieuses en Angleterre et en France,* Tome second. Aalen: Scientia.
Burgmann, V., 1993, *Power and Protest: Movements for Change in Australian Society,* St Leonards: Allen & Unwin,

Burke, E., 1967, 'Burke to Richard Burke, October 1789', in Copeland, T., Cobban, A., and Smith, R., (eds.), *The Correspondence of Edmund Burke. Vol. 6: July 1789–December 1791*, Cambridge: Cambridge University Press, 29–30.

Burke, E., 2001, *Reflections on the Revolution in France*, ed. Clark, J.C.D., Palo Alto, CA: Stanford University Press.

Burnett, J., 2017, *Considering the Relational Contours of Sociological Research Methods Department of Sociology University of British Columbia*, http://www.sociologix.ca/js/ViewerJS/Burnett_Contours%20of%20Relational%20Methods_WEB.pdf.

Burrows, S., 2013, 'Precarious Work, Neo-liberalism and Young People's Experiences of Employment in the Illawarra Region', *The Economic and Labour Relations Review* 24(3): 38–96.

Burrows, J., 1986, *The Ages of Man: a Study in Medieval Writing and Thought*, New York: Clarendon Press of Oxford.

Burt, C., 1925, *The Young Delinquent*, London: University of London Press.

Butterfield, H., 1931, *The Whig Interpretation of History*, London: Bell.

Bye, C., 2019, 'Hardcore Climate Change Activists Coach Children on How to Orchestrate Massive School Walkout', *Daily Telegraph*, 18 February 2019, https://www.dailytelegraph.com.au/news/nsw/hardcore-climate-change-activists-coach-children-on-how-to-orchestrate-massive-school-walkout/news.

Caine, S., 1967, *The Guardian*, 15 March 1967.

Canavan, M., 2018, cited in Hinchliffe, Joe. 'Thousands of School Children Join Melbourne Climate Rally', *The Age*, 30 November 2018, https://www.theage.com.au/national/victoria/thousands-of-schoolchildren-join-melbourne-climate-rally-2018 1130-p50jf7.html.

Canetti, E., 1962, *Crowds and Power*, trans. Stewart, C., New York: Farrar, Straus and Giroux.

Canovan, M., 1998, *Nationhood and Political Theory*, Cheltenham: Edward Elgar Pub.

Caputo, J., 2018, *Hermeneutics: Facts and Interpretation in the Age of Information*, London: Pelican.

Carlisle, J.E., and Patton, R., 2013, 'Is Social Media Changing How We Understand Political Engagement? An Analysis of Facebook and the 2008 Presidential Election', *Political Research Quarterly* 66(4): 883–895, doi:10.1177/1065912913482758.

Carpenter, M., Cited in M. May, 1981, 'Innocence and Experience "The Evolution of the Concept of Juvenile Delinquency in the Mid-Nineteenth Century"', in Dale, R., (ed.), *Education and the State* (Volume 1), London: Falmer Press, 269–283.

Carrington, K., 1993, *Offending Girls: Sex Youth and Justice*, Sydney: Allen & Unwin.

Carroll, J., 1968, 'Paris Gripped By Insurrection', *The Guardian*, 25 May https://www.theguardian.com/century/1960-1969/Story/0,106493,00.html).

Carter, N., 2007, *The Politics of the Environment: Ideas, Activism, Policy*, 2nd ed., New York: Cambridge University Press.

Casey, B., Jones, R., and Hare, T., 2008, 'The Adolescent Brain', *Annals of the New York Academy of Science* 124(March): 111–126.

Cassirer, E., 1923, *Substance and Function*, Chicago, IL: Open Court.

Castoriadis, C., 1987, *The Imaginary Institution of Society*, trans. Blamey, K., Cambridge: MIT Press.

Caute, D., 1988, *The Year of the Barricades: A Journey through 1968*, New York: Harper and Row.

Cavell, S., 2010, 'A Social History of Midshipmen and Quarterdeck Boys in the Royal Navy, 1761–1831', PhD thesis, Exeter: University of Exeter.

Bibliography 269

Caws, P., 1990, *Structuralism: A Philosophy for the Human Sciences*, Atlantic Heights: Humanities Press.

Chakrabarti cited in Dawar, A., 2008, 'Teenager Faces Prosecution for Calling Scientology Cult', *The Guardian*, 20th May, http://www.theguardian.com/uk/2008/may/20/1?gusrc=rss&feed=networkfront.

Charlesworth, M., 1969, 'The Youth Revolution', *Meanjin Quarterly* 3: 391–397.

Chase-Dunn, C., and Almeida, P., 2020, *Global Struggles and Social Change: From Prehistory to World Revolution in the Twenty-First Century*, Baltimore, MD: Johns Hopkins University Press.

Chen, J., 1971, *The May Fourth Movement in Shanghai: The Making of a Social Movement in Modern China*, Leiden: Brill.

Chen, P., 2013, *Australian Politics in a Digital Age*, Canberra: Australian National University Press.

Chesters, J., Smith, J., Cuervo, H., Laughland-Booy, J., Wyn, J., Skrbis, Z., and Woodman, D., 2018, 'Young Adulthood in Uncertain Times: The Association between Sense of Personal Control and Employment, Education, Personal Relationships and Health', *Journal of Sociology* 55(2): 1–20, doi:10.1177/1440783318800767.

Chitty, C., 2007, *Eugenics, Race and Intelligence in Education*, London: Continuum.

Cho, A., Byrne, J., and Pelter, Z., 2020, *Digital Civic Engagement by Young People*, New York: UNICEF Office of Global Insight and Policy.

Cieslik, M., and Simpson, D., (eds.), 2013, *Key Concepts in Youth Studies*, Thousand Oaks: Sage.

Clinton, H., 2012, 'Clinton to Arab Youth: 'The World Ignores You at Its Peril', CNN, 25 February, https://edition.cnn.com/2012/02/25/world/africa/tunisia-clinton/index.html.

Cockburn, T., 1998, 'Children and Citizenship in Britain', *Childhood* 5(1): 99–118.

Cockburn, T., 2007, 'Partners in Power: A Radically Pluralistic Form of Participatory Democracy for Children and Young People', *Children and Society* 21: 446–457.

Cohen, A., 1956, *Delinquent Boys*, New York: The Free Press.

Cohen, E., 2005, 'Neither Seen nor Heard: Children's Citizenship in Contemporary Democracies', *Citizenship Studies* 9(2): 221–240.

Cohen, P., 1972, *Sub-Cultural Conflict and Working Class Community*, Working Papers in Cultural Studies No. 2, Centre for Contemporary Cultural Studies, University of Birmingham.

Cohen, S., 1972, *Folk Devils and Moral Panics: The Creation of the Mods and Rockers*, London: MacGibbon & Kee.

Cohen, S., 1979, *Folk Devils and Moral Panics* (2nd ed.), Oxford: Martin Robertson.

Cohn, B., 1998, *An Anthropologist among the Historians and Other Essays*, Oxford: Oxford University Press.

Coleman, G., 2014, *Hacker, Hoaxer, Whistleblower, Spy: The Many Faces of Anonymous*, London: Verso.

Coleman, S., 2006, *Remixing Citizenship: Democracy and Young People's Use of the Internet*, London: Carnegie YPI.

Collier, P., 2018, *The Future of Capitalism: Facing the New Anxieties*, London: Penguin.

Collin, P., 2015, *Young Citizens and Political Participation in Digital Society*, Basingstoke: Palgrave Macmillan.

Collini, S., Winch, D., and John Burrow, J., 1983, *That Noble Science of Politics: A Study in Nineteenth-Century Intellectual History*, Cambridge: Cambridge University Press.

Collins, P., and Matthews, I., 2021(in press), 'School Strike for Climate: Australian Students Renegotiating Citizenship', in Bessant, J., Mejia Mesinas, A., and Pickard, S., (eds.), *When Students Protest: Secondary and High Schools* (Volume 1), Rowman & Littlefield.

Collins, P., Matthews, I., Churchill, B., and Jackson, S., 2019, 'Australia', in de Moor, J., Uba, K., Wahlström, M., Wennerhag, M., and De Vydt, M., (eds.), *Protest for a Future II: Composition, Mobilization and Motives of the Participants in Fridays for Future Climate Protests on 20–27 September, 2019, in 19 Cities Around the World*, 35–51, https://static1.squarespace.com/static/5a84ed86f09ca48587f14e51/t/5e844e1cf3a8634447407556/1585729151188/Protest+for+a+Future+II+-+2020-02-24.pdf.

Collins, R., 2010, 'Technological Displacement and Capitalist Crises: Escapes and Dead Ends', *Political Conceptology* #1, 23–34, http://politconcept.sfedu.ru/2010.1/05.pdf.

Commission of the European Communities 1993, Growth Competitiveness, Employment; White Paper, http://aei.pitt.edu/1139/1/growth_wp_COM_93_700_Parts_A_B.pdf.

Commission Temporaire of Lyon [1793/1957] 'Instruction adressée aux autorités constituées des départements de Rhône et de Loire, par la' (16 November 1793), reprinted in Markov, W., and Soboul, A., (eds.), *Die Sansculotten von Paris: Dokumente zur Geschichte der Volksbewegung, 1793–1794*, Berlin, 224.

Connell, R., 1971, *The Child's Construction of Politics*, Melbourne: Melbourne University Press.

Connell, R., 1974, 'Patterns of Social and Political Opinion among Sydney Youth', *Australian Journal of Political History* 20(3): 177–185.

Connell, W., 1980, *The Australian Council for Education Research 1930~1980*, Melbourne: Australian Council Education Research.

Connolly, W., 1995, *The Ethos of Pluralization*, Minneapolis: University of Minnesota Press.

Connolly, W., 2005, *Pluralism*, Durham, NC: Duke University Press.

Cook, J., 1995, 'A History of Placing-out: The Orphan Trains', *Child Welfare League of America* 74(1): 181–197.

Coolidge, G., 2016, *Guardianship, Gender, and the Nobility in Early Modern Spain*, London: Routledge.

Costin, L., and Staff Writers, 2018, 'Children across Nation Rally for Action on Climate Change', *Perth Now*, 30th November 2018, https://www.perthnow.com.au/news/environment/children-across-nation-rally-for-action-on-climate-change-ng-b881037394z?fbclid=IwAR1DRAqZhkO0ff56FO8WjZkSQhDWEJF8BQAm5O4QZV2KblViktsoB4j-2S8.

Crick, B., 1998, *Education for Citizenship and the Teaching of Democracy in Schools: Final Report of the Advisory Group on Citizenship*, London: Qualifications and Curriculum Authority.

Critcher, C., 2009, 'Widening the Focus: Moral Panics as Moral Regulation', *British Journal of Sociology* 49(1): 17–34.

Crosby, M., and Olekalns N., 1997, Inflation, Unemployment and the NAIRU in Australia, Research Paper No. 543, Department of Economics, Melbourne: University of Melbourne.

Cross, G., 1989, *A Quest for Time: The Reduction of Work in Britain and France, 1840–1940*, Berkeley: University of California Press.

Crossley, N., 1996, *Intersubjectivity: The Fabric of Social Becoming*, Thousand Oaks: Sage.

Crossley, N., 2002, *Making Sense of Social Movements*, Buckingham: Open University Press.

Cuervo, H., and Wyn, J., 2011, *Rethinking Youth Transitions in Australia: A Historical and Multidimensional Approach*, Melbourne: University of Melbourne.

Cullis-Suzuki, S., 1992, Rio Summit, https://www.youtube.com/watch?v=oJJGuIZVfLM.

Cunningham, K., 1951, *The Adjustment of Youth*, Melbourne: ACER.

Cunningham, S., and Lavalette, M., 2002, 'Children, Politics and Collective Action: School Strikes in Britain', in Goldson, B., Lavalette, M., and McKechnie, J., (eds.), *Children, Welfare and the State*, London: Sage, 169–187.

Cunningham, S., and Lavalette, M., 2004, '"Active Citizens" or "Irresponsible Truants"? School Student Strikes against the War', *Critical Social Policy* 24(2): 255–269.

Dallery, T., 2008, 'Post-Keynesian Theories of the Firm under Financialization', *Review of Radical Political Economics* 41(4): 492–515.

Daniel, T.A., and Kent, C.A., 2005, 'An Assessment of Youth Entrepreneurship Programs in the United States', *Journal of Private Enterprise* 20(2): 15–34.

Danns, D., 2003, 'Chicago High School Students' Movement for Quality Public Education, 1966–1971', *The Journal of African-American History* 88(2): 138–150.

Danziger, K., 1990, *Constructing the Subject: Historical Origins of Psychological Research*, Cambridge: Cambridge University Press.

David, M., Rahloff, A., Petley, J., and Huges, J., 2011, 'The Idea of Moral Panic–Ten Dimensions of Dispute', *Crime, Media and Culture* 7(3): 215–228.

David, P., 1990, 'The Dynamo and the Computer: A Historical Perspective on the Modern Productivity Paradox', *American Economic Review Papers and Proceedings* 80(2): 355–361.

Davies, A., 1998, 'Youth Gangs, Masculinity and Violence in Late Victorian Manchester and Salford', *Journal of Social History* 32: 349–369.

Davies, A., 1999, '"These Viragoes Are No Less Cruel than the Lads": Young Women, Gangs and Violence in Late Victorian Manchester and Salford', *British Journal of Criminology* 39(1): 72–89.

Davis, B., Mausbach, W., Klimke, M., and MacDougall, C., (eds.), 2010, *Changing the World, Changing Oneself: Political Protest and Collective Identities in West Germany and the US in the 1960s and 1970s*, New York: Berghahn Books.

Davis, J., and Shear, M., 2018, 'How Trump Came to Enforce a Practice of Separating Migrant Families', *New York Times*, 16 June, https://www.nytimes.com/2018/06/16/us/politics/family-separation-trump.html.

Davis, N., 1971, 'The Reasons of Misrule: Youth Groups and Charivaris in Sixteenth Century France', *Past and Present* 50: 41–75.

de Moor, J., Uba, K., Wahlström, C.M., Wennerhag, M., and De Vydt, M., (eds.), 2020, *Protest for a Future II: Composition, Mobilization and Motives of the Participants in Fridays for Future Climate Protests on 20–27 September, 2019, in 19 Cities around the World*, https://static1.squarespace.com/static/5a84ed86f09ca48587f14e51/t/5e844e1cf3a8634447407556/1585729151188/Protest+for+a+Future+II+-+2020-02-24.pdf.

De Moor, T., and Van Zanden, J., 2009, 'Girl Power: The European Marriage Pattern and Labour Markets in the North Sea Region in the Late Medieval and Early Modern Period', *The Economic History Review* 63(1): 320–321.

De Munck, B., 2007a, *Technologies of Learning: Apprenticeship in Antwerp Guilds from the 15th Century to the End of the Ancien Regime*, Turnhout: Brepols, 178.

De Munck, B., 2007b, 'Construction and Reproduction: The Training and Skills of Antwerp Cabinetmakers in the Sixteenth and Seventeenth Centuries', in de Munck, B., Kaplan, S., and Soly, H., (eds.), *Learning on the Shop Floor, Historical Perspectives on Apprenticeship, International Studies in Social History*, New York: Berghahn Books, Volume 12, 85–110.

DeGroot, G., 1998, *Student Protest: The Sixties and After*, New York: Addison Wesley Longman.

DeGroot, G., 2008, *The Sixties Unplugged*, Oxford: Macmillian.

Delgado, J., and DeFronzo, J., 2009, 'A Comparative Framework for the Analysis of International Student Movements', *Social Movement Studies* 8: 203–224.

Delgado, S., and Ross, W., 2016, 'Students in Revolt: The Pedagogical Potential of Student Collective Action in the Age of the Corporate University', *Knowledge Cultures* 4(6): 141–158.

Demos, J., and V., 1969, 'Adolescence in Historical Perspective', *Journal of Marriage and the Family* 31: 632–638.

Dennis, J., 2019, *Beyond Slacktivism: Political Participation on Social Media*, London: Palgrave Macmillan.

Dépelteau, F., 2018, 'From the Concept of 'Trans-Action' to a Process-Relational Sociology', in *The Palgrave Handbook of Relational Sociology*, London: Palgrave, 499–519.

Déplanche, N., 2011, 'From Young People to Young Citizens: The Emergence of a Revolutionary Youth in France, 1788–1790', *Journal of Social History* 45(1): 225–237.

Deutsche Boerse Group, 2009, 'The Global Derivatives Market: A Blueprint for Market Safety and Integrity: White Paper', https://deutscheboerse.com/resource/blob/79206/c45b15c5cf7f0531f3664d4304934961/data/the-global-derivatives-market-0909_de.pdf.

Devries, K., 2011, *Joan of Arc: A Military Leader*, Stroud: The History Press.

Dewey, J., and Bentley, A., 1949, *Knowing and the Known*, Boston, MA: Beacon Press.

Dick, W., 1965, *A Bunch of Ratbags*, Melbourne: Collins.

Dickens, C., 1846, 'A Letter on Ragged Schooling', *The Daily News*, 4 February, https://infed.org/mobi/charles-dickens-on-ragged-schooling/.

Diderot, D., 1753/2005, 'Citizen', in *The Encyclopedia of Diderot & d'Alembert Collaborative Translation Project*, trans. Dhanvantari, S., Ann Arbor: Michigan Publishing, University of Michigan Library, http://hdl.handle.net/2027/spo.did2222.0000.070 (accessed 3 July 2020). Originally published as 'Citoyen', *Encyclopédie ou Dictionnaire raisonné des sciences, des arts et des métiers* 3: 488–489 (Paris, 1753).

Dillon, Z., and Cassidy, N., 2018, 'Labour Market Outcomes for Younger People Sydney RBA', https://www.rba.gov.au/publications/bulletin/2018/jun/pdf/labour-market-outcomes-for-younger-people.pdf.

Docker, J., 1998, 'Those Halcyon Days: The Moment of the New Left', in Head, B., and Walter, J., (eds.), *Intellectual Movements and Australian Society*, Melbourne: Oxford University Press, 289–307.

Dolores, D., 1998, 'Grassroots Leadership Reconceptualized: Chicana Oral Histories and the 1968 East Los Angeles School Blowouts', *Frontiers* 19(2): 113–142.

Donson, A., 2010, *Youth in a Fatherless Land: War Pedagogy, Nationalism, and Authority in Germany, 1914–1918*, Cambridge, MA: Harvard University Press.

Donson, A., 2011, 'The Teenagers' Revolution: Schülerräte in the Democratization and Right-Wing Radicalization of Germany, 1918–1923', *Central European History* 44(3): 420–446.

Douglas, R., 2007, 'Cold War Justice? Judicial Responses to Communists and Communism, 1945–1955', *Sydney Law Review* 29(43): 43–84.

Downs, A., 1957, *An Economic Theory of Democracy*, New York: Harper and Row.

Draper, H. (ed.), 1965, *Berkeley: The New Student Revolt*, New York: Grove Press.

Dryzek, J., 2006, *Deliberative Global Politics: Discourse and Democracy in a Divided World*, Cambridge: Polity Press.

du Bois-Reymond, M., 2009, 'Models of Navigation and Life Management', in Furlong, A., (ed.), *Handbook of Youth and Young Adulthood: New Perspectives and Agendas*, Furlong, Abingdon, Oxon: Routledge, 31–38.

Dunleavy, J., 1991, *Democracy, Bureaucracy and Public Choice*, Hemel Hempstead: Harvester-Wheatsheaf.

Dunkels, E., Franberg, G., and Hallgren, C., 2010, *Youth Culture and Net Culture: Online Social Practices*, London: IGI Global.

Durham, D., 2000, 'Youth and the Social Imagination in South Africa Introduction to Parts 1 and 2', *Anthropological Quarterly* 73(3): 113–120.

Durham, D., 2004, 'Disappearing Youth: Youth as a Social Shifter in Botswana', *American Ethnologist* 31(4): 589–605.

Durkheim, E., 1912/1995, *The Elementary Forms of the Religious Life*, trans. Fields, K., New York: Free Press.

Durlauf, S., and Blume, L., (eds.), 2010, *Economic Growth* (2nd ed.), London: Palgrave Macmillan.

Dyhouse, C., 1989, *Girls Growing up in Late Victorian and Edwardian England*, London: Routledge and Kegan Paul.

Eade, S., 1975, 'The Reclaimers: A Study of the Reformatory Movement in England and Wales, 1846–1893', PhD thesis, Canberra: Australian National University.

Eckersley, R., 1988, *Casualties of Change: The Predicament of Youth in Australia: A Report on the Social and Psychological Problems Faced by Young People in Australia*, CSIRO, Canberra: Commission for the Future.

Eckersley, R., 1993, 'The West's Deepening Cultural Crisis', *The Futurist*, November–December: 8–12.

Eckstein, K., Noack, P., and Gniewosz, B., 2012, 'Attitudes toward Political Engagement and Willingness to Participate in Politics: Trajectories throughout Adolescence', *Journal of Adolescence* 35: 485–495.

Eco, U., 1995, *Faith in Fakes: Travels in Hyperreality*, New York: Vintage.

Edwards, K., 2007, 'From Deficit to Disenfranchisement: Reframing Youth Electoral Participation', *Journal of Youth Studies* 10(5): 539–555.

Edwards, K., Saha, L., and Print, M., 2006, *Youth Electoral Study – Report 3: Youth, The Family, and Learning about Politics and Voting*, http://www.aec.gov.au/About_AEC/Publications/youth_study/index.htm.

Eide, K., 1990, 'International Congress on 30 Years of Educational Collaboration in the OECD', *International Congress on Planning and Management of Educational Development, Mexico City*, 74.

Eisenberg, L., 1981, 'Cross-cultural and Historical Perspectives on Child Abuse and Neglect', *Child Abuse and Neglect* 5: 299–308.

Elder, G., 1980, 'Adolescence in Historical Perspective', in Adelson, J., (ed.), *Handbook of Adolescent Psychology*, New York: John Wiley, 3–46.

Elephrame, 2020, https://elephrame.com/textbook/BLM/.

Elias, N., 1978, *What Is Sociology?* Trans. Morrissey, G., Mennell, S., and Jephcott, E., New York: Columbia University Press.

Elias, N., 2012, *On the Process of Civilisation: The Collected Works of Norbert Elias* (Volume 3), Dublin: UCD Press.

Elliott, L., 2016, 'Each Generation Should Be Better Off than Their Parents? Think Again', *The Guardian*, 15 February, https://www.theguardian.com/business/2016/feb/14/economics-viewpoint-baby-boomers-generation-x-generation-rent-gig-economy.

Ellis, R., 2019, 'Hopkins Protestors Are Spoiled Brats', *The Baltimore Sun*, 10th May, https://www.baltimoresun.com/opinion/readers-respond/bs-ed-rr-hopkins-protesters-spoiled-brats-letter-20190510-story.html.

Ellis, S., 1998, 'A Demonstration of British Good Sense?' British Student Protest during the Vietnam War', in de Groot, G., (ed.), *Student Protest: The Sixties and After*, London: Longman, 54–68.

Ellison, R., 1995, 'The World and the Jug', in Callahan, J., (ed.), *The Collected Essays of Ralph Ellison*, New York: Random House, 330–334.

Emirbayer, M., 1997, 'Manifesto for a Relational Sociology', *American Journal of Sociology* 103: 281–317.

Emy, H., 1972, 'The Roots of Australian Politics: A Critique of a Culture', *Politics* 7: 12–30.

Epstein, G., 2005, *Financialisation and the World Economy*, New York: Edward Elgar.

Epstein, S., 1991, *Wage Labor and Guilds in Medieval Europe*, New Jersey: Chapel Hill.

Erikson, E., 1950–1963, *Childhood and Society* (2nd ed.), New York: Norton.

Erturk, I., Froud, J., Johal, S., Leaver, A., and Williams, K., 2007, 'The Democratization of Finance? Promises, Outcomes and Conditions', *Review of International Political Economy* 14(4): 553–575.

Esping-Andersen, G., 1990, *The Three Worlds of Welfare Capitalism*, Princeton, NJ: Princeton University.

Evans, E., 1999, *William Pitt the Younger*, London: Routledge.

Evans, R., and Ferrier, C., 2004, *Radical Brisbane: An Unruly History*, Melbourne: Vulgar Press.

Ewer, P., et al., 1991, *Politics and the Accord*, Sydney: Pluto Press.

Ey, C., 2018, *The Higher Education Loan Program (HELP) and Related Loans: A Chronology*, Canberra: Australian Parliamentary Library, https://parlinfo.aph.gov.au/parlInfo/download/library/prspub/5872304/upload_binary/5872304.pdf.

Eyal, Y., 2007, *The Young America Movement and the Transformation of the Democratic Party 1828–1861*, Cambridge: Cambridge University Press.

Ezell, M., 1983, 'John Locke's Images of Childhood: Early Eighteenth Century Response to Some Thoughts Concerning Education', *Eighteenth-Century Studies* 17(2): xvii.

Fairclough, N., 1989, *Language and Power*, London: Longman.

Fairclough, N., 1992, *Discourse and Social Change*, Cambridge: Polity Press.

Farr, J., and Seidelman, R., (eds.), 1993, *Discipline and History: Political Science in the United States*, Ann Arbor: University of Michigan Press.

Fasianos, A., Guevara, D., and Pierros, C., 2016, 'Have We Been Here Before? Phases of Financialization within the 20th Century in the United States', Levy Economics Institute Working Paper No 869, http://www.levyinstitute.org/pubs/wp_869.pdf.

Fass, P., and Mason, M., (eds.), 2000, *Childhood in America*, New York: New York University Press.

Featherstone, L., 2011, *Lets Talk about Sex: Histories of Sexuality in Australia from Federation to the Pill*, Newcastle: Cambridge Scholars.

Fernandes-Alcantara, A., 2018, *Youth and the Labor Force: Background and Trends*, Washington: Congressional Research Service, www.crs.gov R42519.

Fernandez-Armestos, F., 1997, *Truth: A History and Guide for the Perplexed*, London: Black Swan.

Fernandez-Armesto, F., 2004, *So You Think You're Human? A Brief History of Humankind*, Oxford University Press.

Feuer, L., 1969, *The Conflict of Generations*, New York: Basic Books,

Fierravanti-Wells, C., (@Senator_CFW), 2019, Twitter. 10 March 2019, https://twitter.com/Senator_CFW/status/1104964425511927808.

Financial Stability Board, 2019, 'Monitoring of FinTech', http://www.fsb.org/what-we-do/policy-development/additional-policy-areas/monitoring-of-fintech/.

Fink, C., Gassert, P., and Junker, D., (eds.), *1968: The World Transformed*, Cambridge: Cambridge University Press.

Flacks, R., 1970, 'Social and Cultural Meanings of Student Revolt: Some Informal Comparative Observations', *Social Problems* 17(3): 340–357.

Fletcher, L., 1970, 'Student Unrest: A Retrospect', *Australian Journal of Education* 4(1, December): 13–20.

Fletcher, J., 1997, *Violence and Civilization*, Cambridge: Polity Press.

Foa, R., and Mounk, Y., 2016, 'The Democratic Disconnect', *Journal of Democracy* 27(3): 5–17, http://www.journalofdemocracy.org/sites/default/files/Foa%26Mounk-27-3.pdf.

Foa, R.S., Klassen, A., Slade, M., Rand, A., and Collins, R., 2020, *The Global Satisfaction with Democracy Report 2020*, Cambridge: Centre for the Future of Democracy.

Fordham, B., 'She Should She Should Be Courteous': Tony Abbott on Student's National Anthem Boycott', *2GB Radio*, https://www.2gb.com/she-should-be-courteous-tony-abbott-on-students-national-anthem-boycott/.

Forrester, M., 2002, 'Appropriating Cultural Conceptions of Childhood: Participation in Conversation', *Childhood* 9(3): 255–276.

Foti, A., 2017, *General Theory of the Precariat*, Amsterdam: Institute of Network Cultures.

Foucault, M., 1972, *The Archaeology of Knowledge*, trans. Sheridan, A., New York: Harper and Row.

Foucault, M., 1977, *Discipline and Punish*, London: Penguin Books.

Foucault, M., 1997, 'Governmentality', in Rabinow, P., (ed.), *The Essential Works of Michel Foucault, 1954–1984* (Volume 3), London: Allen Lane, 201–223.

Foyster, E., and Marten, J., 2010, *A Cultural History of Childhood and Family*, Oxford: Bloomsbury.

Frank, R., 1988, *Passions within Reason: The Strategic Role of Emotions*, New York: W.W. Norton.

Franklin, B., 2004, 'Community, Race and Curriculum in Detroit', *History of Education* 33(2): 137–156.

Franklin, V., 2000, 'Black High School Student Activism in the 1960s: An Urban Phenomenon?' *Journal of Research in Education* 10: 3–8.

Franklin, V., 2003, 'Patterns of Student Activism at Historically Black Universities in the United States and South Africa, 1960–1977', *The Journal of African-American History* 88(2): 204–217.

Fraser, R., 1988, *1968: A Student Generation in Revolt*, New York: Pantheon Books.

Freeman, M., 2000, 'The Future of Children's Rights', *Children and Society* 14(4): 277–293.

Fregier, H., 1840, *Des classes dangereuses de la population dans les grandes villes, et des moyens de les rendre meilleures*, Paris: Libraire de l'Academie Royal de Medicine.

Frey, B., and Osborne, M., 2017, 'The Future of Employment: How Susceptible Are Jobs to Computerization', *Technological Forecasting and Social Change* 114: 254–280.

Friedenburg, E., 1959, *The Vanishing Adolescent*, Boston, MA: Beacon Press.

Friedrich, D., 2010, 'Historical Consciousness as a Pedagogical Device in the Production of the Responsible Citizen', *Discourse: Studies in the Cultural Politics of Education* 31(5): 649–663.

Frith, S., 1986, *The Sociology of Youth*, Ormskirk: Causeway Press.

Furet, F., 1981, *Interpreting the French Revolution*, trans Forster, E., Cambridge: Cambridge University Press.

Furlong, A., 2015a, 'Young People and the Post Industrial Economy: Lessons from Japan_Departments/Parliament', in Kamp, A., (ed.), *A Critical Youth Studies for the 21st Century*, Leiden: Brill, 25–37.
Furlong, A., 2015b, July 24, *Change Studies Symposium*, Newcastle: University of Newcastle.
Furlong, A., and Cartmel, F., 2007, *Young People and Social Change: Individualisation and Risk in Late Modernity* (2nd ed.), Maidenhead: Open University Press.
Furlong, A., and Cartmel, F., 2012, 'Social Change and Political Engagement among Young People: Generation and the 2009/2010, British Election Survey', *Parliamentary Affairs* 65(1): 13–28.
Fürst, J., 2010, *Stalin's Last Generation: Soviet Post-War Youth and the Emergence of Mature Socialism*, Oxford: Oxford University Press.
Gadamer, H., 1977, *Philosophical Hermeneutics*, trans. and ed. Linge, D.E., Berkeley: University of California Press.
Gadamer, H., 2004, *Truth and Method* (2nd rev. ed.), London: Continuum International Publishing Group.
Galbraith, J., 1958, *The Affluent Society*, New York: Houghton Mifflin.
Galston, W., 2004, 'Civic Education and Political Participation', *PS: Political Science and Politics* 37(2): 263–266.
Galton, F., 1869, *Hereditary Genius: An Inquiry into Its Laws and Consequences* (1st ed.), London: Macmillan.
Galton, F., 1978, *Hereditary Genius* (reprint of 1892 edition, first published 1869), London: Friedmann.
Galton, F., 1883, *Inquires into Human Faculty and Its Development*, London: Macmillan.
Galton, F., 1890, 'Kinship and Correlation', *North American Review* 150: 419–431.
Garber, P., 1993, 'The Collapse of the Bretton Woods Fixed Exchange Rate System', in Bordo, M., and Eichengreen, B., (eds.), *A Retrospective on the Bretton Woods System: Lessons for International Monetary Reform*, Chicago, IL: University of Chicago Press, 461–494.
Gardiner, L., 2016, *Stagnation Generation: The Case for Renewing the Intergenerational Contract*, London: The Intergenerational Commission/Resolution Foundation.
Gardner, G., Sheil, B., and Taylor, V., 1970, 'Passive Politics: A Survey of Melbourne University Students', *Politics* 1(May): 34–43.
Gass, J., 1988, 'Towards the "active society"', *OECD Observer* 152: 6–8.
Gassert, P., and Klimke, M., (eds.), 2009, *1968: Memories and Legacies of a Global Revolt*, Washington, DC: GHI Bulletin Supplement.
Geertz, C., 1973, 'Thick Decsription: Toward an Interpretative Therapy of Culture', in *The Interpretation of Cultures*, New York: Basic Books, 3–32.
Gelb, S., 1995, 'The Beast in Man: Degenerationism and Mental Retardation, 1900–1920', *Mental Retardation* 33: 1–9.
Gendron, F., 1993, *The Gilded Youth of Thermidor*, Toronto: McGill University.
Geremek, B., 1994, *Poverty: A History*, Oxford: Blackwell.
Gergen, K., 1985, 'The Social Constructionist Movement in Social Psychology', *American Psychologist* 40(3): 266–275.
Gerig, A., 2015, 'High-Frequency Trading Synchronizes Prices in Financial Markets', DERA Working Paper Series, https://www.sec.gov/files/dera-wp-hft-synchronizes.pdf.
Gerster, R., and Bassett, J., 1991, *Seizures of Youth: The Sixties and Australia*, Melbourne: Victoria Hyland House Publishing.
Gibbs, J., 1972, *Social Control*, Andover, MA: Warner Module.

Giddens, A., 1984, *The Constitution of Society: Outline of the Theory of Structuration*, Cambridge: Polity Press.

Giersch, H., 1985, *Eurosclerosis*, Discussion paper No. 112, Kiel: Institut für Weltwirtschaft (IfW), https://www.econstor.eu/bitstream/10419/48070/1/025296167.pdf.

Giersch, J., and Dong, C., 2018, 'Required Civics Courses, Civics Exams, and Voter Turnout', *The Social Science Journal* 55(3): 160–170.

Gill, J., and DeFronzo, J., 2009, 'A Comparative Framework for the Analysis of International Student Movements', *Social Movement Studies* 8(3): 203–224.

Gilliam, L., and Gulløv, E., 2014, 'Making Children "Social": Civilising Institutions in the Danish Welfare State', *Human Figurations* 3(1), http://hdl.handle.net/2027/spo.11217607.0003.103.

Gilligan, C., 1982, *In a Different Voice: Psychological Theory and Women's Development*, Cambridge, MA: Harvard University Press.

Gillis, J., 1974, *Youth and History: Tradition and Change in European Age Relations, 1770–Present*, New York: Harcourt Brace Jovanovich Publishers.

Gillis, J., 1975a, 'The Evolution of Juvenile Delinquency in England, 1890–1914', *Past and Present* 67: 96–126.

Gillis, J., 1975b, *Youth and History: Tradition and Change in European Age Relations, 1750–Present*, Amsterdam: Elsevier.

Ginsborg, P., 1990, *A History of Contemporary Italy: Society and Politics 1943–1988*, London: Penguin.

Gish, C., 1999, *Rescuing the 'waifs and strays' of the City: The Western Emigration Program of the Children's Aid Society*, Fairfax, VA: Peter N. Stearns.

Gitlin, T., 2013, 'Occupy's Predicament: The Moment and the Prospect for the Movement', *British Journal of Sociology* 64(1): 3–25.

Gjelten, T., 2011, 'FBI Tries to Send Message with Hacker Arrests', *National Public Radio*, http://www.npr.org/2011/07/20/138555799/fbi-arrests-alleged-anonymous-hackers.

Glazer, N., 1968, 'Student Power in Berkeley', *Public Interest* 13(1): 3–21.

Gleadle, K., 2016, 'The Juvenile Enlightenment: British Children and Youth During the French Revolution', *Past & Present* 233(1): 143–184.

Gleick, J., 2014, 'Today's Dead End Kids', *The New York Review of Books*, December 18: 36–38.

Global Voices, 2015, 'Sketch Comic Faces Accusations of Glorifying Terrorism in Spain', 15th January, https://globalvoicesonline.org/2015/01/15/catalan-sketch-comic-faces-accusations-of-glorifying-terrorism.

Goffman, E., 2009, *Stigma: Notes on the Management of Spoiled Identity*, New York: Simon and Schuster.

Goldson, B., 2001, 'The Demonization of Children: From the Symbolic to the Institutional', in Foley, P., Roche, J., and Tucker, S., (eds.), *Children in Society: Contemporary Theory, Policy and Practice*, Basingstoke: Palgrave, 34–48.

Goldstone, J., 1991, *Revolution and Rebellion in Early Modern World*, Berkeley, CA: UCP.

Goodin, D., 2018, 'US Service Provider Survives Largest Recorded DDoS Attack in History', *Ars Technica*, 18 March, https://arstechnica.com/information-technology/2018/03/us-service-provider-survives-the-biggest-recorded-ddos-in-history/.

Gordon, B., 1998, 'The Eyes of the Marcher: Paris, May 1968-Theory and Its Consequences' in DeGroot, G.J., (ed.), *Student Protest: The Sixties and After*, London: Addison Wesley Longman, 39–53.

Gordon, F., 2018, *Children, Young People and the Press in a Transitioning Society: Representations, Reactions and Criminalisation*, London: Palgrave.

Gordon, R., (ed.), 1970, *The Australian New Left: Critical Essays and Strategy*, Melbourne: W. Heinemann.

Gorka, S., 2019, @SebGorka, https://twitter.com/SebGorka/status/1176301345151864832.

Gorman, C., 2015, 'Bodgies and African American Influences in Sydney', Sydney: Dictionary of Sydney Trust.

Gorz, A., 1987, *Farewell to the Working Class*, London: Pluto.

Gould, S., 1996, *The Mismeasure of Man*, New York: W.W. Norton & Co.

Graeber, D., 2011, *Debt: The First 5000 Years*, New York: Melville House Publishing.

Graham, G., 2006, *Young Activists: American High School Students in the Age of Protest*, DeKalb: Northern Illinois University.

Graham, J., and Gray, E. (producers) 1995, Transcript of The Orphan Train on the PBS's *The American Experience Series*, WGBH Boston, www.pbs.org/wgbh/amex/orphan/orphants.html.

Grasso, M., 2016, *Generations, Political Participation and Social Change in Western Europe*, London: Routledge.

Gray, J., 2018, 'The Protesters of 1968 Changed the World – But Not in the Way They Hoped', *New Statesman*, 2 April, https://www.newstatesman.com/culture/books/2018/04/protesters-1968-changed-world-not-way-they-hoped.

Green, F., 2013, *Youth Entrepreneurship*, A Background Paper for the OECD Centre for Entrepreneurship, Paris: OECD.

Greenberg, B.S., 1963, '"Operation Abolition" vs. "Operation Correction"', *Audio Visual Communication Review* 11(3): 40–46.

Grieve, V., 2018, *Little Cold Warriors: American Childhood in the 1950s*, New York: Oxford University Press.

Griffin, C., 1993, *Representations of Youth: The Study of Youth and Adolescence in Britain and America*, Cambridge: Polity Press.

Griffin, G., 1977, 'Troubled Teens: Managing Disorders of Transition and Consumption', *Consuming Cultures: Feminist Review* 55: 5–22.

Gullette, M., 2004, *Aged by Culture*, Chicago, IL: University of Chicago.

Gurney, C., 2000, 'A Great Cause: The Origins of the Anti-Apartheid Movement, June 1959–March 1960', *Journal of Southern African Studies* 26(1): 123–144.

Habermas, J., 1971, *Knowledge and Human Interests*, Boston, MA: Beacon Press.

Habermas, J., 1987, *The Philosophical Discourse of Modernity*, trans. Lawrence, F., Cambridge: Polity Press.

Habermas, J., 1989, *The Structural Transformation of the Public Sphere: An Inquiry into a Category of Bourgeois Society*, trans. Burger, T., and Lawrence, F., Cambridge: Polity Press.

Hacking, I., 1983, *Representing and Intervening*, Cambridge: Cambridge University Press.

Hacking, I., 1986, *Historical Ontology*, Cambridge, MA: Harvard University Press.

Hacking, I., 1999, *The Social Construction of What?* Cambridge, MA: Harvard University Press.

Hacking, I., 2002, *Historical Ontology*, Cambridge, MA: Harvard University Press.

Haggman-Laitila, A., Solokekila, P., and Krki, S., 2019, 'Young People's Preparedness for Adult Life and Coping after Foster Care: A Systematic Review of Perceptions and Experiences in the Transition Period', *Child and Youth Care Forum* 48(5): 633–661.

Hall, G., 1905, *Adolescence: Its Psychology and Its Relations to Physiology, Anthropology, Sociology, Sex, Crime, Religion and Education* (Volumes 1 and 2), New York: A Appleton and Company.

Hall, G.S., 1917, *Jesus, the Christ, in the Light of Psychology*, (2 vols), New York: D. Appleton and Sons.

Hall, G.S., 1922, *Senescence: The Last Half of Life*, New York: D. Appleton and Sons.
Hall, S., (ed.) 1997, *Cultural Representations and Signifying Practices*, London: Open University Press.
Hall, S., and Jefferson, T., (eds.), 1976, *Resistance through Rituals: Youth Subcultures in Postwar Britain*, London: Hutchinson.
Hamel-Green, M., 1983, 'The Resisters: A History of the Anti-Conscription Movement', in King, P., (ed.), *Australia's Vietnam: Australia in the Second Indo-China War*, Sydney: George Allen & Unwin, 100–128.
Hammersley, R., 2015, 'Concepts of Citizenship in France during the Long Eighteenth Century', *European Review of History: Revue européenne d'histoire* 22(3): 468–485.
Hanna, E., 2013, *Student Power! The Radical Days of the English Universities*, Cambridge: Cambridge Scholars.
Hansen, P., 2009, *Contesting the French Revolution*, New York: Wiley-Blackwell.
Hanson, P., 2018, 'Schoolgirl Who Refused to Stand for National Anthem Responds to Pauline Hanson', *SBS News*, 13 September, https://www.sbs.com.au/news/schoolgirl-who-refused-to-stand-for-national-anthem-responds-to-pauline-hanson.
Harman, C., Clarke, D., Sayers, A., Kuper, R., Shaw, M., 1968, *Education, Capitalism and the Student Revolt*, London: International Socialism.
Harman, G., 2018, *Object-Oriented Ontology: A New Theory of Everything*, London: Pelican.
Harre, R., 2003, *Social Being* (2nd ed.), Oxford: Blackwell.
Harrington, M., 1962, *The Other American: Poverty in the United States*, New York: Penguin.
Hart, D., and Youniss, J., 2017, *Renewing Democracy in Young America*, New York: Oxford University Press.
Hartley, L., 1952, *The Go Between*, London: Hamish Hamilton.
Hartung, C., 2017, *Conditional Citizens: Rethinking Children and Young People's Participation*, Singapore: Springer.
Harvey, D., 2005, *A Brief History of Neoliberalism*, Oxford: Oxford University Press.
Hastings, M., 2011, 'Years of Liberal Dogma Have Spawned a Generation of Amoral, Uneducated, Welfare Dependent, Brutalised Youngsters', *Daily Mail*, 12 August 2011, http://www.dailymail.co.uk/debate/article-2024284/UK-riots-2011-Liberal-dogma-spawned-generation-brutalised-youths.html (accessed 3 March 2012).
Hayward, J., Barry, B., and Brown, A., (eds.), 1999, *The British Study of Politics in the Twentieth Century*, Oxford: Oxford University Press.
Hazlitt, W., 1978, *The Letters of William Hazlitt*, New York: New York University Press.
Hecht, T., (ed.), 2002, *Minor Omissions: Children in Latin American History and Society (Living in Latin America)*, Wisconsin: University of Wisconsin Press.
Heffernan, M., 2013, *Willful Blindness*, New York: Penguin.
Hein, E., 2009, 'A (Post-) Keynesian Perspective on Financialization', IMK Macroeconomic Policy Institute Studies, No 2009-1. Düsseldorf: Hans Böckler Foundation.
Hein, E., and Mundt, M., 2013, *Financialisation and the Requirements and Potentials for Wage-led Recovery: A Review Focusing on the G20*, ILO Working Paper.
Heineman, K., 2001, *Put Your Bodies upon the Wheels: Student Revolt in the 1960s*, Chicago, IL: I.R. Dee.
Heirich, M., 1970, *The Beginning: Berkeley, 1964*, New York: Columbia University Press.
Heirich, M., 1971, *The Spiral of Conflict, Berkeley*, New York: Columbia University Press.
Hendrick, H., 1990, *Images of Youth: Age, Class, and the Male Youth Problem, 1880–1920*, Oxford: Clarendon Press.
Henn, M., and Weinstein, M., 2006, 'Young People and Political (In)activism: Why Don't Young People Vote?' *Policy & Politics* 34(3): 517–534.

Henn, M., Weinstein, M., and Forrest, S., 2005, 'Uninterested Youth? Young People's Attitudes towards Party Politics in Britain', *Political Studies* 53(3): 556–578.

Henn, M., Weinstein, M., and Wring, D., 2002, 'A Generation Apart? Youth and Political Participation in Britain', *British Journal of Politics and International Relations* 4(2): 167–192.

Hensby, A., 2014, 'Networks, Counter-networks and Political Socialisation – Paths and Barriers to High-cost/risk Activism in the 2010/11 Student Protests against Fees and Cuts', *Contemporary Social Science* 9(1): 92–105.

Hensby, A., 2017, *Participation and Non-Participation in Student Activism: Paths and Barriers*, London: Rowman Littlefield.

Hepburn, B., 2012, 'Justin Trudeau: At 40, Is He Too Young to Lead the Liberals?' *The Star*, 18 July, https://www.thestar.com/opinion/editorialopinion/2012/07/18/justin_trudeau_at_40_is_he_too_young_to_lead_the_liberals.html.

Hernandez, S and Sacks, B 2018, 'Here's How Some Schools Punished Students for Walking Out to Protest Gun Violence', *Buzz Feed News*, 15 March, https://www.buzzfeednews.com/article/salvadorhernandez/how-schools-punished-students-for-gun-walkouts.

Heywood, C., 2001, *A History of Childhood*, Cambridge: Polity Press.

Heywood, A., 2013, *Politics* (4th ed), London: Palgrave Macmillan.

Hier, S., 2008, 'Thinking Beyond Moral Panic: Risk, Responsibility, and the Politics of Moralisation', *Theoretical Criminology* 12(2): 173–190.

Hier, S., 2011, 'Tightening the Focus: Moral Panic, Moral Regulation and Liberal Government', *British Journal of Sociology* 6(3): 523–541.

Higonnet, A., 1998, *Pictures of Innocence: The History and Crisis of Ideal Childhood*, London: Thames and Hudson.

Hill, J., 2019, An Open Letter to Greta Thunberg, 11th November, https://www.frontpagemag.com/fpm/2019/11/open-letter-greta-thunberg-jason-d-hill/?fbclid=IwAR3MWF2uPQIZnXTfP0faqT13C9G3CUNVLyKk8sH7NNqBkhZovzVFMVNrAjA#.Xhe4ff68ONX.facebook.

Hillyer, Q., 2015, 'Coddled College Students Need to Grow Up', *National Review*, 17th November, https://www.nationalreview.com/2015/11/coddled-college-students-should-grow-up.

Hobsbawm, E.J., 1975, 'The Age of Capital 1848–1875', Abacus, London, https://libcom.org/files/Eric%20Hobsbawm%20-%20Age%20Of%20Capital%20-%201848-1875.pdf.

Hockstader, L., 2000, 'Gaza Gains a Martyr, Parents Lose a Son: Slain Youth Hailed as Palestinian Hero While Couple Mourns', *Washington Post*, 11 December, https://twitter.com/realdonaldtrump/status/1205100602025545730?lang=en).

Hoefferle, C.M., 2013, *British Student Activism in the Long Sixties*, Routledge: New York.

Hogg, D., and Kasky, C., 2018, 'Never Again MSD | Real Time with Bill Maher', YouTube. 2 March 2019, https://www.youtube.com/watch?v=jcsKMie6M94.

Hogg, L., @lauren_hoggs https://twitter.com/lauren_hoggs/status/975426857523871745).

Hoijer, B., 2011, 'Social Representations Theory: A New Theory for Media Research', *Nordicom Review* 32(2): 3–16.

Holt, M., 1992, *The Orphan Trains: Placing Out in America*, Lincoln: University of Nebraska Press.

Honig, B., 1993, 'The Politics of Agonism', *Political Theory* 21(3): 528–533.

Honig, B., 2009, *Emergency Politics: Paradox, Law, Democracy*, Princeton, NJ: Princeton University Press.

Honig, B., 2017, *Public Things: Democracy in Disrepair*, New York: Fordham.

Horn, G., 2007, *The Spirit of '68: Rebellion in Western Europe and North America, 1956–1976*, Oxford: Oxford University Press.

Horowitz, D., 1999, *Radical Son: A Generational Odyssey*, New York: Touchstone, http://hdl.handle.net/2027/spo.11217607.0003.103.

Howard-Wagner, D., Bargh, M., and Altamirano-Jiménez. I., 2018, 'From New Paternalism to New Imaginings of Possibilities in Australia, Canada and Aotearoa/New Zealand: Indigenous Rights and Recognition and the State in the Neoliberal Age', in HowardWagner, D., Bargh, M., and AltamiranoJiménez, I. (eds.), *The Neoliberal State, Recognition and Indigenous Rights: New Paternalism to New Imaginings*, Canberra: ANU Press pp. 1–39.

HuffPost, 2019, 13th December, https://twitter.com/huffpost/status/12052119708882411158?s=12.

Humphreys, E., 2018, *How Labour Built Neoliberalism: Australia's Accord, the Labour Movement and the Neoliberal Project*, London: Brill.

Humphries, S., 1981, *Hooligans or Rebels? An Oral History of Working-class Childhood and Youth, 1889–1939*, Oxford: Blackwell.

Hunt Botting, E., 2006, *Family Feuds: Wollstonecraft, Burke, and Rousseau on the Transformation of the Family*, Albany, NY: State University of New York Press, Chap. 5.

Hunt, L., 1989, 'Family Narrative and Political Discourse in Revolutionary France and America', in Mannucci, V., (ed.), *The Languages of Revolution Milan Quaderno 2*, Istituto De Studi Storici, Dipartimento di storia della società e delle istituzioni, Università degli studi di Milano, Milan, 161–176.

Hutter, S., and Kriesi, H., 2013, 'Movements of the Left, Movements of the Right Reconsidered', in Stekelenburg, J., Roggeband, C., and Klandermans, B., (eds.), *The Future of Social Movement Research: Dynamics, Mechanisms, and Processes*, Minneapolis: University of Minnesota Press, 281–298.

Hyde, M., 2010, *All Along the Watchtower: Memoir of a Sixties Revolutionary*, Melbourne: Vulgar Press, 21, 32–33.

Illich, I., 1972, *De-Schooling Society*, London: Pelican.

ILO, 1998, *World Employment Report 1998–99: Employability in the Global Economy – How Training Matters*, Geneva: ILO.

Imhonopi, D., and Urim, U., 2015, 'Shrinking the Ballooning Youth Precariat Class in Nigeria: The Need for Youth Empowerment', *The African Symposium* 15: 69–82.

International Labour Organization (ILO), 2020, *World Employment and Social Outlook Trends 2020*, Geneva: ILO, https://www.ilo.org/wcmsp5/groups/public/---dgreports/---dcomm/---publ/documents/publication/wcms_734455.pdf.

Isin, E., 2002, *Being Political: Genealogies of Citizenship*, Minneapolis: University of Minnesota Press.

Isin, E., 2008, *Recasting the Social in Citizenship*, Toronto: University of Toronto Press.

Isserman, M., and Kazin, M., 2000, *America Divided: The Civil War of the 1960s*, Oxford: Oxford University Press.

Jameson, F., 1984, 'Postmodernism: On Cultural Logic of Late Capitalism', *New Left Review* 146: 55–92.

Jaume, L., 2013: *Tocqueville: The Aristocratic Sources of Liberty*, Princeton, NJ: Princeton University Press.

Jenkins, H., Shresthova, S., Gamber-Thompson, L., Kligler-Vilenchik, N., Zimmerman, A.M., and Soep, E., 2016, *By Any Media Necessary: The New Youth Activism*, New York: New York University Press.

Jenks, C., 1996, *Childhood: Key Ideas*, New York: Routledge.
Jenks, C., 1998, *Childhood*, London: Routledge.
Jessop, B., 1992, 'Fordism and Post-Fordism: A Critical Reformulation', in Storper, M., Scott, A.J. (eds.), *Pathways to Industrialization and Regional Development*, London: Routledge, 42–62.
Jobs, R., 2009, 'Youth Movements: Travel, Protest, and Europe in 1968', *American Historical Review* 114(2): 376–404.
Jodelet, D., 1989, *Madness and Social Representations*, London: Harvester/Wheatsheaf.
Johnson, L., 1983, *The Modern Girl: Girlhood and Growing Up*, St Leonards: Allen and Unwin.
Johnson, N., and Feinberg, W., 1980, 'Youth Protest in the 60s: An Introduction', *Sociological Focus, Special Issue: Youth Protest in the 60s* 13(3): 173–178.
Johnson, C., and Marshall, B., 2004, *Political Engagement among Young People: An Update*, London: Electoral Commission.
Jones, B., 1982, *Sleepers Wake! Technology and the Future of Work*, Melbourne: Oxford University Press.
Jones, G., 2009, *Youth*, Cambridge: Polity Press.
Jones, M., 1983, *The Australian Welfare State: Growth, Crisis and Change*, Sydney: Allen and Unwin.
Jones, P., 1991, *The 1848 Revolutions*, Abingdon: Routledge.
Jose, J., 2017, 'A Brutal Blow against the Democratic Normality: Unlearning the Epistemology of the Political', *Social Identities* 23(6): 718–729.
Jose, J., and Motta, S., 2017, 'Reoccupying the Political: Transforming Political Science', *Social Identities* 23(6): 651–660.
Jowell, R., and Park, A., 1998, *Young People, Politics and Citizenship: A Disengaged Generation?* London: Citizenship Foundation.
Judt, T., 2006, *Postwar: A History of Europe since 1945*, London: Penguin.
Junankar, P., 2015, 'The Impact of the Global Financial Crisis on Youth Unemployment', *The Economic and Labour Relations Review* 26(2): 191–217.
Kahneman, D., 2011, *Thinking, Fast and Slow*, New York: Farrar Strauss and Giroux.
Kandal, D., 1978, 'On Variations in Adolescent Subculture', *Youth and Society* 9(9 June), 373–382.
Kaplan, S., 1993, 'L'apprentissage au XVIIIe siècle: le cas de Paris', *Revue d'histoire moderne et contemporaine* 40: 452.
Katsiaficas, G., 1987, *The Imagination of the New Left: A Global Analysis of 1968*, Boston, MA: South End Press.
Keller, J., 2012, 'Virtual Feminisms', *Information, Communication & Society* 15(3): 429–447.
Keniston, K., 1965, *The Uncommitted: Alienated Youth in American Society*, New York: Harcourt, Brace & World.
Keniston, K., 1968, *Young Radicals*, New York: Harcourt Brace and World.
Keniston, K., 1970, 'Student Activism, Moral Development, and Morality', *American Journal of Orthopsychiatry* 40(4): 577–592.
Keniston, K., 1973a, *Radicals and Militants*, Lexington, MA: Lexington Books.
Keniston, K., 1969, 'Notes on Young Radicals', *Change in Higher Education* 1(6): 25–33.
Keniston, K., 1971, *Youth and Dissent*, New York: Harcourt Brace Jovanovich.
Keniston, K., 1973b, *Radicals and Militants: An Annotated Bibliography of Empirical Research on Campus Unrest*, Lexington, MA: D.C. Heath.
Kerr, S., Kerr, W., and Xu, T., 2017, 'Personality Traits of Entrepreneurs: A Review of Recent Literature, Harvard Business School', Working Paper 18–047, Cambridge, MA: Harvard University.

Kett, J., 1971, 'Adolescence and Youth in Nineteenth-Century America', *The Journal of Interdisciplinary History* 2(2): 283–298.
Kett, J., 1974, *Rites of Passage: Adolescence in America, 1790 to the Present*, New York: Basic Books.
Keynes, J., 1935, *The General Theory of Employment, Interest and Money*, London: Macmillan.
Kimberlee, R., 2002, 'Why Don't British Young People Vote at General Elections?' *Journal of Youth Studies* 5(1): 85–98.
King, P., 2006, *Crime and Law in England: Remaking Justice from the Margins*, Cambridge: Cambridge University Press.
Kinnell, M., 1988, 'Sceptreless, Free, Uncircumscribed? Radicalism, Dissent and Early Children's Books', *British Journal of Educational Studies* 36(1): 49–71.
Kioupkiolis, A., and Pechtelides, Y., 2018, 'Youth Heteropolitics in Crisis-Ridden Greece', in S. Pickard, and J. Bessant (eds.), *Young People Re-Generating Politics in Times of Crises*, Palgrave Studies in Young People and Politics, London: Palgrave, 273–293.
Klapp, O., 1969, *Collective Search for Identity*, New York: Holt, Rinehart and Winston.
Klimke, M., 2010, *The Other Alliance: Student Protest in West Germany and the United States in the Global Sixties*, Princeton, NJ: Princeton University Press,
Klimke, M., and Scharloth, J., (eds.), 2008, *1968 in Europe: A History of Protest and Activism 1958–1977*, London: Palgrave-Macmillan.
Knowles, M., 2019, Fox News Channel, 23 September https://www.youtube.com/watch?v=q8sdDGaWqUY.
Koenker, D., 2001, 'Fathers against Sons/Sons against Fathers: The Problem of Generation in the Early Soviet Workplace', *Journal of Modern History* 73(4): 781–810.
Kohlberg, L., 1963, 'The Development of Children's Orientations toward a Moral Order: Sequence in the Development of Moral Thought', *Vita Humana* 6: 11–33.
Kohlberg, L., 1981, *The Philosophy of Moral Development: The Moral Stages an the Idea of Justice: Essays on Moral Development*, 1, San Francisco, CA: Harper and Row.
Kosselleck, R., 2002, *The Practice of Conceptual History: Timing History, Spacing Concepts*, trans. Samuel Presner, T., Stanford, CA: Stanford University Press.
Kosselleck, R., 2004, *Futures Past: On the Semantics of Historical Time* (Translated and with an introduction by Keith Tribe), New York: Columbia University Press.
Kriesi, H., 2013, 'The Political Consequences of the Economic Crisis in Europe: Electoral Punishment and Popular Protest', in Bermeo, N., and Larry Bartels, L., (eds.), *Mass Politics in Tough Times*, Oxford: Oxford University Press, 297–333.
Krippner, G., 2005, 'The Financialization of the American Economy', *Socio-Economic Review* 3(2): 173–208.
Kuhn, T., [1962] 2012, *The Structure of Scientific Revolutions*, Chicago, IL: University Chicago Press.
Kurlansky, M., 2004, *1968 The Year that Rocked the World*, New York: Random House.
Lacquer, W., 1984, *Young Germany: A History of the German Youth Movement*, London: Routledge.
Lakoff, G., 1999, *Moral Politics: How Conservatives and Liberals Think*, Chicago, IL: University of Chicago Press.
Lambert, M., 2014, *Privatization and the Public Good: Public Universities in the Balance*, Cambridge, MA: Harvard Education Press.
Lancet, 2019, May, 'Editorial: The Emerging Voices of Youth Activists', *The Lancet* 393: 10183, https://www.thelancet.com/journals/lancet/article/PIIS0140-6736(19)30991-2/fulltext.

Lapavitsas, C., 2013, 'The Financialization of Capitalism: 'Profiting without Producing', *City* 17(6): 792–805.
Laslett, P., 1965, *The World We Have Lost*, London: Routledge.
Latour, B., 1999, *Pandora's Hope: Essays on the Reality of Science Studies*, Cambridge, MA: Harvard University Press.
Latour, B., 2013a, *An Inquiry into Modes of Existence: An Anthropology of the Moderns*, trans. Porter, C., Cambridge, MA: Harvard University Press.
Latour, B., 2013b, In Tresch, J., 'Another Turn after ANT: An Interview with Bruno Latour', *Social Studies of Science* 43(2): 302–313.
Latour, B., 2018, *Down to Earth: Politics in the New Climactic Regime*, Cambridge: Polity Press.
Lazerson, M., 1998, 'The Disappointments of Success: Higher Education after World War II', *The Annals of the American Academy of Political and Social Science* 559: 64–76.
Lazonick, W., and O'Sullivan, M., 2000, 'Maximizing Shareholder Value: A New Ideology for Corporate Governance', *Economy and Society* 29(1): 13–35
Le Bon, Gustave, 1960, *The Crowd: A Study of the Popular Mind*, New York: Viking.
Le Bon, G., 1895/2009, *Psychology of Crowds*, Zurich: International Relations and Security Network, https://www.files.ethz.ch/isn/125518/1414_LeBon.pdf.
Lee, J., 1998, 'Overseas Students in Britain: How Their Presence Was Politicised in 1966–1967', *Minerva* 36(4): 305–321.
Lefebvre, H., 1991, *The Production of Space*, Oxford: Blackwell.
Leftwich, A., 2004, *What Is Politics. The Activity and Its study,* Cambridge: Polity.
Leitenberg, M., 2006, 'Deaths in Wars and Conflicts in the 20th Century Cornell University Peace Studies Program', Occasional Paper #29 (3rd ed.), https://www.clingendael.org/sites/default/files/pdfs/20060800_cdsp_occ_leitenberg.pdf.
Lesko, N., 2001, *Act Your Age: A Cultural Construction of Adolescence*, New York: Routledge.
Levene, A., 2012, *The Childhood of the Poor: Welfare in Eighteenth-Century London*, Basingstoke: Palgrave Macmillan, 17.
Liebert, R., 1971, *Radical and Militant: A Psycho-analytic Inquiry*, New York: Praeger.
Linton, O., and Mahmoodzadeh, S., 2018, 'Implications of High-Frequency Trading for Security Markets', *Annual Review of Economics* 10: 237–259, https://www-annualreviews-org.ezproxy.lib.rmit.edu.au/doi/pdf/10.1146/annurev-economics-063016-104407.
Lipset, S.M. (ed.), 1967, *Student Politics*, New York: Basic Books, 97–123.
Lipset, S.M., 1971, *Rebellion in the University*, Chicago, IL: University of Chicago Press.
Lipset, S.M., and Wolin, S., 1965, *The Berkeley Student Revolt*, Garden City, NY: Anchor Books.
Lipsett, S., 1968, 'On the Politics of Conscience and Extreme Commitment', *Encounter* 31(August): 66–71.
Little, G., 1970, *The University Experience*, Melbourne: Melbourne University Press.
Livingstone, S., and Stoilova, M., 2020, 'Understanding Children Online: Theories, Concepts, Debates', *Children Online: Research and Evidence (CORE)*, London: London School of Economics, https://core-evidence.eu/understanding-children-online-theories-concepts-debates.
Lombroso-Ferrero, G., 1972, *Criminal Man According to the Classification of Cesare Lombroso*, Montclair, NJ: Patterson Smith. Original work published 1911.
Loring, B., 2005, *'Race' Is a Four-Letter Word: The Genesis of the Concept*, New York: Oxford University Press.
Lowe, D., 1982, *History of Bourgeois Perception*, Chicago, IL: University of Chicago.
Ludy, B., 2007, *A Brief History of Modern Psychology,*: New York: John Wiley.

Luecke, T., 2009, 'Blast from the Past: The Generation of 1914 and the Causes of World War III', Prepared for the Annual Conference of the American Political Science Association Toronto, Canada, 3–6 September 2009.

Luescher-Mamashela, Thierry M., 2015, 'Theorising Student Activism in and beyond the 20th Century: The Contribution of Philip G Altbach', in Klemenčič, M., Bergan, S., and Primožič, R., (eds.), *Student Engagement in Europe: Society, Higher Education and Student Governance: Council of Europe Higher Education Series No. 20*, Strasbourg: Council of Europe Publishing.

Lumley, K., 1998, 'Teeny Thugs in Blair's Sights: Media Portrayals of Children in Education and their Policy Implications', *Youth and Policy* 61: 1–11.

Luzzatto, S., 1997, 'Young Rebels and Revolutionaries, 1789–1917', in Levi, G., and Schmitt, J.C., (eds.), *A History of Young People*, Cambridge, MA: Belknap Press, 174–231.

Lynch, K., 1988, *Family, Class and Ideology in Early Industrial France: Social Policy and the Working-Class Family, 1825–1848*, Madison: The University of Wisconsin Press.

Macedo, S., (ed.), 1999, *Deliberative Politics: Essays on Democracy and Disagreement*, New York: Oxford University Press.

Macleod, E., 2013, 'British Spectators of the French Revolution: The View from Across the Channel', *The History Journal* 50(3): 377–392.

Macmillan, M., 2013, *The War That Ended Peace: How Europe Abandoned Peace for the First World War*, London: Profile Books.

Magarey, S., 1978, 'The Invention of Juvenile Delinquency in Early Nineteenth-Century England', *History* (34, May): 11–27.

Magarey, S., 1981, 'The Invention of Juvenile Delinquency in Early Nineteenth Century England', in Muncie, J., Hughes, G., and McLaughlin, E., (eds.), *Youth Justice: Critical Readings*, London: Sage, 115–123.

Manly, S., 2007, *Language, Custom and Nation in the 1790s: Locke, Tooke, Wordsworth, Edgeworth*, Aldershot: Ashgate.

Mannheim, K., 1952, 'The Problem of Generations', in Kecskemeti, P., (ed.), *Essays on the Sociology of Knowledge: Collected Works, V.5*, New York: Routledge, 276–322.

Manning, A., 1958, *The Bodgie: A Study in Psychological Abnormality*, Wellington: AH Reed.

Manning, N., 2010, 'Tensions in Young People's Conceptualisation and Practice of Politics', *Sociological Research Online* 15(4): 1–11.

Mason, P., 2017, *Postcapitalism: A Guide to Our Future*, London: Allen Lane.

Marcuse, H., 1964, *One-Dimensional Man: Studies in the Ideology of Advanced Industrial Society*, Boston, MA: Beacon Press.

Marcuse, H., 1967, *One Dimensional Man*, London: Sphere Books.

Marglin, S., and Schor, J., (eds.), 1992, *The Golden Age of Capitalism: Reinterpreting the Postwar Experience*, Oxford: Oxford University Press.

Martin, A., 2012, *Young People and Politics: Political Engagement in the Anglo-American Democracies*, New York: Routledge.

Marwick, A., 1998, *The Sixties: Cultural Revolution in Britain, France, Italy and the United States, c.1958– c.1974*, Oxford: Oxford University Press.

Marx, K., 1990, *The Eighteenth Brumaire of Louis Bonaparte*, trans. Dutt, C.P., New York: International.

Marx, K., and Engels, F., 1967, *The Communist Manifesto*, trans. Moore and Engels, Harmondsworth: Penguin.

Marx, W., 1977, *Introduction to Aristotle's Theory of Being as Being*, The Hague: Martinus Nijhoff.

Mastercard and Kaiser, 2019, *The Global Gig Economy: Capitalizing on a ~$500B Opportunity*, https://newsroom.mastercard.com/wp-content/uploads/2019/05/Gig-Economy-White-Paper-May-2019.pdf.
Matheson, L., 1980, *Still Learning*, Melbourne: Macmillan.
May, M., 1973, 'Innocence and Experience: The Evolution of the Concept of Juvenile Delinquency in the Mid-19th Century', *Victorian Studies* 17(1): 7–29.
Mayall, B., 2002, *Towards a Sociology for Childhood: Thinking from Children's Lives*, Buckingham: Open University Press.
Mayhew, T., 1851, *London Labour and the London Poor* (Volume 1), Dover, 469, 475, 476.
McAdam, D., 1988, *Freedom Summer*, New York: Oxford University Press.
McCallum, D., 1985, 'The Theory of Educational inequality in Australia 1900 1950', Ph.D. thesis, Melbourne: University of Melbourne.
McClelland, J., 1989, *The Crowd and the Mob: From Plato to Canetti*, London: Unwin.
McCloskey, D., 2006, *The Bourgeois Virtues: Ethics for an Age of Commerce*, Chicago, IL: University Chicago Press.
McCurties, E., 2011, 'Red Roots, Radical Fruit: Children of the Old Left in the Civil Rights Movement and the New Left', PhD thesis, Michigan: Michigan State University.
McDonald, J., 1951, 'The Bodgie', Unpublished BA (Hons) thesis, Sydney: University of Sydney.
McDonald, R., (ed.) 1997, *Youth, the Underclass and Social Exclusion*, London: Routledge.
McDonald, R., 2008, 'Disconnected Youth? Social Exclusion, the 'Underclass' & Economic Marginality', *SW&S* 6(2), https://www.socwork.net/sws/article/view/45/358.
McDonald, R., and Giazitzoglu, A., 2019, 'Youth, Enterprise and Precarity: Or, What Is, and What Is Wrong with, the "gig economy"?' *Journal of Sociology* 55(4): 724–740.
McDowell, L., 2002, 'Transitions to Work: Masculine Identities, Youth Inequality and Labour Market Change', *Gender, Place and Culture* 9(1): 39–59.
McRobbie, A., 1980, 'Settling Accounts with Subcultures: A Feminist Critique', *Screen Education* 34: 37–49.
McRobbie, A., 1984, 'Dance and Social Fantasy', in McRobbie, A., and Nava, M., (eds.), *Gender and Generation*, London: Macmillan, 130–161.
McRobbie, A., 1991, *Feminism and Youth Culture*, London: Macmillan.
Melkman, E., 2017, 'Childhood Adversity, Social Support Networks and Well-being among Youth Aging out of Care: An Exploratory Study of Mediation', *Child Abuse and Neglect* 72: 85–97.
Melleuish, G., 2015, 'Australian Politics in the Australian Journal of Political Science: A Review', *Australian Journal of Political Science* 50(4): 719–734.
Mellor, S., 1998, *'What's the Point?': Political Attitudes of Victorian Year 11students*, Camberwell: Australian Council for Educational Research.
Mellor, S., Kennedy, K., and Greenwood, L., 2002, *Citizenship and Democracy: Australian Students' Knowledge and Beliefs*, The IEA Civic Educational Study of Fourteen Year Olds, Melbourne: Australian Council for Educational Research.
Menga, F., 2017, 'Conflicts on the Threshold of Democratic Orders: A Critical Encounter with Mouffe's Theory of Agonistic Politics', *Jurisprudence* 8(3): 532–556.
Merelman, R., 1977, 'Moral Development and Potential Radicalism in Adolescence', *Youth and Society* 9(1): 29–54.
Merriman, J., 1991, *The Margins of City Life: Explorations on the French Urban Frontier, 1815–1851*, Oxford: Oxford University Press.

Mihai, M., McNay, L., Marchart, O., Norval, A., Paipais, V., Prozorov, S., and Thaler, M., 2017, 'Democracy, Critique and the Ontological Turn', *Contemporary Political Theory* 16(4): 501–531.

Milkman, R., Luce, S., and Lewis, P., 2013, *Changing the Subject: A Bottom-up Account of Occupy Wall Street in New York City*, New York: CUNY: The Murphy Institute.

Mill, J.S., 1846, *System of Logic, Ratiocinative and Inductive*, New York: Harper & Brothers.

Miller, D., 1995, *Blackwell Encyclopedia of Political Thought*, Oxford and Cambridge: Blackwell.

Miller, M., and Gilmore, S. (eds.), 1965, *Revolution at Berkley Adventurism of the 1960s Youth Culture*, New York: Dial.

Millin, S., 1917, 'Child Life as a National Asset', *Journal of the Statistical and Social Inquiry Society of Ireland* 13: 301–316.

Minton, H., 1988, *Lewis M. Terman*, New York: New York University Press.

Mintz, S., 2006, *Huck's Raft: A History of American Childhood*, Cambridge: Belknap.

Mirowski, P., 2019, Hell Is Truth Seen Too Late', *Boundary*, 2 February, 1–52, https://read.dukeupress.edu/boundary-2/article-pdf/46/1/1/559165/0460001.pdf.

Mischler, P., 1999, *Raising Reds: The Young Pioneers, Radical Summer Camps, and Communist Political Culture in the United States*, New York: Columbia University Press.

Mitchell, W., and Muysken, J., 2002, 'Why Aggregate Demand Matters for Understanding Unemployment', Centre of Full Employment and Equity Working Paper No. 02-01, March.

Mitterauer, M., 1992, *A History of Youth*, trans. Dunphy G., Oxford: Blackwell.

Mitzman, A., 1987, 'The Civilizing Offensive: Mentalities, High Culture and Individual Psyches', *Journal of Social History* 20(4): 663–687.

Mizen, P., 2003, *The Changing State of Youth*, Basingstoke: Palgrave.

Monkonnen, E., 1975, *The Dangerous Class: Crime and Poverty in Columbus, Ohio, 1860–1885*, Cambridge, MA: Harvard University Press.

Morabito, A., 2016, 'Report: Millennials Won't Meet the Average Standard of Living Until 2034', *Red Alert*, 17 August, http://redalertpolitics.com/2016/08/17/report-millennials-wont-meet-average-standard-living-2034/#fD4uSFjcvEb5e6TZ.99.

Moran, L., and Hall, A., 2011, 'British Youth Are 'the Most Unpleasant and Violent in the World': Damning Verdict of Writer as Globe Reacts to Riots', *Daily Mail*, 10th August 2011, http://www.dailymail.co.uk/news/article-2024486/UK-RIOTS-2011-British-youths-unpleasant-violent-world.html (accessed 3 March 2012).

More, H., 1799, *Strictures on the Modern System of Female Education* (7th ed., 2 volumes), London, i, 147.

More, H., 1809–1995, *Cœlebs in Search of a Wife*, Lewiston: Muller.

Morrison, S., 2018, 'Planned Student Strike for Climate Change Prompts PM's Call for 'More Learning, Less Activism' in Schools', *News.com.au*, 26 November 2018, https://www.news.com.au/video/id-5348771529001-5972440925001/planned-student-strike-for-climate-change-prompts-pms-call-for-more-learning-less-activism-in-schools (accessed 5 July 2019).

Morrissey, S., 2000, 'From Radicalism to Patriotism? Petersburg Students between Two Revolutions, 1905 and 1917', *Revolutionary Russia* 13: 2.

Moscovici, S., 1973, 'Foreword', in Herzlich, C., (ed.), *Health and Illness: A Social Psychological Analysis*, London: Academic Press, ix–xiv.

Moscovici, S., 1981, 'On Social Representations', in Forgas, J.P., (ed.), *Social Cognition: Perspectives on Everyday Understanding*, London: Academic Press, 181–209.

Moscovici, S., 1982, 'The Coming Era of Social Representations', in Codol, J.P., and Leyens, J.P., (eds.), *Cognitive Approaches to Social Behaviour*, The Hague: Nijhoff, 115–150.

Moscovici, S., 1984a, 'The Phenomenon of Social Representations', in Farr, R.M., and Moscovici, S., (eds.), *Social Representations*, Cambridge: Cambridge University Press, 3–69.

Moscovici, S., 1984b, 'The Myth of the Lonely Paradigm: A Rejoinder', *Social Research* 51(4): 939–967.

Moscovici, S., 1988, 'Notes towards the Description of Social Representations', *European Journal of Social Psychology* 18: 211–250.

Moscovici, S., 1989, 'Preface', in Jodelet, D., (ed.), *Folies et Representations Sociales*, Paris: Presses Universitaires de France.

Moscovici, S., 1990, 'Social Psychology and Developmental Psychology: Extending the Conversation', in Duveen, G., and Lloyd, B., (eds.), *Social Representations and the Development of Knowledge*, Cambridge: Cambridge University Press, 164–185.

Moscovici, S., 1993, 'Introductory Address', *Papers on Social Representations* 2(3): 160–170.

Moscovici, S., 1994, 'The Proof of the Pudding Is Still in the Eating', Paper Presented, Second International Conference on Social Representations, Rio de Janeiro.

Moscovici, S., 2000, *Social Representations: Explorations in Social Psychology*, ed. Duveen, G., Cambridge: Polity Press.

Moses, A., and Gardiner, S., 2011, 'LulzSec Hack into Murdoch's British Websites', *Sydney Morning Herald*, 19 July, www.smh.com.au/technology/technology- news/lulzsec-hack-into-murdochs-british-websites-20110719-1hm6r.html.

Moss, D., 2013, 'The Form of Children's Political Engagement in Everyday Life', *Children & Society* 27, 24–34.

Mouffe, C., 1993, *The Return of the Political*, London: Verso.

Mouffe, C., 2005, *On the Political*, London: Routledge.

Muggleton, D., 2005, 'From Classlessness to Club Culture', A Genealogy of Post-war British Youth Cultural Analysis', *Research on Youth and Youth Cultures* 13(2): 205–219, 10.1177/1103308805051322.

Mulcair, T., 2014, 'Prime Minister 'isn't an Entry Level Job,' Mulcair Says of Trudeau', *The Globe and Mail*, August, https://www.theglobeandmail.com/news/politics/prime-minister-isnt-an-entry-level-job-mulcair-says-of-trudeau/article20556381/).

Muller, A., (ed.), 2006, *Fashioning Childhood in the Eighteenth Century: Age and Identity*, Aldershot: Harvester, 43–52.

Müller, J-W., 2016, *What Is Populism?* Philadelphia: University of Pennsylvania.

Muncie, J., 2009, *Youth Crime* (3rd ed.), Los Angeles: Sage.

Murphy, K., 2015, 'In the Backblocks of Capitalism': Australian Student Activism in the Global 1960s', *Australian Historical Studies* 46(2): 252–268.

Nakata, S., 2008, 'Elizabeth Eckford's Appearance at Little Rock: The Possibility of Children's Political Agency', *Politics* 28(1): 19–25.

Nakata, S., 2015, *Childhood Citizenship, Governance and Policy: The Politics of Becoming Adult*, London: Routledge.

Nisbet, R., 1980, *History of the Idea of Progress*, New York: Basic Books.

Nolan, M., 2001, 'Opposition Machen Wir!' Youth and the Contestation of Civic and Political Legitimacy in Germany', *Childhood* 8(2): 293–312.

Norris, P., 1999, *Critical Citizens: Global Support for Democratic Governance*, Oxford: Oxford University Press.

Norris, P., 2002, *Democratic Phoenix: Reinventing Political Activism*, New York: Cambridge University Press.

Nussbaum, M., 2011, *Creating Capabilities: The Human Development Approach*, Cambridge: Belknap Press at Harvard University Press.

O'Brien, J., 1972, 'The Development of the New Left', in Altbach, P.G., and Laufer, R.S., (eds.), *The New Pilgrims: Youth Protest in Transition*, New York: David McKay, 32–45.

O'Connor, R., 1974, 'Political Activism and Moral Reasoning: Politics and Apolitical Students in Great Britain and France', *British Journal of Political Science* 4(January): 53–79.

O'Connor, S., 2001, *Orphan Trains: The Story of Charles Loring Brace and the Children He Saved and Failed*, Chicago, IL: University of Chicago.

O'Hanlon, S., and Luckins, T., (eds.) 2005, *Go! Melbourne in the Sixties*, Melbourne: Circa,

O'Higgins, N., 2001, *Youth Unemployment and Employment Policy a Global Perspective*, Geneva: ILO.

O'Malley, A., 2003, *The Making of the Modern Child: Children's Literature and Childhood in the Late Eighteenth Century*, London: Routledge.

Oberschall, A., 1973, *Social Conflict and Social Movements*, Prentice-Hall: Englewood Cliffs.

Ocasio-Cortes, A., 2020a, Alexandria Ocasio-Cortes @AOC 21 JUNE https://twitter.com/AOC/status/1274499021625794565.

Ocasio-Cortez, A., 2020b, cited in O'Sullivan, D., 2020, 'Trump's Campaign Was Trolled by TikTok Users in Tulsa', *CNN*, 21st June, https://edition.cnn.com/2020/06/21/politics/tiktok-trump-tulsa-rally/index.html.

Ockenden, J., 1985, 'Anti-War Movement and the Student Revolt at Monash: An Examination of Contending Ideologies' Honours thesis, Clayton: Monash University.

OECD, 1988a, *Meeting of the Manpower and Social Affairs Committee at the Ministerial Level*, Paris: OECD.

OECD, 1988b, *The Future of Social Protection*, OECD Social Policy Studies No. 6, Paris: OECD.

OECD, 1992, Press Release Meeting of the Employment, Labour and Social Affairs Committee at Ministerial Level Paris, 8th and 9th December 1992, http://www.oecd.org/officialdocuments/publicdisplaydocumentpdf/?cote=SG/PRESS(92)94&docLanguage=En.

OECD, 2006, 'Comparing the Pension Promises of 30 OECD Countries', ISSA 16 June, https://onlinelibrary.wiley.com/doi/abs/10.1111/j.1468-246X.2006.00247.x.

OECD, 2009, *Good Jobs for All in a Changing World of Work: The OECD Jobs Strategy*, Paris: OECD, https://www.oecd.org/employment/emp/long%20booklet_EN.pdf.

OECD, 2012, *Better Skills, Better Jobs, Better Lives*, Paris: OECD, http://www.oecd.org/education/imhe/IMHEinfos_Jult12_EN%20-%20web.pdf.

OECD, 2017, *Employment Outlook 2017*, Paris: OECD, http://www.oecd.org/employment-outlook.

OECD, 2019, *Pensions at a Glance 2019*, Paris: OECD, https://www.oecd-ilibrary.org/docserver/5ffa7926-en.pdf?expires=1589089648&id=id&accname=guest&checksum=5C44C25A2512AEC4AF1DD7752E641444.

Offer, D., 1969, *The Psychological World of the Teenager: A Study of Normal Adolescent Boys*, New York: Basic Books.

Offer, D., and Offer, J.L., 1975, *From Teenage to Young Manhood: A Psychological Study*, New York: Basic Books.

Oropeza, L., 2005, *Raza Si!, Guerra no!: Chicano Protest and Patriotism During the Vietnam War Era*, Los Angeles: UC Press.

Osler, A., and Starkey, H., 2005, *Changing Citizenship: Democracy and Inclusion in Education*, Maidenhead: Open University Press.

Palley, T., 1994, 'Debt, Aggregate Demand, and the Business Cycle: An Analysis in the Spirit of Kaldor and Minsky', *Journal of Post Keynesian Economics* 16: 371–390.

Palley, T., 2007, 'Financialization: What It Is and Why It Matters', *Political Economy Research Institute Working Paper Series* 153: 1–39.

Palti, E., 2011, 'Reinhart Koselleck: His Concept of the Concept and Neo-Kantianism', *Contributions to the History of Concepts* 6(2): 1–20.

Paris, P., 2018, 'Emboldened by March for Our Lives, Far-Left DC Council Considers Lowering Voting Age to 16', *Infowars*, 9 May 2018, https://www.infowars.com/emboldened-by-march-for-our-lives-far-left-dc-council-considers-lowering-voting-age-to-16 (accessed 5 July 2019).

Parker, I., 1989, *The Crisis in Modern Social Psychology: And How to End It*, London: Routledge.

Parker, L., 2019, 'Kids Suing Governments about Climate: It's a Global Trend', *National Geographic*, June https://www.nationalgeographic.com/environment/2019/06/kids-suing-governments-about-climate-growing-trend

Parkin, F., 1968, *Middle Class Radicalism*, Manchester: Manchester University Press, 46.

Patrick, M., and Trickel, E., 1997, *Orphan Trains to Missouri*, Columbia: University of Missouri Press.

Peacock, T., 2001, *The Letters of Thomas Love Peacock*, Joukovsky, O., (ed.) (2 volumes), Oxford: Oxford University Press, Vol i, 8–9.

Pearson, G., 1983, *Hooligans: A History of Respectable Fears*, London: Macmillan.

Pellowe, D., 2019, 'How the School Student Strike Reduces Kids to Puppets', 14 March, *Spectator Australia*, https://www.spectator.com.au/2019/03/how-the-school-student-strike-reduces-kids-to-puppets/.

Perez, C., 2018, 'School to Suspend Students Who Walked Out for Gun Protest', *New York Post*, 14 March 2018, https://nypost.com/2018/03/14/school-to-suspend-students-who-walked-out-for-gun-protest/ (accessed 5 July 2019).

Perry, M., 2017, 'Fortune 500 Firms 1955 v. 2017: Only 60 Remain, Thanks to the Creative Destruction that Fuels Economic Prosperity', *Carpe Diem*, https://www.aei.org/publication/fortune-500-firms-1955-v-2017-only-12-remain-thanks-to-the-creative-destruction-that-fuels-economic-prosperity.

Pertman, A., 2000, *Adoption Nation: How the Adoption Revolution Is Transforming America*, New York: Basic Books.

Peukert, D., 1993, *The Weimar Republic: The Crisis of Classical Modernity*, New York: Hill & Wang.

Phillips, D., 2003, 'Three Moral Entrepreneurs and the Creation of a Criminal Class in England 1790 1840', *Crime, Histories and Societies* 7(1): 79–107, https://journals.openedition.org/chs/612?lang=e.

Phillips, K., 1996, *Boiling Point: Democrats, Republicans, and the Decline of Middle-Class Prosperity*, New York: Random House.

Phillips, M., 2008, 'Paine, Thomas 1737–1809', *Oxford Dictionary of National Biography*, Oxford University Press, online edn, May.

Phipps, C., 2003, 'Children of the Revolution: Who Can Blame the Decision-makers of the Future for Taking to the Streets?', *Guardian*, 22 March, 20.

Piaget, J., 1932, *The Moral Judgment of the Child*, London: Kegan Paul, Trench and Trubner.

Piaget, J., 1932/1965, *The Moral Judgment of the Child*, New York: Free Press.

Piaget, J., 1940–1967, *The Mental Development of the Child, in Six Psychological Studies*, New York: Vintage Books.

Picini, J., 2013, 'A Whole New World: Global Revolution and Australian Social Movements in the Long Sixties', PhD thesis, Brisbane: University of Queensland.

Pick, D., 1989, *Faces of Degeneration: A European Disorder, c. 1848–c. 1918*, Cambridge: Cambridge University Press.

Pickard, S., 2017, *Young People re Generating Politics in Times of Crisis*, London: Palgrave Macmillan.

Pickard, S., 2019a, *Politics, Protest and Young People. Politics and Dissent in 21st Century Britain*, London: Palgrave Macmillan.

Pickard, S., 2019b, 'Young Environmental Activists Are Doing It Themselves', *Political Insight* 10(4): 4–7.

Pickard, S., and Bessant, J., 2018, France's *#Nuit Debout Social Movement: Young People Rising Up and Moral Emotions, Societies*, special issue: *Youth and Social and Political Action in a Time of Austerity*, 0–21. doi:10.3390/soc8040100 http://www.mdpi.com/journal/societies/special_issues/Youth_and_Social.

Picketty, T., 2014, *Capital in the Twenty First Century*, Harvard: Harvard University Press.

Picketty, T., 2020, *Capital and Ideology*, Trans Goldhammer, Arthur, Cambridge, MA: The Belknap Press of Harvard University.

Pietsch, R., 2004, 'Ships' Boys and Youth Culture in Eighteenth-Century Britain: The Navy Recruits of the London Marine Society', *The Northern Mariner/Le marin du nord*, XIV(4, October): 11–24.

Piketty, T., and Zucman, G., 2013, 'Capital Is Back: Wealth-Income Ratios in Rich Countries, 1700–2010. Data Appendix', 15 December 2013, http://piketty.pse.ens.fr/en/capitalisback.

Pinker, S., 2018, *Enlightenment Now: The Case for Reason, Science, Humanism and Progress*, New York: Viking.

Pitkin, H., 1998, *The Attack of the Blob: Hannah Arendt's Concept of the Social*, Chicago, IL: University of Chicago.

Plumb, J., 1975, 'The New World of Children in Eighteenth-Century England', *Past and Present* 67(May): 64–95.

Pocock, J., 1995, 'The Ideal of Citizenship since Classical Times', in Beiner, R., (ed.), *Theorizing Citizenship*, Albany: State University of New York Press.

Pohl, A., and Walther, A., 2007, 'Activating the Disadvantaged', *International Journal of Lifelong Education* 5: 533–553.

Pontusson, J., and Raess, D., 2012, 'How (and Why) Is This Time Different? The Politics of Economic Crisis in Western Europe and the United States', *Annual Review of Political Science* 15: 13–33.

Poovey, M., 1995, *Making a Social Body: British Cultural Formation, 1830–1864*, Chicago,IL: University of Chicago.

Powell, M., Smith, A., and Taylor, N., 2016, 'Rural Childhood in New Zealand: A Unique Site of Children's Agency and Social Participation', *Children Australia* 41(4): 275–284.

Powell, R., 2013, 'The Theoretical Concept of the 'Civilising Offensive' (*Beschavingsoffensief*): Notes on Its Origins and Uses', *Human Figurations* 2(2): 1–13. https://quod.lib.umich.edu/h/humfig/11217607.0002.203/--theoretical-concept-of-the-civilising-offensive?rgn=main;view=fulltext.

Prager, L., and Donovan, S., 2013, *Suicide by Security Blanket, and Other Stories from the Child Psychiatry Emergency Service: What Happens to Children with Acute Mental Illness*, New York: Praege.

Premo, B., 2005, *Children of the Father King: Youth, Authority, and Legal Minority in Colonial Lima*, Chapel Hill: The University of North Carolina Press.

Print, M., Saha, L., and Edwards, K., 2004, 'Youth Electoral Study _ Report 2: Youth Political Engagement and Voting', Australian Electoral Commission, Sydney.

Prout, A., 2000, 'Children's Participation: Control and Self-Realisation in British Late Modernity', *Children and Society* 14(4): 304–315.

Pujals, S., 2005, 'Fathers and Sons: The Politics and Culture of Generational Class War in Revolutionary Russia, 1918–1935', *Soviet and Post-Soviet Review* 32(2–3): 209–232.

Quiggin, J., 1999, 'Globalisation, Neoliberalism and Inequality in Australia', *The Economic and Labour Relations Review* 10(2): 240–259.

Quinn, J., 2017, *Young Ireland and the Writing of Irish History*, Dublin: University Dublin Press.

Radzinowicz, L., and Hood, R., 1986, *The Emergence of Penal Policy*, London: Steven's and Son.

Ragged School Union, 1857, *Thirteen Annual Report For The Ragged School Union*, London: Ragged School Union.

Rahikainen, M., 2004, *Centuries of Child Labour: European Experiences from the Seventeenth to the Twentieth Century*, Aldershot: Ashgate, 5–6.

Randers-Pehrson, J., 1999, *Germans and the Revolution of 1848–1849: New German-American Studies*, New York: Peter Lang.

Rayner, J., 2016, *Generation Less: How Australia Is Cheating the Young*, Melbourne: Redback Quarterly.

Real Democracy Movement, 2020, *Time's up for Neoliberalism: Manifesto for a Transition to a Real Democracy*, London: Lupus Books.

Reich, R., 1992, *The Work of Nations: Preparing Ourselves for 21st Century Capitalism*, New York: Vintage Books.

Reyna, V., and Farley, F., 2006, 'Risk and Rationality in Adolescent Decision Making: Implications for Theory, Practice, and Public Policy', *Psychological Science in the Public Interest* 7(1): 1–44.

Richey, S., 2003, *Joan of Arc: The Warrior Saint*, Westport, CT: Praeger.

Riddell, M., 2011, 'London Riots: The Underclass Lashes Out', *The Telegraph*, 8th August 2011, http://www.telegraph.co.uk/news/uknews/law-and-order/8630533/Riots-the-underclass-lashes-out.html (accessed 3 March 2012).

Rifkin, J., 1995, *The End of Work*, New York: Putman Publishing Group.

Riots Communities and Victims Panel, 2012, *After the Riots: The Final Report of the Riot Communities and Victims Panel*, http://riotspanel.independent.gov.uk/wp-content/uploads/2012/03/Riots-Panel-Final-Report1.pdf.

Ritchie, G., 1973, 'The Rhetoric of American Studies in Protest during the 1960s: A Study in Ends and Means', PhD thesis, Philadelphia: Temple University.

Roberts, D., 2008, 'The Legend Turns Fifty, Inside Story', 27th November, https://insidestory.org.au/the-legend-turns-fifty/.

Robins, D., 2005, 'Melbourne's Maoists: The Rise of the Monash University Labor Club, 1965–1967', Honours thesis, St Albans: Victoria University.

Roche, J., 1999, 'Children: Rights, Participation and Citizenship', *Childhood* 6(4): 475–493.

Ronald, D., 2015, *Youth, Heroism and War Propaganda: Britain and the Young Maritime Hero, 1745–1820*, London: Bloomsbury Academic.

Rooke, M., 1971, *Anarchy and Apathy: Student Unrest 1968–1970*, London: Hamish Hamilton.

Rootes, C., 1988, 'The Development of Radical Student Movements and Their Sequelae', *Australian Journal of Politics and History* 34(2): 173–186.

Rorabaugh, W., 1989, *Berkeley at War: The 1960s*, Oxford: Oxford University Press.

Rorty, R., 1980, *Philosophy and the Mirror Image*, Princeton, NJ: Princeton University Press.
Rose, L., 1991, *The Erosion of Childhood Child Oppression in Britain 1860–1918*, London: Routledge.
Roseman, M., 1995, *Generations in Conflict: Youth Revolt and Generation Formation in Germany 1770–1968*, Cambridge: Cambridge University Press.
Rosenbrier, G., 1971, 'An Historical Analysis of Student Unrest', PhD Thesis, Boston: Boston University.
Rosenfeld, S., 2013, *Subversives: The FBI's War on Student Radicals and Reagans Rose to Power*, New York: Farrar, Straus and Giroux.
Ross, D., 1991, *The Origins of American Social Science*, Cambridge: Cambridge University Press.
Rothman, D., 1971, 'Documents in Search of a Historian: Toward a History of Children and Youth in America', *Journal of Interdisciplinary History* 2: 367.
Rousseau, J.J., 1979, *Emile or On Education*, New York: Basic Books.
Rowse, T., 1978, *Australian Liberalism and National Character*, Melbourne: Kibble Books.
Roxburgh, N., 2018, 'Five Programs to Help Young People Become Job Creators', *FYA*, https://www.fya.org.au/2018/07/13/5-programs-helping-young-people-become-job-creators.
Rubenstein, B., and Levitt, M., 1969, 'The Student Revolt: Totem and Taboo Revisited', Burton Lecture on Moral Education, Paper Delivered at American Orthopsychiatry Meeting, New York, March 31.
Rubtsova, A., and Dowd, T., 2004, 'Cultural Capital as a Multi-level Concept: The Case of an Advertising Agency', *Legitimacy Processes in Organizations Research: In the Sociology of Organizations* 22: 117–146.
Rury, J., and Hill, S., 2012, *The African-American Struggle for Secondary Schooling, 1940–1980: Closing the Graduation Gap*, New York: Teachers College Press.
Rury, J., and Hill, S., 2013, 'An End of Innocence: African-American High School Protest in the 1960s and 1970s', *Journal of the History of Education Society* 42(4): 468–508.
Russell, L., 1999, 'Today the Students, Tomorrow the Workers! Radical Student Politics and the Australian Labour Movement 1960–1972', PhD thesis, Sydney: University of Technology.
Rutter, M., Giller, H., and Hagill, A., 1998, *Antisocial Behaviour by Young People*, Cambridge: Cambridge University Press.
Saha, L., Edwards, K., Print, M., 2007, *Youth Electoral Study – Report 4: Youth, Political Parties and the Intention to Vote*, http://www.aec.gov.au/About_AEC/Publications/youth_study/index.htm.
Salter, C., 2014, 'Activism as Terrorism: The Green Scare, Radical Environmentalism and Governmentality', *Anarchist Developments in Cultural Studies* 1: 211–238.
Sanderson, E., 2019, 'Youth Transitions to Employment: Longitudinal Evidence from Marginalised Young People in England', *Journal of Youth Studies*, DOI: 10.1080/13676261.2019.1671581.
Sassen, S., 2014, *Expulsions: Brutality and Complexity in the Global Economy*, Cambridge, MA: Harvard University Press.
Savage, J., 2007, *Teenage: The Creation of Youth Culture*, London: Chatto and Windus.
Savio, M., 1965a, 'Introduction', in Draper, H., (ed.), *Berkeley: The New Student Revolt*, New York: Grove Press, 1–8.
Savio, M., 1965b, 'An End to History', in Lipset, S., and Wolin, S., (eds.), *The Berkeley Student Revolt*, Garden City, NY: Anchor Books, 533–551.

Sawyer, M., 2013, 'What Is Financialization?' *International Journal of Political Economy* 42(4): 5–18.

Scalmer, S., 2002, *Dissent Events: Protest, the Media and the Political Gimmick in Australia*, Sydney: UNSW Press.

Scalmer, S., 2011, *Gandhi in the West: The Mahatma and the Rise of Radical Protest*, Cambridge: Cambridge University Press.

Schama, D., 1989, *Citizens: A Chronicle of the French Revolution*, New York: Knopf.

Scheu, J., 2011, 'Dangerous Classes: Tracing Back an Epistemological Fear', *Distinktion: Scandinavian Journal of Social Theory* 12(2): 115–134.

Schindler, N., 1997, 'Guardians of Disorder: Ritual of Youthful Culture at the Dawn of the Modern Age', in Levi, G., and Schmitt, J., (eds.), *A History of Young People* (Volume 1). Trans. Nash, C., Cambridge, MA: Belknap Press of Harvard University Press, 24–282.

Schmidt, J., 2020, 'The German Labour Movement, 1830s–1840s: Early Efforts at Political Transnationalism', *Journal of Ethnic and Migration Studies*, 46(6): 1025–1039. https://doi.org/10.1080/1369183X.2018.1554283 1–15.

Schmidt, S., 2020, cited in O'sullivan, D., 2020, 'Trump's Campaign Was Trolled by TikTok Users in Tulsa', *CNN*, 21 June, https://edition.cnn.com/2020/06/21/politics/tiktok-trump-tulsa-rally/index.html.

Schmitt, C., 1988, *The Crisis of Parliamentary Democracy*, trans. Kennedy, E., Cambridge: MIT Press.

Schmitter, P., 2016, *Politics as a Science (aka politology)*, Central European University, https://www.eui.eu/Documents/DepartmentsCentres/SPS/Profiles/Schmitter/Politics-as-a-science.pdf.

Schnapp, A., and Vidal-Naquet, P., (eds.), 1971, *The French Student Uprising: November 1967–June 1968*, trans. Jolas, M., Boston, MA: Beacon Press.

Schroeder, W., 2016, 'Germany's Industry 4/0 Strategy: Rhine Capitalism in the Age of Digitalisation,' London: The Friedrich-Ebert-Stiftung Foundation, http://www.feslondon.org.uk/cms/files/fes/css/FES-London_Schroeder_Germanys%20Industrie%204.0%20Strategy.pdf.

Schumpeter, J., 1943, *Capitalism, Socialism and Democracy*, London: Routledge.

Schwab, K., 2016, 'The Fourth Industrial Revolution: What it Means, How to Respond', *WEF*, https://www.weforum.org/agenda/2016/01/the-fourth-industrial-revolution-what-it-means-and-how-to-respond.

Scott, E., 2019, 'Response to Greta Thunberg Is a Reminder That No Trump Critic Is Immune from Attacks by President's Supporters', *Washington Post*, 23 September, https://www.washingtonpost.com/politics/2019/09/24/response-greta-thunberg-is-reminder-that-no-trump-critic-is-immune-attacks-by-presidents-supporters/.

Scott-Kemmis, D., 2017, *The Role of VET in the Entrepreneurial Ecosystem*, NCVER Report. NCVER.

SDS, 1962, *The Port Huron Statement*, http://www.progressivefox.com/misc_documents/PortHuronStatement.pdf.

Sears, E., 1986, *The Ages of Man: Medieval Interpretations of the Life Cycle*, Princeton, NJ: Princeton Legacy Library.

Seidman, M., 2004, *The Imaginary Revolution: Parisian Students and Workers in 1968*, New York: Berghahn Books, 2004.

Sen, A., 1999, *Development as Freedom*, New York: Random House.

Sen, A., 2009, *The Idea of Justice*, Cambridge, MA: The Belknap Press of Harvard University Press.

Sercombe, H., 1996, 'Naming Youth the Construction of the Youth Category', Doctor of Philosophy, Murdoch University, Western Australia.

Serres, M., 2015, *Times of Crisis: What the Financial Crisis Revealed and How to Reinvent Our Lives and Future*, New York: Bloomsbury.
Shapiro, I., 1999, *Democratic Justice*, New Haven: Yale University Press.
Shapiro, I., 2016, *Politics Against Domination*, Cambridge, MA: Belknap Press.
Shapiro, L., 1985, 'Beginning the Exploration: Taking Over the Family Business', in Kaplan, J., and Shapiro, L., (eds.), *Red Diaper Babies: Children of the Left*, Washington, DC: Red Diaper Productions, 1–11.
Sheleff, L., 1976, 'Beyond the Oedipus Complex', *Theory and Society* 3(1, Spring): 1–44.
Shildrick, T., and Rucell, J., 2016, *Sociological Perspectives on Poverty*, London: Joseph Rowntree Foundation.
Shildrick, T., MacDonald, R., Webster, C., and Garthwaite, K., 2012, *Poverty, and Insecurity: Life in Low-Pay, No Pay Britain*, Bristol: Policy Press.
Shore, H., 2011, 'Inventing and Re-Inventing the Juvenile Delinquent in British History', *Memoria y Civilización* 14: 105–132.
Siebert, H., 'Labor Market Rigidities: At the Root of Unemployment in Europe', *Journal of Economic Perspectives* 11(3): 37–54.
Sieyes, E., 2003, *Political Writings: Including the Debate between Sieyes and Tom Paine in 1971*, ed. and trans. Sonenscher, M., Cambridge: Hackett Publishing.
Silva, D., 2020, 'Mother of George Floyd's Daughter: 'He Will Never See Her Grow Up'', *Today*, NBC, 3 June, https://www.today.com/news/mother-george-floyd-s-daughter-he-will-never-see-her-t183081.
Skinner, Q., 2002, *Visions of Politics:* Vol I: *Regarding Method*, Cambridge: Cambridge University Press.
Slezak, M., and Sadler, R., 2020, 'Australian Government Sued by 23-year-old Melbourne Student over Financial Risks of Climate Change', *ABC News*, 22 July, https://www.abc.net.au/news/2020-07-22/student-sues-australian-government-over-climate-change/12480612.
Sloam, J., 2016, 'Diversity and Voice: The Political Participation of Young People in the European Union', *British Journal of Politics & International Relations* 18(3): 521–537.
Sloam, J., and Henn, M., 2018, *Youth Quake 2017: The Rise of Young Cosmopolitans in Britain*, Basingstoke: Palgrave Macmillan.
Slobbe, J., and Verberkt, S., 2012, 'Hacktivists: Cyberterrorists or Online Activists? An Exploration of the Digital Right to Assembly', v.org/pdf/1208.4568.pdf.
Smelser, N., 1962, *Theory of Collective Behavior*, London: Routledge and Kegan Paul.
Smelser, N., 1968, *Essays in Social Explanation*, Englewood Cliffs: Prentice Hall.
Smith, K., 2011, 'Producing Governable Subjects: Images of Childhood Old and New', *Childhood* 19(1): 24–37.
Snricek, N., and Williams, A., 2015, *Inventing the Future: Postcapitalism and a World without Work*, London: Verso.
Soboul, A., 1980, *The Sans Culottes: The Popular Movement and Revolutionary Government, 1793–1794*, Princeton, NJ: Princeton University Press.
Social Exclusion Unit, 1998, *Bringing Britain Together: A National Strategy for Neighbourhood Renewal*, London: Social Exclusion Unit.
Solomon, C., and Palmieri, T., (eds.), 2011, *Springtime: The New Student Rebellions*, London: Verso.
Solow, R., 1957, 'Technical Change and the Aggregate Production Function', *Review of Economics and Statistics* 39: 312–320.
Sorin, R., and Galloway, G., 2006, 'Constructs of Childhood: Constructs of Self', *Children Australia* 31(2): 12–21.
Souter, G., 1968, *Sydney Observed*, Sydney: Brio.

Spearman, C., 1904, '"General intelligence" Objectively Determined and Measured', *American Journal of Psychology* 15: 201–293.
Stachura, P., 1975, *Nazi Youth in the Weimar Republic*, Oxford: Clio Books,
Stachura, P., 1981, *The German Youth Movement 1900–1945*, New York: St. Martin's Press.
Stallybrass, P., 1990, 'Marx and Heterogeneity: Thinking the Lumpenproletariat', *Representations* 31: 69–95.
Standing, G., 2011, *The Precariat: The New Dangerous Class*, New York: Bloomsbury.
Standing, G., 2014, *A Precariat Charter: From Denizens to Citizens*, London: Bloomsbury Academic.
Stanton, K., 2019 'Waging a Legal Battle on Climate Change', University of Melbourne, https://law.unimelb.edu.au/alumni/mls-news/issue-21-june-2019/waging-a-legal-battleon-climate-change?fbclid=IwAR1XOtTnw1TqEIKqIxhTa59NBeuC9kO0EiKZuist3GSSaF8GVG1Y9BKDnU.
Statista, 2019, *Number of Listed Companies on Stock Exchanges in the Americas 2018*, https://www.statista.com/statistics/265285/number-of-listed-companies-on-stock-exchange-in-the-americas/.
Stavrakakis, Y., 1999, *Lacan and the Political*, London and New York: Routledge.
Steedman, P., 2019, 'Security Services – Then and Now', *Counterculture Studies* 2(1): 155–157.
Steidl, A., 2007, 'Silk Weaver and Purse Maker Apprentices in Eighteenth- and Nineteenth-Century Vienna', in De Munck, B., Kaplan, S.L., and Soly, H., (eds.), *Learning on the Shop Floor*, New York: Berghahn.
Steinberg, L., 2007, 'Risk Taking in Adolescence: New Perspectives From Brain and Behavioral Science', *Current Directions in Psychological Science* 16(2): 55–59.
Stepan, N., 1982, *The Idea of Race in Science: Great Britain 1800–1960*, London: Macmillan.
Stewart, W., and McCann, W., 1967, *The Educational Innovators, 1750–1880*, London: Palgrave, chap. 2.
Stigler, S.M., 1986, *The History of Statistics*, Cambridge, MA: Harvard University Press.
Stokes, B., 2015, 'Who Are Europe's Millennials?' Pew Research Center. March ww.pewresearch.org/fact-tank/2015/02/09/who-are-europes-millennials/.
Stone, L., 1977, *The Family, Sex, and Marriage in England, 1500–1800*, New York: Harper and Row.
Stone, L., 1981, 'Family History in the 1980s: Past Achievements and Future Trends', *Journal of Interdisciplinary History* 12: 69.
Stout, J., 1965, 'On University Appointments: Thoughts after Knopfelmacher', *Minerva* 4(1): 55–72.
Stout, R., 1970, 'A Study of Alienation on Three Diverse Ohio College Campuses', PhD thesis, Bowling Green: State University Ohio.
Stout, R, 1971, *A Study of Alienation in Three Diverse Ohio College Campuses*, Dissertation Abstracts International 31(11–12).
Stratton, J., 1984, 'Bodgies and Widgies in the 1950s', *Journal of Australian Studies* 8(15): 10–24.
Stratton, J., 1989, 'Beyond Art: Postmodernism and the Case of Popular music', *Theory, Culture and Society* 6(2): 41–53.
Stratton, J., 1992, *The Young Ones*, Perth: Black Swan.
Streeck, W., 2016, *The Future of Capitalism*, London: Verso.
Such, E., and Walker, R., 2003, 'Being Responsible and Responsible Beings: A Study of Children's Understandings of Responsibility', *Children and Society* 17(4): 1–12.

Such, E., Walker, O., and Walker, R., 2005, 'Anti-war Children: Representation of Youth Protests against the Second Iraq War in the British National Press', *Childhood* 12(3): 301–326.

Sukarieh, M., and Tannock, S., 2016, 'On the Political Economy of Youth: A Comment', *Journal of Youth Studies* 19(9): 1281–1289.

Sukarieh, M., and Tannock, S., 2014, *Youth Rising: The Politics of Youth in the Global Economy*, Abingdon: Routledge.

Sullivan, S., and Tuana, N., 2007, *Race and the Epistemologies of Ignorance*, Albany: SUNY Press.

Susskind, R., and Susskind, D., 2015, *The Future of the Professions: How Technology Will Transform the Work of Humans and Experts*, Oxford: Oxford University Press.

Sweet, M., 2018, 'As All Roads Lead to #COP24, it Is the Children Who Provide Leadership', *Croakey*, 3 December, https://croakey.org/as-all-roads-lead-to-cop24-it-is-the-children-who-provide-leadership.

Taleb, N.N., 2007, *The Black Swan: The Impact of the Highly Improbable* (2nd ed.), London and New York: Penguin.

Task Force on Employment Opportunities, 1994, *Restoring Full Employment*, Canberra: AGPS.

Tavan, G., 2018, *The Conversation*, 15th September, https://theconversation.com/outrage-over-schoolgirl-refusing-to-stand-for-anthem-shows-rise-of-aggressive-nationalism-103160.

Taylor, C., 1994, 'The Politics of Recognition', in Gutmann, A., (ed.), *Multiculturalism: Examining the Politics of Recognition*, Princeton, NJ: Princeton University Press, 25–73.

Taylor, cited in McLymore, A., and Wang, E., 2020, 'TikTok Has Its Arab Spring Moment as Teen Activism Overtakes Dance Moves', *Reuters*, 3 June, https://www.reuters.com/article/us-minneapolis-police-tiktok-idUSKBN2392WX.

Tchir, T., 2017, *Hannah Arendt's Theory of Political Action Daimonic Disclosure of the 'Who*, London: Palgrave Macmillan.

Tehan, D., 2019, 'Australian Federal Minister for Education Minister 2019', cited in Bye, C., 2019, 'Hardcore Climate Change Activists Coach Children on How to Orchestrate Massive School Walkout', *Daily Telegraph*, 18 February.

Tenison Woods, M., 1937, *Juvenile Delinquency: With Special References to Institutional Treatment*, Melbourne: Melbourne University Press.

Terman, L., 1919, *The Measurement of Intelligence*, London: Harrap.

Thapar, A., Collishaw, S., and Pine, D., 2012, 'Depression in Adolescence', *The Lancet* 379(9820): 1056–1067.

The Army Children Archive, 2020, http://www.archhistory.co.uk/taca/history.html.

Thomas, N., 1996, 'The British Student Movement 1965–1972', PhD thesis, Warwick: Warwick University.

Thomas, N., 2002, 'Challenging Myths of the 1960s: The Case of Student Protest in Britain', *Twentieth Century British History* 13(3): 277–297.

Thomas, T., 2018, 'Young Minds Filled with Green Mush', *Quadrant*, 6 December 2018, https://quadrant.org.au/opinion/doomed-planet/2018/12/young-minds-filled-with-toxic-green-mush (accessed 5 July 2019).

Thompson, R., 2011, 'Individualisation and Social Exclusion: The Case of Young People not in Education, Employment or Training', *Oxford Review of Education* 37(6): 785–802.

Threadgold, S., 2019, 'Figures of Youth: On the Very Object of Youth Studies', *Journal of Youth Studies* 23(6): 686–701, https://www-tandfonline-com.ezproxy.lib.rmit.edu.au/doi/pdf/10.1080/13676261.2019.1636014?needAccess=true.

Thunberg, G., 2018, @GretaThunberg 26 November 2018, https://twitter.com/gretathunberg/status/1066943533037363200?lang=en.

Thunberg, G., 2019a, Speech at the United Nations, 23 September https://www.npr.org/2019/09/23/763452863/transcript-greta-thunbergs-speech-at-the-u-n-climate-action-summit.

Thunberg, G., 2019b, Transcript: Greta Thunberg's Speech at the UN Climate Action Summit, September 2019,https://www.npr.org/2019/09/23/763452863/transcript-greta-thunbergs-speech-at-the-u-n-climate-action-summit.

Timeline, 2018, 'The 1968 Student Walkout that Galvanized a National Movement for Chicano Rights', https://timeline.com/the-1968-student-walkout-that-galvanized-a-national-movement-for-chicano-rights-1294f1f4508c.

Tobias, J., 1967, *Crime in Industrial Society in the Nineteenth Century*, New York: Schocken Books.

Tognini, G., 2019, 'Gemma Tognini: Kids Are Being Used as Pawns in Climate Wars', *The Western Australian*, 13 March 2019, https://thewest.com.au/opinion/gemma-tognini/gemma-tognini-kids-are-being-used-as-pawns-in-climate-wars-ng-b881132559z.

Tooze, A., 2015, *The Deluge: The Great War, America and the Remaking of the Global Order, 1916–1931*, New York: Random House.

Tort, C., 2008, 'A Schizophrenic yet Useful Monograph on Infanticide', *Journal of Psychohistory* 36(2): 186–189.

Toulalan, S., 2013, 'Child Sexual Abuse in Late Seventeenth and Eighteenth-Century London: Rape, Sexual Assault and the Denial of Agency', in Goose, N., and Honeyman, K., (eds.), *Childhood and Child Labour in Industrial England: Diversity and Agency, 1750–1914*, Farnham: Ashgate, 23–44.

Toumbourou, J., Kypri, K., Jones, S., and Hickie, B., 2014, 'Should the Legal Age Alcohol Purchase be Raised to 21?' *Medical Journal of Australia*, 200(10): 568–570.

Trometter, A., 2013, '"The Fire in the Belly": Aboriginal Black Power and the Rise of the Australian Black Panther Party, 1967–1972', PhD thesis, University of Melbourne.

Trump, D., 2019, @realDonaldTrump 12 December, https://twitter.com/realdonaldtrump/status/1205100602025545730?s=12 13 December.

Tuck, R., 2016, *The Sleeping Sovereign*, Cambridge: Cambridge University Press.

Tully, J., 1995, *Strange Multiplicity: Constitutionalism in an Age of Diversity*, Cambridge: Cambridge University Press.

Tully, J., 2008, *Public Philosophy in a New Key Vol.1 Democracy and Civic Freedom*, Cambridge: Cambridge University Press.

Turban, E., Lediner, D., McLean, E., and Wetherbe, J., 2007, *Information Technology for Management: Transforming Organisations in the Digital Economy*, Hoboken, NJ: Wiley & Sons.

Turner, R., and Killian, L., 1972, *Collective Behaviour* (2nd ed.), Englewood Cliffs, NJ: Pren.

UN Development of Economic and Social Affairs, 2017, Frontier Issues, 31 July, https://www.un.org/development/desa/dpad/wp-content/uploads/sites/45/publication/2017_Aug_Frontier-Issues-1.pdf.

Unger, R., 2014, *The Religion of Future*, Cambridge, MA: Harvard University Press.

Uphof, N., 1989, 'Distinguishing Power, Authority & Legitimacy: Taking Max Weber at His Word by Using Resources-Exchange Analysis', *Polity* 22(2): 295–322.

van Dijk, T., 2013, 'Ideology and Discourse', in Freeden, M., and Stears, M., (eds.), *Oxford Handbook of Political Ideologies*, Oxford: Oxford University Press, 175–196.

Van Ginkel, R., 1996, 'A Dutch Sodom and Gomorrah: Degenerates, Moralists and Authority in Yerseke, 1870–1914', *Crime, Law and Social Change* 24: 223–239.

Van Krieken, R., 1999, 'The Barbarism of Civilization: Cultural Genocide and the "Stolen Generations",', *British Journal of Sociology* 50(2): 297–315.

van Stekelenburg, J., and Teodora Gaidyte, T., 2019, 'The Netherlands', in Wahlström, Mattias, Kocyba Piotr, De Vydt Michiel and de Moor Joost, (eds.), *Protest for a Future: Composition, Mobilization and Motives of the Participants in Fridays For Future Climate Protests on 15 March, 2019 in 13 European Cities*, 53–67, http://eprints.keele.ac.uk/6536/1/Protest%20for%20a%20future_GCS%2015.03.19%20Descriptive%20Report-2.pdf.

Vandenberghe, F., 2001, 'From Structuralism to Culturalism: Ernst Cassirer's Philosophy of Symbolic Forms', *European Journal of Social Theory* 4(4): 479–497, https://doi.org/10.1177/13684310122225271.

Varon, J., 2004, *Bringing the War Home: The Weather Underground, the Red Army Faction, and Revolutionary Violence in the Sixties and Seventies*, Berkeley: University of California Press,

Verrips, K., 1987, 'Noblemen, Farmers and Labourers: A Civilizing Offensive in a Dutch Village', *Netherlands Journal of Sociology* 23(1): 3–17.

Vinen, R., 2018, *The Long '68: Radical Protest and Its Enemies*, London: Allen Lane.

Vromen, A., 2003, 'People Try to Put Us Down…: Participatory Citizenship of "Generation X"', *Australian Journal Political Science* 38(1): 79–99.

Vromen, A., 2007, 'Australian Young People's Participatory Practices and Internet Use', *Information Communication and Society* 10(1): 48–68.

Vromen, A., and Collin, P., 2010, 'Everyday Youth Participation? Contrasting Views from Australian Policymakers and Young People', *Young* 18(1): 97–112.

Wahlström, M., Kocyba, P., De Vydt, M., and de Moor, J., (eds.) 2019, *Protest for a Future: Composition, Mobilization and Motives of the Participants in Fridays for Future Climate Protests on 15 March, 2019 in 13 European Cities*, http://eprints.keele.ac.uk/6536/1/Protest%20for%20a%20future_GCS%2015.03.19%20Descriptive%20Report-2.pdf.

Walkerdine, V., and Lucey, H., 1989, *Democracy in the Kitchen: Regulating Mothers and Socialising Daughters*, London: Virago.

Wallerstein, I., 1974, 'The Rise and Future Demise of the World Capitalist System: Concepts for Comparative', *Comparative Studies in Society and History* 16(4, Sep): 387–415.

Wallerstein, I., 2014, 'Keynote Address Delivered at the 38th Annual Political Economy of the World-System Conference', April 10, Pittsburgh, Pennsylvania, 158–172.

Wallerstein, I., Collins, R., Mann, M., Derluguian, G., and Calhoun, C., 2013, *Does Capitalism Have a Future?* Oxford: Oxford University Press.

Wallis, P., Webb, C., and Minns, C., 2009, *Leaving Home and Entering Service: The Age of Apprenticeship in Early Modern London*, Department of Economic History London School of Economics.

Walvin, J., 1982, *A Child's World: A Social History of English Childhood 1800–1914*, London: Pelican.

Wardley, L., 2019, 'The Biopolitics of Feeling: Race, Sex, and Science in the Nineteenth Century', *Nineteenth Century Contexts* 41(1): 109–112.

Warner, J., 2018, 'High-frequency Trading Explained: Why Has It Decreased?' *IG*, 18 October, https://www.ig.com/au/trading-strategies/high-frequency-trading-explained--why-has-it-decreased--181010.

Waters, C., Zalasiewicz, J., Summerhayes, C., Barnosky, A., Poirier, C., Gałuszka, A., Cearreta, A., Edgeworth, M., Ellis, E., Ellis, M., Jeandel, C., Leinfelder, R., McNeill, R., Richter, D., Steffen, W., Syvitski, J., Vidas, D., Wagreich, M., Williams, M., Zhisheng, A., Grinevald, J., Odada, E., Oreskes, N., and Wolfe, A., 2016, 'The Anthropocene Is Functionally and Stratigraphically Distinct from the Holocene',

Science 351(6269), https://science-sciencemag-org.ezproxy.lib.rmit.edu.au/content/sci/351/6269/aad2622.full.pdf.

Watts, R., 1987, *The Foundations of the National Welfare State*, St Leonards: Allen and Unwin.

Watts, R., 2021, 'Theorizing Student Protest Action', in Bessant, J., Mejia Mesinas, A., and Pickard, S., (eds.), *When Students Protest: Secondary and High Schools* (Volume 1), Rowman and Littlefield in press, Lanham, MD.

Weber, M., 1947, *The Theory of Social and Economic Organization*, trans. Henderson, A.M., and Parsons, T., New York: Oxford University Press.

Webster, S., 2015, 'Protest Activity in the British Student Movement, 1945 to 2011', Unpublished PhD thesis, Manchester: University of Manchester.

Weissbach, L., 1989, *Child Labor Reform in Nineteenth-Century France: Assuring the Future Harvest*, Baton Rouge: Louisiana State University Press.

West, A., 1999, 'They Make Us Out to Be Monsters: Images of Children and Young People in Care', in Franklin, B., (ed.), *Social Policy, the Media and Misrepresentation*, London: Routledge, 253–267.

Whitaker, R., 2002, *Mad in America: Bad Science, Bad Medicine, and the Enduring Mistreatment of the Mentally Ill*, New York: Perseus Books.

White, J., 2006, *Intelligence, Destiny and Education: The Ideological Roots of Intelligence Testing*, London: Routledge.

Whitwell, G., 1986, *The Treasury Line*, Sydney: Allen & Unwin.

Wike, R., and Castillo, A., 2018, 'Many around the World Are Disengaged from Politics, Pew Research Center's Global Attitudes Project, https://www.pewresearch.org/global/2018/10/17/international-political-engagement/.

Wilson, D., and Lyons, L., 2012, *Anxious Kids, Anxious Parents*, Philadelphia, PA and Florida: Health Communications, Deerfield Beach.

Wilson, J., Thomson, A., and McMahon, A., (eds.) 1996, Statement of the Accord, 1983, *The Australian Welfare State: Key Documents and Themes*, Melbourne: Macmillan Education.

Wohl, R., 1979, *The Generation of 1914*, Cambridge, MA: Harvard University Press.

Wood, S., 2017, *Dissent: The Student Press in 1960s Australia*, Melbourne: Scribe.

Wooden, M., 1996, 'The Youth Labour Market: Characteristics and Trends', *Australian Bulletin of Labour* 22(2): 137–160.

Woodley, S., 2009, '"Oh Miserable and Most Ruinous Measure": The Debate between Private and Public Education in Britain, 1760– 1800', in Hilton, M., and Shefrin, J., (eds.), *Educating the Child in Enlightenment Britain: Beliefs, Cultures, Practices*, Farnham.

Woodman, C., 2017, 'Red Warwick versus Warwick University Plc: The Political Economy of Higher Education and Student Protest', https://connorwoodman709698973.files.wordpress.com/2018/02/red-warwick-versus-warwick-university-plc-the-political-economy-of-higher-education-and-student-protest.pdf.

Woodman, D., 2012, 'The Rise of the Temporal Precariat: Conceptualising Inequality among Young People in the Context of Labour-Market Change', TASA Conference https://tasa.org.au/wp-content/uploads/2012/11/Woodman-Dan1.pdfnference.

Woodman, D., and Wyn, J., 2014, *Youth and Generation: Rethinking Change and Inequality in the Lives of Young People*, London: Sage.

Wordsworth, W., 1959, *The Prelude: 1799, 1805, 1850*, New York: W. W. Norton & Company.

World Bank, 2019, *Stocks Traded, Total Value (Current US$)*, https://data.worldbank.org/indicator/CM.MKT.TRAD.CD.

World Economic Forum, 2016, *The Global Information Technology Report 2016 Innovating in the Digital Economy*, Geneva: World Economic Forum.

World Economic Forum, 2017, *Global Risks Report 2017*, http://reports.weforum.org/global-risks-2017.
Wright, D., 2003, 'Black Pride Day, 1968: High School Student Activism in York, Pennsylvania', *The Journal of African-American History* 88(2): 151–162.
Wrightsman, L., (ed.) 1968, *Contemporary Issues in Social Psychology*, Belmont, CA: Brooks Publishing Company.
Yallop, H., 2014, *Age and Identity in Eighteenth Century England*, London: Pickering and Chatto.
York, B., 1983, 'Sources of Student Unrest in Australia with Particular Reference to Latrobe University', MArts thesis, Sydney: University of Sydney.
Zaff, J., Malanchuk, O., Michelesen, E., and Eccles, J., 2003, *Socializing Youth for Citizenship* (CIRCLE Working Paper), College Park, MD: Center for Information and Research on Civic Learning and Engagement.
Zhao, G., 2011, 'The Modern Construction of Childhood: What Does It Do to the Paradox of Modernity?' *Studies in Philosophy and Education* 30: 241–256.
Zhong, R., 2019, 'TikTok Blocks Teen Who Posted about China's Detention Camps', *New York Times*, https://www. nytimes.com/2019/11/26/technology/tiktok-muslims-censorship.html.
Zhou, N., 2018, 'Climate Change Strike: Thousands of School Students Protest across Australia', *The Guardian*, 30 November, https://www.theguardian.com/environment/2018/nov/30/climate-change-strike-thousands-of-students-to-join-national-protest).
Žižek, S., 1989, *The Sublime Object of Ideology*, London: Verso.
Zoran, G., 2015, 'Between Appropriation and Representation: Aristotle and the Concept of Imitation in Greek Thought', *Philosophy and Literature* 39(2): 468–486.
Zuboff, S., 2019, *The Fight for a Human Future at the New Frontier of Power*, New York: Public Affairs.

INDEX

Note: Page numbers followed by "n" refer to endnotes.

action (activism) 150, 153, 154, 156, 165, 168, 170–172, 178, 180, 181n6, 181n7, 213, 223, 224, 226–228, 234, 243, 246, 247, 253
active society model 191–194
adolescence 8, 10, 15, 20–22, 68, 69, 87n5, 91, 108, 109, 114–120, 135, 136, 139, 148, 149, 157, 164, 188, 216, 256
adolescent 2, 8, 9, 13, 15, 18, 21, 22, 33, 34, 40, 46, 48, 67, 87n5, 109, 110, 115–118, 120, 127, 135–140, 146, 149, 164, 169, 215, 243
adolescent development 2, 34, 116, 140, 149
adult power 48, 217, 220
age 3, 8, 9, 22, 23, 31, 33–37, 40, 59, 66–73, 77, 82–84, 87n3, 87n8, 90, 94, 100, 101, 103–105, 108, 113, 115, 116, 120, 136, 153, 163, 188, 206, 212, 215, 216, 218, 225, 235n1, 237–241, 255, 257, 258
Anthropocene 183, 184
anti-austerity campaigns 222–224
anti-gun protests 241
anti-war protests 221–222
Arendt, H. 18, 43–46, 58–64, 74, 86, 92, 93, 105, 217, 231–234, 239
Aries, P. 67, 68, 216
Aristotle 7, 11, 19n12, 54, 56
austerity (anti-austerity) 186, 211, 212, 222–225, 230, 231, 241
Australia: anti-intellectual stereotypes 159; history 170–171; national income support system 192; newspapes 134;

politics 52; psychologists 139; widgies and bodgies 126, 128–132, 140

Berkeley campus 155, 156, 158, 159, 164, 172–176, 178, 179
Binet, A. 113, 114, 120
biological 7, 11, 21, 45, 67, 101, 102, 109, 111, 112, 116, 118, 146, 155–157, 258
Black Lives Matters movement 64, 244
bodgie and widgies *see* widgies
Bourdieu, P. 7, 9–12, 14, 19n13, 24, 25, 31, 40, 41, 42n6, 42n7, 51, 52, 97, 98, 123, 126, 162, 214, 215, 223, 239; relational theory-method 36–39; and representations 31–35; and representations of youth 35–36
boy sailors 84–85
Bray, D. 5, 45, 237, 238
Bretton Woods agreement 186, 190, 207n2
Brocklehurst, H. 45, 57, 217, 238
Brynjolfsson, E. 185
Burt, C. 114, 120, 136, 138

capital 1, 14, 17, 31–36, 38, 40, 43, 97, 127, 140, 178, 183, 186, 187, 190, 197–200, 205, 206, 207n2, 209n12, 217, 223, 237
capitalism 31, 124, 125, 154, 155, 173, 181n3, 196, 197, 199, 204, 206, 220, 236n7
capitalist 12, 16, 17, 23, 31, 115, 124, 197, 201, 206, 207, 216
casualization 4, 184, 199, 202, 205, 208n3, 208n4, 209n13, 212

Centre for the Future of Democracy (2019) 211
child development 15, 48, 49, 216
children 2–6, 8–18, 20, 24, 39, 40, 43–46, 64, 64n2, 67, 68, 76, 86, 87n8, 89–92, 120n1, 123, 132, 134, 136, 139, 140, 145, 153, 158, 166–168, 188, 210, 212–214, 221, 223, 224, 231, 232, 235, 237–247, 249, 250, 253, 255, 256–258; adolescence and Hall 114–119; ages 69–73; Arendt and 58, 60–64; in British navy 82–84; child labour 103–104; citizenship 56–58; civilizing offensive 101–103, 109–111; criminal 104–106; 'dangerous classes' 96–101; eugenics 108–109; French revolution 79–82, 92–95; Galton and eugenics 111–114; intellectuals 97–99; Juvenile Enlightenment 79–82; as minors 47–49; Mouffe and 58–60; paternalism 46–47; politics 51–56, 218–220; schooling 106–108; Young Germany 95–96; Young Ireland 95–96; Young Italy 95; and young people 49–51, 100–103, 214–218
citizen (citizenship) 17, 44–49, 54–58, 60, 74–76, 81, 82, 88n10, 88n11, 93, 94, 97, 119, 133, 134, 136, 151n9, 163, 172, 184, 211, 225, 230, 235n2, 236n9, 238, 242; politics of 76–79
civilizing offensive 101–104, 106, 108, 109, 119, 123
civitas 56, 65n5
climate action 45, 212, 231–234, 248
climate change 2, 206, 221, 233, 234, 239–241, 246, 254
cognitive development 218
Cohen, E. 46, 64n2
Cohen, S. 10, 97, 121n8, 130–131, 135
Cold War 124, 158, 163, 220
colonial 15, 73, 109, 110, 120
communist 16, 93, 98, 154, 157–163, 166, 167, 180
Connell, R. 136, 218, 224
constitutive 9, 28–30, 38, 45, 49, 50, 57, 59–61, 99, 237, 238, 256
construction 8, 21–23, 27, 28, 30, 42n6, 85, 133, 218–220
counter revolutionary 78, 93, 94, 119, 123
courts 58, 101, 105, 106, 119, 132–134, 138, 139, 160, 162, 168, 211, 227, 231, 233, 234, 242, 249
COVID-19 4, 210, 226, 233
creative destruction 194, 204
crime 8, 15, 21, 84, 97–99, 113, 116, 131, 132, 193, 205, 220, 225, 231
crisis 4, 13, 16–18, 50, 63, 174, 175, 197, 201, 205, 211, 231, 232, 252, 253, 256, 258, 259

crisis of democracy 13, 50, 211
Cullis-Suzuki, S. 239, 253

'dangerous classes' 15, 87, 89, 91, 96–102, 108, 111, 119, 123, 135, 193, 202, 203
Dangerous Classes of New York, The (Brace) 97
Darwin, C. 111, 112
Declaration of the Rights of Man and Citizens (Paine) 75, 78, 81, 88n14, 91
degeneracy 98, 109, 111, 113
degeneration 100, 104, 115, 118, 149
delinquency 21, 99–101, 105, 114, 122, 123, 126, 135–140, 146; girls politics and (*see* young women); moral panics and 130–135
deregulation 191, 195, 196, 199, 234
development (adolescent, child development) 2, 15, 34, 48, 49, 116, 140, 149, 216
developmental theory 14, 35, 149
Diderot, D. 76, 81, 94
digital politics 224–227, 229–234
digital revolution 194, 199–201
Dignity and Justice 230, 236n10
discourse 13, 15, 17, 20–25, 37, 41n2, 60, 97, 100, 103, 106, 107, 135, 140, 148, 185, 216, 237
distributed denial of service attacks (DDoS) 227–229, 236n9
double-click model 26
Durham, D. 8, 9
Durkheim, E. 25, 27, 29, 30, 32

Eckford, E. 43, 62, 64
eighteenth century 7, 14, 19n14, 67–73, 75, 82, 84–86, 88n10, 91, 109, 120n1, 213
Elias, N. 7, 37–38, 42n10, 101
Ellison, R. 43, 44, 64
empire 71, 85, 93, 102, 109–111, 123, 149
employment 17, 34, 72, 103, 104, 123, 124, 137, 148, 154, 169, 183–192, 195–199, 201, 202, 206, 207n2, 208n4
enlightenment 13, 73, 80, 81, 93, 108
entrepreneur 17, 97, 98, 103, 135, 162, 195, 204, 205
entrepreneurs (policy) 97, 103
entrepreneur (young) 17, 185, 201, 203–206, 255
epidemic 122, 126, 130, 132, 210
eugenics 15, 108–109, 111–114, 119
expert 6, 7, 10, 13, 15, 16, 20–22, 24, 25, 32, 33, 39, 40, 45, 49, 83, 98, 102, 109, 114, 119, 123, 125–128, 131, 132, 134–142, 148–150, 154–163, 171, 180, 184, 185, 203, 206, 214, 216, 221, 233, 238, 247, 252, 256, 257, 259

Facebook 200, 201, 226, 231
feminine 142, 144, 145, 147–149
Fernandez-Armesto, F. 109, 110
financialisation 194, 196–200, 203, 206, 254
folk devils 20, 130, 131, 135, 203
Foucault, M. 21, 49, 97, 104, 105, 162
fourth industrial revolution 203, 204
freedom 5, 46, 54, 60–64, 70, 76, 86, 92, 95, 108, 144, 164, 171–174, 195, 210, 225, 228, 241, 254, 258
free speech 155, 158–159, 166–168, 171, 172–176, 179, 227
French revolution 14, 15, 66, 67, 73–77, 79–82, 85, 86, 91–96, 99, 100, 119, 123, 153
Freud, S. 25
Fridays For Future 231–233

Galton, F. 108, 111–114, 118–120, 136
gender 8, 23, 35–37, 54, 57, 59, 74, 96, 125–127, 140, 142, 144, 146–149, 154
Gendron, M. 78, 79
generation 4, 31, 63, 64, 74, 113, 118, 135, 146, 154, 155, 165, 167, 168, 181n3, 184, 204, 212, 243–245
Generation Z 212
George III, King 66, 73, 85, 86
gig economy 184–185, 198, 205
Gilded Youth 78–79
Gleadle, K. 69, 73, 79–82, 88n13
Global Climate Strike 212, 231, 232
global democratic recession 211
global financial crisis 198
global warming 17, 183, 233–235
government 2, 8, 13, 14, 16, 29, 45, 50, 52–56, 66, 78, 92–95, 98, 99, 102, 103, 106, 109, 114, 119, 122, 123, 135–137, 139, 140, 158, 159, 162, 166, 169, 171, 178–180, 183–187, 189–195, 198, 201, 203, 205, 206, 210–212, 214, 216, 219–222, 227–231, 233–235, 238, 239, 248, 252, 254, 255, 255n1, 256, 257
Graham, G. 168, 169
Grieve, V. 219–220
Griffin, C. 10, 13, 20–25, 40, 41n2, 216
Gullette, M. 8

Habermas, J. 58
Hacking, I. 9, 28, 49, 97, 256
Hall, G. Stanley 15, 21, 69, 114–119, 121n14, 121n15, 136, 149, 157
Hall, S. 7, 126
Hartung, C. 5, 237, 238
Heartbreak Hotel 134
Heidegger, M. 49
Hensby, A. 223, 224, 235n6
Hill, J. 244–245

history 3, 4, 6, 7, 10, 25, 48, 49, 53, 74, 80, 81, 85, 97, 99, 108, 109, 117, 118, 121n7, 126, 127, 139, 153, 154, 167, 170, 186, 193, 196, 204, 214–216, 220, 221, 227, 229, 231, 252, 255

ideology 21–25, 37, 41n2, 41n3, 155, 237
indigenous 7, 40, 47, 110, 248
'Industry 4.0' 203–206
inequality 17, 31, 32, 195, 196, 198, 231, 235
inferior 47, 102, 108, 110, 111, 240, 250, 251, 253
innocence 100, 215, 220
intellectual 6, 12, 24, 29, 31, 32, 34, 36, 70, 71, 74, 88n13, 94, 96–100, 107–113, 115, 116, 118, 119, 121n7, 127, 135–137, 139, 154, 159, 160, 166, 184, 256–258
International Labour Organisation (ILO) 188
International Monetary Fund (IMF) 203, 207n2
Isin, E. 56–58, 65n5, 102

juvenile delinquency *see* delinquency
Juvenile Enlightenment 79–82

Keynes, J. M. 123, 183, 186, 187, 190, 194
Kohlberg, L. 149, 164
Kosselleck, R. 10, 49
Krippner, G. 209n12

labour flexibility 195–196
labour market programs 192, 193
Lakoff, G. 240–241
Latour, B. 26, 49, 124, 234
leadership 14, 17, 18, 76, 83, 85, 136, 175, 222, 253
Le Bon, G. 99, 121n7, 156
Lefebvre, H. 218–219
Leftwich, A. 53–56
liberal-democracy 16, 46, 47, 54, 58–60, 64, 95, 108, 153, 228
Locke, J. 47, 70
Luckmann, H. 26–28, 41n5

McCloskey, D. 256
McDonald, J. 129, 133, 141, 151n6
McDonald, R. 185, 192
McRobbie, A. 127, 142
make up (making up) 6–11, 13, 97, 125
Mannheim, K. 42, 184
March For Our Lives 3, 247, 248, 251, 252
Marx, K. 23, 25, 31, 32, 41n3, 98, 108, 154, 165
media 2–4, 10, 16, 17, 21, 43, 50, 58, 96, 130, 131, 135, 141, 150, 154, 158–162,

193, 201, 218, 219, 221, 224, 225, 227–229, 237, 239, 241–246, 252–254
medical metaphors 135, 258
millennials 212, 216
Mill, J. S. 109
Mitterauer, M. 216
Mitzman, A. 102
modern child 46, 110
moral panic 97, 149, 150, 160, 193, 241; and delinquents 130–135
Moscovici, S. 7, 10, 13, 21, 24–33, 40, 97, 123, 214
Mouffe, C. 58–62
Muncie, J. 114–115

Nakata, S. 5, 45, 237, 238
Napoleon 66, 67, 73, 85, 86, 87n4, 93, 119
natality 18, 58, 61–63, 74, 92, 93, 105, 217, 232
navy 79, 82–85
Nelson, H. 66–67, 73, 79, 82, 85, 86
neo-classical economics 59, 190, 199
neoliberal 17, 194, 195, 199, 202–206, 211, 212, 221, 234, 238
neoliberalism 194–197
New Climactic Regime (Latour) 234–235
nineteenth century 8, 12, 15, 18, 66, 67, 69, 73, 82, 83, 86, 91–96, 99–102, 106–109, 111, 114, 115, 118, 119, 121n11, 127, 134, 135, 153, 204, 238
Nisbet, R. 108
Not in Education or Training (NEET) 192, 205
novelty 14, 58, 62, 74–77, 86, 92, 93, 180, 181, 188

Organisation for Economic Co-operation and Development (OECD) 188–189, 191, 192, 196, 197, 199, 203, 205, 208n6, 208n7
Origin of Species, The (Darwin) 111, 112
Orphan Trains 89–91

Parkland massacre 252
participation 3, 44, 45, 50, 62, 63, 76, 86, 92, 137, 173, 175–177, 188, 192, 208n4, 211, 213, 214, 219, 220, 223, 254, 256, 257
paternalism 46–48
pathological 156, 157, 245
Pellowe, D. 243, 244
philanthropy 84, 89, 98, 106
Piaget, J. 25, 39, 218
Picketty, T. 183, 195, 198
Pitt, William 66, 67, 73, 79, 85, 86, 87n2

police 4, 17, 43, 48, 56, 90, 96, 103, 105, 106, 128, 130–134, 151n9, 155, 158, 160–162, 169, 171, 174, 175, 178, 180, 191, 210, 217, 222, 223, 227, 228, 231, 242, 244, 248, 251, 253
political 2–7, 9–18, 23, 24, 32–36, 40, 66, 67, 70, 73–77, 79–83, 85–87, 87n3, 91–95, 97, 108, 110, 111, 119, 123, 126, 127, 131, 133, 140, 143, 144, 148, 150, 153–160, 162–165, 167–169, 171–177, 179, 180, 185, 187, 188, 194, 195, 202, 203, 205–207, 210–214, 235n3, 236n9; children as minors 47–49; digital 229–234; identity 85, 218, 224; Mouffe and Arendt 58–64; paternalism 46–47; responses 246–247; *see also* politics
politics 2, 3, 5, 6, 9, 10, 12–15, 18, 24, 30, 31, 40, 41, 44–47, 50–64, 67, 73, 74, 76–79, 81, 86, 91–94, 97, 153, 185, 201, 203, 205, 210, 211, 213–215; Bourdieu and 51–52; character and regulatory functions of government 52; children 218–220; of citizenship 76–79; digital 224–227, 229–234; Leftwich and 53–56; media reactions 241–246; of misrecognition 250–253; student (*see* student politics); truancy 247–250; young people 220–224; young women (*see* young women)
Poovey, M. 8, 256
Popular Party is Dissolved, The 230–231
post-war boom 124, 183, 190, 194
poverty 11, 15, 33, 34, 45, 90, 98, 99, 114, 123, 136, 137, 238
power 5, 9–12, 14, 18, 24, 25, 29, 32, 34–36, 38, 39, 41n4, 54–56, 59, 61, 65, 84, 85, 93, 100, 120n2, 121n7, 127, 144, 150, 164, 172, 173, 178, 192, 213, 215, 217, 219, 220, 241, 242, 245, 249, 251, 257, 259
precariat 17, 185, 201–203, 205, 216, 255
professionals 15, 16, 25, 29, 40, 51, 68, 74, 83, 95, 97, 114, 119, 123, 132, 137, 142, 144, 150, 152n10, 162, 214, 216
progress 13, 108–111, 117, 184, 185, 204, 230, 237
protest psychosis 156
protests (student) 16, 17, 153–168, 170, 171, 174, 175, 179, 180, 181n9, 223, 235n6, 241, 247, 255n2
psychologist 7, 13, 24, 25, 28, 101, 111, 112, 114, 115, 126, 135–139, 142, 149, 152n10, 157, 164

racial 15, 64, 102, 108, 110, 111, 115, 116, 118, 119, 123, 148
racial fitness 15, 108, 111–115, 118, 120, 150
racism 167, 169, 173, 175, 229
radical 60, 64, 73, 77–81, 92, 93, 95, 96, 98, 155–162, 172, 173, 181n5, 181n9, 223, 241
recapitulation 115, 117–119
recognition (misrecognition) 5, 14, 31, 39, 42n7, 47, 53, 57, 62, 64, 102, 164, 165, 206, 235, 239, 250–255
recursive 9
Red Diaper Babies 158, 166, 170
reductionism 124–125
regeneration 74, 78, 118
relational 6, 9, 11–12, 14, 29, 33, 36–40, 51, 55, 65n3, 76, 223
relational theory-method 36–39
representation 5–18, 19n13, 20–37, 39, 40, 41n1, 41n3, 41n5, 41n7, 45–51, 67–69, 71, 85–87, 91, 96, 97, 99, 100, 107–110, 115, 116, 119, 120, 123, 127, 128, 131, 133–135, 139, 144, 150, 155, 157, 158, 160–162, 164, 166, 180, 185, 192, 193, 201, 203–207, 214–217, 220, 231, 232, 235, 237–240, 242, 245, 250–257
representations (collective) 29
Representations of Youth (Griffin) 13, 20–21
revolution 14, 15, 67, 73–81, 85–87, 91–96, 98–100, 119, 121n6, 123, 153, 154, 156, 181, 189, 194, 199–201, 203–205, 213, 225
revolution (Glorious) 92
revolutionary movements 74, 92, 93
risk 52, 146, 148, 160, 193, 204, 205, 208n5, 216, 234, 245
Robespierre, M. 73, 77–79, 93
Rousseau, J. -J. 19n14, 70, 77, 80, 81, 251

sans culottes 77, 78
schooling 47, 103, 104, 106–109, 115, 137, 169, 238, 249
SchoolStrike4Climate 231, 232, 246
school strikes 168, 213, 222, 232, 247
Schumpeter, J. 204
scientific 2, 7, 10, 12–15, 19n13, 19n14, 26, 31, 33, 34, 36, 40, 49, 51, 80, 87n5, 108, 109, 111–113, 115, 117, 118, 120, 129, 136–139, 155, 189, 257
Secondary Heads Association (SHA) 247
Second World War 183, 188
sex and widgie 140–142
Shore, H. 101, 121n8

Snap Chat 226
snowflakes 243, 244
social constructionism 28, 42n6
social media 3, 4, 201, 224, 227, 246, 254
social movements 2, 16–18, 29, 57, 86, 102, 150, 214
sociogram 134–135
sociology of knowledge 25–28, 165
soldiers 82, 129, 247
Spearman, C. 112–113, 136
stadial theory 48, 110, 216
stages of life 68, 70, 109, 120, 216, 240, 256
Standing, G. 185, 201–203
state 5, 10, 14, 15, 17, 34, 35, 39, 43, 46, 48, 51, 52, 54–56, 58, 60, 63, 74, 78, 79, 81, 83, 89, 93, 96–98, 102, 103, 105, 107, 108, 110, 113, 117, 118, 121n7, 123, 136, 139, 150, 156–158, 161, 162, 175, 187, 190, 195, 205, 210, 211, 216, 220, 224, 227, 229, 235, 236n9, 237, 238, 241, 249, 254, 256, 258
Stop Online Piracy (SOPA) Bill 228
Student Non-violent Coordinating Committee (SNCC) 167, 172, 174
student politics 153–154; activism 167–171; Berkeley, free speech in 172–175; communist 157–163; Leeds University 175–178; Monash University 178–180; protest 154–157, 163–167
students 16, 17, 43, 69, 74, 136, 138, 146, 151n6, 181n2, 181n4–181n6, 181n9, 182n10, 198, 205, 212, 213, 220–224, 231, 232, 234, 241, 242, 244–248, 251, 252; *see also* student politics
Students for a Democratic Society (SDS) 167, 172, 173, 176
Student Underground 170
substantialist approach 6, 11, 14, 19n12, 36–38, 54, 65n3
surveillance capital 200, 236n7
Sydney 128–130, 132–134, 140, 151n6, 171, 179
symbolic order 10, 14, 22, 24, 32, 40, 74, 97, 148, 150, 239
symbolic violence 38, 162

Taylor, C. 226, 239, 250, 251
technology 2, 28, 39, 108, 164, 185, 199–201, 204, 225, 226, 229, 233, 253, 254, 258, 259
teen brain 3, 40
Terman, L. 113, 114, 136
Thatcher, M. 191, 213, 249
Threadgold, S. 20, 184–185, 206–207

Thunberg, G. 1–3, 5, 231–234, 240, 244–246, 253, 255n4
TikTok 226, 227, 233, 236n7
transition 21, 72, 116–119, 137, 138, 140, 149, 157, 186, 191, 202, 206, 216, 256
truancy 242, 247–250
Trump, D. 3, 226, 238, 245, 255n4
Twitter 225, 226, 231, 233, 252

UN Convention of the Rights of the Child 220
underclass 16, 34, 192, 193, 207
underemployment 186, 208n3
unemployment 10, 13, 15–17, 21, 33, 45, 98, 102, 114, 123, 154, 185–191, 193–195, 199, 204, 207, 208n3, 208n6, 208n8, 212, 231
Unger, R. 255
United Nations (UN) 1, 5, 8, 204, 232, 253
United Nations Climate action Summit 232
university, universities 10, 16, 45, 74, 115, 148, 150, 153–162, 164, 166, 167, 171–173, 175–179, 186, 198, 205, 210, 221–222, 224, 242, 244; Berkeley 155, 156, 158, 159, 164, 172–176, 178, 179; Leeds University 175–178; Monash University 178–180
urbs 65n5

Vietnam war 164, 166, 170, 171, 178–180, 213

Wacquant, L. 98
Wallerstein, I. 93, 120n2, 206
war 16, 18, 66, 79, 83, 85, 93, 94, 100, 110, 123–129, 131, 136, 149, 154, 155, 158, 161–164, 166, 168, 170, 171, 178–180, 183, 186–188, 190, 194, 213, 214, 220–223, 237, 242, 243, 246, 249
Weber, M. 24, 41n4, 55, 65n3
welfare state 17, 103, 123, 187, 205
Wellington, Duke of 67, 73, 82, 85, 86
White Paper on Full Employment in Australia 187
widgies 15, 16, 135–150, 151n3, 151n6, 151n8, 225; and bodgies 122, 124–126, 128–135, 138–141, 147, 151n5; gender 146–148
work 7, 13, 16, 19n14, 20–22, 24–26, 28–31, 34, 36, 45, 46, 49, 59, 67, 68, 72, 80, 81, 88n11, 89, 96–98, 100–106, 113–117, 126, 134, 137, 141, 147, 148, 158, 159, 167, 170, 185, 186, 188, 189, 191–193, 199–207, 208n4, 210, 212, 215, 216, 230, 243–245, 249, 250, 258
working-class 23, 33, 35, 77, 91, 93–96, 98, 99, 101, 103, 104, 120n2, 122, 124, 126–128, 130, 133, 137, 138, 141, 150, 157, 167, 201
World Bank 207n2
World Economic Forum (WEF) 203, 211
Wyn, J. 202, 246

young entrepreneur 17, 185, 201, 203–206, 255
young Germany 95–96, 153, 212
young Ireland 95–96, 153
young Italy 95–6, 153
young people 2–6, 8–18, 20–24, 26, 34, 36–41, 44–46, 53, 56, 58, 60, 62–64, 66–67, 85–87, 90–93, 95, 96, 100, 109, 110, 114–116, 118–120, 121n15, 151n9, 151n10, 153, 154, 156, 157, 162, 164, 165, 167, 168, 171, 172, 180, 181n2, 183–189, 191–194, 201, 208n4, 210–214, 219–235, 238–259; ages 69–73; in British navy 82–84; children as minors 47–49; civilising offensive 101–108; contested politics of citizenship 76–79; dangerous classes 100–101; and French Revolution 73–76, 80–82; heroes 84–85; historians 67–69; Juvenile Enlightenment 79–82; paternalism 46–47; politics 220–224, 237 (*see also* politics); representations of 49–51, 201–207, 214–218
young precariat 17, 185, 201–203, 205, 216, 255
young women 122–123, 148–150; experts 135–139; gender 146–148; moral panic and delinquents 130–135; and post-war affluence 123–128; sex and widgie 140–142; style, space and politics 142–146; widgies and bodgies 128–130, 140
youth 2, 5, 8–16, 18, 20–25, 35, 37, 45–49, 67–69, 74, 78, 79, 81, 84, 85, 91, 96, 101, 108, 115, 116, 118–120, 151n9, 159, 160–162, 164–167, 169, 184, 185, 192–194, 202–205, 207, 208n3, 212, 217, 226, 231, 234, 237, 242, 243, 245, 252, 254–257, 259; ages of child and 69–73; Bourdieu and representations 35–36; empires 109–111; labour market 185–189; unemployment 189–191
youth culture 15, 79, 125–127, 143
youth labour market 184, 185–189, 194, 208n3
youth participation 254, 257
Youth Strike for Climate 2, 231

Žižek, S. 23, 59
Zuboff, S. 196, 197, 205
Zubov, S. 200–201